THE GUIDE TO TEXTILES

FOR INTERIORS

3RD EDITION

JACKMAN • DIXON • CONDRA

PORTAGE & MAIN PRESS

© 2003 Dianne Jackman, Mary Dixon, Jill Condra
Published 1983, Second Edition 1990

Portage & Main Press acknowledges the financial support of the
Government of Canada through the Book Publishing Industry
Development (BPIDP) for our publishing activities.

Printed and bound in Canada by Friesens, Altona
Book and cover design 3rd edition: Relish Design Studio Ltd.
Book and cover design 2nd edition: Pat Stanton
Illustrations: Jess Dixon, Brenda Le Blanc, Avril Goodall

05 06 07 08   5 4 3 2

National Library of Canada Cataloguing in Publication Data

Jackman, Dianne R. (Dianne Rose), 1934-
    The guide to textiles for interiors / Dianne R. Jackman, Mary
Dixon, Jill Condra.

Previous ed., by Dianne R. Jackman and Mary K. Dixon, has title:
The guide to textiles for interior designers.
    Includes bibliographical references and index.
    ISBN 1-895411-97-1

1. Textile fabrics in interior decoration. 2. Textile fabrics. 3. Textile
fibers. I. Dixon, Mary K. (Mary Katherine), 1936- II. Condra, Jillian,
1968- III. Jackman, Dianne R. (Dianne Rose), 1934- Guide to textiles
for interior designers. IV. Title.
NK2115.5.F3J32 2003   684'.3   C2003-910379-X

PORTAGE & MAIN PRESS

318 McDermot Avenue
Winnipeg, Manitoba Canada R3A 0A2
E-mail: books@portageandmainpress.com
Tel: (204) 987-3500
Toll free: (800) 667-9673
Fax: (866) 734-8477

Printed on 100% recycled paper (50% PCW)

CONTENTS

NEW LEAF PAPER

ENVIRONMENTAL BENEFITS STATEMENT

Guide to Textiles for Interiors is printed on New Leaf Reincarnation Matte, made with 100% recycled fiber, 50% post-consumer waste, processed chlorine free. By using this environmental paper, Portage and Main Press saved the following resources:

trees	water	energy	solid waste	greenhouse gases
73 fully grown	15,898 gallons	33 million BTUs	3,478 pounds	5,877 pounds

Calculated based on research done by Environmental Defense and other members of the Paper Task Force.

© New Leaf Paper   www.newleafpaper.com   888.989.5323

PREFACE

It has been an amazing twenty years since the first edition of *The Guide to Textiles* was published. We are grateful for the book's long-term acceptance, and thank the hundreds of instructors and thousands of students who have used the information over the years.

Most of the information from previous editions is still current. But this edition includes the latest information from research, literature, institutions, and industry associations. We address environmental issues and put deserved emphasis on concerns for the occupants of spaces. We acknowledge health and safety and sick building syndrome, and emphasize the three Rs—reduce, reuse, recycle.

We know changes in the format and the addition of more charts will make it easier to access vital information. The new full-color format allows the addition of photographs and illustrations to further clarify concepts.

Our goal for this edition is to create another 'must-have' resource. The first edition of *The Guide* won the ASID Joel Polsky Prize, and the book was listed with the NCIDQ as the textiles study guide for the interior design qualification exam; it is invaluable as a teaching and learning tool; and we are told that it is one textbook that remains in a student's library long after graduation. Facility managers are acknowledged and accepted as a sensible and much-needed member of the design community. We are delighted it has such a good reputation as a textile reference.

This edition includes the work of Jill Condra for the first time, and Dianne and Mary welcome her experience with textile testing, research and teaching at the university level.

Finally, we acknowledge and thank our editors and long-time publisher. Known in previous editions as Peguis Publishers, the same company is now called Portage & Main Press.

Dianne Jackman
Mary Dixon
Jill Condra

Winnipeg, 2003

INTRODUCTION

The Latin verb *texere* means to weave, braid, or construct fabrics, and *textilis* is the Latin root noun for the now commonly used term *textile*. Textiles are made from fibers that are processed into yarns, then into woven, knit, or nonwoven fabrics. Artwork, carpeting, casements, draperies, upholstery, and wall coverings are all interior uses for textiles, and join hundreds of other familiar and unfamiliar products that are also textiles.

> Textiles hold society together. If this seems too bold and general a statement, try to imagine a world without them! From swaddling infants to dressing armies, from catching the wind with a sail to clothing astonauts in space, textiles are involved. Textiles help stabilize the roads you drive on, keep you insulated against heat and cold, and serve many other functions that you cannot actually see. Our daily contact with textiles is often taken for granted—like the automobile upholstery we casually slide over as we get in the car. Our clothing, bedding, linens, carpeting, drapery and furniture coverings are necessities but also sometimes luxuries. The clues we get from textiles—the mail carrier's uniform, the clothing choices of others—help to shape and identify our world. The textiles in other environments—homes, offices, stores, restaurants, schools—are full of diversity and may appall or delight, or may be taken for granted.

In order to supply fibers, yarns, and fabrics for the myriad end uses—fashion, interior spaces, industrial textiles—the industry is organized to facilitate the supply and flow of textiles worldwide. The textile complex is a web of interconnected industries that collectively produce textiles, but also produce the necessary machinery and software to handle that production. Textile research, product development, and marketing are all part of the textile complex.

The Textile Complex

Today's textile industry is comprised of many interdependent sectors. While each segment of the production process is a separate activity, together they are part of a succession of stages whereby each process depends on the one before. Many different textile components go into the production of one upholstered chair: filler, lining, finishing fabric, trim. Each of these textiles has a unique source, fiber shape, fiber content, yarn type, fabric structure, color, texture, and finish. The task of bringing all the components together to produce a final product requires cooperation among all sectors of the textile complex.

Today, the textile industry produces trillions of meters (yards) of product per year and employs millions of

The Textile Complex

Fiber Producers	Natural, manufactured, research and development
Yarn Producers	Spun yarn Filament yarn: multifilament, monofilament, composite
Fabrics Producers	Woven, knits, nonwoven, leather, and fur
Finishers	Mechanical, chemical, aesthetic, functional Dyes and prints
Product Manufacturers	Floor coverings: rugs, carpets, backings, padding Window coverings: curtains, drapes, valences
Sales	Direct to job Distributors Retailers Commercial, residential
Consumers	Individual, family, industrial/commercial (office, hospital, hotels, schools, retailers)
Disposal/Recycling	Recovery (de-installation), reuse, recycling, landfill sites

people worldwide. The textile industry is affected, either positively or negatively, by general **economic factors.** Economics slowdowns impact the retail and luxury goods market and will, in turn, affect sales of interior fabrics for housing design. Commercial design is not as affected by economic slowdown, and demand for textiles in hospitals, hotels, airports, offices—where they can not afford to look shabby—may remain more stable. Some 'bad times' such as war can benefit the textile industry, as uniforms and myriad other cloth products are needed in great quantity, while at the same time consumer purchasing of textile products might decline.

ENERGY COSTS affect the textile industry, as it is an intensive user of power, and fluctuations in the cost or supply of energy influence the bottom line of textile firms. The supply and cost of essential energy have forced many manufacturers to analyze the amount and kinds of energy they use. More efficient and economical techniques are needed to help sustain the increasing production volumes that are expected in the industry.

ENVIRONMENTAL CONCERNS are becoming an important part of the textile complex. Besides power usage, the processing of fibers, yarns, fabrics, finishes, and dyes is also resource intensive, especially in water use. The industry has been criticized for this in the past; today concerns with environmental sustainability are more evident. The carpet industry in particular is leading the way in creating programs for recycling and reusing old carpet fibers. In an effort to reduce the amount of used carpet ending up in landfill sites, the carpet industry has worked together toward solutions. Others in the textile industry are seeking to reduce the use of chemicals that produce 'off gases' and affect the quality of air inside buildings. Reuse of material is innovative: fibers from recycled soda pop bottles are being reprocessed into upholstery and drapery fabrics. These products and some nylon carpet fibers are certified *green* products, and are labeled for easy identification by design professionals and end users. Being environmentally conscious is not only necessary for the preservation of our environment, but it also appeals to consumers and can be an advantage in the marketing of interior textile products.

Geography of the Textile Industry

The textile industry is worldwide. Virtually all nations have some textile manufacturing. Research, development, mass production, and marketing occur mainly in the developed world, while fabric is produced all over the world in various forms and quantities. The wool industry, for example, is concentrated in Australia, New Zealand, and Argentina where sheep are commercially raised and concerted efforts are made to develop quality fibers.

Textile industries may operate on a local basis. Many countries produce their own textiles for domestic use. Centuries-old techniques for fabric making and coloring are still used in many countries, using readily available natural fiber sources and natural dyes. Small-scale production is extremely important and is relatively easy to do; spinning yarn and weaving fabric can be done by hand and in small spaces.

Conversely, the scale of textile production in North America, Europe, and Asia is immense. **Mass production** requires a supply of capital, space, highly technical and efficient equipment, dependable energy sources, and many experienced workers. Increasingly, advanced software for design and automated production needed. Demand for textiles can be accommodated quickly and easily with reduced **lead time**—the amount of time between placing an order and delivering the goods.

Horizontal Operation/Vertical Integration

Textile firms may produce goods at several, if not all, stages of the production process. The largest of these **vertical operations** are generally known as **conglomerates**—the size and scope of their operations may include everything from fiber processing to marketing and retailing finished goods. They may own and operate the agricultural source of fibers and have diversified interests in textile machinery, retail outlets, transportation, and equipment. A vertically integrated firm can manufacture a product from fiber to finish in one location.

Alternately, textile firms may be single-task oriented (for instance, spinning raw cotton into basic yarn). This is known as a **horizontal operation.** For ease of understanding, the following assumes each step as a horizontal operation.

Processing

All textiles start as raw materials, either natural or manufactured, so the first step is to produce usable fiber. Processing is specific to each fiber (cleaning, combing, and other treatments to produce natural fibers, blending chemical components, and spinning continuous filaments of synthetic fibers). Fibers may be blended to introduce other qualities to a yarn and fabric.

Fibers are sent to the **spinning mill** where the fibers are transformed into useable yarns. The manufacturers produce yarn types as specified for the final piece goods (the actual fabric). Yarns are then sent to a fabric producer and made into woven, knit, or nonwoven fabrics.

A **production mill** may produce basic **greige** or gray goods (unfinished, undyed fabric), which need further processing, or, working closely with their buyers, the mill may produce a finished cloth of specific weight, weave, color, and design. Mills sell to **converters** or **jobbers.**

If the mill has produced greige goods, the fabrics are sold to a converter. Fabric conversion involves all the post-construction processes such as bleaching, dyeing, finishing, printing, adding texture, along with chemical treatments to enhance or modify performance. The converter must be aware of current trends in colors and patterns and sensitive to market fluctuations. The converter produces finished piece goods, which are then used by product manufacturers. Many converters also manufacture items such as towels, sheets, ready-made draperies and bed covers, etc. Converters may operate on a huge scale, or they may work with small quantities for special or exclusive use.

The **textile jobber** buys from either the mill or the converter. The name derives from *job lot*, which is the quantity produced at one production run—this may be tens or hundreds of thousands of meters (yards). Jobbers buy and stock goods, cut and distribute samples to a range of textile product manufacturers and regional jobbers, and then sell **piece goods** (one or more bolts of fabric) to these customers.

Regional jobbers, who buy multiple bolts of finished goods, sell cut orders or specific yardage to regional manufacturers, designers, or local retailers. Not wanting to be left with unsold goods, the small regional jobber usually stocks common, popular, mid-priced fabrics.

The bigger regional jobbers—those located in Manhattan, Chicago, and Atlanta—are generally classified as fabric houses. These fabric houses may specialize in a particular price range or type of goods, or they may carry a wide general range. In New York, fabric houses are classified as **downtown** or **uptown**. Downtown houses sell to retailers, furniture manufacturers, regional and uptown houses, and may also have contract divisions specializing in institutional or hotel work. Uptown houses sell cut orders to the trade—interior designers, architects, special order retailers, contract departments of major department stores, and furniture manufacturers. Uptown houses sell only decorative fabrics through showroom samples. Whether 'open' or 'closed,' sales are only made to those within the trade.

While all of the above deal with goods produced domestically in the United States, a thriving business is done in most countries with **imports**. Imports may enter a country at any stage of production, from fiber to finished goods. **Import houses** deal exclusively in imports of finished goods and are an extension to the range of goods available.

Marketing

One of the most important factors in the textile industry is the buying and/or selling at each stage of production. Fibers are marketed as **commodities, brand** or **trade name fibers,** or **controlled brand name fibers.** Fibers marketed as commodities are used without identification of source and are sold to any buyer on the open market. A drapery fabric labeled '100% polyester' is fabric that has been made with commodity polyester fibers. Brand name fibers are identified by source through the brand name used. The fiber producer has a marketing budget that is used for promotion and to establish the brand name and expects manufacturers, wholesalers, and retailers to promote the brand name through the entire chain of production and sales. The fiber producer does not always have complete control over the use of a brand name after the mill has purchased the fiber.

The **controlled brand name** approach enables the fiber maker to rigidly control the subsequent use of the fiber. Controlled brand names usually infer licensing. Under a licensed brand name, the licensed producer allows its brand name or trademark to be used by subsequent companies in return for a specified remuneration. In some cases, the licensed fiber producer carefully checks the final product for quality. The licensed brand name is an assurance to consumers that the product has satisfactorily passed various tests related to its end use. The tests are specified by the licensor and require the maintenance of a quality control program to ensure certain levels of performance.

In today's market, user assurance is more vital than ever because of the proliferation and confusion of brands, claims, and performance characteristics. Frequently there are no visible differences between fabrics, yet performance can vary significantly. In addition to the manufacturer's desire to produce both a quality product and one that will attract repeat business, various government departments and independent consumer groups act as watchdogs to make sure that claims about performance and product longevity are not erroneous or overstated.

Finished goods are marketed either by written specifications or from samples. If a fabric is purchased based on written specifications, then the seller must ship the fabric exactly as specified. Such details as the number of yarns per centimeter (inch), weight, thickness, breaking strength, and degree of colorfastness are examples of possible specifications.

Sample Formats

Fabric sales representatives use various sample forms to show their products. These include:

COLOR CARD: This is a card on which a swatch of each color is shown. A print fabric is usually sold in three or four colorways; a solid color might be available in many different colors.

SALES TYPE OR CAP SET: These are swatches of one fabric in many different color combinations. The set is held together with a cardboard holder that contains important information about the fiber content, color numbers, and design details.

HEADENT: This sample is larger than the sales sample; it usually measures one quarter of a meter (yard) and is the entire width of the fabric.

BOOK: A book is a set of 10 cm x 15 cm (4" x 6") swatches that show a number of fabric designs and colors. A book is usually organized in themes or lines available from one manufacturer.

SQUARE: These swatches measure 30 cm^2 to 60 cm^2 (12 inches^2 to 245 inches^2) and show the full pattern repeat.

ONE-METER SWATCHES (ONE-YARD SWATCHES): These large samples show the full pattern repeat and allow the designer to see the draping quality of the fabric.

MEMO SAMPLES: Manufacturers who prefer not to send out free samples 'cold,' let it be known that they will respond to an e-mail or fax request from a design professional, and that they will courier a specific sample or samples, which must later be returned or paid for.

Overview of *The Guide to Textiles for Interiors*

In Part I, textiles are introduced and discussed in the contexts of the future and the past. All sectors of the textile industry are constantly conducting research and developing new products. These may be to meet requirements or laws regarding environmental or life safety issues, to meet requests from the design community, to satisfy various desires from end users, or simply to create new markets through advertising. New fiber types, new uses for old fiber types, and innovative ways of finishing fabrics all contribute to the evolution of the world of textiles.

Understanding the present and future is often easier when an historical context is given. The evolution of the textile industry is traced from an agricultural, economic, and political perspective. Understanding how events influenced and were influenced by different aspects of the industry helps give perspective for further study in this area.

Part II concentrates on the processing of textiles from fibers to finished products. Fiber basics are explained and the character and performance of each fiber type is outlined in easy-to-follow charts. Yarn processing and various yarn types are explained. Fabric structures are outlined and processes of weaving, knitting, and creating nonwoven fabrics are explained. The inherent characteristics of fabrics can be drastically altered with chemical, mechanical, and aesthetic finishes applied after the fabric is constructed. Two of the more important aspects of textiles for interiors are color and design. Dye classifications and application are discussed.

Part III deals with issues that design professionals must address when they select and specify textiles for interiors. Textile products for drapery, upholstery, and carpeting are assessed for performance, costing, health, safety, and installation. Building and safety codes are discussed as part of a chapter on professional responsibility.

In Part IV, future textile innovations are explored as research and development continues. The future world of textiles includes innovative uses for fiber optics, creating smart fabrics and new synthetic fabric structures.

PART

ONE

TEXTILES FOR INTERIORS: TODAY AND TOMORROW

The future use of interior textiles has always been assured. Textiles are versatile, easy to handle, economical, and aesthetically pleasing. They are an essential part of the built environment as well as an integral part of the personal environment of each of us.

The future of textiles is mind-boggling. In many instances practical improvements and consumer demand have been surpassed by the magic of innovation. Textile scientists are posing "What if..." questions and developing textile products the public could never have imagined twenty years ago. Consider these:

- Built-in electronic capabilities in textiles that enable fabrics to become extensions of our senses and of how we interact with our built environment.

- 'Smart fabrics' that can sense heart rates or even hormone levels are already in use in the medical profession.

- Information technology blended with textile products, to produce wearable computers and cellular telephones, are in research and development stages.

- Color-enhancing finishes can be encapsulated in fibers that react in different ways depending on the ambient temperatures.

- Scented fibers may add to the pleasure and functionality of using certain textiles.

- Sleep enhancers in fabrics for bedding and nightwear to help with insomnia.

- Medically charged fibers—with vitamins, minerals, and even mosquito repellent—may soon be available in everyday fabrics.

- New fabrics are being manufactured from recycled tires and soda pop bottles.

- Compostable, recyclable, and reclaimable fibers and textiles made from corn, rice, beets, and other raw materials are all possible.

- Chitin, a renewable resource made from crustacean shells (e.g., crab), is likely to become a mainstay of future textiles. Fibers designed with chitin are resistant to chemicals; have antibacterial, antifungal, and antiviral properties; and are nonallergenic. Chitin is also completely biodegradable.

More detail on these developments may be found in chapter 14.

Recent Developments

The benefits of the Internet are now well established, and the web is widely used. It is worth reviewing the impact of computer technology on the design community and the textile industry.

The Internet provides an instant source of product information from manufacturers. It is easily cross-checked for product accuracy, and specifications can easily be compared and assessed. Pricing policies and other details can quickly be obtained through web sites or e-mail. Designers, who tend to be visually attuned, can use web sites to see product samples and obtain their specifications. Besides product information, various codes in the locality of design work can be found. Design professionals can order samples, request and receive price quotes, place orders, and coordinate product delivery to job sites. Contact with clients for approvals, time frames, and progress reports can be accomplished easily and quickly.

Artists can display and sell their work over the Internet, gaining valuable exposure worldwide. Small commercial firms may also have a site on the web to advertise their unique specialty furnishings, including fabrics.

Computer aided design programs (CAD) are used by both interior and textile designers and have helped to significantly end waste in the design process. Designs can be accurately seen on screen without the wasteful sampling processes. The speed of communication is such that designers in various locations around the world can meet on-line and work through problems, come up with solutions, and so on.

Sick building syndrome occurs when there is 'off-gassing' (the release of toxic fumes) from building components, paint, carpeting, and furnishings. Sealed buildings with inadequate ventilation and fresh-air exchange are most likely to cause sickness in its occupants. For example, using new high-performance fiber technology can help improve indoor air quality (IAQ) by reducing the types and amounts of adhesives needed to secure carpet to its backing, or to the floor.

Our growing familiarity with all parts of our world is leading to some adoption of region-based design. We see this most clearly in fashion, but global cultural influences are also evident in household accessories like cushions made from Indian sari fabric, Indonesian batik patterned fabrics, bold colors and patterns found in southern African and South American countries. This familiarity helps add color to interiors.

Another recent trend is the greater degree of cooperation within the design community or 'blurring of the professions.' Architects, interior designers, landscape architects, and artist are seen as integral to good overall building design; and the professional facility managers add insight and practical on-site knowledge.

Design has long looked to the past for inspiration for contemporary interiors. A general audience is coming to appreciate some of the collectibles of the past and to look at dated furniture with new eyes—thanks in part to television shows like *The Antiques Roadshow*. The principles of modernism, introduced by the European Bauhaus movement—that were interrupted by World War II and never fully realized—are finding new expression in good design at affordable prices. House accessory design has improved and become more widely available in part due to design professionals providing guidance to mass market suppliers. Examples are Michael Graves' designs for Target stores and the popular and affordable IKEA lines of furniture and accessories. The mass appeal and influence of Martha Stewart must be acknowledged for helping to popularize good design.

The textile field has always been connected to society. In the past—as chapter 3 relates—the production of textiles was closely related to the economies of nations, the settlement of people, agricultural practices, and fair labor laws. Today, textiles are increasingly involved in questions of human rights and globalization. Questions that were rarely asked twenty years ago are now relevant, and answers are required. Who is manufacturing this product? Where? At what wages and in what working conditions? Is this inexpensive, mass-produced product replacing the output and livelihood of a developing nation? What resources are used? Wasted? How does the manufacture affect the environment? Is recyling/re-use feasible? Globalization may well be the panacea it is sometimes portrayed to be; yet there are many issues to consider before the economic, free-trade model is adopted worldwide. Thoughtful design professionals will keep these concerns in mind.

The Green Scene: Textiles and Environmental Sustainability—

In the last twenty years, concern with environmental issues has become evident. There has been overuse of natural resources and of chemicals both in manufacturing techniques and finished products. Use and disposal of interior textiles, such as carpets and upholstery have become increasingly important, and design professions and the textile industries are working together to find ways and means to overcome wasteful and polluting practices. Many strands remain to be woven into the green textile complex but there is momentum in the green building movement that is encouraging.

Five critical areas influence the work of design professionals: (1) the health, safety, and welfare of the users, (2) the function of the proposed space, (3) the client's budget, (4) law and ethics, and (5) design synthesis. Environmental issues play a part in all these areas. Professionals make decisions, in tandem with clients, that have an impact on the entire community, not only on those who will directly use the space.

The United States Federal Trade Commission (FTC) controls how manufacturers market green products. Strict rules must be followed to protect the consumer from misleading advertising or *green wash*. There was a time when statements commonly made about products and their environmental sustainability were not necessarily true. Consumers were demanding these products; manufacturers recognized a marketing advantage and started claiming their products were environmentally sustainable when, sometimes, they were not. Now, according to the FTC, environmental marketing claims must be clear, understandable, and substantiated. Disclaimers and qualifications must be clearly marked on the product labels. Claims of an environmental nature must explain what makes the product green. These claims must be credible and supported by unbiased evidence. Terms such as *degradable, biodegradable,* and *photodegradable* must be clearly marked. Products that need light or oxygen in order to decompose (e.g., photodegradable) are not likely to successfully break down if they are covered with tons of garbage in a landfill site. The ultimate aim is **perpetual recycling**, or a closed loop. The questions to consider are: Is the product recyclable once, or more than once? Will it never find its way to the landfill site? Is the product 100 percent recyclable, or are parts of the product not recyclable? Byproducts from the manufacturing process that are normally part of future production cannot be advertised as part of the recycled content.

All claims of ecological sustainability must be made in a way that is understandable to the typical consumer. Misleading advertising, even if unintentional, is not acceptable. Disclaimers must be easy to see and read, clearly made in association with the claim of environmental safety. Type size should be legible, the disclaimers should be close to the rest of the claim and should not be a contrary claim, which will lead to confusion on the part of the consumer. Companies cannot say that a product has recycled content and then, in less obvious or less well-distributed material, say that the company has the right, at any time, to substitute that recycled material for virgin material. This is misleading and confusing for the consumer. Terratex®, Earth Square®, and Climatex® are systems that aim to reduce the imprint of the production process on the environment. These systems address the complete lifecycle of the product through production and use, then disposal.

Statistically, the built environment profoundly affects our natural surroundings. According to the United States Green Buildings Council (USGBC), buildings emit 30 percent of greenhouse gases, account for 30 percent of raw material use, and generate 30 percent of the waste that finds its way to landfill sites across the United States. New industrial ecology means that **manufacturers are accountable** for their choices of raw material and how they are processed. The way new buildings are constructed is being rethought. Clients and designers need to focus on reducing the impact the built environment has on our natural environment. Often clients are surprised by the economic benefits of a green building. Operating costs are reduced, employee health is better in nonpolluted interiors, absenteeism is reduced, and productivity is higher. Many building professionals are committed to reducing the negative impacts of construction and actively contributing to community wellness.

Consumers want high-performance fabrics and a safe indoor work environment. **Indoor air quality** (IAQ) is as important to our health as outdoor air quality.

We spend most of our life inside buildings, after all. Carpeting, wall treatments, office cubicle constructions and fabrics may contribute to sick building syndrome. Bad indoor air can affect the health of anyone who works or lives in such an interior. Professional designers respect the health and well being of the occupants by respecting the environmental impact (interior and exterior) of all materials that they select. Consultations with clients, design team members, and representatives from companies that sell textile products help make the design process more sustainable. Clients who are not aware of the environmental options may select environmentally unsustainable products. Designers need to convince clients, with the help of sound scientific data, that there are benefits to using green products and that cost, in the long run, is lower when green products are used.

Carpeting constitutes a large part of interior textile materials, and carpeting with adhesives and other volatile organic compounds contribute to poor indoor air quality. When carpet is removed, it makes up a large part of the waste associated with a building. Fortunately, carpeting is one segment of the textile industry that has taken a pro-active approach in developing production methods that reduce impact on the natural environment. It is possible to recycle carpet, with intense cleaning of old materials, melting and reprocessing fiber solutions through the entire production. All of these processes use energy and water, which, some believe, is also harmful and costly. Some carpet manufacturers opt, instead, to convert parts of used carpeting into new designs. These **modular carpet systems** cut useable portions directly from areas where the fiber has not worn down. The useable portions undergo a cleaning process, and are either made into carpet tiles or shapes that will be incorporated into new carpet installations. Special logos and designs can be created, or new patterns can be overprinted onto the old carpet. Fewer steps are involved in this process, and it gives old carpet extended life and significantly reduces waste.

Carpet backing may be manufactured from other industrial or post-consumer waste. Used car and truck tires, for example, are recycled and used for carpet backing. This process requires no new materials, and no additional resources are exploited. Used carpet backing may be removed and used again in a new installation.

Interior fabrics such as upholstery and drapery products are sometimes made from recycled materials. Polyester fiber can be made from post-consumer waste or post-industrial waste. Post-consumer waste is leftover packaging products such as soda pop bottles. Post-industrial waste is generated from industrial processes, before consumer use. Using these recycled polyesters reduces waste in landfill sites and reduces demand on finite petroleum products that are needed to produce new polyester fibers. Recycled polyester can be used for both apparel and interior textiles. Carpets, upholstery, and drapery fabrics can all be made of post-consumer recycled polyester.

Regenerated cellulose fibers such as **lyocell** (Tencel®) satisfy environmental, performance, and aesthetic needs. The natural cellulose base (such as wood chips) are chemically engineered into fibers. Lyocell is recyclable and biodegradable, which makes it an excellent environmentally sustainable textile choice. The performance characteristics are comparable to rayon and cotton. Unlike most manufactured fiber, lyocell is spun in a continuous process. Any solvents are either re-used or evaporated in the process so it produces no hazardous waste. The cross section of lyocell can be altered, luster can be controlled, and it has excellent wet tenacity, and excellent dye uptake. There is minimal shrinkage. As a newer manufactured fiber, lyocell satisfies many of the environmental goals of future textile research. It is truly a fiber for today and the future—environmentally sound, high-performance, and aesthetically pleasing.

Natural products may be environmentally sustainable. Natural and unbleached cotton, for instance, is eco-sensitive if it has been grown without chemical fertilizers or pesticides. It is claimed that 100 percent natural fibers do not emit the same kinds of toxins some synthetic fibers might. Cotton, wool, silk, and linen fabrics may be left untreated, omitting the use of bleaches, dyes, or finishes. These fabrics are necessary for those with allergies to the chemicals normally used in textile production. On the other hand, some people cannot tolerate natural fibers such as wool, which can cause skin irritation and breathing difficulties. Some might also argue that natural fibers are susceptible to bacteria and dust mites infestations, which would also cause those with allergies to react badly. Labeling must be clear when cotton, feather, wool, hemp, or other untreated natural fiber is used.

Environmental Sustainability Programs

Life cycle assessment is a process that looks at the environmental impact of products. A green product must have minimal impact on the natural environment. A holistic approach to sustainability includes looking at the environment, economics, and social structures.

Life cycle assessment of a product depends on many factors. How the production and use affect the following should be considered in textile product specification.

• water and energy used

• global warming potential

• ozone depletion potential

• acidification potential

• petrochemical oxidant potential

• water and soil ecotoxicity potential

• human toxicity potential

Some of the most important considerations are also the most basic. Is the product needed at all? Does the need justify the financial and environmental costs? Do natural resources need to be consumed? How will the product be used? How will the product be disposed of? An emphasis on the costs (financial and environmental) and on the added value that the technology brings to the product should be considered before anything else. Sustainable methods to replace products that do not completely deteriorate can be done through recycling and reuse programs. The furniture company, Herman Miller, for example, incorporates environmental departments in-house, where research is done, and programs are developed to promote environmental design. Green supplies are chosen over conventional materials, and each product has a series of numbers on its component parts that can later be mixed and matched with other parts in the recycling process. Designs have low environmental impact, fewer steps in processing than conventional production, and use the fewest possible number of components. This is design for disassembly.

Reclamation programs are followed by many manufacturers. These programs help reduce their environmental footprint but are still working within a competitive atmosphere. Competition among manufacturers, formerly based on high speed and competitive pricing, now also concentrates on environmental programs. As consumers demand more green products, designers, clients, purchasers, manufacturers, and reclaimers all work together to promote thoughtful use and reuse of building products. The FTC's guidelines are taken as a baseline for manufacturers to follow. The triple bottom line considers the economic, environmental, and social concerns of choosing certain products. The social responsibility of some manufacturers goes beyond simple improvements of its physical processing of textile products. For example:

Duracolor® (from Lee's Carpets) is a stain-resistant finishing system for carpets that are cleanable with less water and mild detergents. The finish helps carpeting resist up to 99 percent of common stains that occur in the workplace, and is permanent and integral to the fiber.

Unibond® is a thermoplastic backing system for carpets. Unlike traditional latex backings, it is mold and mildew resistant. Instead of using traditional adhesive installation methods, this process uses a hot melt backing that adheres to the carpet with no toxic welds or sealers needed. This system gives the materials greater recycling potential and meets the Carpet and Rug Institute's *green label* standards.

LEED® (Leadership in Energy and Environmental Design)

LEED® is a self-assessing system implemented by the United States Green Buildings Council (USGBC) to rate major renovations and new building construction of commercial buildings, schools, government buildings, apartment complexes, and retail. The entire design process is assessed with respect to the overall impact on the environment. Site selection through occupancy is rated according to the standard guidelines. A building is awarded points or credits for choosing a green option over a conventional one, and the points add up to particular levels of LEED® certification (bronze, silver, gold, platinum).

Six categories address different aspects of a project:

1. sustainability of site selection

2. water efficiency

3. energy and atmosphere
4. materials and resources
5. indoor environment quality
6. innovation in the design process

In each area, points are given for environmental sustainability addressed by the design and reducing the imprint on the environment. The rating system deals with the building envelope and mechanical systems that offer more sustainable energy sources. Materials are part of the rating system but do not yield as many points as the larger elements of the building's structure.

Green interior design is more difficult to assess. Interior rating systems will soon be part of the LEED program, and parts of the program are already contributing to better green design. Professional interior designers can become LEED certified following a period of education. In the textile industry, there is room to work on green production and more conciencious use of materials. Because interior spaces in commercial buildings are likely to be redesigned many times throughout the life of the building, environmental sustainability of materials should be considered from the beginning of a project.

Textiles contribute points toward attaining LEED certification under materials selection. Carpeting is the largest textile component in most commercial interiors. **The Carpet and Rug Institute** (CRI) has a *green label* program that addresses indoor air quality in relation to carpets and rugs. If a carpet meets the standards set by CRI, it gets a LEED credit. An environmentally sustainable carpet will attain the LEED point if it contains some percentage of post-consumer content (e.g., 20 percent or more) and incorporates a backing system that contains bio-based materials. Coloring systems should have little impact on the environment, and the carpet should be certified by the CRI or some other unbiased scientific certification system. More information on LEED can be found through the USGBC.

CARE℠

CARE (Carpet America Recovery Effort) is a joint industry/government effort to reduce the amount of post-consumer carpet that ends up in landfill sites. CARE's goal is to increase recycling and reuse of carpets. It is a nationwide agreement of members of the carpet industry, representatives from government agencies at the federal, state, and municipal levels, and nongovernmental agencies (NGOs). Systems have been devised whereby manufacturers can remove old carpet, break it down, and either recycle or reuse the components. By 2002, over 85 million pounds of carpet had been recovered.

Sustainable Future

The movement to 'build green' is gaining ground in North America. The synergy among scientists, engineers, architects, interior designers, facility managers, contractors, and builders from around the world is essential in order to move away from conventional production and for innovative solutions to become accepted. Reinforcing the financial impact and cost savings of environmentally sustainable building will create the support and cooperation needed to maximize the benefits to the industries involved. Clients must be convinced that it is in their best interest to build green.

Traditional production and use of take-and-make-waste no longer apply. The life cycle of a product must become a closed loop, endless system where materials are continually diverted back into the production of future materials. It is everyone's responsibility to look at a product's impact and demands on nature, and ask questions.

HISTORY OF TEXTILES

The development of textiles can truly be said to be the fabric of history. Cloth in all its forms is closely interwoven with social, cultural, and economic progress. The finding and trading of raw materials for fabric and the manufacturing and selling of cloth have played key roles in exploitation and settlement, trade routes and transportation, industrialization and labor practices, the wealth of some nations and the exploitation of others, work ethics, culture, democracy and the rights of individuals. The following important dates and times in history show how textiles have helped shape culture and influenced many modern economic structures and practices. Globalization and industrialization are not new concepts. Production of and global trade in textiles have occurred for centuries. Using the textile industry as a vehicle to study political, social, and economic history allows us to see how one industry affected—and was affected by—laws and events that shape our world. In some cases, the textile industry was the core reason for change and advancement in society.

Felt, a flat warm material made of wool fibers, was probably the first cloth made by humans. The earliest attempts at weaving are thought to have been made by interlacing tree branches for shelter. Soon, materials such as reeds, grasses, or strips of animal hide were being used for weaving. We do not know when humans invented methods of forming crude fibers and, subsequently, weaving cloth. However, spinning fiber and weaving cloth can be traced back nearly 6000 years.

The art of textiles was known in the earliest era of the Stone Age. In the ruins of the Swiss Lake Dwellers (an archeological discovery of 1853-54), yarns of linen and wool were found in plaited and woven construction, along with string, cordage, and rope.

Around 4000 B.C.E., sheep were kept and wool was being traded in the Tigris-Euphrates basin (now the Iranian Gulf). Around 3000 B.C.E., people living in Britain wore crude forms of woolen garments. As early as 2640 B.C.E., according to Chinese legend, the Empress Shi-Ling-Chi discovered that a particular caterpillar produced an incredible thread with which to make its cocoon. She planted mulberry trees and nurtured the precious insects, and so began the sericulture, the production of silk.

Egyptian tombs are a source of historical textiles. Linen cloth, measuring 1.5 by 18 meters (5 x 60 feet), dates from approximately 3000 B.C.E., and the quality, reportedly, compares with today's fine sheeting. Tomb drawings, dating from 2000 B.C.E., depict ornamental textiles believed to have had their designs either painted or embroidered on plain woven textiles.

The Judeo-Christian scriptures and the sacred writings of other religions hold many references to sheep, shepherds, cotton, linen, wool, and weaving. In India, people were raising cotton, spinning yarn, weaving fabric and trading textiles by 1500 B.C.E. By 1000 B.C.E., traffic in the Mediterranean was considerable, with the Phoenicians the principal seafarers and traders in raw wool and all types of woven goods. Their 'exclusive,' though, was the coveted purple dye extracted from the *Murex branndaris* and *Purpura*

haemastoma molluscs, which were found around ancient Tyre. This purple dye was possibly the first permanent dye and was so costly and rare that, by sumptuary law, only those of royal or imperial rank could wear garmets of purple. In the early Roman Catholic Church, centuries later, 'elevation to the purple' meant promotion to the rank of Cardinal. Their robes are still the purple color of the ancient mollusc dye. Around 700 B.C.E. wool dyeing was established as a craft in Rome.

HISTORY AT A GLANCE

Every event, discovery, and invention takes place in context of all other events, human knowledge and behavior. This timeline provides a glimpse of events surrounding the history of textiles.

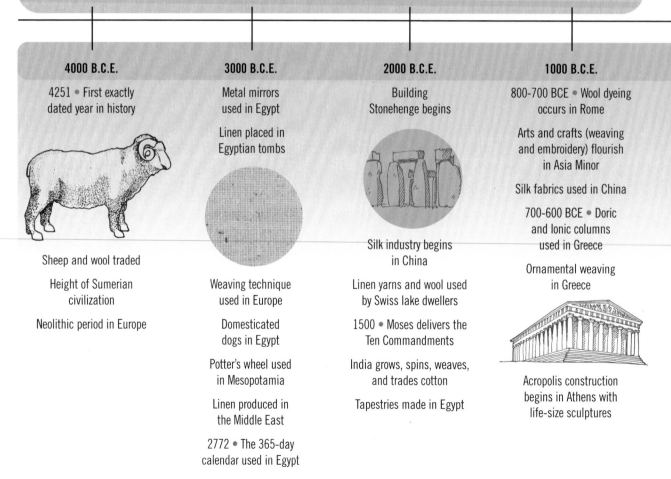

4000 B.C.E.

4251 • First exactly dated year in history

Sheep and wool traded

Height of Sumerian civilization

Neolithic period in Europe

3000 B.C.E.

Metal mirrors used in Egypt

Linen placed in Egyptian tombs

Weaving technique used in Europe

Domesticated dogs in Egypt

Potter's wheel used in Mesopotamia

Linen produced in the Middle East

2772 • The 365-day calendar used in Egypt

2000 B.C.E.

Building Stonehenge begins

Silk industry begins in China

Linen yarns and wool used by Swiss lake dwellers

1500 • Moses delivers the Ten Commandments

India grows, spins, weaves, and trades cotton

Tapestries made in Egypt

1000 B.C.E.

800-700 BCE • Wool dyeing occurs in Rome

Arts and crafts (weaving and embroidery) flourish in Asia Minor

Silk fabrics used in China

700-600 BCE • Doric and Ionic columns used in Greece

Ornamental weaving in Greece

Acropolis construction begins in Athens with life-size sculptures

At the height of the Roman Empire, there was tremendous demand for greater variety and richness in textiles in order to satisfy the affluent tastes of the Roman elite. Romans practiced scientific sheep raising and selective breeding and developed the Tarrentine sheep, a forerunner of the present Merino breed. The Roman armies had to be clothed, and this led to efficient wool producing and cloth making.

When Alexander the Great invaded India in 327 B.C.E., he was taken with the extent and beauty of the cotton prints. Cotton soon became the main apparel fabric along the Mediterranean shores.

The **Silk Road**, a 9600 kilometer (6000 mile) trail from Asia to Italy, opened sometime around 125 B.C.E. and was the transport route for silk from China to the Roman Empire. Interior textiles, bed fabrics, window coverings, and household linens were common in affluent homes, and, in 63 B.C.E., cotton awnings were devised and used in Rome.

Ovid, Pliny, the Romans, and Seneca all wrote about raising and breeding sheep, the culture of cotton, and

speculation about the silk industry. While silk was known and coveted, its origins were a well-kept secret. Seneca thought the lustrous threads were gathered from trees. Pausanius, a Greek traveler, believed silk came from a spider-like insect twice the size of a large beetle. He thought the Chinese fed the insects green reeds until they burst, whereupon the filaments were

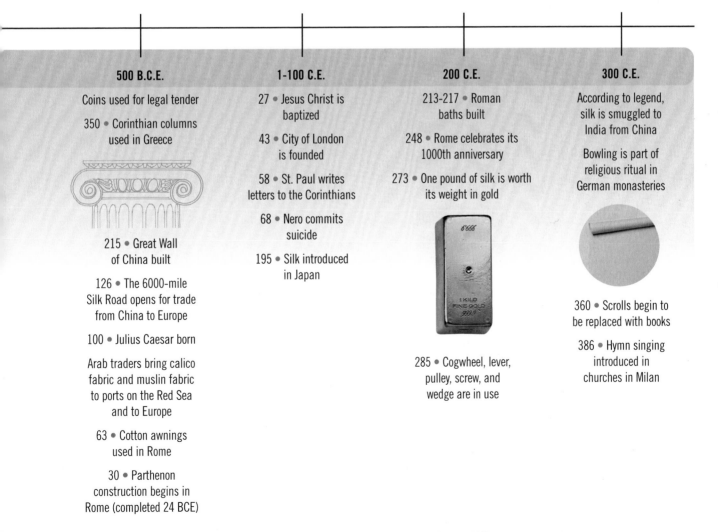

500 B.C.E.

Coins used for legal tender

350 • Corinthian columns used in Greece

215 • Great Wall of China built

126 • The 6000-mile Silk Road opens for trade from China to Europe

100 • Julius Caesar born

Arab traders bring calico fabric and muslin fabric to ports on the Red Sea and to Europe

63 • Cotton awnings used in Rome

30 • Parthenon construction begins in Rome (completed 24 BCE)

1-100 C.E.

27 • Jesus Christ is baptized

43 • City of London is founded

58 • St. Paul writes letters to the Corinthians

68 • Nero commits suicide

195 • Silk introduced in Japan

200 C.E.

213-217 • Roman baths built

248 • Rome celebrates its 1000th anniversary

273 • One pound of silk is worth its weight in gold

285 • Cogwheel, lever, pulley, screw, and wedge are in use

300 C.E.

According to legend, silk is smuggled to India from China

Bowling is part of religious ritual in German monasteries

360 • Scrolls begin to be replaced with books

386 • Hymn singing introduced in churches in Milan

extracted from the body. As late as the fourth century C.E., a Roman historian advanced the theory that Chinese soil itself was so soft it could be watered and combed and somehow made into silk cloth.

In the second century, Greece was the first European country to grow cotton crops. India remained the principal source of this fiber, however. Arab traders dealt in calico, muslin, and other cotton fabrics across the Red Sea and overland to Mediterranean ports, then to Europe. The source of cotton fiber was also a great mystery, and speculations similar to those about the source of silk fibers were common.

The fall of the Roman Empire brought an abrupt end to innovation and production of textiles. The impetus for progress was gone and was not fully revitalized for another thousand years. Fabric making continued on a smaller scale in the home during this time so the skill was not lost.

By the third century C.E., Japan had developed a **sericulture** (silkworm farming and silk harvesting) and provided an additional source of the precious material. A pound of silk at that time was worth its weight in gold. Silk was a highly protected industry in China, which meant that export of the silkworm was illegal. The Indian silk industry, according to legend, developed when a Chinese princess, given in marriage to an Indian prince, brought him silkworm eggs and mulberry tree seeds hidden in the lining of her head-dress. The same sort of devious action brought sericulture to Europe when two Nestorian monks hid silkworm eggs and mulberry tree seeds in their hollowed-out canes and presented this bounty to the Emperor Justinian in 552 C.E. Under the monks' guidance, mulberry trees were planted near Constantinople (Istanbul), eggs were hatched, fiber was cultivated and a center for silk production was founded.

In 768 C.E., Charlemagne saw the possibilities for a French textile industry and established manufacturing centers in Lyons and Rouen. Lyons is still an eminent silk designing and weaving center. Soon after, Charlemagne instituted cloth fairs throughout western Europe. These centers still serve as clearing houses for the world textile trade.

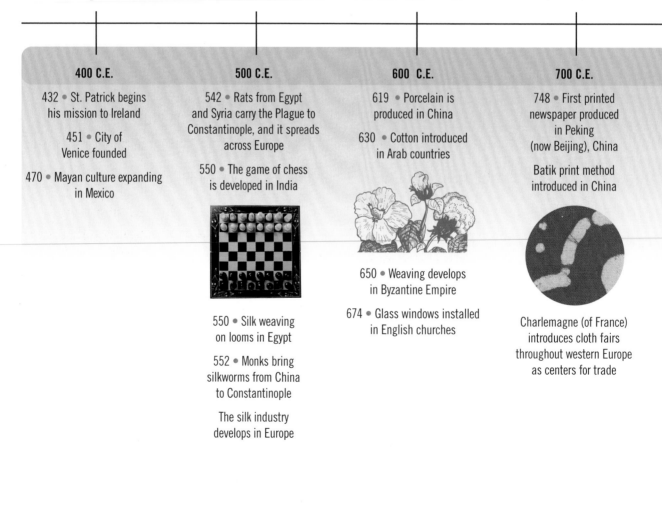

400 C.E.

432 • St. Patrick begins his mission to Ireland

451 • City of Venice founded

470 • Mayan culture expanding in Mexico

500 C.E.

542 • Rats from Egypt and Syria carry the Plague to Constantinople, and it spreads across Europe

550 • The game of chess is developed in India

550 • Silk weaving on looms in Egypt

552 • Monks bring silkworms from China to Constantinople

The silk industry develops in Europe

600 C.E.

619 • Porcelain is produced in China

630 • Cotton introduced in Arab countries

650 • Weaving develops in Byzantine Empire

674 • Glass windows installed in English churches

700 C.E.

748 • First printed newspaper produced in Peking (now Beijing), China

Batik print method introduced in China

Charlemagne (of France) introduces cloth fairs throughout western Europe as centers for trade

Despite competition from other world silk producers, China stayed in the forefront of luxury fabrics. The Chinese devised the method of resist dyeing, now known as batik, which allowed them to produce intricately patterned silk. By the ninth century, silk production had extended farther into Europe.

Making textiles depended on human labor: raising and caring for plants, animals, and insects; harvesting the fiber; spinning and weaving. Transport was by animal-drawn caravans or wind-powered ships. Fabrication into clothing or household goods was done not by machines, but by needle and thread and human effort, by natural light or oil lamps. A finished cloak of woven wool was the result of hundreds of hours of work by many people.

Agricultural Patterns

Early textile production was closely related to agriculture. Natural fibers and dyes all have their origins in the land or from animals that feed off the land. Sheep were raised for wool; crops for the dyes, mulberry trees, and silkworms; and flax and cotton were the main agricultural pursuits alongside the production of food.

Wool was the favored fiber in Europe, and sheep were valuable commodities. By 1275, demand for wool was so great that even serfs owned an average of fifty sheep per family. By the fourteenth century, sheep raising was England's most profitable pursuit. In Spain, Pedro IV imported Barbary rams for use in crossbreeding to improve the fiber quality. Spanish wool was reputed to be the highest quality anywhere by the sixteenth century. The Spanish Conquistadores brought sheep to Mexico, and Native American Indians, particularly the Pueblo and Navajo, began to use wool to weave distinctive patterns into blankets.

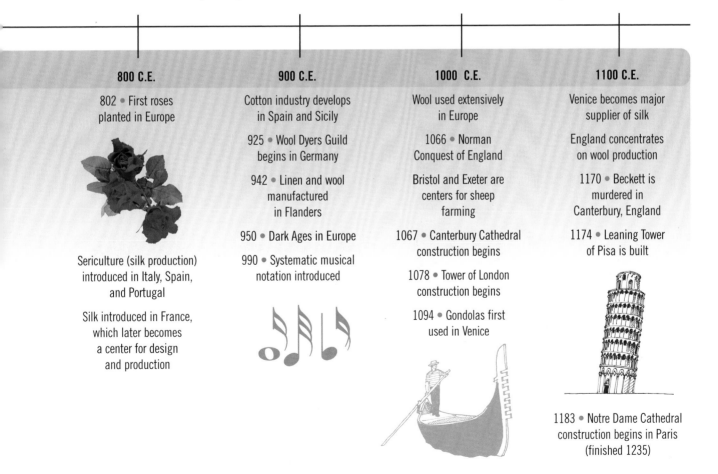

800 C.E.

802 • First roses planted in Europe

Sericulture (silk production) introduced in Italy, Spain, and Portugal

Silk introduced in France, which later becomes a center for design and production

900 C.E.

Cotton industry develops in Spain and Sicily

925 • Wool Dyers Guild begins in Germany

942 • Linen and wool manufactured in Flanders

950 • Dark Ages in Europe

990 • Systematic musical notation introduced

1000 C.E.

Wool used extensively in Europe

1066 • Norman Conquest of England

Bristol and Exeter are centers for sheep farming

1067 • Canterbury Cathedral construction begins

1078 • Tower of London construction begins

1094 • Gondolas first used in Venice

1100 C.E.

Venice becomes major supplier of silk

England concentrates on wool production

1170 • Beckett is murdered in Canterbury, England

1174 • Leaning Tower of Pisa is built

1183 • Notre Dame Cathedral construction begins in Paris (finished 1235)

In Spain, Merino sheep were a closely guarded monopoly until the English defeated the Spanish Armada in 1588. It was not until 1765, however, that other nations managed to secure Merino sheep from Spain.

The Dutch and English sent sheep to the United States at the beginning of the seventeenth century.

- In 1607, the London Company sent a flock to Virginia.
- In 1625, the Dutch East India Company sent a flock to New York City.
- The Massachusetts colony received its first sheep in 1633.
- In 1635, Dutch Texel sheep were brought from Holland to improve the breed.
- By 1640, there were three thousand sheep in the American colonies.

Until 1656, various trade embargoes prevented skilled English weavers from settling in Massachusetts. After that, English weavers were granted land in exchange for training the colonists how to breed sheep and produce cloth in Lowell, Mass. The islands around Nantucket were excellent breeding grounds for the sheep, where they were safe from Aboriginal hunters and the British Crown. The colonists were, by this time, nearly self-sufficient in raw wool and finished garments, much to the dismay of the English government.

European imperial aspirations allowed for trade in textile goods as exploration and settlement were taking place in other parts of the world. The Dutch occupied South Africa by 1724, and Merino sheep were soon introduced. Then the British took over South Africa. Over the next two hundred years, the wool industry continued to grow. Today, South Africa still produces wool and exports it worldwide.

Sheep were first introduced to Australia in 1780 with the arrival of settlers from England. One English settler, Captain MacArthur, was instrumental in starting Australia's wool industry. He purchased rams and ewes of various types and crossbred them to adapt to the Australian climate. He founded and

1200 C.E.	1300 C.E.	1400 C.E.	1500 C.E.
1220 • Salisbury Cathedral construction begins (finished 1258)	Spanish Merino wool known as the highest quality	1429 • First published book on textile dyeing	1506 • Cotton produced to North America
1253 • Linen manufacture begins in England	The silk industry in Lyons develops	1455 • Silk is manufactured in England	1516 • Leonardo da Vinci invents the spinning flyer for yarn manufacturing
1278 • Flemish textile workers rebel in Flanders	Black Death in Europe kills thousands	1470 • War of the Roses disrupts wool production	Indigo dye imported from Japan to Europe
Spain manufactures cotton	1309-1438 • Doge's Palace built in Venice	1480 • Leonardo da Vinci invents the parachute	1589 • The use of forks for eating introduced in French courts
Glass mirrors introduced	1387 • Chaucer writes 'The Canterbury Tales'	1492 • Columbus sails the Atlantic Ocean and arrives in America	
		Modern banking system established in Italy	1594 • Shakespeare writes the play 'Romeo and Juliet'
			Elizabethan-style houses built in England

promoted the Pastoral Company of English Investors to help with his plans for colonization and to further his aims to make Australia a world class sheep-raising region. Wool production continues today in both Australia and New Zealand.

By 1765, Americans began to trade sheep to the West Indies for molasses, sugar, and rum. In 1770, George Washington imported Merino lambs to increase and improve his Mount Vernon flock. Sometimes, mistakes were made. Andrew Craigie of Cambridge, Mass., received a gift of three Spanish Merino sheep. Not knowing the true value of the gift, the Craigies enjoyed the sheep very much—for dinner! Ten years later, Mr. Craigie paid $1000 for one Merino ram.

Until the War of 1812, the textile industry in the United States had mainly produced household textiles. With the onset of war, the industry was hard-pressed to supply enough cloth and blankets for the army. Broadcloth sold for $8-$12 per yard, and the price of wool fleece rose to $4 per pound. Sheep husbandry gained new impetus, and by 1814 the sheep population was roughly fourteen million head. After

the war, increased cotton production in the southeast and population shifts forced sheep farmers to move west. In the southwest, free public land was available to settlers. Land was used for animal grazing, and there was little need for shelter and fodder thanks to the warm climate. Producing wool became a profitable venture. Texas, California, and Oregon offered incentives to sheep farmers, and, by 1865, the sheep population was estimated to be thirty-six million.

The Industrial Revolution changed everything. New spinning and weaving machines replaced household production of wool. Although raising sheep for wool continues worldwide, much of the innovation in the early part of the industrial age was in making textile production more efficient and less labor intensive.

While silk was being produced in China, Japan, India, and east of the Mediterranean, it was just being introduced in Europe by 1000. In 1147, the first white mulberry trees were brought from Syria and successfully planted in France. In 1520, Francis I had more silkworms brought from Milan to the Rhone Valley, where they have been cultivated ever since.

1600 C.E.

1626 • New Amsterdam founded in North America

1634 • Cotton manufactured in Massachusetts

1641 • English cotton manufactured in Manchester

Wool woven in American colonies

1670 • Hudson's Bay Company incorporated by British Royal Charter

1677 • Ice cream becomes popular in Paris

1682 • Amsterdam weaving factory established with 100 looms

1682 • Palais de Versailles becomes a French royal residence

1685 • Huguenots manufacture silk in Britain

1688 • Plate glass is cast

1700 C.E.

Georgian period in England

1701 • Axminster and Wilton carpets introduced

1709 • Pianoforte invented

1720 • Papering walls is popular

1720s • Amish decorative arts and quilt making become popular

1730 • Rococo style popular

1760 • Wedgwood pottery factory opens

1771 • Sir Richard Arkwright opens a yarn spinning mill in Scotland

1789 • French Revolution

1793 • Eli Whitney invents the cotton gin

1792-1801 • Jacquard loom invented in France

1800 C.E.

1795-1820 • Empire period

1813 • Jane Austen writes 'Pride and Prejudice'

1837 • Victorian era begins

1840 • Ireland becomes important exporter of linen

1845 • Bigelow constructs power loom fo carpets

Elias Howe patents sewing machine

300,000 British cotton workers

Workday limited to twelve hours for children

1851 • London Great Exhibition at Crystal Palace; new textile technology introduced

1861-65 • American Civil War

1874 • William Morris heads the Arts and Crafts Movement in England

late 1800s • Bentwood furniture

Silk production in North America was attempted in Virginia in 1607, where plantation owners were fined ten pounds sterling if they did not produce at least ten mulberry trees for each of their one hundred acres.

In 1633 there was disagreement about the origins of cotton fibers, when the famous English diarist Samuel Pepys wrote,

> Sir Martin Noell told us of the dispute between him as a farmer of the additional duty and the East India Co., whether calico be linen or no; which he says it is, having been ever esteemed so; they say it is made of cotton woole that grows upon trees, not like flax or hemp. But it was carried against the Company though they stand out against the verdict.

By 1656, silk production was still encouraged in the North American colonies, and the Virginia Assembly offered 10 000 pounds of tobacco to any planter who exported raw silk or cocoons to the value of two hundred pounds per year. No claims were presented. Though sericulture was not successful in Virginia, Georgia and South Carolina fared better. By 1759,

Georgia was able to produce 10 000 pounds of silk cocoons. Despite this apparent success in producing silk, tobacco and cotton production was preferred. By 1772, Georgia's silk industry was nearly nonexistent.

Cotton is an indigenous plant to North America, and in 1650 the first American cotton plantation was established in Virginia. The first mention of cotton growing in Georgia was in 1735. The indigo plant, used for the production of blue dye, was a profitable crop in South Carolina and continued to do well until after the American Revolution, when indigo imports from the East Indies were found to be cheaper. The need for field workers in the cotton industry is often used as a rationale for the extensive slave trade. The War of 1812 meant a boom in production of all textiles, and in 1820, cotton growers produced 125 million pounds of the fiber. The American cotton industry has sustained itself despite war and the Great Depression of the 1930s. The American south remains one of the largest suppliers of cotton, followed by China and India.

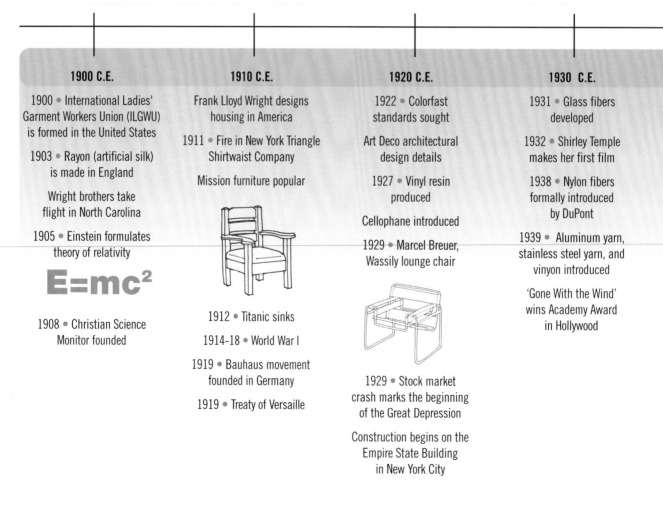

1900 C.E.

1900 • International Ladies' Garment Workers Union (ILGWU) is formed in the United States

1903 • Rayon (artificial silk) is made in England

Wright brothers take flight in North Carolina

1905 • Einstein formulates theory of relativity

$$E=mc^2$$

1908 • Christian Science Monitor founded

1910 C.E.

Frank Lloyd Wright designs housing in America

1911 • Fire in New York Triangle Shirtwaist Company

Mission furniture popular

1912 • Titanic sinks

1914-18 • World War I

1919 • Bauhaus movement founded in Germany

1919 • Treaty of Versaille

1920 C.E.

1922 • Colorfast standards sought

Art Deco architectural design details

1927 • Vinyl resin produced

Cellophane introduced

1929 • Marcel Breuer, Wassily lounge chair

1929 • Stock market crash marks the beginning of the Great Depression

Construction begins on the Empire State Building in New York City

1930 C.E.

1931 • Glass fibers developed

1932 • Shirley Temple makes her first film

1938 • Nylon fibers formally introduced by DuPont

1939 • Aluminum yarn, stainless steel yarn, and vinyon introduced

'Gone With the Wind' wins Academy Award in Hollywood

In the twentieth century, the textile industry became less dependent on agriculture to provide the raw materials needed to produce fabrics. Early synthetic fibers began appearing in world expositions near the end of the nineteenth century, with a viscose solution that later became rayon. Rayon ('Artificial Silk') was used in the early part of the 1900s to replace silk fibers, which were too expensive for most women to afford. The 1920s and 1930s saw dramatic fashion changes that, for the first time, showed the true body shape of women. Clingy, natural silhouettes were popular. Rayon was the ideal fabric for this trend, as it has soft drape, similar to weighted silk fabric.

Nylon was introduced during World War II (1939-45). This extremely strong fiber revolutionized fashion trends, especially for women. Silk stockings were replaced by nylon stockings, which were less expensive and more durable. This fiber was also a welcome addition to fabrics used for soldiers and in fighting during the war. Nylon fibers are extremely durable and strong, and have largely replaced wool fibers in commercial carpeting. Its excellent resiliency and ability to maintain color make it a long-lasting fiber, perfect for carpets and rugs.

People were awed by the miracle of nylon in the 1940s, but they were even more impressed with polyester when it was introduced with unprecedented marketing schemes in 1951. A suit made from polyester fibers was worn for three months, after which time it was shown in a press conference; it was still wrinkle-free. The emergence of polyester allowed for new fashion trends to develop, and its ability to be dyed in extremely bold colors helped inspire upholstery and fashion designers of the 1960s and 1970s to offer fabrics in psychedelic colors. Polyester was not without its faults and its oleophilic nature (ability to absorb oil) and lack of breathability meant scientists had to refine the fabric in order to make it more comfortable. By the late 1960s, polyester outsold all other synthetic fibers including rayon and nylon. Late in the twentieth century, polyester and nylon both saw resurgence in sales thanks to microfiber technology, which allows fibers to be spun in tiny diameters. These fibers are still extremely strong but are also very soft and allow fabric manufacturers to produce new, softer, more breathable fabrics.

1940 B.C.E.

1939-45 • World War II

1946 • Eames molded
plywood lounge chair

1948 • Saran, orlon, veral,
and quiana fibers
introduced

Textiles is the second
largest industry in
the United States

1950 B.C.E.

1950 • Acrylic fibers introduced

1950 • 1.5 million television
sets in the United States

1950-1953 • Korean War

1951 • 15 million television
sets in the United States

1952 • Alexander Gerard
made Director of Textiles
for Herman Miller

1953-58 • various polyester
and acrylic fibers trademarked

1955 • Frank Lloyd Wright
designs the Guggenheim
Museum in New York City

1956 • Tufted carpets are 46 percent
of carpet sales in the United States

1958 • National Aeronautics
and Space Administration
(NASA) established

1960 B.C.E.

Vietnam War

1961 • Berlin Wall erected
in Germany

1962 • Antron® nylon, Orlon®
acrylic, and Herculon®
olefin introduced

1964 • Beatlemania

1965 • Saarinen designs the
'Gateway Arch' in St. Louis, Missouri

1966 • Color televisions
replace black and white
televisions across America

1969 • First artificial grass
floor covering produced

Economic Values

Before the Industrial Revolution, the textile industry was labor intensive. Every step of the production process was performed by men, women, and children. As early as 1300 C.E., several thousand people were involved in the silk business in cities such as Bologna, Genoa, and Milan, not including those responsible for raising silkworms.

Jewish communities had long been in textile trading and, while any form of money lending or financing was forbidden to Christians, Jewish merchants developed what was later to become 'capital financing' and 'bank drafts' for the necessary funding of raw textile production and the sale of finished goods. Around 1300, in Italy, modern banking and financial systems developed. The first banking law on record was passed in Venice, to protect depositors in textile transactions. In 1285, Florentine banking houses were making cash advances to English abbeys

in return for their entire raw wool output. This was terminated by Edward II in 1311, on the pretext that foreign creditors must be abolished. The English king confiscated all the English property of the 'financial aggressors.' By 1320, most of the Florentine merchant bankers had left England. The Medici family banking houses were pre-eminent in the fourteenth century, and are usually credited with founding 'world scale' banking.

Textile production, and the attendant labor and financing systems, continued through the fifteenth century. Control over production and processing became increasingly restricted to various textile guilds. By 1620, Europe was overcome by periodic economic depression, which forced textile prices to drop, reduced exports, and increased unemployment in England and European textile centers. It was not until after 1630 that recovery began.

1970 C.E.	1980 C.E.	1990 C.E.	2000 C.E.
Advances in textiles include: adding texture, cross-section modification, and high-speed production	Environmental concerns include depletion of ozone layer and the greenhouse effect	Berlin Wall comes down—reunification of Germany	Emphasis continues on human rights issues in textile industry
1972 • Consumer Product Safety Agency responsible for research and testing of flammability in textiles	1981 • Prince Charles and Lady Diana Spencer marry	New generation of engineered textiles appears	Global trade means more products are available to more people worldwide
1974 • Aramid polyamide fiber introduced	1983 • Airline industry establishes new performance standard for flammability following Air Canada Flight 797 fire	Production in the textile industry moves east	Design practice become more international
Kevlar protective clothing used by law enforcement agencies	1984 • Apple personal computers become popular	Questions of human rights and environmental sustainability in building and textile industries	Textile specialists are important part of the design team
1978 • Manufactured fibers outsell cotton and wool fibers	1986 • 3500-year-old tomb of Tutankhamen discovered		Environmental sustainability emphasized in design and textile production
	1988 • The musical 'Phantom of the Opera' opens on Broadway		
	1989 • Eighty nations declare that chlorofluorocarbons must be banned by the year 2000		

By the seventeenth century, trading between Europe (and England) and the colonies was a significant economic boost for both. Textiles were a large segment of import and export economies, and by 1675 the Massachusetts Bay Colony was trading wool to France in exchange for linen, and to Spain and Portugal for wine. This did not please the English, and restrictive trade laws were enacted in order to protect their interest in the colonies. American colonies were not deterred from increasing trade with Europe, and protectionist policies further encouraged their independence from England.

England diversified its textile industry in the eighteenth century by promoting linen production in Ireland and silk production in England. John Lombe is credited with developing the silk industry in Derby, England, in 1718. His early 'industrial espionage' involved disguising himself as a laborer and working in leading silk throwing mills in Italy. He surreptitiously made drawings of machines and learned how to work them. His efforts were discovered in the early 1700s but he managed to escape capture by boarding a ship bound for England. The Spitalfields silk industry grew throughout the eighteenth century with fabrics of intricate floral patterns, which were often used as upholstery fabric.

England was importing cotton in limited quantities, and restrictions against further import, formulated to protect the domestic wool industry, were common. The Irish linen mills had no labor codes to control the length of a worker's day or conditions inside the factories. These factories were dangerous and unhealthy for workers. These were the first of the 'sweatshops' about which much has been written.

In the United States, the woolen textile industry was burgeoning and the price of Merino grease wool went from 75 cents to over $3.00 a pound by 1812. When the war was over, British wool reappeared in America, forcing a decline in prices. The eighteenth century was one of invention and mechanization. Mechanical looms and knitting machines took the place of hand weavers and knitters. Mechanical spinning replaced manual spinning wheels, and yarn could be produced much more quickly, with consistently higher quality. In 1818, the first mill for weaving silk ribbons, trimmings, and fringes was established in Philadelphia. With faster production, lower costs, and increased quantities of textiles on the market, fabric became cheaper to buy. Ready-to-wear and premade fabrics were offered to the consuming public.

In the nineteenth century, large factories were needed to house the large mechanical looms and knitting machines. Skilled textile workers were needed to run the machines and control quality. Sewing operations had largely been a home-based endeavor for women. The new factories had rows and rows of sewing machines. The new factory system provided consistent quality and mass production of goods. In New York, these factories were notoriously dangerous for workers. The spaces were small and crowded, there was inefficient temperature control, and poor ventilation. Factories had lint hanging in the air, which created conditions that were ideal for flames to catch and spread. Indeed, devastating fires did occur. A lack of windows and few exits meant tragedy for many of the women who worked in these factories. Over time, labor unions recognized the danger faced by the workers in the textile industry, and codes were established to help improve the working conditions in North America and Europe.

Textiles and Politics

Textiles, as a major economic segment of each nation, were subject to the vagaries of politics. Innumerable laws to encourage, protect, restrict, and curtail production were enacted. Rulers, who were anxious to see the best economic return from the industry in their country, regulated use and trade of textiles. Early Sumptuary Laws restricted who could wear certain garments and colors and, later, manufacturers were restricted in terms of types and quantities of textiles they were allowed to produce. In 1111, Henry I of

England established the Scottish woolen industry at the mouth of the Tweed River. In 1221, Henry III, in an effort to foster home production of wool, ordered the Mayor of London to burn every piece of cloth that contained Spanish wool. Edward II further forbade all use of foreign cloth. By 1337, Edward III declared wool a Crown commodity and he would buy only English wool. Not all producers were in favor of this action and, refusing the edict, were subject to having their wool seized in return for promissory notes.

British parliament passed laws prohibiting the export of raw wool, which led to rampant smuggling of the fibers. This illegal trade is said to have contributed greatly to the rise of the British merchant navy. The struggle between the Crown and English, woolen producers lasted well into the fifteenth century. In 1483, Edward IV ended the dispute when he reversed all restrictive laws and allowed shipments of raw wool out of the country. These were then distributed from Calais, France.

In order to improve relations between England and Spain, in the late 1400s, Edward IV allowed a shipment of sheep to go to Spain. Not wanting to give too much of an advantage to this sometime enemy, the King made sure the sheep designated for export were of poor quality, far below the quality of the Spanish Merino. Spain, at the time, was a textile power, particularly in wool fabrics.

After crossing the Atlantic in 1492, Columbus discovered that the North American Native peoples used cotton cloth. This became a prized sample of a New World commodity and was sent back to Europe. Later expeditions (around the 1520s) into Central and South America, by Pizarro and Cortez, also found cotton used in abundance. They discovered that block printing and coloring cotton textiles were well-developed crafts. Red cochineal was taken from Mexico and Peru and became a new 'Spanish' textile dye. In 1533, Pizarro declared the Peruvian woven fabrics were superior to those made in Spain and were equal to the fine fabrics of Egypt.

In England, Henry VIII was engaged in a dispute with the Roman Catholic Church. In 1539, two hundred abbeys and monasteries were suppressed. This resulted in the demise of English Monastery Wool, which had been a great source of income for the church.

Northern Ireland, taken over by England and settled with English and Scottish Protestants, supported a strong flax spinning base for mills in Manchester. The Irish mills employed women and children, in deplorable conditions, and profits were siphoned off to the English owners.

During Oliver Cromwell's rule as Lord Protector of England (1649-58), the export of sheep, raw wool, and yarn to the American colonies was forbidden. This action was designed to limit the growth of the colonies' strength. Instead, it led to increased trade between America and Holland and Spain, and ultimately to colonial independence. Colonial trade in textiles and its growing power alarmed the British; in 1669, a British law was passed forbidding all export of wool or textile products from the colonies. It even prohibited the trade of textiles between colonies. It could not be properly enforced, however, and trade continued. Similar legislation in 1698 forbade shipments of wool from the colonies to England, even though England was in need of raw wool for domestic use.

England's relations with Ireland had also deteriorated. England had tried and failed to upgrade their Irish-based flax and linen business. Britain allowed Ireland to control its own linen industry, and much to the chagrin of England, the Irish succeeded. The English, though, then forbade the import of woolens from Ireland, and any Irish goods found in England were to be confiscated and destroyed.

The cotton industry had grown in America, and, in 1770, cotton goods were forbidden in England in an effort to enforce the exclusive use of British woolens by English people. In 1701, silk imports to England were also forbidden. These restrictions were not effective, and in 1712 English law forbade wearing cotton fabrics. By 1716, there were thirty separate laws prohibiting the import of calico alone, yet the fashionable prints continued to gain in popularity. The restrictions had little effect on the colonies' growth in textile production; in 1768, all graduates of Harvard College wore colonial-made fabrics. In 1770, Ben Franklin was in the forefront of encouraging many facets of American textile manufacturing. In 1774, England forbade the export of cotton textile machinery to America, but this did little to curb production and export of cotton from the colonies.

During the American Civil War (1861-65), the woolen industry expanded as the demand for military blankets and uniforms increased. The end of the conflict saw a thriving garment industry in New York and the beginning of America's great textile mills in the south. For the remainder of the nineteenth century, textile production and trade expanded worldwide.

Textile Workers ━━━━━━━━━━━━━━

Historically, employment, work ethics, and labor laws have been closely connected with the textile industry. The provision of the basic necessities of life such as shelter, food, and clothing has been the main concern for centuries. Textiles have played a role in all of these areas. Fabric was used as window coverings in early shelters and for padding benches and beds. Foods, mostly grains, were stored and traded in woven cloth sacks. Transportation overseas depended on wind-powered ships with cloth sails. And, of course, apparel is made of cloth.

In 1100, Flemish textile workers moved to England seeking work, and Henry I (1100-1135) accepted them but scattered and relocated them among the villages and hamlets so that their skills could be used throughout the country. In 1128, the French Cistercian monks arrived in England: by 1143, fifty abbeys were established, and led the country's wool production. Monks were the textile workers in this period, which lasted until Henry VIII enforced the closure of monasteries throughout England.

Persecution forced Jewish families to leave Flanders and settle in England by the mid-twelfth century, where they were active traders in wool. By 1271, Henry III of England declared that all workers, male and female, were welcome in England if they came to work in the cloth industry.

By the fourteenth century, Venice had over 17 000 woolen cloth workers. Florence had about 200 wool dyers, fullers, cloth cutters, and tailors. Louvain, in Flanders, boasted 150 000 journeyman weavers. Edward III offered protection to all foreigners working in the wool industry in England, and took an active part in promoting commerce in woolen goods. When Flemish rulers decided that the quality of their cloth was diminishing, they set up a Cloth Examining Boards. This resulted in a slowdown in production in Flanders, and forced many Flemish weavers to seek work in England, where they were welcomed.

The Protestant Reformation in the sixteenth century caused general disruption in England and Europe. Edward VI urged Protestants to come to England to work in the textile industry. Workers came from Germany, France, Italy, Poland, and Switzerland. Elizabeth I consolidated the English woolen industry, welcoming textile workers from the Netherlands, who were fleeing the Spanish invasion. To remind knights of England's economic base (wool), they were made to kneel on a woolsack when they were knighted.

The Spanish invasions of Europe, under Philip II, caused thousands of workers to flee for their lives. Many went to Ireland, others to parts of France and England. By 1763, silk making had developed in England and 40 000 men, women, and children worked in and around London—in Spitalfields, for example. Settlement of North America was under way by this time, and householders were required, by decree, to spin yarn and weave cloth in proportion to the number of females in the family, giving rise to the term 'spinster.'

Mennonites, from the Rhenish Palatinate, immigrated to America and soon set up textile weaving and knitting operators in Germantown, Pennsylvania, then part of the city of Philadelphia. The War of 1812 brought about the introduction of trousers, a symbol of revolt against the British, whose men dressed in knee breeches and hose.

The waves of Irish immigrants coming to the United States, fleeing famine in their homeland early in the nineteenth century, included many skilled linen workers. By 1850, up to 50 000 people found work in woolen factories. Conditions were deplorable and working hours long. In 1852, in New York, the conditions of the average worker started to improve when state law eliminated child labor. Technical advances provided another boon; the development of the self-threading shuttle, in 1868, eased the hazard of contracting the 'kiss of death'—a respiratory disease caused by sucking the filling yarn through a hole to thread the shuttle.

Labor unions fought long, bitter struggles to gain the right to represent textile workers. In 1900, the International Ladies' Garment Workers Union (ILGWS) was formed. New York City had 475 shirt-waist factories, employing 18 000 workers—mostly girls. The economic crash of 1929 and the subsequent Depression of the 1930s followed the prosperous, fun-loving, carefree *Roaring Twenties*. New York City lost 1100 dress manufacturing facilities between 1929 and 1932, and contract shops declined 80 percent. World War II led to a renewal of the textile industry; with high demand for textile products, employment opportunities were better than ever.

In the twentieth century, labor concerns in North America focused on job security. By the late 1900s, cheaper manufacturing could be found offshore in Asia, Africa, and India. Many manufacturers moved their production from the 'West' to these low-cost countries. Protecting the domestic textile industry has increasingly become a concern with the implementation of massive economic and trading communities, such as those found in North America and Europe.

The North American Free Trade Agreement (NAFTA) signed by Canada, the United States, and Mexico was designed to improve movement of goods through the borders at reduced rates, or tariff- or duty-free. This agreement has caused debate among textile producers as to how it affects their business.

Central America and South America participate widely in all sectors of manufacturing with 'Maquila Doras' (free-trade zones in Honduras, Costa Rica, and Mexico among others). Labor issues abound in factories in these countries. In North America, where the idea of child labor is abhorred (and illegal), the 'maquilas' are seen to exploit young women. Many fashion companies have been forced to address ethical production policies with workers' rights at the top of the list.

Factories in Asia and India all face scrutiny over their production practices. At the same time, the North American textile industry is seen to suffer from having to pay high wages by comparison. The clothing industry, in particular, contends that consumers demand low-cost products and are not willing to pay more. In order to satisfy that need, and to stay profitable, manufacturers see no other choice but to move production offshore to lower-cost countries where the labor laws are less stringent, and workers are plentiful and willing to work for low wages. The industry constantly faces the dilemma of serving both interests, causing tension and debate. Since the 1980s, many in the design profession have demanded that human rights be considered when sourcing textiles from other countries. With increasing global trade and specialization of manufacturing, labor issues and ethical production will continue to be debated.

PART
TWO

FIBER BASICS

Fibers are the basic components of fabrics. As such, their characteristics and particular properties form the bases for determining the final character of the fabric. Yarn and fabric manufacturers choose the fiber or fibers that most closely meet the requirements for the planned end use, and then proceed to modify, maximize, or minimize those properties to suit their purpose. They may, in addition, add totally new properties. Fiber, yarn, fabric construction, and finishes are interdependent and together give the finished product its final distinguishing characteristics. A common error is to search for a mythical absolute—one fiber to satisfy all needs. No single fiber has the capacity to meet all needs; often functions overlap and the performance of one fiber must be compared to the slightly different performance of another. This 'knowledgeable juggling' results in the selection of the best fiber(s) for a particular purpose. Familiarity with fibers and their basic properties helps the design team to anticipate the performance that a particular fiber will contribute to a textile.

Fibers fall into two general categories:

* **Natural:** found in nature and used in the same form in which it was found. Examples include wool, cotton, silk, and linen.

* **Manufactured:** contains products from other substances found in nature (such as oil and wood), which are altered drastically before being made into fibers.

Fiber Composition

A fiber is like a hair—a pliable strand with a minute diameter in relation to its length (a high length-to-width ratio). All fibers are composed of simple molecules, or **monomers**, built in a chain-like formation to form giant molecules called **polymers**. The process of forming polymers from molecules is called **polymerization**, and the **degree of polymerization** (dp) identifies the number of molecular units joined together end to end to form the polymer.

Fibrous polymers are characterized by a high degree of polymerization, usually between 500-10000. The size and complexity of the polymer means that their properties are radically different from those of the individual molecules.

Other characteristics of a polymer are:

* high molecular weight
* great stability
* a high degree of intramolecular force, which prevents easy destruction

Sugar and cotton are both composed of glucose units. Sugar is a relatively simple combination of glucose elements, and it may be dissolved in water. The cellulose that forms cotton is composed of up to 10 000 glucose molecules joined by polymerization and produces a product that is both water insoluble and resistant to many strong chemicals.

The polymerization of various chemicals into fibers occurs in nature to produce cotton, wool, silk, and linen. The same process is synthesized and amplified in the laboratory, then transferred to the mill, to produce manufactured fibers.

Fiber Qualifications

To be suitable for use as a textile fiber, a polymer must meet the following basic qualifications (sometimes known as primary characteristics):

- high length-to-width ratio
- adequate strength, or tenacity
- flexibility, or pliability
- cohesiveness, or spinning quality
- uniformity

These basic qualifications are determined by the nature of the fiber's external structure, its chemical composition, and the fiber's internal structure.

These properties are essential, and production of yarns does not proceed if any one property is absent. The design team can, therefore, safely assume that these qualities are present in any commercially produced fiber or yarn.

High Length-to-Width Ratio

A minimum of 100:1 is usually considered essential, and most fibers have much higher ratios. Fibers shorter than 1.5 cm (approx. 1/2") are seldom used for yarn. The fiber molecules and the fiber itself are usually long and extremely thin. Bundles of long thin monomers form long thin polymer chains through systematic repetition (polymerization) to become fibers.

STAPLE FIBERS are short fibers, measured in centimeters or inches. Natural fibers, except silk, are naturally staple length and vary from 1.3 cm to 1 meter (1/2-39").

FILAMENT FIBERS are long, continuous fiber strands of indefinite length, measured in meters (yards) or even kilometers (miles). They may be made into **monofilament** or **multifilament** yarn. A common monofilament yarn is fishing line. Multifilament yarns have a number of filament fibers loosely twisted together to form a yarn.

Silk is the only natural filament fiber. It is usually about 1450 m (1600 yrds.) long. Natural rubber and metal are made into filament form but are not naturally found in that condition. All manufactured fibers are produced as filament fibers. Depending on the end use, they may be transformed into short lengths to become staple fibers. The filament-to-staple process involves grouping thousands of filaments together to form a thick rope called a *filament tow* that is then cut or broken into the required lengths. The staple fibers are then spun into yarn in the same way cotton or wool might be.

Adequate Strength, or Tenacity

While this quality varies for different fibers, they must all possess sufficient tenacity to withstand processing (spinning and fabric construction) and to give adequate durability in the end use to which the fibers are allocated. The American Society for Testing and Materials (ASTM) defines tenacity as: "the tensile stress expressed as force per unit linear density of the unstrained specimen."

Tenacity is determined by mechanical testing and mathematical conversion formulae. It may be expressed as grams of force per denier. **Denier** is a unit of yarn measurement equal to the weight in grams of 9000 meters of the yarn. Fiber strength does not always indicate comparable yarn or fabric strength. Most fabrics require a minimum fiber tenacity of 2.5 grams per denier (gpd). However, some weak fibers— like wool with strength less than 2.5 gpd—can be used in durable textiles due to compensating properties such as superior elasticity and resilience. The strongest yarns are those made of strong filament fibers; staple fibers in yarns may slip under stress.

Flexibility, or Pliability

This is the capacity to bend a fiber repeatedly without breaking it. Flexibility is important in durability. Fiber size may determine the flexibility of a fabric. Thick fibers are relatively inflexible and give crispness, roughness, body, and stiffness. They also resist crushing, which is important for fibers used in carpeting. Fine or thin fibers are very flexible and give softness and better drape to a fabric.

Cohesiveness, or Spinning Quality

Spinning quality or cohesiveness is the ability of fibers to stick together in the yarn manufacturing process. The necessary cohesion may occur because of the longitudinal contour or the cross-sectional shape of the fibers. Fibers like wool have a textured surface with scales that allow the fibers to interlock in the twisting process in yarn spinning. Cotton fibers have a kidney-shaped cross section that looks like a flattened ribbon along the longitude. This allows the fibers to fit into one another in the twisting process of yarn spinning. When the shape or surface does not have good spinning quality, fibers of sufficient filament length are used so they can be twisted into yarns more easily.

Uniformity

To successfully spin a group of fibers into yarn they must be similar in:

- length and width
- flexibility
- spinning quality

Manufactured fibers can be controlled during production to maintain a high degree of uniformity. Textile manufacturers prefer yarns composed of uniform fibers because the fibers have a smooth and regular appearance, handle well in machinery, and accept dyes more evenly.

Natural fibers may lack uniformity and vary slightly in quality because they are affected by natural elements like weather, nutrients, insects, and disease. Blending the same fibers from different sources often compensates for this lack of uniformity.

Fiber Classification

It is practically impossible to remember all the properties and characteristics of each individual fiber. Since the advent of manufactured fibers, scientists have arranged or classified them into groups. Design professionals need, first, to become acquainted with the general properties of each group. Then, for intelligent selection, use, and care of any textile product, access to knowledge concerning special qualities of individual fibers is necessary. The system for classification is generally based on the following:

- the origin of the fiber:
  - natural
  - manufactured
- the general chemical type:
  - cellulosic
  - protein
  - mineral
  - synthesized
- the generic term:
  - natural
  - manufactured (synthesized), as specified by the Textile Fiber Products Identification Act (e.g., spandex)

- the trade name:
  - Lycra® (spandex)
  - Antron® (nylon carpet fiber)

Fiber Origin

The broad classifications for fiber origin are **natural** and **manufactured.**

NATURAL FIBERS: Natural fibers are obtained from plants, animals, or minerals. Fibers from this group are the product of thousands of years of selection and cross breeding. They are produced seasonally and stored until used. Although carefully controlled, they are still to some extent subject to the vagaries of nature—weather, insects, nutrients or the lack of them. Natural fibers are divided into **cellulosic**, plant source; **protein**, animal source; **mineral**; and **natural rubber.**

MANUFACTURED FIBERS (synthetic fibers): Close observation of the silkworm building its cocoon led to the discovery of how silk was made. As early as the seventeenth century, it was predicted that if a proper liquid were forced through a small aperture and allowed to congeal, a fiber similar to silk might be produced. It was not until 300 years later, however, that the first filament was made from a solution of cellulose—an inferior fiber called *artificial silk*. By 1910, these fibers were in limited commercial production in the United States. Improvements followed and the fiber was renamed rayon in 1924.

• *Spinneret, manufactured fibers*

The process of polymerization is used to manufacture synthetic fibers. The fibers are made from various chemical solutions that are forced through the tiny holes of a spinneret—a device similar to a showerhead but much smaller. The fine liquid streams of solution harden into continuous strands of filament fiber. The properties of the fiber depend on the exact spinning conditions. The number of holes in the spinneret, their shape, and size, vary with the filament fiber and the yarn desired.

A small spinneret may be the size of a large thimble and have up to ten holes, while a large one has more than 10 000 holes. The spinneret is usually round and made of platinum or iridium. Extruded filaments may be single, or monofilament, such as nylon fishing line. More often the filaments are extruded in groups or bundles of multifilaments. The orifice shape can be varied, which changes the cross section of the fiber. A triangular hole will produce a trilobal fiber, a round hole will produce a smooth rod-like fiber, a star-shaped hole will produce a multilobal fiber. The size is varied to make filaments finer than silk or heavier than horsehair.

Three basic techniques are used to produce filament fibers. In the **dry spinning method**, the polymer solution is combined with a solvent, then forced through the spinneret into warm air where the solvent evaporates, leaving the liquid stream to immediately solidify. In the **wet spinning method**, the polymer solution is forced through the spinneret into a wet solution where it immediately coagulates into a continuous filament. In the **melt spinning method**, a solid polymer is melted and forced

Microfiber is an extremely fine fiber—finer than silk. The spinning process requires very high-quality polymer, and the fiber is often produced in a bicomponent process using two different polymers that do not mix. Two or more fiber solutions are forced through the spinneret. The fibers are treated immediately to dissolve or shrink away the binding materials, leaving the fine microfiber. It is very soft and drapable, and the bicomponent spinning method reduces the stress on the fiber.

Microfiber can be made out of nylon or polyester and is used in upholstery fabrics.

Microfibers

• *Pie Wedge*   • *Islands/sea*

through the spinneret into cool air where it solidifies. The combination of chemicals and mechanical extrusion often produces a filament that is too smooth or lustrous, especially if it is extruded through round holes. This is sometimes tempered by the addition of a chemical delustering agent to the solution. The effect is usually to pit the surface of the fiber, resulting in a more diffused reflection of light and a softer, less lustrous, look.

After extrusion, the polymer chains in the filament must be oriented (made parallel to each other). This is done by a drawing or stretching process, and it is important for the ultimate strength and elasticity of the fiber. Manufactured filaments may be used for textile production without further processing into yarn, or they may be further twisted or spun into yarns, either in their filament form or cut into staple form.

Textile Fibers

| General Chemical Type | Natural | | Manufactured | |
	Generic Term	Source	Generic Term	Source
CELLULOSIC	Abaca	abaca leaves	Acetate	Wood, cotton
	Coir	coconut husk	Rayon	Wood, cotton
	Cotton	seed hairs		modified
	Linen	flax stalk		
	Hemp	hemp stalk	Triacetate	Wood, cotton
	Jute	jute stalk		modified
	Kapok	seed hairs	Lyocell	Wood, cotton
	Pina	pinapple leaves		modified
	Ramie	ramie stalk		
	Sisal	agave leaves		
PROTEIN	Wool	sheep		
	Silk	moth larvae secretion		
	Alpaca	alpaca		
	Angora fur	angora rabbit		
	Camel hair	Bactrian camel		
	Horsehair	horse		
	Llama	llama		
	Mohair	angora goat		
	Vicuna	vicuna		
MINERAL			Glass	silica sand
			Metal	various metals
			Carbon	
ELASTOMERIC	Rubber	rubber tree	Spandex	segmented polyurethane
SYNTHESIZED			Acrylic	manufactured polymers
			Aramid	manufactured polymers
			Modacrylic	manufactured polymers
			Olefin	manufactured polymers
			PBI (polybenzimidazole polymer)	
			Polyamide Nylon	manufactured polymers
			Polyester	manufactured polymers
			Saran	manufactured polymers
			Sulfar	manufactured polymers
			Vinal	manufactured polymers
			Vinyon	manufactured polymers

General Chemical Types

Fibers of both natural and manufactured origin may be classified by chemical type.

Cellulosic

NATURAL CELLULOSE fibers are obtained from vegetable sources. These fibers may come from the **plant stem**, as in linen (flax) or hemp; from the **leaves**, as in sisal; from the **seed hairs**, as in cotton; or from **nut husks**, as in coir.

MANUFACTURED CELLULOSIC fibers are significantly different in degree and combination of properties to natural cellulosic fibers. These fibers burn easily and quickly, and are damaged by acids and resistant to alkalies. They are low in elasticity and resilience and are soft and absorbent.

MODIFIED CELLULOSIC fibers combine cellulose with acetic acid. Specific manufacturing techniques and finishes give this group a variety of properties in addition to, or instead of, the basic properties of other cellulose-based fibers.

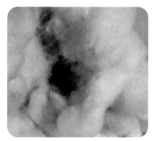

• cotton fibers   • wool fibers

Protein

Fibers in this group are natural in origin and are derived from animal hair (wool and variants) and, in lesser quantity, from the secretions of animals (silk). These fibers, as a group, are relatively weak and less resistant to certain chemicals and environmental factors. Protein fibers have good resiliency and elasticity and excellent moisture absorbency. They burn slowly and are self-extinguishing.

PROTEIN FIBERS have not been successfully synthesized in the same way as cellulosic fibers. **Spider silk** has been a fascination for generations, and it is generally thought to be stronger than silk fibers from a *bombyx mori* (silkworm). Harvesting spider silk is much more difficult than harvesting silk from a worm, as spiders are more territorial, therefore, harder to breed, and once the fiber is spun by the spider, it is too fine and weak to use as a commercial fiber.

Advances in biotechnology research and development have resulted in a solution to producing commercially usable spider's silk. Nexia's BioSteele® Extreme Performance Fibers is the manufactured spider 'dragline' (one of four types of silk spun by spiders), similar to that used to build a spider's web. Transgenics research and deeper understanding of silk protein have resulted in the first manufactured spider silk.

The silk is only produced after it has been extruded from the spider and exposed to air where it then hardens. Using the similarities in mammary glands of goats and spider silk glands—both have epithelial cells that manufacture and secrete water soluble, complex proteins—the spider silk gene has been successfully transferred to the goat's numerous mammary cells. This process works well because the goat can tolerate the silk gene, and excretes milk from the mammary glands along with the spider's silk. Uses for spider silk are mainly in health care (sutures and prosthetic ligaments), but because of its awesome strength (the strongest known material) cordage and protective fabrics will soon follow.

Mineral

ASBESTOS: Asbestos is obtained from a fibrous form of serpentine rock mined extensively in Canada. Today, very few products contain asbestos; the fibers are hazardous if inhaled into the lungs. It was popular in building construction because it is completely fire resistant.

MANUFACTURED MINERAL FIBERS: Fiber such as glass manufactured from silica sand and limestone, or metallic fibers, usually aluminum but sometimes gold or silver, have very specific properties and uses. Variations of glass and metallic fibers are used extensively in furnishings.

RUBBER AND ELASTOMERS: The liquid sap from the rubber tree (Hevea species) is the source of natural rubber fibers. Manufactured elastomeric fibers like spandex are formed of a variety of chemicals.

Synthesized

New developments, new techniques, and new combinations are continually being assessed, and new fibers and textiles are the results of this research. Innovation and modification are ongoing activities for textile chemists. The significant distinguishing fact about these fibers is that they are 'invented', devised in the lab and built without recourse to traditional fiber sources. Processes involve extracting molecules from sources such as petrochemical waste, water, and air; inducing the formation of macromolecules; and creating long-chain polymers suitable for extruding into fibers. DuPont organized and funded the first research and development in this area in 1928, not knowing what the result of the fundamental investigation would be.

> The development of nylon, which commenced commercial production in 1939, was one of the results of DuPont's research. It has been said, in this regard, that the first pound of nylon fibers cost DuPont 27 million dollars.

Generic Terms

The generic terms for the natural fibers are well known: cotton, wool, etc. Once manufactured fibers were widely accepted, generic terms became confusing. By the mid 1950s a wide range of manufactured fibers were being produced so, in 1958, the Textile Fiber Products Identification Act (TFPIA) was passed in the United States. It became effective in 1960. This law established generic, or family names, and definitions for all manufactured fibers. A generic name is used for a group of fibers having similar chemical composition. New generic names are adopted only when a fiber is developed that is different in chemical composition from other fibers. It also must reflect significantly different properties. The generic classifications are universal and are always written in lower case. The law also requires textile products sold at retail to have labels stating the fiber content in generic terms.

Specific Trade Names

Under natural fiber generic terms, origin or additional detail usually comprises the specific name (Indian Head cotton, for instance). For manufactured or synthetic fibers, there are also fiber **trade names** owned and promoted by manufacturers (e.g., Lycra® from DuPont). Trade names are given to various fibers manufactured by specific textile firms and are written as proper nouns. Fiber content labels must always use the generic name, not the trade name (e.g., spandex, NOT Lycra®).

Manufactured fibers are not subject to the limitations of nature; they are usually uniform in quality because the entire production process can be controlled. When fibers are spun, constructed, finished, and styled for the mass market, however, that quality may be compromised to save time and money. The trade name, therefore, can be a good consumer guarantee of quality.

Inherent Fiber Characteristics

Each individual fiber is characterized by a number of inherent properties. These distinctive attributes apply to the basic fiber before it is transformed into yarn and eventually into textile products. A finished fabric will likely have some of the inherent properties of raw fibers. Depending on the end use, however, a fabric might not resemble its fiber base at all. Cotton, for example, is hydrophilic, but a finished fabric might be resistant to water. How closely the finished fabric resembles the original fibers depends on many factors:

- the type of yarn
- the method of construction (weave, knit, nonwoven)
- the weight of the final product
- the types of finishes, dyes, or treatments

Inherent fiber characteristics or properties may be changed or removed, and other properties may be added. (These will be introduced in the chapters on yarn production, fabric construction, and finishing.) Nevertheless, just as fibers are the 'ingredients' of textiles, so their particular characteristics determine, to a large extent, the 'flavor' of the final product.

The terms used for identifying fiber properties are divided into three categories:

- inherent characteristics

- reactions to chemicals
- environmental sensitivities

Inherent characteristics are those properties that are general, constant, and integral to a fiber before it has been processed into yarn or fabric. These might be tenacity, elasticity, or resiliency. Chemical reactivity refers to a fiber's reaction to alkalis, acids, solvents, or other agents. Environmental sensitivities refer to a fiber's sensitivity to sun, heat, fire, water, moisture, microorganisms, insects, and aging.

Inherent Characteristics

Fiber Description	**Fiber size** is the width of a fiber measured in microns; one micron is 1/1000 millimeter (1/25400 inch).
	Degree of uniformity of fibers means that the fibers must be relatively the same length and diameter as one another for spinning.
	Natural color in fibers ranges from black to brown to white or translucent depending on their source.
	Degree of luster is judged on the amount of light reflected by a fiber. High luster indicates a bright sheen, low luster a dull or matte appearance.
Strength	**Tenacity** is expressed in grams per denier (gpd), with 1.5-2.0 gpd being relatively weak, 2.5-4.0 gpd relatively strong, and 5-8 gpd exceptionally strong.
	Flexibility refers to the ability of a fiber to be flexed or bent repeatedly without breaking.
Dimensional Stability	**Elongation** is a fiber's ability to be stretched or extended, and is expressed as a percentage of the fiber's length taken at standard conditions—21.1°C (70°F) and 65% relative humidity.
	Elastic recovery is expressed as a percentage of return to original length after elongation of 2% or 5%. Elasticity is perfect if the recovery after elongation is 100%, but is rated poor if recovery is 75% or less.
	Resiliency is the fiber's ability to return to its original shape after bending, compressing, or crushing. Fabrics that wrinkle or crease easily and carpet fibers that compress under pressure and do not return to their original shape have poor resiliency.
Density	**Density** is expressed in grams per cubic centimeter and indicates the mass per unit volume. The higher the density, the greater the weight of the fiber. Lower density indicates loft, lightness, or buoyancy. The range is from 0.9 gpcc, exceptionally low, through 1.3 light, 1.45 medium, to 1.5-2.5 high.
Absorbency	**Absorbency** is measured through **moisture regain** and **moisture absorption.** Fibers usually contain a certain amount of water; **moisture regain** indicates this normal moisture level at standard conditions and is expressed as a percentage of the weight of a moisture-free sample.
	Moisture absorption indicates the amount of water the fiber is capable of holding at 100% humidity, and is expressed as a percentage of the weight of the bone-dry specimen. Absorbency influences the dyeability of fibers (affects uptake of water based dyes) and is an important aspect of comfort against the skin.
	Some synthetic fibers are completely **hydrophobic** and repel water completely. Natural fibers are **hydrophilic** and accept water; they generally have higher moisture regain, with wool the highest at 16%. Good absorbency ranges from around 6-14%.
	Oil absorption is also a concern in terms of staining and harming fibers. Nylon, for example, absorbs little water, but readily accepts oil into its core. This can be important for upholstery and carpet fibers.

Inherent Characteristics, cont'd	
Reactions to Chemicals	These refer to a fiber's reaction to **alkalis, acids**, and **solvents**.
Environmental Sensitivities	Each fiber has particular sensitivity to certain elements of the environment. Our concern is with **sun, heat, cold, fire, microorganisms, insects**, and **aging**.

Fiber Modifications

Modification of natural fibers is limited to chemical or mechanical treatment of the yarn or fabric made from a particular fiber. These are discussed in chapter 8.

Modification of the manufactured fibers, however, is practically limitless and can literally be engineered to fit almost any application. Manufactured fibers were originally made to simulate silk, the only natural filament. Rayon, nylon, polyester, acrylics, etc., were first made as round fibers spun from a spinneret having simple round orifices, with only the size of the round hole as a variable.

Modifications
Second Generation Fibers

Fiber Cross Sections

The first modifications were accomplished by changing the orifice shape in the spinneret. Trilobal, triangular, rectangular, dogbone, mushroom, pentalobal, and other shaped orifices produce continuous filaments with variations in aesthetics and performance. The changes

- expose more surface on the fibers
- aid in their capacity to be spun into yarns (improve spinning quality and cohesiveness)
- alter sheen or luster and dullness
- affect smoothness, roughness, and opacity

All of the alterations better matched the natural characteristics of silk, wool, linen, and cotton.

Cross section is further modified by the production of **thick-and-thin fibers**, which show variation along the length of the fiber. This modification is accomplished by uneven drawing out of the fibers, and allows for subtle color effects, with the thicker portions accepting greater quantities of dye. Texture, as well, is affected.

Altering the cross-section provide many advantages. These include:

- improved soil resistance
- increased bulk and cover
- smoother feel, and
- reduced pilling

The trilobal cross-section fiber, in particular, greatly improves soil resistance, a decided asset in carpeting.

Molecular Structure

The basic strength of a fiber may be modified in two ways:

- by a change in chemical constituents to increase the degree of polymerization
- by increased stretching of the fiber, which results in a greater alignment of the molecules

The speed of extrusion from the spinneret can also affect the strength, with greater tenacity resulting from faster spinning. Reducing the molecular weight may produce low-pilling fibers. This reduces the flex life and results in a weaker fiber, but where pilling is an unattractive feature, it is preferable.

Color and Properties

Color can be added to the fiber solution, fibers, yarns, fabrics, or finished products. Color can be added to the fibers solution by adding compatible pigments before spinning into filaments. Alternately, incorporating dye-catching chemicals to the solution may modify a fiber that normally does not accept dyestuff, so that once it is spun, dyes can be added later. These chemicals are formulated to accept only certain types or classes of dyes (basic, acid, disperse, etc., as discussed chapter 9). Yarns and fabrics manufactured from a blend of fibers can be given one dye bath with

Typical Synthetic Filament Cross Sections

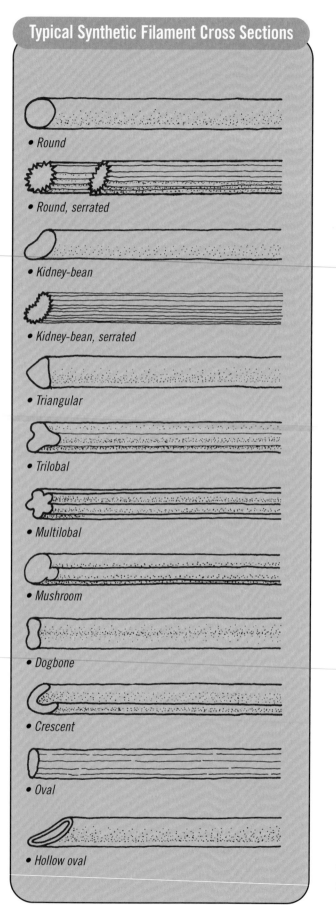

- Round
- Round, serrated
- Kidney-bean
- Kidney-bean, serrated
- Triangular
- Trilobal
- Multilobal
- Mushroom
- Dogbone
- Crescent
- Oval
- Hollow oval

the end result being several subtle tones of color within the one blended yarn or fabric.

To add, remove, enhance, or minimize inherent characteristics, fiber chemists have devised special techniques. Soil release, flame resistance, anti-static properties, and resistance to sunlight are just a few modifications that can alter textiles. These modifications require the addition of various chemical stabilizers or compounds. Improved or modified fibers are often labeled by the manufacturer.

Delustering

Synthetic and manufactured fibers are usually lustrous in their raw unfinished form. In general, this is not a desirable quality (although fashions change), so manufacturers will add delustering agents (usually titanium dioxide) to the solution prior to spinning. These are only evident under microscopic examination, but the effect is to dull the reflecting capacity of the fiber and, therefore, results in a less lustrous surface.

Texturizing

To produce bulkier (or loftier) yarns and fabrics, more air space is incorporated within the filament or along its length. This can be done by introducing air into the spinning solution, or by adding chemical elements that are subsequently evaporated or washed out. Such fibers have a lower density, or weight, per unit volume.

Filaments may also be crimped after spinning. This procedure sets a permanent kink, curl, or wave in the individual filaments so that when they are spun into yarn they form a thicker, more resilient strand. The effect of the crimp is to force each filament to make more space for itself within a yarn structure.

Crimp may be introduced through:

- modification of the spinneret shape
- adjusting the air flow at the spinneret
- vibration
- the addition of chemicals, which may produce either immediate or latent crimp— latent crimp needs an additional process step to produce the effect

Crimp is also commonly set by heat, and many methods are used. The filaments may be fed through intermeshing gears, or into a variously sized tunnel in such a way as to produce a sinuous set. **The stuffer-box method** produces the greatest amount of bulk. In this process, filaments are mechanically fed through crimping gears into the stuffer-box, forcing them into a saw-toothed crimp that is then heat set. These processes may be introduced at either the filament manufacturing or yarn producing stage.

Staple and Tow

While not a modification of the filament per se, cutting the filaments into short lengths, or **staple**, is often done at point of production. The staple fibers are then packed in bales and sold to yarn manufacturers. At this point, the fibers are treated much like cotton or wool. Alternately, the hundreds of thousands of filaments produced simultaneously may be drawn into thick ropes, or **slivers**, and packaged in that form, which is called **filament tow.** Yarn manufacturers then have the option of modifying and/or treating the fibers, processing the filaments directly into yarn, or cutting the tow into staple form as part of their integrated yarn production.

• *Sliver*

Advanced Fiber Engineering
Third Generation Fibers

While changes are still being made to fibers under the general classifications described above, newer technology focuses on the so-called 'third generation' fibers. Ingenuity and research are producing fibers to meet very particular needs, literally **custom tailoring fibers** for specialized end uses.

The objective of these modifications is to create fibers, or filament yarns, with texture to more closely simulate the unevenness of natural fibers. This produces the desired hand, or appearance, while maintaining the performance features of strength, soil resistance, shape retention, dyeability, wrinkle-resistance, or other desirable characteristics that have been engineered into the basic synthesized fiber. Three methods are currently used to create these effects:

- Bi-component fibers
- Bi-constituent fibers
- Combination filaments

Bi-component Fibers

Bi-component fibers are composed of two generically similar but chemically different polymers, physically joined during production into a single filament. The first conception of this technique was to join two polymers of different shrinkage rates so during yarn processing, as one component shrank more than the other, crimping would occur, giving greater bulk to the yarn. The technique for conjugate spinning was developed by American Viscose in 1940 when two rayon solutions, one aged and one unaged, were extruded through a single divided spinneret. The two halves joined and had a straight configuration until immersed in water, which caused one half to shrink, drawing the whole into a three-dimensional helical crimp. Later techniques with other fibers used heat, or a combination of moisture and heat, to produce the desired crimp. Side-by-side bi-components may also be produced with differing dye reactions, so that one dye bath can produce a two-color fiber.

Bi-components are also made by a 'pipe-in-pipe' extrusion procedure, which produces a fiber with a sheath different from the core. Most recent technology has expanded from the components to include multi-component fibers, but the focus must still be on compatible polymers with good surface-to-surface adhesion.

Bi-constituent Fibers

Bi-constituent fibers are composed of two generically different polymers physically joined in the solution stage before extrusion through the spinneret. The first bi-constituent was devised by Allied Chemical in 1968 and introduced the 'matrix-fibril' technique. One polymer is in solution form—the matrix—while the second is in very short, fine filament form—the fibril. These are combined and extruded together to produce a new fiber. Allied Chemical's innovation produced a 70% nylon, 30% polyester blend called Source®.

Bi-constituents are produced in three distinct ways:

- by mixing two polymers to produce an entirely different fiber, as in the matrix-fibril technique

- by adding chemical ingredients to change a particular function or property of one of the component polymers

- by adding ingredients that can be removed at a further processing step to leave desired voids in the finished filament. This is often a water-soluble ingredient that washes or leaches out in water, leaving pits or hollow spaces on the filament's surface

The bi-constituent fiber is the most difficult fiber to engineer.

Some Bi-component and Bi-constituent Fibers

Trade Names

SOURCE®, introduced by Allied Chemical, is a 70% nylon, 30% polyester matrix-fibril bi-constituent fiber. Inherent characteristics of nylon have been retained with improvements in appearance, which give the fiber a unique silky sheen and luminosity. It is used in carpeting, and is easily maintained.

MONVELLE®, developed by Monsanto, is a side-by-side bi-component fiber with 50% each of nylon and spandex. It is principally used in hosiery.

CORDELAN®, a Japanese import, is a matrix-fibril bi-constituent of 50% vinal and 50% vinyon. It retains the inherent characteristics of its two components and does not absorb stains. It is easily maintained and has a pleasant hand. Most important, it will not support combustion, and does not give off toxic fumes, as do many other flame-retardant fibers. Its uses include draperies, bedspreads, upholstery and blankets, as well as children's sleepwear, work clothes, and industrial fabrics.

Structures

Concentric Sheath/Core

Typically used in binder fibers with a low-melting sheath around a higher-melting core. A nonwoven fabric is made with these fibers, then heated to melt the sheath, which bonds the fabric together upon cooling. The concentric sheath/core can also be used to deliver an outer layer of a high value (and/or low strength) polymer around a lower-cost, yet stronger, core.

Eccentric Sheath/Core

Similar to the concentric sheath/core, but with the core shifted off-center. The different shrinkage rates of the two polymers cause the fiber to curl into a helix when heated under relaxation.

Side-by-Side

Both polymers occupy part of the fiber surface. Proper polymer selection can mean higher levels of latent crimp than the eccentric sheath/core.

Pie Wedge

A round cross section made of up to sixteen adjacent wedges, similar to slices of pizza. The polymers alternate side by side around the pie. These fibers are designed to be split into the component wedges by mechanical agitation (typically hydroentangling), and result in microfibers of 0.1 to 0.2 denier in the final fabric.

Hollow Pie Wedge

Has a hollow center core to the inner tips of the wedges from joining, which makes splitting easier. Hollow centers can be used in other fibers, too, but are particularly useful here.

Islands/Sea

Also known as the "pepperoni pizza" configuration, where one polymer is the pepperoni and the other is the cheese. This fiber allows the placement of many fine strands of a fiber polymer within a matrix of soluble polymer that is subsequently dissolved, leaving only the fine filaments. This allows the production of a fabric made of very fine microfibers. Staple fibers can be made with thirty-seven holes in each spinneret, producing fibers as low as 0.04 denier.

Three Islands

This configuration can be described as either three islands in a sea or as a **sheath/core arrangement** with three cores instead of one. It can be used to reduce the cost by filling the cores with a low-cost polymer while still maintaining strength. Alternately, a high-strength material in the core can reinforce a weak polymer used for its surface properties.

Combination Filaments

Combination filaments are composed of manufactured filament fibers physically joined after each is produced, not in the production stage as in the bi-component, or in the solution stage as in the bi-constituent. This method has a greater range of possible combinations than either of the previous two. The combining of component fibers is accomplished by twisting or interlacing in a separate manufacturing step. While production of this fiber does not require the delicate chemical balancing techniques of the bi-component or bi-constituent, its potential for creating new and specialized fibers is broader, and a much greater range can be joined by this method. This technology has added greatly to the whole field of fiber blending.

Fiber Blending

The blending of fibers is certainly not new. First, blends combined different weights of the same natural fiber, such as wool, for a new texture or look. Next came blends of naturals, cotton/wool, wool/silk, silk/cotton, cotton/linen, etc., for new textures, new weights, and new performance standards. Viyella, an English blend of 55% wool and 45% cotton, has been widely used for many years. Today, blends of natural fibers, natural with manufactured fibers, and blends of different manufactured fibers based on the combination filament principle, are the dominant factor in the fabric-producing industries.

Blends are, by definition, 'intimate blends' in which specific proportions (by weight) of two or more component fibers are combined at the start of the textile process.

There are many reasons for blending fibers:

- to obtain cross-dyed effects
- to improve uniformity in manufacturing or finishing
- for economic reasons
- to extend the effect, or prestige, of expensive fibers by adding less costly ones
- to improve appearance or touch
- to produce fabrics with improved performance

While all reasons are viable, the last two are perhaps the most important and have provided the impetus for most of the significant advances in this area. Fiber characteristics and user needs are assessed and a combination plotted that will complement each component fiber and meet as many requirements as possible.

Blend levels are an important factor, and this area is the subject of much study. It has been found, for instance, that 15 percent of nylon blended with wool improves the overall strength of the fabric, but 60 percent of nylon is needed to significantly improve the strength of rayon. The industry is conscientious in setting its own standards in this area, but it is important to know that these variables exist.

Performance-based blends produce, in effect, a new fiber that combines functional properties. For instance, the superior hand of one fiber blended with the strength of a second fiber produces a 'new' fiber with hand plus strength. A good example of this is the first successful combination filament, Arnel®-plus-nylon. In various proportions, it creates fibers with the bulk, texture, and aesthetic qualities of the tri-acetate Amel®, without greatly diminishing the strength that nylon contributes.

Textile chemists have assigned functions to many of the manufactured fibers based on outstanding properties or special strengths. These fibers may be depended upon to contribute that particular characteristic to the finished yarn or textile product. Some of the dependable fibers and their functions are as follows:

ACRYLIC provides dimensional stability, creates bulk without weight, and adds versatility to surface texturing.

NYLON adds strength and abrasion resistance. Often used as the core of the filament, it gives durability, dimensional stability, and press retention to the finished textile.

POLYESTER is the fiber for unrivalled wash-and-wear performance. It adds wrinkle resistance and press retention, as well as strength and abrasion resistance.

RAYON contributes a 'natural hand', eases processing of a textile, and is easily given decorative effects.

Blending is largely an automated process, though four **basic methods** are still employed depending on size of operation and fibers being combined. All of these methods blend the component fibers before, or as, they are being spun into yarn.

HAND FEEDING is the least reliable for establishing exact proportions. As implied, the fibers are hand fed from behind the hopper line.

SLIVER BLENDING combines slivers of staple fibers through a process of doubling and drafting.

HOPPER BLENDING has the different components hand weighed and spread in layers, and then fed into the hopper line from the cross section.

AUTOMATIC BLENDING is the same as hopper blending, except fully automated, and is the most common form of staple fiber blending.

Mixture yarns are similar to, but distinct from, blended yarns. They are less intimate blends of two or more fibers twisted together after each is in strand or continuous filament form.

An additional distinction in this area are **mixture fabrics.** These may be made from mixture yarn, from different component strands laid side by side, from different yarns in the warp and weft directions, or from some other fabric construction method.

These techniques of blending, along with previous modifications through technology and chemistry, make it possible to design a fiber to any specification. Textile chemists are able to improve luster, improve hand, modify or improve dyeability, improve flame resistance, reduce static conductivity, improve whiteness retention, reduce pilling, improve laundering performance, increase moisture absorbency, impart stretch, and can manufacture fibers with bulk, moldability, or temperature sensitivity. Having these performance factors 'on order' gives fibers a staggering range.

The continuing challenge for textile technologists is to be able to combine performance requirements, to produce new textiles in sufficient quantity to meet needs, and to keep costs competitive. There is no one perfect fiber that satisfies all needs, though many of the synthetic blends do, quite literally, look, feel, and perform perfectly for the required use, and generally may be easily maintained almost indefinitely. We often grow tired of the textile product (drapes, upholstery, or clothing) long before the fabric actually shows signs of wear. Competition between natural and manufactured fibers is a thing of the past, and each fiber is assessed and valued for its own best qualities.

FIBERS

COTTON • Natural Fiber • Cellulose	Spanish: Algodon • French: Coton

Cotton is the most important natural fiber for use in environmental textiles, either alone or as a component of a blended fabric. It is a cellulosic fiber derived from seed hairs of the cotton plant.

Cotton grows in warm climates where there is sufficient rain and irrigation and a growing period of six to seven months with twelve hours of sunlight per day.

Cotton is a bushy annual plant that produces a characteristic boll of fleecy fibers.

Bolls are picked either by hand or mechanically (the fibers only) or stripped (the entire boll) from the plant.

The cotton gin separates the cotton fibers from the seed and removes some of the dirt, twigs, and leaves.

The fibers from each bale are classified by length, grade, and character.

The grade is based on: color (white, gray, yellow), the brightness and dullness, and the quantity of foreign matter.

Quality and price are determined on the commodity market and are governed by fluctuations in demand and other market forces. The ginned cotton is packed in 227 kg (500 lb) bales and shipped to yarn producers. The fiber is generally bleached and cleaned, often boiled to reduce any chance of bacteria buildup. They are dyed in the fiber, yarn, or fabric stage.

• Cotton Boll

cuticle   layers of secondary cell wall   growth rings

• Cotton Fiber   primary wall   fibrils   lumen

- Microscopic view shows convolutions, unique to cotton.
- The fiber looks like a flattened twisted ribbon.
- The center of the fiber is hollow and is called the lumen.
- The cross section of cotton is kidney shaped.

convolutions

• Regular Cotton Fiber

• Mercerized Cotton Fiber

FIBER PROPERTIES

INHERENT CHARACTERISTICS	
Fiber Description	• uniform fiber 12–20 microns in width • natural color range: cream-white, can be grown red, yellow, green, gray with hybrid genetically modified seeds • low luster • staple fiber: 1.9 cm (less than .75") to 6.35 cm (about 2.5") • Shorter fibers are used for lesser quality fabrics, are rougher in appearance and less expensive • Longer fibers allow for increased cohesiveness and smoother refined fabrics
Strength	• dry tenacity is moderate, 3–5 grams per denier • tenacity increases 10-20% when wet
Dimensional Stability	• very poor elastic recovery (65–75% with 2% elongation) • elongation at break point 3–7% • resiliency poor—creases easily
Density	• high: 1.54–1.56 gpcc

COTTON • Natural Fiber • Cellulose	Spanish: Algodon • French: Coton

FIBER PROPERTIES

Absorbency	• hydrophilic and absorbs water easily • can absorb up to 20% water vapor without feeling wet, and up to 65% of its weight without dripping • dries slowly • high moisture regain

REACTION TO CHEMICALS

Alkalis	• high resistance
Acids	• good: cool dilute acids (will slowly degrade) • low: hot dilute acids • poor: all concentrates
Solvents	• good: most organic solvents • poor: cuprammonium hydroxide and cupriethylene diamine

ENVIRONMENTAL SENSITIVITIES

Flammability and Thermal Performance	• burns very easily • decomposes in prolonged exposure to heat (150°C/300°F)
Cold	• unaffected
UV Light Resistance	• medium: will decompose with prolonged exposure
Microorganisms	• due to moisture content mildew will grow on and damage fiber, especially in a humid climate
Insects	• good (except silverfish)

COTTON SYMBOL

♲ GREEN COTTON

The cotton industry is experiencing a surge in popularity for **organic** or **green** cotton. As with any agricultural commodity there is great debate about how to produce cotton with the least impact on the environment. Some suggest sustainability will be achieved through genetically modified (GM) crops. GM cotton seeds (like Monsanto's INGARD®) are resistant to all natural pests and help reduce dependence on fertilizers, pesticides, and herbicides. 78% of U.S. cotton was genetically modified in 2001. Others argue that GM cotton crops are harmful to the rest of the food chain, as cottonseeds are incorporated into cattle feed.

Organic cotton crops, on the other hand, are crops where no GM seeds are used and no chemical fertilizers, pesticides, or herbicides are used. These plantations must be free of these chemical pest controls for 3 years and must satisfy certain standards in order to use the term 'certified organic cotton'. Cotton that is picked but has little further processing (such as chlorine bleaching or chemical dyeing) is considered to be 'green' cotton. Conventional cotton production uses .45 kg (1 lb) of chemicals to produce 1.36 kg (3 lbs) of fabric.

Cotton can also be grown in different colors eliminating the need for dyeing, which is a very resource-intensive process. Cotton fibers can be grown in a full range of muted colors (achieving vibrant colors is still difficult) like mocha, tan, gray, red-brown, yellow, and green.

The green and organic cotton industries are experiencing rapid growth and expect an increase of 44% by 2008.

LINEN • Natural Fiber • Cellulose	Spanish: Lino • French: Lin

Flax is the plant source of linen. Most flax for fiber (as opposed to flax for seed) is grown in eastern Europe, Ireland, and New Zealand. Flax is a bast fiber derived from the stalk of the plant.

Flax is pulled from the ground, rather than cut, as the usable fibers extend into the roots. To gain access to the fibers inside the plant's stalk, the outer woody portion of the stalk must be rotted away. This process is called *retting* and can be accomplished by several means.

Dew retting: The flax is laid out on the ground to gradually rot. Takes up to six weeks.

Pool or stream retting: Bundles of flax are placed in either stagnant or slow-moving water. Takes up to six weeks.

Tank retting: The flax is placed in a tank of warm water that hastens the decay of the outer fibers. This takes a few days.

Chemical retting: The flax is placed in a tank of warm water and chemicals to speed up the decay. This process must be carefully controlled to avoid damage to the fiber.

Breaking: After retting, the rotted stalks are bundled and passed through fluted rollers to break up the outer woody portions of the stalks.

Scutching mechanically separates the usable fiber from the broken outer covering.

Hackling can be compared to the carding and combing of cotton. This process draws the fibers over increasingly fine sets of pins, which rid the fibers of waste, separate the long fibers (called line fibers) and the shorter fibers (called tow fibers), clean and straighten them, and draw out the fibers into a sliver in preparation for yarn manufacture.

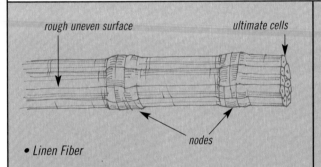

rough uneven surface — ultimate cells

nodes

• Linen Fiber

- Microscopic view shows a rough surface with regular nodes along the longitudinal axis.
- The width of the fiber varies along its length.
- The cross section shows a multi-cellular fiber with 10–40 cells called *ultimates* or *ultimate cells*. Each cell is polygonal and has a lumen (hollow center). Nodes are created by overlapping ultimate cells (which are approximately 33 mm/1.29" long).

FIBER PROPERTIES

INHERENT CHARACTERISTICS

Fiber Description	• 15-20 microns in width • fairly uniform • color: light ivory to dark tan or gray • luster: improves with cleaning • higher than cotton • 10–100 cm (4-40") in length, averaging about 50 cm (19.6")
Strength	• tenacity: 5.5–6.5 gpd, but may vary from 2.6–7.7 gpd • moderate to very strong • wet tenacity increases by about 20% • poor resistance to flexing
Dimensional Stability	• elongation is from 2.7–3.3% before breaking • 65% recovery at 2% elongation • elasticity and resilience poor

LINEN • Natural Fiber • Cellulose	Spanish: Lino • French: Lin

FIBER PROPERTIES

Density	• high: 1.5 grams per cu. cm
Absorbency	• moisture regain at standard conditions is 12% • hydrophillic—absorbs moisture • superior wicking ability: affected by changes in humidity; therefore, not for use in an area with changing humidity where a consistent size is essential (e.g., draperies)

REACTION TO CHEMICALS

Alkalis	• high resistance
Acids	• resistant to cold diluted acids, but concentrated or hot acid solutions cause deterioration
Solvents	• high resistance

ENVIRONMENTAL SENSITIVITIES

Flammability and Thermal Performance	• burns very easily • smells of burnt paper, and leaves a fluffy gray ash residue • decomposes in prolonged exposure to heat 150°C (300°F)
Cold	• high resistance
UV light resistance	• highly resistant to UV damage, although long exposure to direct sunlight causes gradual loss of strength
Microorganisms	• more resistant to fungi and mildew than cotton, but extreme humidity will allow mildew to grow on damp fibers, which will cause eventual deterioration
Insects	• high resistance
Aging	• excellent if stored in dry, dark environment

LINEN SYMBOL

Lin Leinen Linnen Lino Linen
100% 100% 100% 100%
Lino Linen Lin Leinen Linnen
100% % 100%
Linen nen Lino
100% % 100%
Linnen in Leinen
100% % 100%
Leinen en Lin
100% 100%
Lin Lein Linen
100% 100%
Lino Linen nnen
100% 100%
Linen Lin Leinen Linnen Lino
100% 100% 100% 100%

JUTE • Natural Fiber • Cellulose

Jute produces a bast fiber, commonly made into burlap.

- integrated into wall coverings or linoleum
- used as carpet backing
- used in furniture construction as webbing and base fabric

The plants are grown widely in Asia, and about 7 times more jute is produced than flax.

Jute grows to a height of 4.6–6.1 meters (15 to 20 feet). Extraction of the fibers is by the same basic method as is used for flax; that is, retting, breaking, and scutching.

FIBER PROPERTIES

INHERENT CHARACTERISTICS

Fiber Description	• microscopic view shows a very rough surface • the width of the fiber varies along its length • the cross section, like linen, shows a multi-cellular fiber with 20 ultimate cells • on average 10x larger than cotton • less uniform than flax • color: yellow, brown, or gray • luster: high • has a strong natural odor • grows 4.6–6.1 meters (15–20 feet)
Strength	• 3–5 gpd • poor flexibility
Dimensional Stability	• low elongation before breaking, less than 2% • low elastic recovery
Absorbency	• hydrophillic: absorbs moisture readily • on exposure to water becomes weaker and brittle
Density	• high: 1.5 gpcc

REACTION TO CHEMICALS

Alkalis	• highly resistant
Acids	• good: cool dilute acids (will slowly degrade) • low: hot dilute acids • poor: all concentrates
Solvents	• highly resistant • fibers are hard to bleach, so are often left in natural color, or are dyed bright or dark colors

JUTE • Natural Fiber • Cellulose

FIBER PROPERTIES	
ENVIRONMENTAL SENSITIVITIES	
Flammability and Thermal Performance	• burns very easily • smells of burnt paper, and leaves a fluffy gray ash residue • decomposes in prolonged exposure to heat 150°C (300°F)
Cold	• unaffected
UV Light Resistance	• highly resistant to UV damage
Microorganisms	• resists mildew very well
Insects	• highly resistant
Aging	• excellent unless exposed to water

HEMP • Natural Fiber • Cellulose

Hemp is a bast fiber from a hardy plant *(cannabis sativa)*, that can be cultivated in many climates throughout the world. The plants are cut by hand and thereafter handled like flax (retting, breaking, and scutching) to extract the fibers. Hemp is used for wall coverings and draperies.

Hemp is imported into the United States; since World War II, cultivation has been illegal because it is a subspecies of the cannabis plant from which marijuana is derived. Hemp plants, however, do not contain the same hallucinogenic substance and smoking it makes a person ill. In Canada, hemp is recognized as a nonhallucinogenic subspecies of the cannabis plant and is easily grown in all regions of the country.

Industrial hemp has experienced an increase in demand over the past decade. It has many excellent performance properties.

FIBER PROPERTIES	
INHERENT CHARACTERISTICS	
Fiber Description	• microscopic view shows a slightly rough fiber surface • the width of the fiber is consistent along its length • the cross section, like linen, shows a multi-cellular fiber with ultimate cells • similar to linen in texture and feel • dark tan to brown • not as fine as flax fibers • length to width ratio varies with each fiber, can be several centimeters (inches) long

HEMP • Natural Fiber • Cellulose

FIBER PROPERTIES	
INHERENT CHARACTERISTICS	
Strength	• tenacity: high, very strong: 5.2 gpd • poor flexibility
Dimensional Stability	• low elongation before breaking • poor elastic recovery
Density	• high: 1.48 gpcc
Absorbency	• 12% moisture regain • can absorb moisture up to 30% of its weight at 100% humidity • dries quickly
REACTION TO CHEMICALS	
Alkalis	• hot concentrated alkalis will dissolve fiber • hot or cold dilute will not damage • cold concentrate will not damage
Acids	• cool weak dilute acids will not damage • mineral acids will reduce tenacity and eventually destroy fiber
Solvents	• resistant with careful handling
ENVIRONMENTAL SENSITIVITIES	
Flammability and Thermal Performance	• burns very easily • smells of burnt paper, and leaves a fluffy gray ash residue
Cold	• unaffected
UV Light Resistance	• medium: will decompose with prolonged exposure
Microorganisms	• damaged by mildew
Insects	• highly resistant (except silverfish)
Aging	• excellent when stored in dark, dry conditions

RAMIE • Natural Fiber • Cellulose

A bast fiber, extracted from the ramie plant, grown mainly in Asia, but also cultivated in Egypt, France, Italy and Russia. It is a perennial shrub that can be cut several times per season. Fibers are extracted by decorticating, to remove the outer woody covering, and are de-gummed in a caustic soda solution to remove the pectins and waxes. They are then rinsed in dilute acid to neutralize the caustic and bleach the fibers. Ramie textiles may be like fine linen or as coarse as canvas. Because of its stiffness and strength the fiber is often blended with cotton or rayon fibers.

FIBER PROPERTIES

INHERENT CHARACTERISTICS

Fiber Description	• microscopic view shows a smooth surface with very subtle nodes • the width of the fiber is consistent along its length • the cross-section, like linen, shows a multi cellular fiber with ultimate cells approximately 40–250 mm (1.6–9.8") long • somewhat stiff • higher luster than flax • pure white • length: 150 cm (59 inches)
Strength	• tenacity: very strong: 5.3–7.4 gpd • flexibility: poor
Dimensional Stability	• low elongation before breaking: 3–7% • low elastic recovery
Absorbency	• hydrophilic, dries quickly • moisture regain 6%, relatively low
Density	• high: 1.5 gpcc

REACTION TO CHEMICALS

Alkalis	• highly resistant
Acids	• good: cool dilute acids (will slowly degrade) • good: cold concentrate mineral acids • low: hot dilute acids • poor: all concentrates
Solvents	• highly resistant

RAMIE • Natural Fiber • Cellulose

FIBER PROPERTIES	
ENVIRONMENTAL SENSITIVITIES	
Flammability and Thermal Performance	• burns very easily • smells of burnt paper, and leaves a fluffy gray ash residue
Cold	• unaffected
UV Light Resistance	• highly resistant to UV damage
Microorganisms	• highly resistant to mildew
Insects	• highly resistant
Aging	• excellent

OTHER CELLULOSE FIBERS

LEAF FIBERS

ABACA

This plant is indigenous to the Philippines and is a member of the banana family. It is also grown as a decorative plant in other warm climates. Fibers are extracted from the leaf stalk and may be as long as 4.5 meters (15'). It has a natural luster and is off-white to dark gray or brown. Main use is for rope and cordage; some regional environmental use for table coverings, or place mats for indoor/outdoor use.

AGAVE—SISAL

The agave plant is grown in warm climates, and its leaves are the source of sisal. The fibers are obtained from the large evergreen leaves when they are about four years old, and must be separated from fleshy leaf parts. Naturally brown and stiff in character, the fibers do not bleach but are sometimes dyed. Interior use is for matting or carpeting

COIR

Obtained from the fibrous mass between the outer shell and the husk of coconuts, coir is a stiff, strong, cinnamon brown fiber. It is impervious to abrasion and weather and is not affected by water. Use is principally for outdoor carpets, floor mats, and patio coverings.

KAPOK

This interesting fiber is obtained from the seed hairs of the Java kapok tree. Difficult to spin into yarn, the fiber is extremely light, soft, and buoyant. Once used extensively for pillow filling and upholstery padding, its major use now is for life preservers where it will support up to 30 times the weight of the preserver without becoming waterlogged.

PINA

The fiber is extracted from pineapple leaves and is mainly produced in the Philippines. White or ivory in color, it is fine, lustrous, soft, flexible, and strong. Often used for elaborately embroidered table covers, as well as clothing.

SILK • Natural Fiber • Protein	Spanish: Seda • French: Soie

WILD SILK, TUSSAH SILK, CULTURED SILK

Silk is mainly produced in China, Japan, and India.

Sericulture, the growth and production of moths for their silk, takes patience and exact conditions to produce acceptable quality fibers. It is extremely labor intensive and requires considerable skill. The Bombyx Mori is the only commercially viable silkworm.

Silk factories are immaculate 'farms' where the insects are raised from egg to moth.

Eggs hatch within a week and the worms eat a steady supply of mulberry leaves for 35 days, increasing their weight 10 000 times and molting four times.

Once full grown the larvae spins its cocoon by forcing out viscous solution through two tiny orifices. The cocoon is spun from the outside in and the worm lies dormant as a chrysalis.

The cocoon is heated to kill the chrysalis, but leaves the fiber unaffected. The cocoon remains hard and is approximately the size of a large almond.

At the filature, the cocoon is reeled (unwound) by soaking in warm water to soften the cocoon and remove the sericin (the gluey substance holding the cocoon together). The ends of the fibers are found and carefully fed through a guide and wound on a reel.

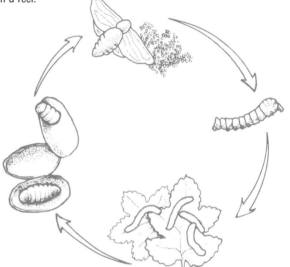

striations

fibrillar structure

• Single Silk Fiber

individual fibers

microfibril

sericin gum

fibrillar bundle

• Silk Fiber as Spun

- Silk is a filament fiber.
- Silk protein is called *fibroin*.
- Made up of 15 different amino acids in molecular chains.
- Under a microscope, degummed silk is smooth and transparent (some black speks might appear, this is the residual sericin gum).
- Cultivated silk has a triangular cross section.
- To the naked eye, cultivated silk fibers are fine and smooth.
- Raw/wild/Tussah silk is rougher and thicker than cultured silk.
- Short remnants from the cocoon can be used for spun silk. *(Wild silk is darker and rougher than cultivated silk and has a more random cross section.)*

FIBER PROPERTIES

INHERENT CHARACTERISTICS	
Fiber Description	• thin, smooth, long continuous filament, cream colored • high luster • width 9–11 microns • length ranges from 915-2750 meters (1000-3000 yards)
Strength	• tenacity: very strong: 2.4–5.1 gpd dry • wet tenacity is 80–85% of dry strength

SILK • Natural Fiber • Protein	Spanish: Seda • French: Soie

FIBER PROPERTIES

		SILK SYMBOL
Dimensional Stability	• elongation dry is 10–25% • elongation wet is 33–35% • elastic recovery is 92% at 2% elongation • medium resiliency	
Density	• medium: 1.25–1.35 gpcc	
Absorbency	• moisture regain is 11% • can absorb 33% of its weight without feeling wet	

REACTION TO CHEMICALS

Alkalis	• very low resistance to alkalis-heated caustic soda will dissolve silk (protein) • weak alkalis such as soap, borax, and ammonia are not harmful except with prolonged exposure
Acids	• resistant to organic acids • little resistance to quick absorbing mineral acids
Solvents	• high resistance

ENVIRONMENTAL SENSITIVITIES

Flammability and Thermal Performance	• burns in flame, self extinguishes when removed from flame • smells like burning hair • leaves a brittle ash • unaffected by long periods of exposure at 135°C (275°F) • will scorch and decompose at 177°C (350°F)
Cold	• unaffected
UV Light Resistance	• low resistance • exposure will cause fiber degradation and destruction
Microorganisms	• highly resistant to mildew • rot-producing conditions (soil and moisture) will cause decomposition
Insects	• highly resistant to moths and silverfish • low resistance to carpet beetles
Aging	• oxygen causes gradual loss of tenacity and the fiber will shatter • should be stored in sealed temperature/humidity controlled environment

WILD SILK

This fiber is collected in the wild in the cocoons of other moth species. The Antheraea myllita and apemyi feed on oak leaves in China and India and produce tussah silk, which is tan or light brown, less uniform than Bombyx Mori silk, and cannot be bleached. Other moths in warm climates yield silk fiber, but the limited quantities are not of significance.

WOOL • Natural Fiber • Protein | Spanish: Lana • French: Laine

WORSTED, WOOLEN, MERINO, SHETLAND, LAMBSWOOL, CASHMERE, MOHAIR, ALPACA, PASHMINA

Most wool is obtained from hundreds of different breeds of sheep specially bred for the quality of their fleece and raised in temperate climates (Australia, New Zealand, Argentina, and the former Soviet Union).

Different breeds of sheep produce different fibers—very soft to very rough.

Processing:
- Wool is sheared from the living animals and is called *fleece*, *clip wool*, or *virgin wool*. It is sometimes pulled from hides of slaughtered sheep, and is then called pulled wool.
- Sheep shearing occurs once a year.
- Preliminary grading is done, and then it is bundled and shipped 'in the fleece.'
- An expert grader opens the fleece and pulls, sorts, and grades the fiber according to:

  fineness, length, crimp, impurities, color, and strength

  (1-best quality, 4-worst quality)

The best fleece comes from the sheep's sides and shoulder area, while the most contaminated fibers come from the sheep's belly.

- Fine, long fibers are used for fine wool fabrics and worsteds.
- Medium fibers are used for woolens.
- Coarse fibers are used for carpeting or rough fabrics.
- Once classified, wool is:
  - scoured (cleaned) to remove oil, dirt, and excrement
  - rinsed
  - dried
- The cleaned wool is:
  - carded—a combing process that aligns the fibers and removes burrs and twigs. In the woolen system, the carded fibers proceed directly to the yarn spinning process.
  OR
  - combed—the fibers are combed again to further orient the fibers leaving the finer, smoother fibers for use in worsted yarn.
- The fibers are delivered to the yarn producers in a pulled, thick, untwisted bundle of fibers called *top*.

surface scales
cuticle
cortical cells
microfibril
polpeptide
protofibril
macrofibril
• Wool Fiber

- Made of protein molecules known as *keratin*.
- Fibrils form the long helical chain of protein molecules into fibrillar bundles.
- These make up the mass of cells in the fiber and are the reason wool is crimped.
- The structure (fibrils spiral around one another) gives the wool fiber its crimp.
- The fiber's surface is covered scales with a water repellent (hydrophobic) layer called the *epicuticle*.
- Depending on the type of wool, the scales are larger or finer. Course wool has few large scales and is thicker. Finer, softer fibers have many fine scales, and the fiber is thinner.

FIBER PROPERTIES

INHERENT CHARACTERISTICS	
Fiber Description	• fibers have three-dimensional crimp • color can range from black to brown tan or most often ivory • fiber ranges from very fine (15–17 microns) to very coarse (40 microns) • length depends on breed of animal: range from 3.8–38 cm (1.5–15") • low luster due to coarseness and crimp
Strength	• tenacity: very weak 1.0–1.7 gpd (dry), 0.8–1.6 gpd (wet)

WOOL • Natural Fiber • Protein	Spanish: Lana • French: Laine

FIBER PROPERTIES

Dimensional Stability	• exceptional flexibility (can bend 20 000 times before breaking) • elongation is 25% (dry) and 35% (wet) • excellent elastic recovery: 99% at 2% extension, 50% at 10% extension note: dimensional stability of wool yarn and fabric is not good. Moisture and agitation may cause felting shrinkage. Yarn and fabric production stretch the wool fibers, making them dimensionally unstable. • excellent resiliency compensates for poor tenacity • wool only creases if crushed then exposed to heated steam or water • will maintain creases thanks to strong chemical bonds
Density	• low: 1.30–1.32 gpcc
Absorbency	• high absorbency: initially water will be repelled due to epicuticle (waxy surface) and scales • water resistent to light moisture (mist) • moisture regain is 13.6–16% (helps to reduce electrical conductivity) • will eventually absorb 30% of its weight in moisture • hygroscopic: has high heat wetting (heat wetting is the ability to release heat as water is absorbed into the fiber core) • once saturated, wool dries very slowly

REACTION TO CHEMICALS

Alkalis	• low resistance: a 5% solution of sodium hydroxide will dissolve wool
Acids	• fair resistance to mild or dilute acids • concentrate mineral acids will decompose fibers
Solvents	• resistant to cleaning solvents

ENVIRONMENTAL SENSITIVITIES

Flammability and Thermal Performance	• unlike cotton, wool is not especially combustible • burns slowly in direct contact with flames • self extinguishes once removed • smells of burning hair • leaves a brittle black bead • dry heat over 132°C (270°F) causes yellowing and decomposition • wet heat causes fibers to stiffen and weaken

PURE WOOL SYMBOL

Cold	• unaffected
UV Light Resistance	• prolonged exposure causes degradation and eventual destruction
Microorganisms	• good resistance to bacteria and fungi • low resistance to mildew • eventual destruction will occur with exposure to prolonged moisture.
Insects	• very low to certain insects (moths) • protein fibers are food for insects who will eat the fibers, causing holes to appear in the fabric. Finishes can be applied to prevent this. Moths and carpet beetles are particularly damaging to wool.

OTHER PROTEIN FIBERS

ALPACA

The alpaca is a member of the camel family, and is native to the mountainous regions of South America. They are sheared only once every two years, and the fine fibers, when separated from the coarse guard hairs, are used in fabric production.

Alpaca is similar to mohair:
- strong glossy fibers sometimes used for plush upholstery
- natural colors range from white to brown and black and are often used without dyeing

CAMEL HAIR

The Bactrian camel sheds about 2.2 kilograms (5 pounds) of fiber per year. The outer hairs are used in industry and for artists' brushes; the fine, short underhairs are as soft and fine as top-quality sheep's wool. Very limited interior use, occasionally found in blankets made of coarse fibers.

CASHMERE

Cashmere is one of the softest, most expensive fibers, and is most often used for clothing production. It comes from the Kashmir goat, which is combed to yield about 114 grams (4 ounces) of fiber in total, of which only a percentage is used. Many different qualities of cashmere are available in Europe and China. Generally, cost is directly reflective of the quality.

LLAMA

Similar in characteristics to alpaca. Both are members of the camel family and native to South American mountains. Llamas are sheared once a year. The fibers are weaker than alpaca fibers, and most are used by South American Indian weavers. Some fiber is exported and blended with wool, other specialty fibers, or manufactured fibers. Very limited use, although llama farming is increasingly popular in the United States and Canada.

MOHAIR

Mohair fibers, which come from the Angora goat, are fine and silky.

Mohair is similar to wool except:
- it is more lustrous
- it has greater abrasion resistance
- it has better resiliency
- it has good adaptability to complex yarn spinning techniques

Upholstery, rugs and draperies may be made of mohair or mohair blends.

VICUNA

This is a rare hair fiber. It is taken from the small, camel-related animal found only in the high reaches of the Andes Mountains. The dog-sized animals are wild, and the fiber can only be obtained by killing the animal. Attempts at domestication have not been successful, and Peru wisely limits the yearly kill.

Each animal yields about 114 g (4 oz) of fine fiber and 284-340 g (10–12 oz) of shorter, less fine fiber. The fiber is one of the softest known and is strong and lustrous. Its limited yield makes it impractical for interior use, and a coat of vicuna cloth is as costly as a fine fur.

SPECIALTY FUR FIBERS

ANGORA

The Angora rabbit is raised for its white, fluffy, silky fur. The fur is combed and clipped every three months and provides a supply of fine, lustrous, and resilient fibers. Principally used in knitting yarns and knitted fabrics or blended with other fibers to obtain a specific appearance. Angora and fur fibers derived from any other fur-bearing animals are occasionally used for blending with wool, primarily to add softness, color interest, or prestige value.

MANUFACTURED FIBERS • CELLULOSIC FIBERS

Robert Hooke of England first mentioned the possibility of producing a silk-like filament in 1664. Silk had long been too expensive, and there had always been a desire to produce a cheap substitute. Credit for the invention of rayon is usually given to Count Hilaire Chardonnet. He used a cellulose nitrate solution dissolved in alcohol. This solution was forced through the spinneret, the fibers stretched to introduce strength, and then denitrated to reduce flammability.

In England in the late 1800s, cotton linters were treated with sodium hydroxide and carbon disulphide, which produced a thick viscose fluid that was extruded through a tiny hole and into a bath where it coagulated. In 1883, J. W. Swan, an English weaver, used a solution of cellulose nitrate in glacial acetic acid to produce fibers, which he exhibited in London in 1884. These fibers were used as the filaments for the first electric light bulbs. Further cellulose products, such as acetate and triacetate, were synthesized throughout the twentieth century.

The first American rayon plant, the American Viscose Company (so named because of the thick viscose solution used to produce the fiber), was opened in 1910, and is still a major force in rayon production as part of the FMC Corporation. In 1926, American Bemberg introduced the cuprammonium process. Rayon was first used for tire cord in 1937, and it is still in wide use for this purpose.

Rayon replaced silk in ladies stockings after World War I. Artificial silk lingerie also took the place of real silk by mid-century. Rayon's heavy silky drapability allowed for the flapper look of the 1920s. Rayon and viscose rayon have remained popular fabrics for women's clothing, and further refinements were made in the late 1900s to improve production processes and make them less environmentally harmful (i.e. Tencel®). Also in demand are high-strength rayon, carpet rayon, high-wet-modulus rayon, and flame-retardant rayon.

RAYON • Manufactured Regenerated • Cellulose

Trade Names: Viscose rayon, Avril®, Coloray®, Enkrome®, Fibro®, Tencel®, BeauGrip®, Coloray®, Encel®, Englo®, Fibro, Jetspun®, Kolorban®, Sayfr high-wet-modulus rayon (Avril®, Nupron®, Vincal, Xena, Zantrel 200®), Cuprammonium rayon (Bemberg®, Cupioni®), and Saponified cellulose rayon (Fortisan®)

Rayon is defined by the Textile Fiber Products Identification Act (TFPIA) as: "a manufactured fiber composed of regenerated cellulose, as well as manufactured fibers composed of regenerated cellulose in which substituents have replaced not more than 15% of the hydrogen of the hydroxyl groups."

Wet Spinning Process
- raw materials (cotton linters, wood pulp) are transformed into sheets of solid pure cellulose
- shredded (1)
- mixed and dissolved in a solution (2)
- filtered then aged (3, 4)
- forced through the spinneret and drawn into a coagulating bath to harden (5)
- drawn and wound onto reels in continuous filaments (6, 7, 8)

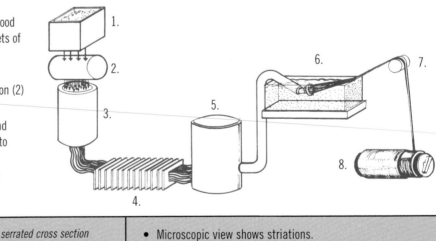

striations   *serrated cross section*   *core*   *skin*

• *Rayon Fiber*

- Microscopic view shows striations.
- Sometimes delustrants are visible as dark flecks.
- Cross section is serrated.
- Can be manipulated to different shaped cross sections to alter the behavior and aesthetics.

RAYON • Manufactured Regenerated • Cellulose

FIBER PROPERTIES

INHERENT CHARACTERISTICS

Fiber Description	• can be produced in any length • depending on the configuration of the spinneret, fibers can be made in a variety of sizes and shapes • fibers are translucent, but can be colored before spinning • if a delustering agent has been added, the fibers are white • fibers range from 12–100 microns • can be filament or staple length
Strength	• low (1.5–2.4 gpd) for regular viscose rayon and cuprammonium rayon • medium to high (2.4–5.0 gpd) for medium-to high-tenacity rayon • high (3.4–5.5 gpd) for high-wet-modulus rayon • very high (6.0–7.0 gpd) for saponified cellulose rayon • rayon is weaker when wet • good flexibility
Dimensional Stability	• regular viscose rayon: 15–30% elongation with 82% recovery at 2% • stronger rayon fibers have approximately 6–30% elongation • elastic recovery of 95–100% at 2% elongation • elongation increases by 20% when wet • regular rayon stretches easily in yarn and fabric • subject to relaxation shrinkage (fabric shrinkage after the fabric is removed from the loom's continual stress) • resiliency is low, especially in warm humid conditions
Density	• medium: 1.5–1.52 gpcc
Absorbency	• high • will swell 50–113% of original size when wet (4x more than cotton) • will lengthen • moisture regain varies from 10.7–16% at standard conditions • absorption is 20–27% of weight

REACTION TO CHEMICALS

Alkalis	• resistant to dilute alkalis • concentrated alkalis cause gradual loss of fiber weight and stiffening of the fiber
Acids	• good resistance: cold dilute acids (fibers will weaken with prolonged exposure) • poor resistance: concentrates, hot dilute acids, and cold concentrates cause disintegration; hot dilute acids cause deterioration
Solvents	• good resistance

viscose rayon

high-tenacity rayon

cuprammonium rayon

Tencel® lyocell

RAYON • Manufactured Regenerated • Cellulose

FIBER PROPERTIES

ENVIRONMENTAL SENSITIVITIES	
Flammability and Thermal Performance	• burns readily like other cellulose fibers • smells like burning paper • fluffy ash residue • resistant to heat at temperatures up to 177°C (350°F), but long exposure to higher temperatures results in degradation
Cold	• unaffected
Light resistance	• low resistance, exposure causes gradual deterioration
Microorganisms	• mildew will damage fibers especially if soiled or damp • rot-producing bacteria will damage fiber
Insects	• good resistance except for silverfish
Aging	• good resistance

MODIFIED CELLULOSIC FIBERS

Henri and Camille Dreyfus developed the first successful cellulose acetate, an ester of cellulose and acetic acid, in 1904 in England. Their early product was used for lacquers, films, and 'dope' used as early airplane wing fabric. In 1913, they made the solution into filaments, but it was not until 1921 that production of acetate fibers began in England and, in 1924, in the United States.

ACETATE AND TRIACITATE • Modified Cellulosic Fibers

The TFPIA defines acetate as:

"a manufactured fiber in which the fiber forming substance is cellulose acetate. Where not less than 92% of the hydroxyl groups are acetylated, the term triacetate may be used as a generic description of the fiber."

Acetate is composed of cellulose, acetic acid, and acetic anhydride, with sulphuric acid as a catalyst. The fibers are formed by the dry spinning method.

Triacetate has the same composition as acetate. Changes to the process result in a fiber with greater stability to aging and resistance to sunlight.

striations

multilobal cross section

• Acetate Fiber

- Microscopic view similar to both acetate and triacetate.
- Longitudinal view shows striations.
- Sometimes delustrants are visible as dark flecks.
- Cross section has an irregular, multilobal shape.
- Generally the cross section is not altered.

ACETATE AND TRIACITATE • Modified Cellulosic Fibers

FIBER PROPERTIES		
CHEMICAL REACTIONS		*acetate*
Fiber Description	• transluscent • delustrants may be added to deflect light • can be filament or cut to staple lengths	
Strength	• tenacity: low • dry: 1.1–1.7 gpd • wet: 0.8–1.0 gpd • good flexibility	
Dimensional Stability	• elongation is from 23–45% • elastic recovery is 90–94% at 2% elongation • acetate permanently deforms at 5% elongation • resiliency: low, especially in warn humid conditions • modified to perform under compressions in carpet form	
Density	• low: 1.31 gpcc	
Absorbency	• low • moisture regain ranges from 3.2–6.5% • absorption is 9–14% • heat treated triacetate has moisture regain of 2.5–3.0%	
ENVIRONMENTAL SENSITIVITIES		
Flammability and Thermal Performance	• melts and burns • has a chemical smell • leaves hard, black bead residue • may be treated for flame retardance • acetate softens at temperatures above 177°C (350°F) • heat-treated triacetate may withstand temperatures of 232°C (450°F) without damage	
Cold	• unaffected	
UV Light Resistance	• acetate loses strength and may disintegrate with prolonged exposure • triacetate has greater resistance to sunlight	
Microorganisms	• mildew will grow on damp fibers and discolor them • acetate may be weakened, but triacetate retains strength	
Insects	• good resistance	
Aging	• acetate weakens with age • triacetate has excellent resistance to aging	

SYNTHESIZED FIBERS

Synthesized fibers are truly invented. Manufacturers turned from imitating the silkworm or using known fiber- producing elements, like cellulose, to creating fibers through chemistry and their own basic knowledge.

The DuPont organization initiated and funded, almost without restriction, the development of this entirely new field. Investigative research started in 1928 when Wallace Carothers, a brilliant young organic chemist, was selected by DuPont to head a team to study possible uses for the gummy waste by-products of various existing manufacturing operations. No particular end use was designated, and the research team was given carte blanche to see what could be developed.

From this study came, among other things, the ability to manufacture controlled linear polymers (macromolecules composed of molecular units linked end-to-end). One of these substances was found, in 1930, to have the ability to form a filament. This was discovered by dipping a glass rod into one of the solutions and drawing out material that did not simply slide off the rod and fall back into the solution but immediately hardened into a solid strand. This strand could be stretched, and the resultant fine thread was attractive, strong, and flexible. The next few years were then devoted to improving the polymer solution, finding methods of forming the threads economically, and developing the necessary machinery to produce the fiber in quantity. Concurrently, testing of the fiber progressed, and the team soon found it had developed a fantastic new filament.

In 1939, DuPont invested in a large-scale plant in Seaford, Delaware, and nylon was introduced in a well-planned and coordinated advertising and marketing promotion. Nylon stockings were introduced in 1940 and received immediate widespread acceptance. After World War II, development of synthesized fibers was accelerated and is still a vital research field. The following introduces the generic fibers within this broad category. The intricate chemistry and production processes of these fibers are beyond the scope of this book.

NYLON • Manufactured Fiber • Polyamide

Trade Names:
Antron®, Dacron®, Perlon®, Tactel®, Astroturf®, Blue "C"®, Celenese®, Cumaloft®, Enka®, Grilon®

Nylon is manufactured in a number of types, and under hundreds of trade names.

Early advertising claimed that nylon was made of coal, water and air. This simplification, which caught the public's fancy, was accurate—to a degree. The coal used in nylon is phenol, which is derived from benzene, which in turn is a product of the distillation of coal tar, or petroleum. 'Water' and 'air' indicated the elements of carbon, hydrogen, oxygen, and nitrogen. Even this breakdown is a simplification; the actual chemical process to produce nylon is complex.

The fiber is derived from natural elements but is synthetic or manufactured.

Polyamides are linear polymers of amide groups occurring at regular intervals. Nylon is often referred to as Nylon 6 or Nylon 6,6. These designations refer to the number of monomers in a nylon polymer, and the manner in which they were polymerized (condensation polymerization or not).

Nylon 6 has six carbon atoms in repeating units.
Nylon 6,6 has two sets of repeating six-carbon atoms.

Nylon is melt spun—chips of nylon polymer are melted by heat and extruded through the spinneret. The spinning process can be regulated to make nylon in any cross-sectional shape. The fiber can have a flattened, round, or hollow cross section. It can be smooth or crimped, creating different effects for different end uses. The fiber is normally made into long continuous filaments that are perfectly uniform along the length.

Sometimes nylon is cut as it cools to form staple fibers for spun yarn uses. Normally this is blended with other (usually natural) fibers.

smooth, rodlike

round cross section

• *Nylon Fiber*

- Microscopic view is smooth and rodlike.
- Often delustrants are added.
- Fiber can be altered by trilobal and multilobal cross section.
- Altered cross section causes striated surface.

NYLON • Manufactured Fiber • Polyamide

FIBER PROPERTIES

INHERENT CHARACTERISTICS

Fiber Description	• size is variable, produced as continuous filament • may be cut into staple lengths for some end uses • can be lustrous or delustered with chemical finishes • translucent unless pigment is added to the spinning solution • Nylon 6,6 will accept a wider range of color dyes than other forms of nylon. It has greater anti-static properties and improved soil resistance.
Strength	• tenacity: exceptional 3.5–9 gpd • wet nylon loses 10–20% of its strength • Nylon 6, 6 is stronger than any natural fiber
Dimensional Stability	• excellent • elasticity: will extend 16–50% dry and 18–55% wet • elastic recovery: at 4% extension, will recover 100% • resiliency: good • Nylon 6,6 resiliency is excellent (recovers from crushing and stretching)
Density	• low: 1.14 gpcc
Absorbency	• moisture absorption: low (hydrophobic) • moisture regain: low, from 3.5–5% at standard conditions or 8% at 95% relative humidity • Nylon 6,6 moisture regain is 3.8–4.5%, absorbs little moisture even in high humidity • dries very quickly

REACTION TO CHEMICALS

Alkalis	• resistant
Acids	• not resistant to mineral acids (can destroy nylon even in very weak dilutions) • acid fumes may weaken or eventually destroy the fiber
Solvents	• excellent resistance to most organic solvents, except phenol

ENVIRONMENTAL SENSITIVITIES

Flammability and Thermal Performance	• fiber is thermoplastic (heat sensitive) • will withstand temperatures up to 149°C (300°F) for long periods. Exceeding this temperature will cause discoloration. • at 177–205°C (350–400°F) fibers soften • at 210–25°C (410–480°F) fibers will melt • can be permanently heatset to any shape • shrinks away from flame, melts and burns in direct contact with flame, forms a gummy gray or tan residue that hardens • fiber self-extinguishes once removed from the flame

NYLON • Manufactured Fiber • Polyamide

FIBER PROPERTIES	
ENVIRONMENTAL SENSITIVITIES	
Cold	• becomes hard in extreme cold
UV Light Resistance	• low resistance • extended exposure causes loss of strength and eventual decomposition • finishes can add to sun resistance
Insects	• resistant to all insects
Microorganisms	• resistant to microorganisms • not affected by fungi or bacteria
Aging	• unaffected

ARAMID • Manufactured Fiber • Polyamide

Trade Names: Kevlar®, Nomex®

- Fibers are produced by the dry spinning method.
- Fibers are polyamides made of aromatic compounds.
- Their main overall feature is a magnification of nylon's strength and exceptional heat resistance.

- Aramid fibers have wide industrial use (tire cord, aircraft components, parachutes, firefighters protective clothing, spacesuits, and bullet-proof armor—Kevlar will rebound a .38 caliber bullet fired from 3 meters/10 feet away.

FIBER PROPERTIES

INHERENT CHARACTERISTICS	
Fiber Description	<ul><li>fibers have either round or dogbone-shaped cross section</li><li>size depends on the manufacturer and desired end use</li><li>fibers are difficult to dye, but some accept a limited range of medium to dark shades</li><li>solution dyed (pigment is added to the polymer solution before spinning)</li><li>uniform fiber</li><li>smooth surface</li></ul>
Strength	<ul><li>may be 4–5.3 gpd</li><li>can be as high as 13–18 gpd (3x stronger than nylon)</li><li>stronger than steel of comparable size</li></ul>
Dimensional Stability	<ul><li>elongation: excellent, 10–31%</li></ul>
Density	<ul><li>medium to high: 1.38–1.44 gpcc</li></ul>
Absorbency	<ul><li>very low</li><li>moisture regain is 3.5%</li></ul>
REACTION TO CHEMICALS	<ul><li>resists all alkalis, acids, and solvents</li></ul>
ENVIRONMENTAL SENSITIVITIES	
Flammability and Thermal Performance	<ul><li>resistant to fire and heat</li><li>will start to degrade with prolonged exposure to 370°C (700°F) heat</li></ul>
UV Light Resistance	<ul><li>unaffected</li></ul>
Microorganisms	<ul><li>unaffected</li></ul>
Insects	<ul><li>highly resistant</li></ul>
Aging	<ul><li>unaffected</li></ul>

POLYESTER • Manufactured Fiber

Trade Names: Polyester, Dacron®, Diolen®, Trevira®, Tefgel®, Fortrel®, Fiber-fill®

One of the most successful and well-used manufactured fibers, polyester accounts for a huge proportion of fibers used today. The first commercially acceptable polyester fibers were developed in England in 1941. Under the name Terylene, polyester was reintroduced in England after the war. Licensing arrangements with the original inventors brought polyester manufacture to DuPont in the United States in 1951, and many firms now produce their own versions of the fiber under various trademarks.

The outstanding property was initially the ease of maintenance and excellent resilience and crease resistance. Early promotion of polyester fabric featured a man's suit; it was worn for 67 consecutive days without need for pressing,

during which time it was washed frequently in an automatic washing machine without showing much wear. At the time it was a fantastic innovation.

- Polyester is produced mainly using the melt spun method.
- Polyester chips are melted at 280°C (536°F) and then extruded through the spinneret.
- The fiber solidifies on contact with cool air.
- Crimp or other textures can be incorporated into the fiber through heat setting.
- These finishes will reduce the luster of the fiber.

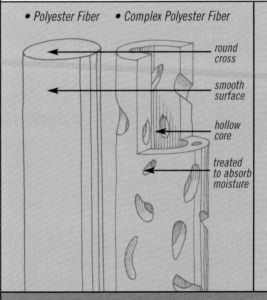

• *Polyester Fiber* • *Complex Polyester Fiber*

round cross

smooth surface

hollow core

treated to absorb moisture

- Polyester is a polymer chain that contains many (poly) ester groups at intervals along the length.
- The ester groups are created by the reaction of dihydric alcohol and dicarboxylic acid.
- Polyester is smooth and even along its length.
- The cross section can be altered to fit the intended end use.
- Trilobal or pentelobal shapes are often used to deflect light and reduce luster.
- Polyester is often made into microfiber, spun very thin, making an extremely soft and breathable knit fabric suitable for upholstery end uses.
- Fiber is often blended with cotton to help increase the tenacity of cotton, and the comfort of polyester against the skin.
- Fiber is normally spun into filament form, but is often cut to staple length to blend with other fibers.
- Staple fibers used as fill for pillows and comforters.

FIBER PROPERTIES

INHERENT CHARACTERISTICS	
Fiber Description	• smooth and uniform • translucent unless pigment is added to the spinning solution
Strength	• variable • range from 2.5–9.5 gpd • unaffected when wet
Dimensional Stability	• excellent • elongation ranges from 8–67% • elastic recovery is 75–100% • exceptional resiliency

POLYESTER • Manufactured Fiber

FIBER PROPERTIES	
Density	• 1.38 gpcc
Absorbency	• very low: hydrophobic, unless treated with special finishes • moisture regain 0.4–0.8% at standard conditions • 0.6–0.8 at 100% relative humidity • because of low absorption fiber wicks (moisture passes between the fibers) • fiber is oleophilic: absorbs and holds oily material, which is very hard to remove. Eventually bacteria is attracted to the oils causing the fiber to develop an odor. • heat setting prevents stretching, sagging, and wrinkling

REACTION TO CHEMICALS	
Alkalis	• good resistance to weak alkalis (hot or cold) • moderate: strong alkalis at room temperature • poor: hot strong alkalis degrade the fiber
Acids	• excellent: hot and cold acids • poor: prolonged exposure to boiling acids will destroy or disintegrate the fiber
Solvents	• resistant to organic solvents, oxidizing agents, and bleaches, and those used in cleaning and stain removal. Certain phenol mixures will dissolve the fibers.

ENVIRONMENTAL SENSITIVITIES	
Flammability and Thermal Performance	• thermoplastic fiber • fiber burns slowly, melts, and drips • produces a dark smoke • chemical odor • leaves hard, golden-brown bead • resistant to prolonged heat up to 120°C (250°F) • at 150°C (300°F) loses up to 20–30% of strength • fiber melts at 238°C (460°F) • polyester can be heat set with permanent creases that are impossible to remove unless heated and reformed in a new position
UV Light Resistance	• excellent • resist sunlight behind glass • prolonged exposure to direct sunlight will weaken fiber
Microorganisms	• microorganisms often feed on the oils trapped inside the fiber, causing the fabric to develop an unpleasant odor • fiber itself is unaffected by microorganisms • if oil is absorbed into the fiber, it is very hard to remove (thanks to hydrophobic nature of the fiber, laundering does not get inside to remove the oil)
Insects	• resistant
Aging	• unaffected

ACRYLIC • Manufactured Fiber

Trade Names: Acrilan®, Creslan®, Courtelle®, Dralon®, Orion®, and Zefran®.

The first acrylic fibers evolved out of the early DuPont research, and the first acrylic fabric, Orlon®, was introduced in 1950. The fiber was touted as a replacement of either wool, which it could, in staple form, be made to resemble, or silk, which it closely resembled in filament form.

Its most significant feature is a warm 'hand,' particularly when mechanically 'bulked' and cut into staple length. Early use was largely as a replacement for wool, either in knitted or woven fabrics, where it combined the softness and bulk of wool without the problems of felting and shrinkage.

Its use has since greatly expanded to include furnishing fabrics, blankets, carpeting, special flooring, and it is often used in blended fabrics.

- fiber is formed with 85% acrylonitril (vinyl cyanide) and 15% of one other comonomer
- there are various combinations all of which produce a type of acrylic
- polymerization occurs and the polymer is dissolved in dimethyl formamide
- wet spinning (or sometimes dry spinning) occurs, and crimp is often added during this process

FIBER PROPERTIES

INHERENT CHARACTERISTICS	
Fiber Description	• microscopic view is smooth and rod-like • crimp is often added • cross section can be round, dog bone, or kidney bean shaped • the fiber surface depends on the cross sectional shape • size is variable • can be lustrous or delustered • transluscent white unless pigment is added to the spinning solution • most often used in staple form
Strength	• high: 2.0–4.2 gpd • very slight loss of strength when wet
Dimensional Stability	• elongation varies from 20–55% • elastic recovery is 97–99% at 2% elongation • wet elongation is slightly higher • higher elongation (5–10%) reduces recovery • need pretreatment and appropriate care to avoid shrinkage and/or stretching
Density	• low: 1.16 gpcc
Absorbency	• low: 1.0–2.5% moisture regain at standard conditions • only 1–2% greater at saturation level
REACTION TO CHEMICALS	
Alkalis	• good: weak alkalis • poor: concentrates

ACRYLIC • Manufactured Fiber

FIBER PROPERTIES	
Acids	<ul><li>good: mineral and organic acids</li><li>poor: concentrates (may cause loss of strength)</li><li>nitric acid (cold concentrate) dissolves fiber</li></ul>
Solvents	<ul><li>excellent</li></ul>
ENVIRONMENTAL SENSITIVITIES	
Flammability and Thermal Performance	<ul><li>burns easily</li><li>forms a gummy residue that retains sufficient heat to ignite other combustible products</li><li>cools and hardens in black irregular bead</li><li>heat up to 150°C (300°F) has no effect</li><li>higher temperatures cause discoloration, degradation, disintegration, and melting at 232°C (450°F)</li></ul>
Cold	<ul><li>unaffected</li></ul>
UV Light Resistance	<ul><li>excellent resistance</li></ul>
Insects	<ul><li>resistant to all insects</li></ul>
Microorganisms	<ul><li>resistant to microorganisms</li></ul>
Aging	<ul><li>unaffected</li></ul>

MODACRYLIC • Manufactured Fiber

Trade Names: Dynel®, Verel®, SEF®

Modacrylics were introduced in 1956 when Union Carbide introduced Dynel®.

They are similar to acrylics but withstand higher temperatures and do not burn. Resistance to fire is the outstanding property and makes the fiber desirable for draperies, casements, blankets, industrial fabrics, and specialty uses such as 'fake fur,' wigs, and molded fabrics (e.g., speaker grilles).

- Composition is similar to acrylic.
- Fiber is formed with less than 85% but more than 35% acrylonitril (vinyl cyanide) and one other compound such as vinyl chloride, vinylidene chloride, or vinyl bromide.
- Polymers are dissolved in solvent and are either dry or wet spun.
- Fibers are mostly cut into staple form, and crimp is added.

surface striations

• Modacrylic Fiber

dogbone cross section

- Fiber is flat.
- It is irregular along the length.
- Crimp is often added.

FIBER PROPERTIES

INHERENT CHARACTERISTICS	
Fiber Description	• size is variable • translucent cream or white • most often used in staple form • may be lustrous or dull • usually staple length • sometimes filament form
Strength	• very good • 2.3–3.1 gpd
Dimensional Stability	• elongation varies from 30–48% • good to excellent recovery • no change when wet
Density	• low: 1.35–1.37 gpcc
Absorbency	• low: 2.5–4% moisture regain at standard conditions
REACTION TO CHEMICALS	
Alkalis	• excellent resistance
Acids	• excellent resistance
Solvents	• good resistance except to acetone and formic acid

MODACRYLIC • Manufactured Fiber

FIBER PROPERTIES

ENVIRONMENTAL SENSITIVITIES	
Flammability and Thermal Performance	• unlike acrylic, will not support combustion • self extinguishes when removed from flame • no dripping occurs • leaves hard black residue • fiber is heat sensitive • softens and shrinks at 150°C (300°F)
Cold	• unaffected
UV Light Resistance	• excellent resistance except Dynel®, which discolors after prolonged exposure
Insects	• resistant to all insects
Microorganisms	• resistant to microorganisms
Aging	• unaffected

SARAN® • Manufactured Fiber

Dow Chemical first introduced Saran in 1940.

It is a relatively expensive fiber and for that reason production is limited, with olefin fibers a common replacement.

Saran fibers are stronger and heavier than olefin, however, they are usually tough and durable and easy to maintain.

Fiber is composed of at least 80% vinylidene chloride units.

Used particularly for upholstery, draperies, and outdoor furniture applications.

Fibers are melt spun and cooled quickly in water.

FIBER PROPERTIES

INHERENT CHARACTERISTICS	
Fiber Description	• may be white or yellowish • may be colored with pigment added to the spinning solution • fibers are round and smooth • high luster
Strength	• moderate • 1.4–2.4 gpd
Dimensional Stability	• good • elongation varies from 15–20% • near perfect recovery • good resilience

SARAN® • Manufactured Fiber

FIBER PROPERTIES	
Density	• high: 1.7 gpcc
Absorbency	• virtually no moisture regain or absorption
REACTION TO CHEMICALS	
Alkalis	• resistant except to sodium hydroxide, which causes deterioration
Acids	• unaffected
Solvents	• good resistance
ENVIRONMENTAL SENSITIVITIES	
Flammability and Thermal Performance	• fibers melt and burn slowly in direct flame • self extinguishes when removed from flame • sensitive to heat • fibers soften at 115°C (240°F) • fibers melt at 177°C (350°F)
UV Light Performance	• resistant to sunlight • white or light colors may darken
Insects	• resistant to all insects
Microorganisms	• resistant to microorganisms
Aging	• unaffected • outdoor furniture retains appearance for 8-10 years

OLEFIN • Manufactured Fiber

Trade Names: Chevron®, DLP, Fibretex®, Fibrilon®, Herculon®, Loktuft®, Marvess®, Montrel®, Patlon®, Poly-bac®, Plycrest®, Poly-loom®, Plymacrame®, Poly-ty®, Supertuft®, Typar®, Tyvek®, Vectra®

There are two major categories of olefin fibers: polypropylene and polyethylene.

Polypropylene is used more often in textiles because of its high thermal stability.

Olefin fibers are made from 85% or more of ethylene or propane gas. High pressure and catalysts induce polymerization. Fibers are produced by the melt spin process, or, alternately, a film or sheet of material is made and then cut into narrow strips and twisted to form a yarn similar to a filament fiber. This alternate method is less expensive than melt spinning.

In either case, olefin fibers are:

- relatively low in cost
- have characteristics that are desirable for use in upholstery fabric carpeting, carpet tiles, and carpet backing
- often heat set into various molded applications; one unusual application is the creation of flexible, resilient surfacing for use as artificial ski slopes.

FIBER PROPERTIES

INHERENT CHARACTERISTICS	
Fiber Description	<ul><li>fiber is usually round</li><li>fiber is regular and even along the length</li><li>fibers are manufactured as multifilament yarns</li><li>size is constant and uniform</li><li>polyethylene fibers are waxy to the touch</li><li>polyethylene is white</li><li>polypropylene is less waxy feeling</li><li>usually filament form</li></ul>
Strength	<ul><li>varies depending on manufacturing technique</li><li>weak: 1.5 gpd</li><li>strong: 8 gpd</li></ul>
Dimensional Stability	<ul><li>elongation varies from 20–80%</li><li>excellent recovery (good for carpet backing)</li><li>resilient</li><li>fibers shrink in heat</li></ul>
Density	<ul><li>exceptionally low (0.90–0.96 gpcc)</li><li>olefin fibers float in water</li></ul>
Absorbency	<ul><li>virtually no moisture regain or absorption</li></ul>
REACTION TO CHEMICALS	
Alkalis	<ul><li>unaffected</li></ul>
Acids	<ul><li>excellent resistance, except to strong oxidizing acids, which cause loss of strength</li></ul>

OLEFIN • Manufactured Fiber

FIBER PROPERTIES	
Solvents	• low resistance • should be cleaned with water
Oil and Grease	• fibers stain easily, but water, soap, and detergent will remove greasy material
ENVIRONMENTAL SENSITIVITIES	
Flammability and Thermal Performance	• burns slowly • sooty smoke • leaves a hard, brown residue • highly sensitive to heat • shrinkage occurs at 75°C (165°F) • polyethylene fibers melt at 105–125°C (221–257°F) • polypropylene melts at 170°C (335°F)
UV Light Resistance	• no resistance to sunlight • UV protecting finishes may be added
Insects	• resistant to all insects
Microorganisms	• resistant to microorganisms
Aging	• unaffected

VINYON® • Manufactured Fiber

Trade Names: Fibravyi®, HH®, Leavil®, PeCe®, PVC, Phovyi®, Teviron®, Thermovyi®, Valcren®, Vinyon®

This fiber was introduced in 1939 by the American Viscose Company. The fiber is a polyvinyl chloride fiber (at least 85%) produced by either a dry or wet spinning method. It is used principally in industrial applications, but also to heat seal or bond some needle constructed fabrics.

FIBER PROPERTIES

INHERENT CHARACTERISTICS	
Fiber Description	• smooth • white or semi-transparent • usually round, but also produced in dogbone shape • high luster
Strength	• great variation depending on polymerization process • 0.7–3.8 gpd
Dimensional Stability	• good to excellent • elongation varies from 12–125%
Density	• .34–1.43 gpcc
Absorbency	• virtually no moisture regain or absorption
REACTION TO CHEMICALS	
Alkalis	• unaffected
Acids	• unaffected
Solvents	• no effect, except to acetone, aromatic hydrocarbons, and ether
ENVIRONMENTAL SENSITIVITIES	
Flammability and Thermal Performance	• will not support combustion, but will burn in direct flame • very sensitive to heat • fibers soften at 65°C (150°F)
UV Light Resistance	• resistant to sunlight
Insects	• resistant to all insects
Microorganisms	• resistant to microorganisms

ELASTOMERIC FIBERS

Elastomers are rubber-like substances, and the fiber forms are characterized by exceptional elongation, from 200-800%, with excellent recovery. The two main fibers in this category are rubber and spandex. Rubber is rarely used thanks to the drastically improved characteristics of spandex. Elastomeric fibers have adequate performance characteristics, with spandex significantly better than rubber in all areas.

Spandex • Manufactured • Elastomeric Fiber

Trade Names: Duraspan®, Estane®, Fulflex®, Glospan®, Interspan®, Lycra®, Numa®, Spanzeile®, Unel®, Vyrene®

Spandex fibers are composed primarily (85%) of segmented polyurethane. Other elements are added, and production techniques vary considerably. These technical processes are largely classified information, closely guarded by manufacturers.

The fiber is spun with hard and soft segments, which allow the fiber its excellent elongation. Dry spinning is the most common technique for extruding the spandex fiber, but different manufacturers also use wet, melt, or reaction spinning.

The fiber may be used in its filament form, as a wrapped or core spun yarn, with other filament fibers, or with staple fibers wrapped in a spiral around the spandex core. Normally, fabric will contain 2–10% spandex depending on the end use.

coalesced fibers   *round cross sections*

• *Spandex Fiber*

- Microscopic view shows a number of tiny fibers joined (coalesced) along the length.
- Fibers are very fine.
- Fibers are white.
- Cross section is round.

FIBER PROPERTIES

INHERENT CHARACTERISTICS	
Fiber Description	- multifilament fibers fused along the length - fibers are rarely colored - very flexible - high luster
Strength	- low: 0.5–1.03 gpd
Dimensional Stability	- lack of strength is compensated for by extremely high elasticity - 500–800% elongation - elastic recovery 100%
Density	- low: 1.20–1.25 gpcc
Absorbency	- moisture regain is low: 0.3–1.2% - fibers have an affinity for a wide range of dyes

Spandex • Manufactured • Elastomeric Fiber

FIBER PROPERTIES	
REACTION TO CHEMICALS	
Alkalis, Acids, Solvents	• poor: concentrate alkalis at high temperatures cause loss of strength • poor: concentrated bleaches cause yellowing and loss of strength • compared to natural rubber, these fibers have greater resistance to smog, oils, perspiration, and body oils
ENVIRONMENTAL SENSITIVITIES	
Flammability and Thermal Performance	• burns in flame • forms a gummy residue • heat resistant to 150°C (300°F)
UV Light Resistance	• resistant
Insects	• unaffected
Microorganisms	• unaffected
Aging	• unaffected

MINERAL FIBERS • Glass Fiber • Mineral Fiber

Trade Names: Beta®, Fiberglas®, Ferro®, Modiglass®, Pittsburgh PPG®, Unifab®, Unistrand®

Venetian artisans in the Middle Ages were the first to draw molten glass into fiber form, which they used to decorate blown glassware. Many attempts were made in the ninteenth century to produce glass fiber, but coarseness, weakness, and lack of flexibility were early characteristics and were certainly not desirable for fabric use. In the 1930s, Owens-Illinois Glass and Corning Glass did considerable separate research on glass fiber production. In 1938, they joined forces as the Owens Corning Fiberglas Corp. and produced the first commercially acceptable glass fiber, Fiberglas®.

There are two methods of producing glass fiber.

Method one:

- the raw materials are silica sand and limestone
- these are combined with small quantities of selected other elements and melted together at about 1650°C (3000°F) to form clear glass marbles, called cullet
- cullet is reheated to the molten stage and fed by gravity through a rectangular platinum bushing (similar to a spinneret) with 400–1600 tiny holes
- the filaments harden immediately in the air they are lubricated, dried, and wound
- One 28 gram (1 ounce) cullet may produce as much as 160 km (100 miles) of glass fiber.

Method two: The direct method

- the cullet step is eliminated
- the silica and limestone are measured
- they are blended, and fed through the furnace
- then extruded as molten glass through the bushing

This method, understandably, is of economic advantage, and conversion to this procedure is widespread.

Staple fibers may be manufactured by the addition of high-pressured blasts of steam directed at the filaments as they drop from the bushing. This causes breakage into varying lengths 12–38 cm (5–15"). The resultant staple fibers are collected on a revolving drum, carded, and pulled into a sliver. Staple fibers can also be cut from longer filament fibers.

In part because of their fire resistance glass fibers are used in sheer casement fabric, draperies, bedspreads, table coverings, and some upholstery fabrics. The broken or cut ends, however, can be irritating to human contact, and loose fibers may be accidentally ingested. Beta®, a 1960 introduction by Owens-Corning, is the finest fiber, and blends well with other fibers.

Fabrics of fiber glass launder easily and resist wrinkling. Glass fibers are also widely used in industry as insulation, filters, electrical tapes, fillers, and as reinforcement for various materials such as boat hulls, car bodies, furniture, and vaulting poles.

FIBER PROPERTIES

INHERENT CHARACTERISTICS	
Fiber Description	• microscopic view shows smooth surface • cross section is round • can be produced in any length, filament, or any size staple • fibers are transparent but can be colored before spinning • high luster
Strength	• exceptionally high: 6.3–6.9 gpd • exceptional resistance to pressure and stress • lacks abrasion resistance
Dimensional Stability	• 3% elongation • elastic recovery 100% • excellent resiliency

MINERAL FIBERS • Glass Fiber • Mineral Fiber

FIBER PROPERTIES	
Density	• high: 2.54 gpcc
Absorbency	• completely hydrophobic
REACTION TO CHEMICALS	
Alkalis	• poor: cold strong alkalis and hot weak alkalis
Acids	• good to all except hydrofluoric acid or hot phosphoric acid
Solvents	• no effect
ENVIRONMENTAL SENSITIVITIES	
Flammability and Thermal Performance	• noncombustible • extremely heat resistant • will lose strength at 315°C (600°F) • will soften at 815°C (1500°F)
UV Ligth Resistance	• unaffected
Insects	• unaffected
Microorganisms	• unaffected
Aging	• unaffected

MINERAL FIBERS • Metallic Fiber

Trade Names : Bekinox®, Brunsmet®, Lurex®, Mylar®

Gold, silver, and aluminum are often used in textile products. The fibers are usually produced by slicing very thin sheets of the metal into narrow ribbons. They are very expensive, and because they are weak and soft, are most often used as a wrapping around a stronger core fiber. Gold tends to discolor and silver to tarnish. Aluminum, colored in a variety of shades, is more commonly used.

Polyester may be used as a coating for aluminum fiber to produce fibers such as Mylar®. Finely ground aluminum, color, and polyester may be mixed in the spinning solution to produce effective, bright, tarnish-free fibers. Metallic-polyester fibers are somewhat delicate.

Stainless steel, as a metallic fiber in fabrics, contributes strength, tear, and abrasion resistance, and helps reduce static build-up. The fibers are also used to transmit and radiate heat when connected to a power source.

Ceramic fibers from various mineral compounds are also produced for very specific applications, such as the aerospace industry's rockets, fittings, and related structures.

YARNS

Yarn is a generic term for a continuous strand suitable for weaving, knitting, or otherwise intertwining to form a textile fabric. There are two main types of yarn and many variations of them. **Spun yarn** is made from staple fibers and **filament yarn** is made from filament fibers. Filament fibers may also be spun after being cut into staple lengths. All natural fibers, with the exception of silk, are made into spun yarn; most manufactured fibers are either multifilament or monofilament yarns.

Chapters four and five detailed the general characteristics of each fiber used for textile production and discussed how usable fibers are obtained from natural sources. This section briefly examines the theory, practice, and current status of spinning yarn. With this basic information in mind, the production and character of yarn in all its diversity is discussed.

Spinning—Past to Present

The process of spinning yarn predates written history by many centuries. The principle is easily demonstrated by lifting a layer of ordinary cotton batting, gradually pulling the fibers apart, and rolling or twisting them between the thumb and forefinger to form a continuous strand. This method was the basis of early spinning of wool, cotton, and flax.

The earliest 'inventions' in the textile industry were two sticks: one, called the *distaff*, to which the mass of raw fibers was tied, and the other, a shorter stick, notched at one end and pointed at the other. Near the pointed end a round of clay or wood, called the *whorl*, was attached, and this combination formed the spindle. To spin yarn, the distaff was held under the arm, and a lead of fibers twisted out and attached to the spindle. As both hands fed out the fibers and formed them into a thread, the weight of the spindle drew the strand downward, and the spindle was

rotated to impart a firm twist to the attached strand. As the spindle approached the ground, it would be taken up and the yarn wound around it, secured in the notch, and the motion repeated.

Earliest spun yarn was probably rather uneven and coarse, yet this simple procedure developed into a fine art. Hand-spun threads have been discovered that have not been equaled for delicacy even today. Dacca muslin was reportedly so fine that it could not withstand weight of a suspended spindle, but was instead wound on a bamboo needle lightly weighted with clay and rotated on a supporting shell.

The spinning wheel appeared in Europe in the thirteenth century. The distaff was mounted in an upright position, and the spindle mounted horizontally within a frame. A wheel was rotated by hand and was connected to a spindle by a band that caused it to revolve. Leonardo da Vinci invented a flyer that twisted the strand and a companion device that fed the yarn evenly across a bobbin mounted on the spindle. In 1533, the Saxony Wheel added a foot treadle to operate the wheel, and the first continuous motion spinning was made possible.

The Saxony Wheel was used exclusively for over two hundred years, and it is still used in fiber arts. During the Industrial Revolution, spinning and weaving methods underwent many advances. By 1812, there were five million spindles being operated in Britain, giving employment to 70 000 spinners and 150 000 weavers.

It is worth remembering that four Englishmen—Lewis Paul, James Hargreaves, Richard Arkwright, and Samuel Crompton—devised the methods upon which all modern spinning is based.

Mechanized Spinning

Drawing • This step involves combining and subsequently redrawing out several slivers. There are usually two passes through this mechanical process, and the result is a longer, thinner strand of fibers.

Roving • This operation is generally one continuous step, with the task of further drawing out the drawn sliver and imparting a slight twist. The resulting product is called the *roving*.

Winding and Twisting • Yarns have to be wound onto large packages suitable for subsequent fabric manufacturing steps.

Spinning Methods

There are six methods of spinning: **flyer, mule, cap, ring, open-end,** and **air jet.**

Flyer Spinning	This system is used to spin flax and jute. The yarn is drawn from an elevated delivery roll of roving down to the top of the flyer, where it is twisted around the flyer leg, through an eye, and onto a bobbin. This is a slow process and only rotates 3000 revolutions per minute. The main disadvantage of this system is its lack of speed.
Mule Spinning	This production method involves three distinct steps—drawing the strand, twisting, and winding. Slightly faster than flyer spinning, mule spinning is capable of producing very fine yarns. It has, nonetheless, been largely replaced by other methods, although cotton waste and some woolen and worsted yarns are still spun commercially by this system.
Cap Spinning	Cap spinning is an adaptation of flyer spinning, with the flyer replaced by a 'cap' within which the bobbin rises and falls while spinning. The action of the bobbin is powered from below. The roving is delivered from above the cap and drags over the lower edge to be wound on the bobbin inside, at about 7000 rpm. This method was used extensively for worsted yarn, but it, too, is gradually being replaced.
Ring Spinning	Ring spinning is currently the most commonly used system to employ the spindle. Action is fast and continuous—the method uses a ring and traveler to spin and feed the strand on to the high-speed (15000 rpm) spindle. Ring spinning places considerable strain on the yarn, but it is the principal method of producing fine yarns.
Open-ended Spinning	Open-ended spinning was introduced in 1967, and it is the first machine that does not use a spindle. Slivers are fed directly into the spinning frame where suction pulls the fibers into a spinning chamber containing a rotor revolving at speeds as high as 45000 rpm. The yarn forms continuously inside the rotor and is simultaneously pulled out and wound onto large packages. The speed, degree of automation, and floor space savings are attractive to manufacturers. The major drawback is that only relatively coarse yarns can be produced by open-end spinning.

Spinning Methods, cont'd

Air Jet Spinning	Yarn is manufactured on air jet spinning equipment. The sliver is fed through the draft zone to determine the size of the yarn. It is fed into two sets of nozzles where air jets release high-pressure air currents in a certain direction. The second nozzle directs the air jets in the opposite direction. The air jets make the protruding fibers on the outside of the yarn wind around the strand, giving it cohesion and strength. This method is especially good for blending cotton and polyester fibers, but also nonblended acrylic, cotton, rayon, and polyester. It can deliver yarn as quickly as 100-200 meters (110-220 yards) per minute. This rate can be as high as ten times the speed of ring spinning and twice that of open-ended spinning. Yarns are characterized by low pilling propensity, good resiliency, better dye affinity, and excellent uniformity and smoothness. These fibers are generally weaker and have lower breaking strength and elongation than ring-spun yarns.

Other Yarn Methods

Automated Fiber to Sliver	The steps detailed earlier may be accomplished as one automatic operation involving several types of machinery. All hand operations, packaging, and transporting are eliminated. Production speed is greater, labor costs are lower, and cleaner plant makes for a healthier environment. The product is more uniform and stronger as a result of the tight control and high standards.
Automated Sliver to Yarn	This highly automated method eliminates separate drawing, roving, and twisting operations. Each step is performed in one continuous operation with little human input.
Automated Tow to Yarn	This system eliminates the separate cutting or breaking of manufactured filaments into staple form. In the tow to yarn system, the alignment of the mass of filament fibers is not lost; breaking into staple is done by passing the tow through rollers operating at different speeds, and the staple lengths are varied rather than identical. These are distinct advantages. The fibers then proceed through the usual drawing and spinning machinery to become yarn. This system reduces fiber waste, introduces considerable economy, and produces either very uniform yarns or, if desired, special-effect yarns.

Classification of Yarns

The method of conversion into yarn depends on the characteristic of the fibers. Silk and all manufactured fibers are in filament form and are used to produce 'thrown' yarns. The origin of the term *throwing* is Anglo-Saxon and the original word, *thrawan*, meant to twist or revolve. The process of throwing, then, is to twist two or more filaments together to form one yarn. The process originally applied only to silk, but it now also describes the process of making yarn from manufactured filaments.

Yarn is also produced from tapes, which are exceedingly thin strips of a fine sheet of manufactured material. This alternate to extruding a solution through a spinneret results in a product similar to, and treated as, a manufactured filament fiber.

Other spinning systems include twistless yarns held together by adhesive rather than twist, self-twist yarns, fasciated yarns, and fibrillated yarns, each of which are manufactured in unconventional ways.

Yarn Types

Spun Yarns	*single* *ply* *cord*	**Singles, Ply, Cord** Yarn as it comes from the spinning frame is called a **single** yarn. It may have very little twist and be quite soft and weak, or it may be moderately twisted to impart more strength and a crisper feel. Twisting two or more single yarns together produces a **ply** yarn, with the number of single yarns designating the number of plies (2-3-or 4-ply, etc.). The individual yarns of a ply are usually slightly more twisted than plain single yarns. The fibers do not slip as readily within the yarn, the yarn's diameter is more uniform, and strength is gained by the additional plys. **Cord** yarn is made of two or more ply yarns twisted together. To identify a cord, the number of plies and then the number of their constituent single yarns are given. A 3,5 cord yarn count indicates that the yarn is composed of three, five-ply yarns twisted together to form one.

• *single yarn*

• *ply yarn*

Filament Yarns	*monofilament* *multifilament*	Filament fibers (silk and manufactured fibers) are continuous strands in variable sizes and shapes. The two basic filament yarns are **monofilament** and **multifilament.** They are generally smooth, strong, and lustrous. **Monofilament** yarns are single filament yarns. They may be as thick as fishing line or as fine as a nylon stocking yarn. **Multifilament** yarns are much more commonly used and composed of many fine filaments thrown, or twisted, to form one yarn. Most are low twist, as very little is needed to hold the fibers together, but a tight twist may be used to give a special effect in the finished fabric. Multifilament yarns may be single or ply, but there are few reasons for, or benefits from, ply filament yarn. Plying does not help increase strength or uniformity, both of which happen when the fiber is spun. Plying filament yarns is generally used to produce specialty yarns.
Tape Yarns		Tape yarns are also called *split film yarns*. They are produced by slitting very thin sheets (or films) of polymer into narrow strips. In production, the following steps would be fully automated: • extrusion of a polymer sheet • cooling in a 'quench tank' of cold water or other medium, over a set of guides • through a slitting unit, through an oven, or over a heat source • around tensioning rolls to draw the tapes • through separating guides directly to the yarn winders The polymer film may be as fine as plastic wrap, or coarser, depending on the intended end use. The finished yarn may retain a flat, tape appearance. With finer tapes, drawing tends to cause longitudinal breakage (or fibrillation), and forming these long fibrils causes the yarn to resemble a coarse filament. Tape yarns are strong, stable, and have good abrasion resistance. While the system can be used to produce yarns from any manufactured fiber polymer, olefin (polypropylene or polyethylene) is most often used. Tape yarns are used for carpet backing, furniture webbing, awnings and blinds, as well as for tarpaulins, sacking, travel goods, and swimming pool covers.

Yarn Types, cont'd

Twistless Yarns		Twistless yarns describe a product that is held together by adhesives rather than by twisting. The roving is attenuated into a fine strand; however, rather than being spun and twisted, the strand is passed between rollers that apply an adhesive. Fibers in twistless yarns lie parallel to one another. These yarns make fabrics with excellent covering power and an attractive appearance. The fabrics have good strength. The adhesive may or may not be removed in subsequent finishing operations.
Self-twist Yarns		These are 2-ply yarns. The yarns are made by standard methods, except an alternate twist is applied along the length, first left hand (counterclockwise or Z twist) and then right hand (clockwise S twist). When two yarns are combined, the alternating twists cause them to 'grab' or twist together, resulting in one 2-ply yarn without a separate twisting operation. The yarns are unstable, so use is limited.
Fasciated Yarns		Tying a continuous bundle of fibers together at irregular intervals produces fasciated yarns. These yarns are surprisingly strong and inexpensive to produce.
Sheath Yarns		Creating sheath yarns involves extrusion of a polymer core into which loose fibrils are embedded. The extended fibers form a sheath around the filament core.

Basic Yarns

Basic yarns make up most textile products. They are smooth, uniform, and stable, with varying size, quality, and twist. Basic fiber may be made of any natural or manufactured yarn or a blend.

SPUN YARNS		
Blended Yarns		Cotton, cut filaments, and blended yarns are widely used in textiles for interiors. The blending processes provide slivers of fibers blended by weight. Textiles labeled '70% polyester, 30% cotton' indicate the percentage by weight of the blend.
Carded Yarns		Carded yarns are spun from a carded sliver and have only the very short fibers removed. The remaining ones are brought into general alignment. This term is used in reference to cotton.
Combed Yarns		Combed yarns are comprised of longer fibers that have had an extra combing process after carding. The yarn is better aligned and is strong and smooth. Combed yarns are used for shirting, bedding, or where smooth fine fabric is required. This term is also most often used when referring to cotton.
Woolen and Worsted Yarns		These terms apply to wool or wool blends. **Woolen** is the equivalent of carded cotton, with one combing application only. Woolen yarn (and fabric) is bulky, fuzzy, and uneven. Tweed is a good example of a woolen fabric. **Worsted wool** is combed twice leaving only the longest, highest quality fibers. Worsted yarn (and fabrics) are smooth, even, and have little surface fuzz. Worsted yarn has higher twist and more uniform fibers, and it is more expensive than woolen yarn. Gabardine is a worsted fabric. In use, woolen fabrics provide better insulation and bulk, and have a soft, napped appearance. Worsted yarns and fabrics are firmer and denser and will hold their shape and creases better. The surface of worsted fabrics clearly reveals the weave, but it is more prone to develop a shine from wear or pressing. A fulling finish slightly naps the surface, and is sometimes used on worsteds to reduce the signs of wear.

Basic Yarns, cont'd

Tow and Line Linen Yarns		Flax produces two qualities of linen fiber. **Tow yarns** are composed of the shorter fibers, and are used for rougher fabrics. **Line yarns** are made of smooth, long flax fibers and are used for fine table linens and handkerchiefs.
Thread		Thread is a basic yarn, but the term is used to designate a yarn that joins pieces of fabric in the sewing process. It is frequently a ply construction. Thread can be made of any fiber with the most common being cotton, polyester, and polyester/cotton blend. The thread used for assembling apparel or furniture needs to be selected carefully to ensure seam stability. Selecting a thread with opposite behavior to the fabric could result in puckering when washed. Using cotton thread with polyester, for example, does not work well because each has such different reactions to use and care.
Crêpe Yarns		Crêpe yarns are simply ply yarns that have been given a very high degree of twist. Made into fabrics of the same name, crêpe yarn produces a characteristic textured surface. A crêpe yarn detached from the fabric and slackened will twist back on itself.

Textured Yarns

The term *textured yarns* belongs to: *"that group of filament or spun yarns that have been given notably greater apparent volume than conventional yarn of similar fiber (filament) count and linear density...."* – American Society for Testing and Materials

Wool is the only naturally bulky fiber. The greater volume of woolen yarn and fabric is a result of wool's inherent crimp. First attempts at introducing bulk to manufactured fibers came with cross sectional modifications.

Thermoplasticity (capacity to soften in heat, harden in cold) of manufactured fibers allows heat setting to create texture, and this was first done with viscose rayon by the Swiss firm, Heberlein & Co. After World War II, their researchers adapted the process of mechanically crimping and heat setting nylon, and introduced Helanca® stretch nylon. Early success was in the manufacture of ski clothes, and lay the groundwork for accelerated research with other fibers in other countries.

Advantages

There are many other advantages to adding texture to yarns and fabrics. Textured yarns, or yarns made of textured fibers, make more comfortable, versatile, and attractive fabrics than their nontextured counterparts. Regular nylon, for instance, constructed into a moderately firm woven or knit fabric, is sleek and tightly packed, preventing the movement of air and moisture. Texturing the nylon creates bulk and space between the filaments, so that the same construction will result in a fabric that 'breathes' and looks more interesting. Textured yarns are more opaque and, therefore, cover better than a nontextured yarn of the same weight. Textured yarns are dry and warmer to the touch, without the cool slick feel of straight filament yarns. Fabrics made of textured yarns have greater abrasion resistance and do not pill or snag as easily.

Texturing Methods

Texturing of manufactured filaments is an exacting procedure, but one that is now performed quickly and efficiently. New machinery and specific improvements are an ongoing process of equipment producers in the United States, Europe, and Japan. Generally speaking, the large quantity, high-speed conversion of smooth thermoplastic fibers into textured filament yarns is done on continuous (feed-in to wind-up), fully automated machinery. Each texturing procedure has appropriate equipment, and each results in a different texturing effect.

False Twist	This method is used to produce both textured and stretch yarns. The simple filament yarn is twisted around a spindle and heat set. The degree of twist is controlled by the size of the spindle and the closeness of the yarns as they are wound around it. Yarns may be twisted to have 400% elongation and perfect recovery. The twisted yarn is then untwisted and cooled, and is wound on take-up spools. This produces stretch yarn. If it is given an additional heat-set-cool after it is untwisted, the result is a textured yarn with a minimum of stretch and is called a *set* or *stabilized yarn*. As twist is one-sided in this method, there

Textured Yarns, cont'd

False Twist, cont'd	is a tendency toward a torque effect, which may result in distortion. A counteracting procedure twists two simple yarns in opposite directions to form a 2-ply balanced yarn. Helanca® and ARTC® are trade names of stretch yarns produced by the false twist method. Set or stabilized yarns textured by this method are Fluflon®, Saaba®, and Superloft®.
Knife-edge	Here, the system draws the simple yarn over a heated knife-edge, which sets a helical twist (like a gift ribbon curled by drawing against a sharp edge). The twist reverses at random so there is no problem of unbalance. Agilon® is a trade name example.
Stuffer Box	The stuffer box method produces the greatest amount of bulk. Straight yarns are passed through crimping rollers and stuffed into a heated box where the crimp is set. BanLon® is a popular trade name yarn prepared by this method.
Gear Crimping	As the name implies, this method crimps yarns by passing them through heated, rotating, and intermeshing gears (similar to the inner workings of a clock). The gear sizes are variable and any degree of crimp is possible.
Tunnel Crimping	This method feeds yarn into a heated tunnel in such a way that it arranges itself into a sinuous coil.
Knit Deknit	Texture is introduced by machine knitting yarn into a tube shape, heat setting the knit material, and then unraveling the yarn. This creates a wavy texture in the yarn, which adds bulk to the fabric.
Air Jet Method	This is one of the few texturing methods that does not employ heat. The system simply passes straight yarn by a turbulent stream of compressed air. The air blows the fibers apart within the yarn, leaving fiber loops on the surface. The result is a bulky yarn, but with no stretch potential. Controlling the air jet allows yarns to be textured to resemble complex yarns, such as bouclé. The special feature of the air jet method is that fibers other than those that are thermoplastic can be textured. Glass fibers are bulked by this method. Trade names are Taslan® and Skyloft®.

Generally, basic yarns produce smooth, plain, durable textiles. However, the generalization must not be taken too literally because differences in fibers, fabric construction, finishes, and coloring may also produce uneven, fancy, or delicate fabrics.

Novelty Yarns

Specialty Yarns

This category includes complex novelty yarns and yarns designed specifically for their stretch and recovery potential.

Complex Yarns

Complex yarns are manufactured for their appearance. In general, the structure is uneven, rather than even, and deliberate irregularities are built in. They contribute interest and decorative surface to fabrics and are widely used for interior textiles. Fabrics made of novelty yarns are generally not as durable as those made with even yarns, and they require greater care in maintenance. Their interesting appearance takes precedence, however, in many applications where durability is not a prime consideration.

Novelty Yarns, cont'd

SINGLE YARNS		
Slub Yarns		Slub yarns are staple yarns that have the twist interrupted at irregular intervals. This produces a yarn with softer, bulky sections along its length.
Thick-and-Thin Yarns		Thick-and-thin yarns are filament yarns composed of fibers that have irregular thick and thin areas along the length, produced by deliberate changes in pressure at the point of extrusion from the spinneret.
Flock Yarns		Flock yarns (sometimes called flake yarns) are characterized by nubs or tufts of fiber protruding from the surface. This is accomplished by mechanically inserting tufts at irregular intervals as the yarn is being twisted. The twists hold the tufts in place.
PLY YARNS		

The addition of strands or plys makes more complex effects possible. 'Novelty yarns' are produced regularly, but the following complex ply yarns cover all types of effects.

Bouclé Yarns		Bouclé yarns are 3-ply, with tight loops projecting from the strand at fairly regular intervals. Construction is as follows: a base yarn remains straight, the effect yarn forms multiple loops, and the binder yarn twists around the base securing the effect yarn.
Ratiné and Gimp Yarns		Ratiné and gimp yarns are variations of bouclé yarns; they are formed in the same manner. Ratiné yarns have closer set loops than bouclé, which are produced by twisting the finished yarn in the opposite direction. Gimp has loops slightly softer than ratiné and is not double-twisted.
Loop (or Curl) Yarns		Loop yarns are at least 3-ply and may be more. As in bouclé, an effect yarn forms the loops, which are larger and more pronounced than in bouclé, on a rather heavy base yarn. The effect yarn is secured by one or more binder yarns.
Nub (Spot, Knot) Yarns		Nub yarns are ply yarns that are manufactured on a special machine that holds the base yarn securely and wraps the effect yarn in such a manner as to form nubs, or enlarged segments, along the length. Sometimes colored fibers are inserted in the nub, which gives a flocked effect as well. Seed or splash yarns are variations of nub yarns. Seed yarns have a very tiny nub. Splash yarns have an elongated nub.
Spiral or Corkscrew Yarns		Spiral yarns are composed of different yarns twisted together. Differences may be in diameter, size, or fiber content. Spiral yarn has two components, a bulky, slack twist yarn that is spirally wound around a fine yarn with a hard twist. Corkscrew yarns twist yarns of different sizes, twist yarns irregularly, or corkscrew a fine yarn around a bulky one.
Chenille Yarns		Chenille yarns are made in an unusual manner: a leno weave fabric (see chapter 8) is constructed and then slit lengthwise into narrow strips and serves as yarn. The soft filling yarns of the fabric form the characteristic fuzzy pile, and the warp yarns prevent the pile from falling apart when the fabric is slit to form chenille yarn. In constructing fabric or rugs with this yarn, the pile can be made to appear on either or both sides.

Novelty Yarns, cont'd		
METALLIC YARNS		
		Metallic yarns for decorative use are usually constructed by either a sandwich or lamination technique. In the first method, aluminum foil and pigment are sandwiched between plastic layers; in the second method, metallized polyester is laminated to clear polyester. Both methods use the tape technique to produce the final yarn, and in both cases the 'metal' is durable and tarnish-proof thanks to the lamination.
		A core yarn technique is also used, with fine extruded metal wrapped around a core of a stronger material. This procedure does not protect the metal, however, and dulling and tarnishing are inevitable.
STRETCH YARNS		
		The principal used to produce textured yarns by false twist is used to produce stretch yarns. Adding false twist is a very reliable, yet unobtrusive, stretch effect in constructed textiles. The 'give' inherent in fabrics made of these yarns is called *comfort stretch*, which implies an easy yielding to body movement or pressure and good recovery with no loss of appearance. Method of fabric construction and the degree of tension contribute greatly to the overall stretching and recovery capacity of any textile product.
		Power stretch is a term given to the high elasticity and full recovery of fabrics composed of elastomeric yarns. These yarns usually covered (wrapped) yarns. Bare elastic yarns are uncomfortable and never used on their own. Covered elastic yarns are made of spandex, anidex, or, rarely, natural rubber, wrapped with spun or filament yarn. These yarns are used for apparel or specialty applications where fit is important.

Yarn Specifications

Yarns are described in many ways, and a yarn specification may include one or several of the descriptions below.

Fiber Content—Labeling

Fiber content is listed generically and may also include a trade name. If the yarn and fabric is made of a blend of fibers, these are stated as percentages.

    50% Wool
    30% Rayon
    16% Polyester
    4% Spandex

STAPLE FIBERS (natural fibers, except silk; blends of natural with manufactured) are made into **spun yarns.** The type or quality of the fibers may also be identified (for instance, 100% combed pima cotton). 'Spun' is not stated.

FILAMENT STAPLE FIBERS (silk or manufactured) are made into **spun yarns** and state 'spun' as part of their description (for instance, spun rayon).

FILAMENT FIBERS (silk or manufactured) are made into **filament yarns.** 'Filament' is not stated on the label.

SINGLE YARNS AND PLY YARNS Single is the yarn as it is spun or thrown. Ply refers to the subsequent joining of two or more single yarns.

Yarn Twist

Yarn twist is the most common method of holding fibers together to form a single strand. The amount of twist to accomplish this holding action depends on the diameter of the yarn, but it is relatively low. Twist is measured in **turns-per-inch** (TPI.)

The direction of the twist is designated as S or Z.

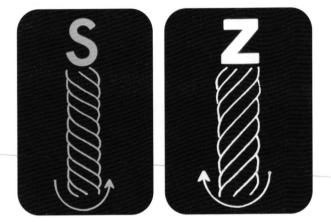

- S twist is right-handed, or clockwise
- Z twist is left-handed, or counterclockwise

Twist adds strength, and yarn is often twisted considerably more than is needed to hold the fibers together. The degree of optimum twist possible for increasing strength is a mathematical computation based on a factor called the **twist multiplier** (TM). Balanced yarns are those in which the amount of twist does not exceed the optimum level. A balanced yarn will hang in a loop without kinking or doubling. An unbalanced yarn has too much twist. Hung in a loop, it will twist back on itself. Yarns that have too much twist loose their tenacity, so the optimum twist calculation is important when deciding on how much twist to add to a yarn. Crêpe is one example of a yarn twisted far beyond its optimum, but tenacity is not a consideration for this fiber.

Yarn Count

Over the centuries, many systems have been devised for measuring yarn for purposes of buying and selling, and for estimating its size.

Weight is a factor and yarn numbers express a relationship between a particular quantity of yarn and a unit of weight. These systems evolved over time and were not standard. A **direct yarn number** is the mass per unit length: an **indirect yarn number** is the length per unit mass.

As an example of the **indirect yarn numbering system**, cotton is numbered by measuring the weight in pounds of one 840-yard hank. In this system the higher the number, the finer the yarn. A 50 spun cotton yarn indicates that fifty 840-yard hanks weigh one pound, a 100-count yarn would need one hundred 840-yard hanks to make up one pound. Woolen yarn is measured in 300-yard hanks, worsted yarn is measured in 560-yard hanks per pound. When identifying spun cotton or cotton blends, the yarn count is followed by 's' if the yarn is a single, or 2, 3, etc. to indicate the number of plys. Wool is described in a reverse fashion with the ply count first, followed by the yarn count.

The **direct yarn numbering system** is used with silk and manufactured filament yarns, and is called the **denier system**. (The denier was a Roman coin.) The denier number represents the weight in grams of 9000 meters of the yarn. 9000 meters of a 10-denier yarn weighs 10 grams. In this system, the yarn number correlates directly with the weight; so the **higher the number, the heavier the weight.**

Filament yarns are also expressed by indicating the number of filaments in the yarn. If combined with the denier number, the denier comes first, the filament number comes second, and the degree and direction of twist, if given, comes last. A 300-20-2S nylon yarn indicates that 9000 meters weighs 300 grams, that the yarn is made up of 20 filaments, and that it has been twisted clockwise (S twist) two turns per inch. To obtain the denier number per filament, the total denier is divided by the number of filaments. In this example, 15 denier is the yarn count of each filament.

THE TEX SYSTEM is the only internationally standardized yarn measuring system. It is a universal metric numbering system in which the yarn number is determined by the weight in grams of 1 kilometer of yarn (g/km). The finer the yarn, the smaller the number.

- 20 tex means that 1 km of yarn weighs 20 g.

Comparison of Properties

SPUN AND FILAMENT YARNS

Fabrics made of spun yarns are generally warm, soft, and light weight. Fabrics of filament yarns are smooth, lustrous, and have a cool hand. Some fabrics combine spun and filament yarns to take advantage of the best characteristics of each. Yarn type, fabric structure, and finishing processes (such as adding texture) can modify any of these generalizations.

The basic differences between spun yarns and filament yarns may be generalized as follows:

	SPUN	FILAMENT
Strength	The fibers in a spun yarn will slip past one another causing the yarn to break.	With all fibers in a filament yarn continuous, more force is needed to break the yarn as the fibers do not slip past one another easily.
Flexibility	Spun yarns are flexible except when exceptionally bulky.	Monofilament yarns are often less flexible; multifilaments are equally flexible to spun yarn or may be more flexible.
Uniformity	Spun yarns are less uniform.	Filament yarns are more uniform.
Smoothness and Luster	Spun yarns are less lustrous. They have protruding fibers and a rougher surface.	Filament yarns are smoother and more lustrous because there are no fibers protruding from the yarn surface.

FABRIC CONSTRUCTION

The construction of fabrics is a blend of ancient arts and modern technology. Automated equipment and new methods of bonding make entirely new fabrics possible. Felting and weaving, the oldest fabric construction methods, are still viable today.

This chapter examines each of the fabric construction techniques and the particular characteristics of the fabrics each technique produces.

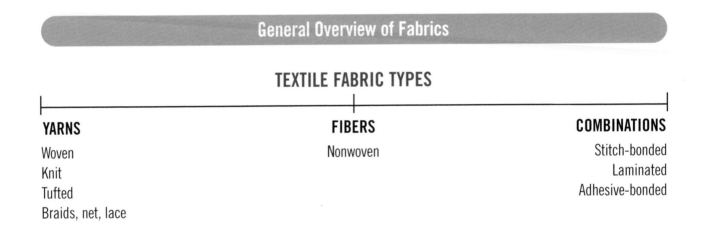

General Overview of Fabrics

TEXTILE FABRIC TYPES

YARNS	FIBERS	COMBINATIONS
Woven	Nonwoven	Stitch-bonded
Knit		Laminated
Tufted		Adhesive-bonded
Braids, net, lace		

Woven Fabrics

Weaving is the interlacing of two sets of yarns at right angles to each other. It is an ancient technique that continues to be the best and most commonly used method of fabric construction. The three basic weaves were devised at an early date, and samples of expertly woven materials have been found in Egypt, Europe, Asia, and South America dating back as far as 5000 B.C.E. Looms are depicted on vases, in wall hangings, and in other pictorial records on all continents.

The Loom

Early weaving on a loom was a fairly simple procedure. The lengthwise yarns, called the *warp*, were separated and secured at each end of the loom to remain taut. A device called a *reed*, which resembled a comb with long teeth, was fixed at the weaving end to keep the warp yarns separated, and used to push each filling yarn into place. The crosswise yarns, called the *filling, pick,* or *weft*, were wound around a stick, woven

• *Loom*

over and under alternate warp yarns to form the inter-lacing, and then pushed together with the reed to form a firm cloth. Early improvements in this proce-dure were the inventions of the *heddle* and the *shuttle*. The heddles are held in a wooden bar (harness) that raises alternate yarns of the warp, creating a triangu-lar opening called a *shed* through which the filling can more easily be passed. The shuttle, an improve-ment on the ball of filling yarn wrapped around a stick, is a smooth boat-shaped device, pointed at both ends, which holds a removable spindle wound with filling yarns.

This general procedure, with the addition of power, automation, size, and speed, is still followed and is the basis of the textile industry's capacity to supply fabrics to billions of consumers.

Weaving

Weaving entails only four separate motions, mechanically performed on a loom with **ten working parts**. The names of these parts, and their functions, are as follows:

1. The warp beam is the cylinder around which the warp yarns are wound in a parallel arrangement. The unwinding of the yarns from the warp beam is part of the letting-off and taking-up motion.

2. The whip roll is a guide roller, over which the warp moves.

3. The lease rods are two rods set between the whip roll and the heddles. Alternate warp yarns are guided over and under the lease rods.

4&5. The heddles are steel wires secured between the top and bottom bars of a harness, which is a movable wooden frame secured to a roller at the top of the loom and connected to a power source. Each heddle contains a central eye through which one warp yarn is threaded. A minimum of two harnesses are required, and yarns are alternated between them. The raising and lowering of each harness with its threaded heddles is the shedding motion and creates the shed (triangular space) through which the filling is inserted.

• *Parts of the loom*

6. The shuttle and bobbin is the combination carrier and holder of the filling yarn, or pick. Passage of the shuttle and bobbin through the shed is called the *picking motion*, which deposits the filling between the alternately raised and lowered warp yarns.

7. The reed is the comb-like device and serves two purposes:

   a. It keeps the warp yarns parallel and separated.

   b. It pushes the filling yarn into place.

The mechanical action of the reed is called the beating motion (also called battening, beating-up, or beating-in).

8. The temples are devices at either side of the newly formed cloth, and help to maintain the fixed width.

9&10. The breast beam is a bar fixed across the front of the loom over which the new cloth passes before being rolled on the cloth roller. This is the companion part of the mechanized letting-off and taking-up motion, and its function completes the weaving process.

Key Terms

In addition to the terms introduced in the preceding discussion about looms, the following definitions will help in understanding the discussions of weaving.

WARP AND FILLING YARNS have definite characteristics apart from being the lengthwise and crosswise yarns respectively. Warp yarns (sometimes called *ends*) are stronger, or of better quality, and usually have higher twist. Filling yarns are weaker and are more apt to be the decorative yarn.

FLOATS are formed when one yarn crosses over more than one other yarn at a time (in either direction).

GRAIN indicates the warp and filling directions. Lengthwise grain is the direction of the warp, crosswise grain is the direction of the filling yarns. Off-grain is a problem that indicates that the weaving has gone off square producing *skewed*—where the 90° angle is not found, or *bowed*—fabric where the center lags behind the sides. Using skewed fabric will result in difficulties in sewing, pressing, drape, and aesthetics. If the fabric is printed the design will not be straight. This is known as *off-grain*. (Off-grain can sometimes be corrected in the finishing procedure).

TRUE BIAS is the diagonal of a square, 45° from either the warp or filling yarns. Garment bias is any position between true bias and either the lengthwise or crosswise grain and gives a clingy, more elegant look.

THREAD COUNT (or cloth count) is the number of warp and filling yarns per square inch (2.54 cm) of fabric, before finishing. If two numbers are given, the warp count is first. If one number is given, it is usually the total of both warp and filling. The higher the thread count the finer and stronger and better quality the fabric. (This thread count should not be confused with the yarn number, which is the measure of yarn size as discussed in chap. 6.)

BALANCE is the ratio of warp yarns to filling yarns. Balanced fabrics have a 1:1 ratio, unbalanced fabrics may have 2:1, 3:1,1:3, etc. Both balanced and unbalanced fabrics may be of poor or good quality, but the aesthetics will vary depending on ratio.

SELVAGE is the lengthwise edge of the fabric. A conventional loom makes identical selvages on both sides of the fabric, and the filling yarns can be seen to have reversed direction. *Plain selvages* are similar to the rest of the fabric and do not shrink. *Tape selvages* have larger and/or ply warp yarns to give more strength, and may be basket woven for flatness. *Split selvages* occur when items such as towels are woven side by side and then cut apart, with the cut edges then finished by machine. Shuttleless looms produce

either a *fringed selvage*, a *cut and tucked selvage* in which the filling yarn ends are cut and tucked back into the fabric, or a *fused selvage* in which the cut ends are fused by heat.

CREELING is the procedure that winds the warp yarns from their individual spools onto the warp beam in readiness for weaving. Before being affixed to the loom, the warp yarns may be run through a *slash bath* of sizing solution, then dried and rewound. Sizing is often necessary to protect the yarns from the mechanical actions of the loom such as tension, friction, and heat.

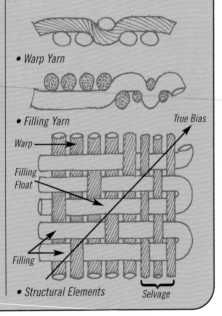

• Warp Yarn

• Filling Yarn

Warp →

Filling Float

True Bias

Filling

• Structural Elements   Selvage

Looms and the weaving motions are sufficient for constructing basic weaves. Improvements to the loom over the years have focused on three areas:

- devices for separating the warp for more intricate designs

- computers and electronic systems for directing and monitoring the weaving motions

- faster and different methods of placing the filling yarns

Electronics are very much part of mass production weaving in designing, programming, and controlling the process. Today, looms operate almost entirely on computer-controlled systems.

Shuttleless looms use a water-jet, air-jet, and the rapier system to place the filling yarn. Shuttle action looms were limited to placing the filling at approximately 200 picks per minute. The *water-jet loom* can place filling yarns at a speed of up to 600 picks per minute. In this system, measured lengths of filling yarn are delivered to a water nozzle where a jet of water carries it through the shed. The process produces a 'fringed' selvage, and the cloth must be dried prior to rolling. Speed is increased dramatically, and it is much quieter than traditional mechanized looms. The *air-jet loom* operates on the same principle, with a blast of air carrying the filling through the shed. This method is considerably slower, at 300 picks per minute.

The *rapier-type loom* weaves at about 300 picks per minute, using two metal arms, called dummy shuttles. The right arm carries the measured filling to the center of the warp where it meets the left arm that takes the filling from the right arm and carries it to the left edge.

Classification of Weaves

There are three basic weaves from which all woven fabrics are constructed. These are *plain weave, twill weave,* and *satin weave.* All other special-effect woven fabrics use the basic weaves, alone or in combination, but need complex loom attachments and techniques to achieve the desired appearance.

Basic Weaves

Plain Weave

The simplest plain weave is one in which warp and filling yarns are the same size and are interwoven one-to-one. This is a *balanced plain weave* and may be constructed of light-, medium-, or heavy-weight yarns. Both sides of the fabric are identical.

An *unbalanced plain weave* is one in which the warp and filling yarns are unequal in number or thickness. The number of warp yarns may be doubled, with the result that only warp yarns show on the top surface, or *face,* of the fabric, or the warp may be increased but not doubled to produce any one of several specific fabrics.

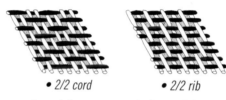

- *2/2 cord*   - *2/2 rib*

Basket weave is a plain weave variation in which two or more warp yarns are used as one. If an equal number of filling yarns are used, the result is a balanced basket weave (2x2, 3x3, 4x4).

Waffle weave is produced by using two or more warp yarns with one or more filling yarns to create an unbalanced basket weave in which the shapes of squares or rectangles vary.

Twill Weave

Twill weaves, a variation of plain weave, are constructed so that each warp or filling yarn floats across two or more filling or warp yarns, with a progression of one yarn to the right or left to form a distinct diagonal line or *wale.* Twills have a right side and a wrong side, and are designated by the direction of the wale. *Right-hand twills* show the line from lower left to upper right; *left-hand twills* are from lower right to upper left. The degree of the angle of the slope also affects the appearance of the fabric. *Steep twill* (steeper than 45°) indicates a fabric with a high warp count. It is stronger than a fabric with *reclining twill* (less than 45°), which indicates a higher filling yarn count. *Even-sided twill* has a 45° slant or a true diagonal and is a balanced weave.

- *2/2 twill*
- *3/3 twill*

Warp-faced twills have a predominance of warp yarns on the face of the fabric.

- *2/1 warp twill*
- *3/1 warp twill*

Filling-faced twills have a predominance of filling yarns on the face of the fabric.

Herringbone fabrics are a twill variation having the twill line reversed at regular intervals.

- *2/2 twill, herringbone*

Satin Weave

Warp-faced satin weaves have each warp yarn floated over four filling yarns (4/1) and interlaced with the fifth, with a progression of interfacings by two to the right or left. The face of the fabric shows a predominance of warp

- *8 thread satin*
- *5 thread satin*
- *Filling faced satin*

yarns. *Filling-faced satin* weaves are the reverse of the warp-faced satin weave (1/4), with the filling yarns predominant on the face of the fabric.

Satin weaves have a definite right and wrong side. The face is lustrous, caused by the long floats of yarns and high thread count.

Special-Effect Weaves

Crepe Weave

Crepe was originally a French word meaning *crinkle*. In English, crepe is used to describe a particular fabric with a pebbly or crinkled texture. True crepe fabrics are obtained by plain weaving extremely high-twist (over-twisted) yarns. Wool is often used for true crepe, where the yarn is twisted so tightly that it loops back on itself which, when woven, creates the pebbled texture. Crepe weaves may be *warp crepes, filling crepes,* or *balanced crepes*. The crepe effect can also be created on manufactured fabrics by heat setting the texture/effect directly onto the surface. Woven crepe may be warp crepe, balanced crepe, or other variations.

Pile Weave

Woven pile fabrics are constructed by weaving an extra set of warp or filling yarns into the basic or *ground* yarns to produce a characteristic three-dimensional effect. Pile yarns can be cut or uncut. Bedford corduroy is an example of uncut pile, while velvet is a cut pile fabric.

Filling pile fabrics are made by weaving a second set of filling yarns so that they float over rows of warp and are cut in a separate operation to form the pile. Corduroy is an example of this.

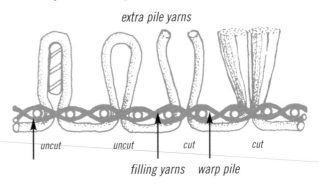

extra pile yarns

uncut — uncut — cut — cut

filling yarns — warp pile

- *Pile yarns*

Warp pile fabrics are made with two sets of warp yarns and one set of filling yarn.

The *double cloth* method simultaneously weaves two fabrics with the extra set of warp woven into each. The fabrics are then cut apart and the extra warp forms the pile.

• *Double Cloth*

In the *over-wire* method, a single cloth is woven with wires placed across the loom over the ground warp and under the pile warp. The over-wire loops may be cut or uncut.

In the *slack-tension pile* method, a special weaving arrangement forces the pile warp to form loops on either side, or both sides, of the fabric. These may then be cut or left uncut. Terrycloth is made this way.

Jacquard Weave

Joseph-Marie Charles Jacquard (1757-1834) developed the loom that bears his name. His loom was one of the great inventions of the Industrial Revolution, and it revolutionized the weaving of a wide range of fabrics and carpets.

Today, jacquard weaves are produced on a loom equipped with a special overhead mechanism called the jacquard head-motion. The whole is called the *Jacquard loom*, a complex machine with two or more sets of both warp and filling yarns, in which every warp yarn is individually controlled and operated by computer. The warp yarn passes through a hole in the pattern card; lack of a hole prevents a particular yarn from being taken up. This selective formation of each shed before each filling yarn is placed results in the capacity to duplicate multicolored, intricate designs into the fabric. Extremely elaborate patterns, whole scenes, typography, and photographs are possible on the Jacquard loom.

Dobby Weave

Dobby weaves are fabrics with small figures (dots, geometric shapes, or florals) and are produced on a loom with a dobby attachment, usually called a dobby loom. The multiple warp yarns are computer-controlled by up to thirty-two separate harnesses that control the raising and lowering of the warp yarns to create the desired shed and pattern.

Cord weaves are also woven on the dobby loom and produce fabrics with defined cords, wales, or ridges. In pique weaves (after the French word for 'quilted') the cords are crosswise; in bedford cord, the wales are lengthwise and uncut. Cords may also be constructed with stiffer yarns running beneath the wales to give them greater definition.

Leno Weave

Leno weaves have warp yarns that do not lie parallel, but are in pairs, with one yarn crossed over the other before the filling yarn is inserted. This effect is obtained with a *doup attachment* that may be mounted on a plain or dobby loom. One of the two warp yarns in each pair is threaded through the doup needle attached to each of the two heddles. When one heddle is raised, the doup yarn is drawn across to the left; when the other heddle is raised, the doup yarn is drawn across to the right. The criss-crossed yarn gives greater strength than plain weaves and allows for an open, lace-like fabric. *Marquisette* and some thermal blankets are leno. Leno weaves may be fairly simple, or more complex doup attachments may allow for very complex and interesting designs.

Surface Figure Weave

Extra warp or filling may be used to produce simple or complex patterns on a dobby or Jacquard loom.

Lappet weave gives the effect of hand embroidery on a base fabric. It is constructed with extra warp yarns that are threaded on needles mounted on a frame near the reed. The frame presses the threaded needles to the bottom of the shed and holds them while the yarns are secured by the filling yarn. The frame is movable from side to side and is moved to create the overall design.

In a *swivel weave*, extra filling yarns are used to weave in a design. Each extra filling yarn is wound on its own shuttle and enters the shed at predetermined spacings to deposit the yarn. Between pattern repeats, the extra yarn is carried on the wrong side of the fabric.

In *spot* (or *dot*) *weaves*, either extra warp or extra filling yarns may provide the yarn patterns, and the weaving takes place on a dobby or jacquard loom. The wrong sides of such fabrics carry the extra yarn floats, and these may be cut or uncut. Occasionally, the floats are carried on the face of the fabric and later clipped to form a fringed, or eyelash, effect.

This technique is also used to weave reversible fabrics with closely spaced designs that are 'right,' though different, on both sides of the fabric.

Hand-loomed Weave

The production of hand-woven textiles is limited to small-scale fabric makers (artist or craftspeople), but as a source of unique fabrics hand-woven textiles are important both in use and as a source of inspiration for commercial production. Capable of producing the three basic weaves, the powered handloom requires the expertise and creativity of the individual operator. Knowledge of yarns and an eye for new color or texture combinations often result in outstanding textiles that may be used for special applications or as accent hangings in their own right.

Triaxial Weave

Triaxial weaving, developed in the late 1960s, was devised specifically for the space industry's need for a dimensionally stable, lightweight fabric. Construction is based on three yarn directions rather than two. Two warp yarns and one filling yarn meet at 60° angles to form a textile with more stability than any other fabric. It is produced only on a special triaxial loom.

Triaxial construction permits lighter yarns to be used, resulting in a lighter fabric. The choice of three rather than two components increases the performance possibilities. It has excellent resistance to tearing and raveling, and is equally strong in all directions. Application in interiors is mainly for upholstered furniture, where its ability to mold into tight corners and to resist tearing are desired.

Common Woven Fabric Names

The following list of fabrics is characterized by the type of weave. It is not all-inclusive but does indicate the principal fabrics produced in each category.

PLAIN WEAVE: greige (gray goods), barathea, barkcloth, batiste, butcher rayon, calico, chambray, chintz, cretonne, flannel, gingham, homespun, lawn, muslin, ninon, organdy, percale, plaid, sailcloth, sheeting, tweed.

BASKET WEAVE: canvas, duck, hopsacking, monks cloth, oxford cloth, sailcloth.

WAFFLE WEAVE: honeycomb, waffle weave.

TWILL WEAVE: *Even,* or *balanced twills:* cavalry twill, cheviot, damask, flannel, foulard, hounds-tooth, serge, surah, tapestry. *Warp face twills:* covert, denim, gabardine, herringbone. *Filling face twills:* herringbone. *Novelty twills:* bird's eye, diaper, goose-eye (reverse herringbone).

SATIN WEAVE: *Warp face satin:* satin. *Filling face satins:* antique satin, sateen (cotton).

CREPE WEAVE: Bemberg, chiffon, georgette, granite cloth, moss crepe, sand crepe, voile.

PILE WEAVE: *Warp face:* panne, velour, velvet, plush. *Filling face:* corduroy, velveteen. *Doublecloth:* matelasse. *Over-wire:* frieze, grosgrain. *Slack-tension:* shagbark gingham, seersucker, terrycloth.

JACQUARD WEAVE: brocade, brocatelle, damask, tapestry.

DOBBY WEAVE: bird's eye, dotted Swiss, huck-a-back, lappet, swivel. *Cords:* bengaline, broadcloth, faille, grosgrain, ottoman, poplin, rep, shuntung, taffeta.

LENO WEAVE: chenille yarn, marquisette

Knit Construction

Knits are the principal fabrics constructed with needles. Unlike weaves, knits are composed, in their basic form, of one yarn rather than two. More knits are being used as textiles for interiors; a field previously occupied almost exclusively by woven goods.

Knitting as a fabrication technique is both faster (about four times faster per square meter [or yard]) and more efficient than weaving. Knitted fabrics are in great demand for upholstering contoured furniture because of the inherent stretch capacity of knitted fabric. Less time and skill are required to obtain a tailored appearance.

Hand knitting as a craft is not as old as weaving; the earliest knit fragments date from around C.E. 200. The type of knitting done by hand is called *weft knitting*, which means that the structure is formed by horizontal (crosswise) passes of the needles and yarn. Warp knitting is an invention of the late 18th century and can only be accomplished by machine. In this type of knit, the loops are formed in a vertical (or lengthwise) direction. The horizontal row of loops is called the *course*. The vertical column of loops is called the *wale*.

In the 1960s, with the possibility of greatly expand-ed markets, there was a boom in new needle machinery. Adaptability to a wide range of yarns, combination knit-weave and knit-sew techniques, electronic programming, and original stitch con-cepts adapted to mass production. These greatly increased the range of needle constructed fabrics. Increasing automation and computerization has continued to add to and improve the possibilities with knitted fabrics.

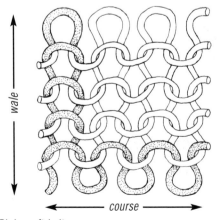

• *Plain weft knit*

Weft Knitting

In 1589, an English minister, the Reverend William Lee, M.A., St. John's College, Cambridge, invented and built an original flat-bed machine for knitting hosiery fabric. The machine could knit ten times faster than an individual, and it used long flexible hooks ending in a sharp needle that are now called *'spring-beard' type*.

• *Spring Beard Needle*

For two hundred years, this was the only type of knitting machine available. In 1758, Englishman Jedediah Strutt built on the original design, and was able to do rib knitting on a machine he called the Derby Rib Hosiery Frame.

In 1816, Marc Brunei invented the first *circular-knitting machine*, and in 1847, Matthew Townshend patented a *latch needle*. These two machines, the flatbed and the circular, and the two needle types, are the basic equipment for current weft knitting.

• *Latch Needle*

Flat-bed Knitting

The machine for knitting flat, open-width fabric has its needles arranged in a straight crosswise fashion. The row of needles can knit simultaneously or knitting can proceed from side to side. The full-fashioned machine can also shape materials by automatically increasing and decreasing the num-ber of stitches.

Circular Knitting

This machine has needles arranged around the circumference of a cylinder. As the cylinder revolves, the needles knit courses of loops, and fabric is produced in a tubular form. Most knitting is now done on a circular machine, and the tubular knits are then slit to form flat fabric, or used as tubes.

Reverend Lee's machine knitted at about 600 stitches per minute; a modern automatic knitting machine produces over 4 million stitches per minute.

Weft Knit Types

Machine knit goods are produced as either single knits or double knits.

Single Knits

Single knits may be plain, ribbed, or patterned. Three types of loops may be formed, depending on the programmed action of the needles. A knit loop forms the basic stitch, a tuck loop forms a new stitch while retaining the loop from the previous course, and a float loop misses that course but retains the previous loop.

Three basic stitches familiar to hand knitters, and one stitch particular to machine knitting, are used to produce machine-knitted goods.

> **THE STOCKINETTE STITCH** (also called plain, flat, or jersey) is the most common, producing a flat face with a characteristic vertical row appearance, and a reverse displaying a horizontal row appearance.
>
> **THE PURL STITCH** produces fabric that is identical on the face and reverse, and resembles the reverse side of stockinette stitch.
>
> **THE RIB STITCH** produces fabric with greater stretch and is machine knit with two sets of needles facing each other so that the stockinette stitch alternates on the face and reverse of the fabric. Rib knits are reversible, and can be even (1 x 1, 2 x 2, etc.) or uneven (1 x 2, 1 x 3, 2 x 3 etc.).
>
> **THE INTERLOCK STITCH** is a variation of the rib stitch and is formed with two sets of needles that interknit two separate 1 x 1 rib fabrics.

Double Knits

The basis of double-knit fabrics is the interlock stitch, and it is produced by two sets of needles at right angles. Decorative effects and patterns can be obtained by using a jacquard attachment for individual needle control. Double knits can also be made by knitting two separate fabrics simultaneously and using periodic binding stitches to hold the two layers together. Besides the basic double knit, the plain interlock, there are variations such as *pique*, *pintuck*, and *double pique*. Production of double knits is very fast, with up to 48 yarns feeding to over 1000 needles, and complex design changes can be accomplished electronically.

Knitted Pile Fabrics

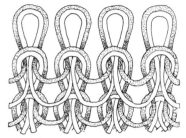

Weft knitting machines are used in the production of pile fabrics. The pile is knitted in from an extra set of yarns that are then drawn out in long loops. The loops may be left or cut. Some pile fabrics also use a sliver of fibers rather than a yarn, and this produces a very rich, luxurious pile. 'Fake furs,' for instance, are sliver knit fabrics.

Weft Knits in Use

Single knits done in stockinette stitch are the most common knit fabrics and can be manufactured in a wide range of weights and tensions. Besides their wide use in apparel from hosiery and underwear to winter coats, casement and drapery fabrics (either plain or patterned) are frequently made. Snags and subsequent runs are drawbacks of this type of construction, but the composition of the yarn and the tightness of the knit can be compensating factors. Double knits are much sturdier, with excellent dimensional stability and run resistance. Compared to single knits, they are heavier, more firm, less stretchable, and more resilient. Their apparel use is well known, and they also make very durable upholstery fabric.

Warp Knitting

Warp knitting can only be done by machine. As in weaving, the warp yarns are those that run lengthwise. The warp yarns are each manipulated by one needle, and loops are formed simultaneously across the width by interlocking each yarn with an adjacent or close warp yarn. Warp knitting is very rapid.

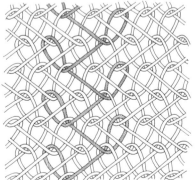

The machine used to produce them is what classifies warp knits. There are several types of warp knits, the most important being the tricot and the raschel.

Tricot Knits

The first tricot (pronounced treeko) machines were designed and made in England in 1775. Their basic operation and the knits they produced were very similar to those machines used today. Modern tricot machinery is classified as single guide bar, 2-Bar, 3-Bar, or more. The single machine produces only basic stockinette stitch; addition of guide bars indicates greater flexibility in pattern as the number of yarns is determined in this manner. The number of stitch variations also increases, depending on the number of guide bars.

Plain and decorative tricot fabrics are made on the same machine, making them economical to produce. Lightweight, sheer, or lace-like fabrics are the usual production as the machinery works most efficiently in this area.

Raschel Knits

This versatile machine appeared in the 1960s. The machine is capable of producing fabrics from the finest netting and trimming delicate lace to heavy industrial goods. It uses multiple guide bars (4-56), which makes it possible to lay in a large number of yarns. Openwork and dense fabrics, stable or elastic, textured or plain, plush fabrics and carpeting, are all possible.

A *'Chaine' raschel* machine knits and tucks on the face, and then reverses to create an alternating surface design. The *jacquard raschel* uses a jacquard attachment to produce intricate eyelet stitch patterns,

Warp Knits in Use

Tricot knits are generally soft, crease resistant and run resistant, with good drapability. Thickness of the fabric is determined by the yarn used, and elongation is affected by the construction. Tight knits have lower elongation, knits of fine gauge have greater elongation ('gauge' is stitches per unit of width; 'fine' indicates many stitches). The strength of tricot is variable; strong yarns, fine gauge, and balanced construction all contribute to strength.

Raschel knits combine the characteristics of tricots with their capacity to be produced in virtually any yarn and in a multitude of patterns and designs.

> **MILANESE:** The knits are fairly dense with a fine rib on the face and a diagonal structure on the reverse; used mainly for lingerie and gloves.
>
> **MARRATI:** This variation of the Milanese produces fabrics on a circular frame.
>
> **SIMPLEX:** This machine produces double-faced fabrics that are used mainly for gloves.
>
> **CIDEGA:** This knits crochet-like or openwork fabrics.

Knitting Variations

To make fabrics more interesting, knitting machines can be manipulated. By inserting extra warp or weft yarns, for example, fabrics will have an extra set of yarns contributing to aesthetic appeal or tenacity. Inserting warp and weft yarns in either warp or weft knits creates a fabric called 'knit-weave.' Knit-sew techniques form fabrics by simultaneously forming loops and stitching through the fabric.

Weft Insertion

Warp knitting machines can be adapted with attachments to lay in weft yarns. This may be one weft carried across the knitter or, with more complex attachments, a sheet of twenty or more weft yarns can be used as filling. Where warp knits may only be knitted with lengthwise stripes or color variations, weft insertion can produce crosswise variations as well. The finished fabric is more stable across the grain than an ordinary warp knit fabric.

Warp Insertion

This technique involves inserting warp yarns into the crosswise knitted structure of the weft knit. The warps are 'woven' in; that is, interlaced on a 1 x 1 basis with the weft knit yarns. The procedure gives greater dimensional stability in the lengthwise grain.

Knit-Weave

Machines, adapted from both weft and warp knitting machines, are able to insert both warp and weft yarns into the basic structure. The Co-We-Knit machine, an adaptation of the raschel warp knitter, is perhaps the most versatile. Fabrics may be quite fine, but the machine tends to be used mostly for fairly rigid, coarse fabrics.

Knit-Sew

This procedure is also called 'stitch-through' or 'stitch-bonded,' and the main principal machines are the Mali and the Arachne, and their variations.

MALIMO technology forms fabrics with three sets of yarns. Warp yarns are fed from a warp beam. Weft yarns are threaded into a carrier that moves back and forth across the machine and simultaneously forward, placing the filling yarns at an angle to the warp. The sewing yarns are fed from a beam through compound needles that sew between the warp and across the filling, and interlock with the warp yarns in a tricot-like stitch. Variation in the fabric on the basic machine is possible through variation in the yarns used.

ARACHNE AND MALI machines form fabric in a variety of ways. One uses a web of fibers stitched through with a binding thread carried by a knitting needle. Another produces a looped pile fabric, while another warp-knits and simultaneously sews fabric. Still another variation produces fabric by forming interlocking loops in the web without a binder yarn.

Some uses of the Mali and Arachne variations are as backing fabrics, floor coverings, upholstery fabrics, wall coverings, sound deadening and/or thermal insulation, household cloths, packaging, and carpet backing.

THE KRAFTAMATIC machine is a cross between a warp knitter and a tuft sewing machine. The knitter works above and the sewing machine below to produce a double-sided pile fabric without grain, and with the tufts securely locked in place. Blankets and carpets can be produced by this method.

Knit-Weave and Knit-Sewn Fabric

Fabrics in Use

The procedures outlined produce fabrics with the best properties of both knitted and woven textiles, and the fabrics are economical to construct. Weft or warp insertions in knits produce fabrics that are stronger and have greater dimensional stability than either knits or weaves. They cover better with no greater bulk, and have the comfort and easy draping qualities of knits. Weft and warp insertions in the true 'knit-weaves' have, in addition, great recovery from stress.

The knit-sew fabrics combine the above properties with an absence of grain that allow fabrics to be cut and sewn in any direction.

'New Frontiers' of Knitting

Computers control, with solid state integrated circuit memory, all machine functions, including individual needle selection on all needle beds. Memory boards can carry control functions for 64,000 stitches at one time. All other machine operations, such as yarn feed, tension, direction, and take-up can be similarly programmed.

The advances in fiber technology go hand-in-hand with machinery development. Textured filaments and new blends mean expanding possibilities in all areas.

The field of upholstery, in general, is open to new knits and their variations. The controlled stretch and good recovery features of knits in the past were limited by a lack of fabric stability, but stability is now a feature of the knit-weaves and knit-sewn fabrics. The resulting better fit and simplified tailoring are important new considerations.

Similarly, the field of draperies, bedspreads, and blankets has been opened to knits. With knitted carpets made on raschel machines, 100 percent of the yarn contributes to wear or appearance. Compare this to woven carpets in which 20-30 percent of the yarn lies on the back and is virtually unused. Knitted carpets, however, do not have the same appearance as tufted woven carpeting, and this is, so far, a drawback to wide consumer acceptance. Progress in all these areas is constant and will undoubtedly continue.

Tufted Fabrics

Tufting was first a handcraft, developed in the southeastern United States. *Candlewick* was used as a tufting yarn to work intricate designs in bedspreads. Hooked rugs were made by a similar technique.

The handcraft involved working yarns into already woven fabric. The automatic tufting procedure practiced today works on the same principle. The method is flexible in that any weight of backing and tufting yarns may be used.

In the automated system, backing (woven or knit) is secured in a horizontal position, and rows of threaded needles are pushed through the fabric from above. Beneath the fabric, companion hooks catch the yarn and hold it in a predetermined position while the threaded needle is retracted. For cut loop pile, blades are attached to the catching hooks and sever the loops once they are fully made.

When the tufting is completed, the tufts of yarn are untwisted and teased open. This 'blooming' of the yarn helps to hold the tufts in place. As well, the backing fabric is often shrunk in the finishing process, which further tightens the tufts in place. Quality tufting is very dense. Knits are the best backing fabric, with more flexibility than weaves. Woven backing sometimes 'grins' through the tufting when the fabric is folded.

Tufting is a very fast process and less expensive than other methods of producing pile fabrics. Variations in pattern, pile height, and density are matters of simple machine adjustment.

Tufted Fabrics in Use

Carpeting is one of the most commonly used tufted fabrics, with over 95 percent of all carpeting made by this method. A tufting machine produces some 700 square meters (765.51 yards) of carpeting per hour and it applies a heavy backing, usually with a latex compound that thoroughly locks the tufts in place.

The tufted construction is also used extensively for blankets and bedspreads, as well as for apparel and fake fur fabrics.

Braids, Nets, and Laces

Braids

Braids are primarily a trimming fabric with three or more yarns interlaced diagonally.

Braids are very strong in the lengthwise direction. Shoelaces are circular braids. Flat braids are used as trims for interior applications. Occasionally braids are made into interesting fabrics by sewing lengths together. Braided rugs are made by braiding various materials and sewing them together in a circular fashion from the center outward.

• *Braided Fabric*

Nets

Nets are open meshed fabrics made by knotting or knitting. Knotted nets are traditional, with geometric mesh in a range of sizes. Knitted nets are constructed on tricot or raschel machines, using very fine filament yarns.

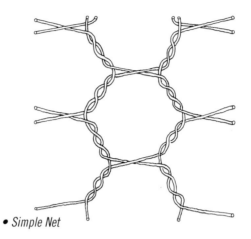

• *Simple Net*

Laces

Lace may be knotted, interlaced, twisted, or knit. Lace is fabric with a decorative design on an open-mesh backing.

Making lace by hand is a traditional home craft, using hooks, needles, bobbins, or shuttles. Handmade lace is called *real lace*. Since its early use in churches as altar cloths and priestly ornaments, handmade lace has had many periods of high fashion. In Elizabethan times, lace cuffs became very popular. The fashion eventually got out of control, with some 'cuffs' measring up to 61 cm (24") deep, and using some 22 meters (25 yards) of handmade lace.

Lace fabrics may now be constructed by a weaving technique on a complex piece of equipment called the *Leavers Lace Machine*. With 40,000 moving parts, and hundreds of miles of threads, the machine duplicates the most complicated handmade lace. The pattern is controlled by a jacquard attachment. Lace fabrics have specialty uses as casements or window hangings.

Nonwoven Fabrics

While the term *nonwoven* might seem to imply any fabric that is not woven on a loom (including knits), it refers to all *fabrics that are neither woven nor knit*. These fabrics are produced in a number of ways, often from fibers rather than yarns. Felt was the first, and for centuries the only, nonwoven fabric. Now a wealth of fabrics are produced from fibers bonded or joined in some way, and by an equally high number of films, foams, laminates, and extrusions.

Nonwoven fabrics are manufactured very economically and at high speed, and it is this factor that presents a great opportunities for future production.

Felt

The inherent structure of wool fiber gives it the ability to curl, shrink, and interlock when exposed to moisture, heat and agitation, and pressure. The wool fibers used for felting may be short—new, reprocessed, or reused—and 40-50% of nonfelting (not wool) fibers can be added to the mixture. Alternate applications of warm moisture, agitation, pressure, and relaxation are usually sufficient for felting to occur, but sulphuric acid and soap are sometimes added to increase the felting action. The fabric thickness may be less than a millimeter or close to 100 mm (about 1/32" to 3").

Felts are inelastic and relatively weak, especially when they are thin. However, their dense structure contributes to good insulating and sound deadening properties. Thick felts are used as rug pads; thinner, more flexible felts are useful for wall coverings, pillow and table covers, and, occasionally, draperies.

Fiber Web Fabrics

Fiber web fabrics are used for a relatively large field of textile products. These fabrics are produced in a variety of ways, all of which include the formation of a web of fibers. The fibers may be oriented (made parallel) in any direction; layers of *oriented* webs may be *crosslaid* in alternate directions; the web may be formed of cross-laced fibers; or the web may consist of a *random* mat. As will be seen, techniques vary, but the following four basic steps are common to the manufacture of all fiber web fabrics:

1. preparing the fiber
2. web formation
3. bonding the web
4. drying and curing the fabric

Needle Punched Fabrics

Needle punched fabrics are those made by mechanical bonding the fiber web; specifically, by using a bed of barbed needles that intimately tangle the fibers into a felt-like configuration.

NEEDLE FELTS resemble felt in appearance, but are made of fibers other than wool. Fibers are blended, and the web is formed using forced air on a moving screen. The fiber mat is laid on a moving belt, and it is mechanically bonded by repeatedly punching hundreds of barbed needles (often heated) set in a board that rises and falls on the fiber web up to 2,500 times. The effect of the needle punching is to push and distort the fibers into a thin, tangled mat. Variations of the needle punching technique may also produce fabrics with one surface resembling a loop pile. Uses for needle felts include carpeting, wall covering, insulation, padding, and blankets.

Bonded Fabrics

Bonded fabrics are fiber mats held together by adhesives, fusing, chemicals, or thermal means. Advances in thermoplastic manufactured fibers and adhesives have made such fabric-forming techniques more popular than ever.

ADHESIVE-BONDED FABRICS developed in the 1930s as textile manufacturers looked for ways of using cotton waste fibers. After World War II, interest shifted to manufactured fibers when fabric producers realized that the same techniques that had been used for cotton could be applied to the newer synthetic fibers. Since then, the thermoplastic qualities of most manufactured fibers have led to a booming industry of *thermal-bonded* fabrics.

DRY-LAY WEBBED FABRICS are made when dry fibers are formed into a web by air dispersion, or by a moving screen or belt. Fibers may be random or oriented in one  direction. Pressure compresses the mat, and bonding occurs either with the application of adhesive resin (wet or dry) or by blending a small proportion of fibers with a low melt point (called 'binder fibers'). In both cases, the fiber mat is then subjected to heat and/or chemical action, which fuses the fibers. Cooling and drying complete the fabric process.

WET-LAY WEBBED FABRICS are made by a method that copies techniques used for papermaking. Fibers are suspended in water, then deposited on a screen surface that drains the water and leaves the fibers in a damp web. The fibers are bonded with either adhesives or binder fibers. Sometimes the adhesive is suspended along with the fibers in the water; once the water is drained, the fibers settle and adhere as they dry.

SOLVENT BONDING uses a solvent that is applied to the web of fibers. It attacks the fibers and causes them to 'spot weld' at points of contact. Before the solvent can destroy the fibers, it is evaporated at higher temperatures leaving behind the bonded fabric structure. This method produces a softer fabric than one in which adhesives are impregnated.

PRINT BONDING, an adaptation of adhesive bonding, uses a roller or screen printer to lay on a design of adhesive, either clear or colored. The print design must be close enough to effect bonding, but the spaces left provide air circulation and greater flexibility in the fabric. J-cloths are print bonded fiber web fabrics.

SPUNBONDS are the product of a four-step integrated polymer-to-fabric process. The fiber is extruded in filament form, drawn to introduce strength, formed into a web on a moving surface, and bonded. Although different bonding techniques are used, the easiest bond is accomplished when two polymers, differing in thermal reactivity, are simultaneously extruded and formed into a web. Later exposure to heat melts one group of fibers, which serves to bond them all together.

Spunbonded fabrics are used as tufted carpet backing, reinforcing, interlining, and substrates for various extruded film fabrics. Some trade names are Cerex®, Reemay®, Typar®, and Tyvek®.

SPUNLACED FABRICS are made by a fluid fiber entanglement process. Extruded and drawn fibers are formed into a web on a moving frame (often one with an intricate pattern) and entangled with fluids under high pressure. No adhesive or binding agent is needed. Nexus® is one trade name.

Fiber Web Fabrics—Uses and Applications

Most fiber web fabrics are used 'as is,' but may be dyed or printed. They have wide home and industrial uses such as: diapers, interfacings, bandages, surgical gowns, and decontamination clothing; upholstery and carpet backing, carpeting, blankets, window shades, curtains, placemats, and napkins.

Nontextiles

Foams

Foams are complex cross-linked polymers formed by a chemical reaction that causes the formation of bubbles within a viscose solution. Subsequent drying and curing results in huge, solid blocks or cylinders of dry, flexible, spongy material. The rolls or blocks are then blade cut into the desired thickness, which may be as thin as 0.06 cm (0.024").

Contents of the solution dictate the size of bubbles (cells) and also the eventual range of physical properties. Foams may be nearly rigid or very flexible, and may be produced in many colors. Flexible urethane foams are used as cushions, padding, carpet backing, and as an integral part of laminated fabrics.

Some properties of flexible urethane foam have good tensile strength, with excellent abrasion resistance and tear strength, and excellent dimensional stability. There is easy, though limited, elongation, with perfect recovery; it does not sag, mat, or become lumpy. Foam is unharmed by solvents, soaps, and detergents, and is unaffected by water, mildew, and microorganisms. It is odorless and hypoallergenic. It has excellent insulating properties, and remains pliable in extreme cold or heat. Sunlight causes yellowing but no loss of durability.

Films

Films are polymers formed into continuous flat sheets. Most are made of vinyl or polyurethane, although many of the same chemicals used for fibers are also applicable as films (like polyester or acetate). Films may be plain, expanded, supported, or unsupported. They may be clear, colored, translucent, opaque, or clear colored. Films may be as thin as plastic wrap or as thick as heavy upholstery.

Extruded Fabrics/Films

Extruded fabrics are variations of films. They are produced from polymer solutions in a sheet-like film, but they are neither continuous nor flat.

First application of the technique was for practical vegetable wraps, and these may still be seen (around heads of lettuce, for instance). The fabrics are formed by piercing, slitting, and/or punching out shapes in a film, then stretching, and sometimes embossing. The resulting fabric is a lace-like structure with durability, airiness, and texture.

A polymer film fabric or coating has little or no porosity. Because of this lack of breathability, many people find these fabrics uncomfortable to sit on, especially in hot or humid weather.

Simulated Suede

Two "finish" operations are used to produce simulated suede and suede-like fabrics: flocking and sueding. Flocking involves electrostatic deposition of the flock (cut fibers) followed by the sueding process.

In the sueding operation, sandpaper-covered disks revolve against the flocked surface, pulling up the fibers, resulting in a roughing of the surface, generally orienting the flock in every direction. Ultrasuede®, a simulated suede material, is given a directional lay or nap.

Ultrasuede®

This fabric was devised in Japan and has had wide acceptance for high-fashion apparel as well as upholstery for quality furniture and wall covering. There is also a high performance Ultrasuede®, known as Ultrasuede® HP, which was created specifically for the interior design industry.

Ultrasuede® and Ultrasuede® HP are compound structures using several techniques. The final components are polyester and polyurethane. The fabric is a rich, complex, nonwoven structure that begins with ultra-microfibers (islands-in-the-sea formation). The fibers are ironed, curled, cut, and needle punched into a soft felt, which is then bonded by adhesive. The fabric is covered with a protective coating that is then dissolved to create the softness and suppleness of real suede. These products have the look and feel of genuine suede and are strong, durable, and easily maintained. Unlike genuine suede, Ultrasuede® is completely washable with soap and water. It is designed not to crock, pill, or fray and is available in a full color range.

LABELING GUIDELINES apply specifically to non-leather upholstery coverings that resemble genuine leather or suede. They are advisory in nature and are used to prevent unfair and deceptive marketing practices. Look for information disclosing the facts of the composition of nonleather upholstery coverings.

Trade names denoting nonleather coverings may not include the words "hide," "skin," or "leather." Homophones of these words, such as "hyde" may be used as long as the true composition of the fabric is disclosed.

> **PLAIN FILMS** are dense, firm, smooth, and uniform. They have innumerable industrial, agricultural, and household uses, from drop sheets to moisture barriers.
>
> **EXPANDED FILMS** are soft and spongy, with tiny air cells formed through the addition of a 'blowing agent' to the solution. They are often used as alternates for leather or suede. They are light and pliable, with a good hand.
>
> **SUPPORTED FILMS** have a woven, knit, or bonded backing, and there are many applications; for example, upholstery, wall coverings, automobile seat covers, and luggage. Naugahyde® is a well-known trade name.
>
> **UNSUPPORTED FILMS** may have application in any of the areas mentioned above. Colored and/ or printed, and with a paper backing, they become wallpaper. Textured, they may be almost anything: rainwear, shower curtains, window blinds, tablecloths, outdoor furniture covers, etc.

Leather and Tapa

Leather

Leather fabrics are converted from raw skins and the hides of animals. While leather is composed of a network of tiny fibers, it should be noted that these fibers are not classified as textile fibers. The animal skins or hides go through four major operations to produce the finished leather product: curing and cleaning, tanning, coloring, and finishing.

Curing involves salting the raw hides. If the hides are thick enough, they may also be split at this stage. *Tanning* is done naturally or with chemical tanning solutions that work more quickly. After tanning, leather is soft, water- and mildew-resistant, and pliable. *Coloring* may be necessary to camouflage an uneven natural color or to produce a current fashion color. Finally, leather can be *finished* by applying lubricants, resins, or waxes or by embossing it to add texture.

FINISHED LEATHER FABRICS are labeled with such terms as *full-grain leather*, which means the natural grain markings have not been altered in any way; *top-grain leather*, which means the fabric has undergone minor corrections; and, finally, *split leather*, which is produced from the central portion of the hide. No natural markings appear on split leather because the top layer of the skin is removed. It may not be as durable as full-grain and top-grain leathers.

GENUINE SUEDE is leather fabric produced with the flesh side of the hide exposed. Genuine suede is not used in upholstery because of a tendency toward crocking or rubbing off of color.

Tapa

Tapa is one of the earliest fabrics created from a solid layer. The source of tapa is the inner bark of the paper mulberry tree in the South Sea Islands or of the fig tree in the Mediterranean and Central America. Cloth is made by soaking the bark, then beating it with wooden mallets into a smooth, paper-thin sheet. The natural color is light tan. Traditionally, tapa was block printed in shades of brown and black.

Compound Fabrics

Many fabrics, both ancient and modern, are composed of more than one component. The category includes:

- embroidery: yarns stitched on a ground or base fabric
- appliqué and patchwork: small pieces of fabric used to decorate, or to form, large pieces
- quilting: fabrics and filling stitched together
- laminated (or bonded) fabrics: layers of fabrics, films, or fabrics and films stuck together

Embroidery

Embellishing a fabric with yarn, feathers, quills, bangles, or sequins is, in many cultures, as old as cloth-making itself. Embroidery is one of the most popular handcrafts. Dominant in furnishings are Kashmir crewel embroideries, in which wool yarns are chain-stitched onto homespun cotton. The paisley motifs are as traditional as the technique.

Most mass produced embroidery is machine embroidery, made on a Schiffli machine, and called Schiffli embroidery. Characteristic of this embroidery is the technique used, in which the decorative yarn does not penetrate the cloth but is held in place with binding threads stitched through from the back. Thousands of needles stitch simultaneously, working from a computerized guide, which directs the placement of each stitch and the number of repeats in an overall pattern. Embroidered goods are produced in relatively short lengths, as the machinery works from selvage to selvage.

A variation is Schiffli lace, achieved by embroidering a grill-like pattern with very compact stitches, and then burning away the ground fabric with acid so that only the 'lace' remains.

Appliqué, Patchwork, and Quilting

In the recent past, there has been an astonishing growth of interest in handcrafts, folk arts, and quilting. Quilt making was an accepted and necessary function of North American households from the earliest days. It was a craft with a soul, engaging not only the eyes and hands, but also the imagination and often a sense of history. The art declined when improved means of heating made layers of bedding less essential and as machine-made blankets became available. Handcrafts lost favor for several generations, and it is only recently that we have come to revalue the work of human hands (and domestic sewing machines!).

Home quilting, appliqué, and patchwork, are made easier with new materials, and are once again becoming treasured textiles for the interior. The textile industry has found ways to mass produce these goods. While the emotional attachment and significance of genuine handwork cannot be duplicated, the appearance may be similar. Even mass produced, these goods certainly add a comfortable ambience to home interiors and institutional settings.

Appliqué

Appliqué is the process of sewing small pieces of fabric onto a larger piece to create interesting patterns or designs.

Patchwork

Patchwork is the sewing together of different pieces of fabric to make a large piece. Patchwork, the art of making whole cloth from bits and pieces of scraps or worn-out clothing, was born of necessity. Patchwork was common when money and material goods were scarce, but time and labor could be given to such a task.

Home patchwork is now done, either by hand or on home sewing machines, using new materials. The appeal of modern patchwork fabrics is in the originality of the design, pattern, or the combination of colors and textures.

Appliqué and patchwork have not been widely adapted to mass production. Occasionally, cloth is printed to resemble these fabrics.

Quilting

Quilting is the stitching together of two or more layers of fabric and filling. In earlier times, the filling was made of wool or cotton, usually well worn. The top side was given a decorative treatment with designs in patchwork of scraps or 'hardly worn' fabrics. The underside was a simple presentable backing, most often cotton. Quilting was periodically used in high fashion; quilting for formal attire was *de rigueur* during the Spanish Bombast period in Europe (1545-1620), when it was the fashion to adorn clothing so heavily with ornaments, a single layer of fabric could not support them. It is said that England's Queen Elizabeth I wore skirts so heavy with jewels that the skirts had to be equipped with little wheels to allow her to walk. Furnishings in comfortable seventeenth and eighteenth century homes often included complete sets of matching quilts, quilted canopies, and side curtains.

Today, home quilt makers use any long-lasting fabric as both top and bottom, synthetic batting (usually polyester), and sew the fabrics and filling together with cotton-polyester, polyester, twistless nylon, or silicone-coated thread. Machine-made quilted fabrics use similar components and several methods of joining the layers together.

Machine Quilting

Machine quilting is done by several methods, effectively joining the layers of fabric and filling, and varying in their appearance from old fashioned to modern.

HAND-GUIDED QUILTING is the most versatile and by far the most costly. It is done with industrial-sized single-needle sewing machines by individual operators. The three most popular types of quilting are (1) *outline quilting*, in which the quilting stitches follow the motif of a printed fabric; (2) *trapunto* quilting, in which only portions of the cloth are quilted and stuffed (often in a centered design); (3) *vermicelli*, an all-over, noodle-like quilting pattern.

AUTOMATED QUILTING is a procedure in which a whole width of cloth is passed through a multiple-needle machine, producing a variety of simple geometric patterns.

STITCHLESS QUILTING fuses or bonds layers of fabric in a quilted pattern, using adhesives or heat. The Pinsonic Thermal Joining Machine welds layers together by heat from ultrasonic vibrations. Baby change pads are quilted in this way.

Quilting Materials

Any relatively stable fabric can be used for the coverings. Depending on the end use, the top may be a quality upholstery fabric, a fashion fabric, or white goods. If a reversible fabric is required, the underside is also a show fabric. If the quilted fabric is intended for bedspreads, a nonslip backing is often used. If it is intended as upholstery, the back is often black or white cheesecloth. Batting may be cotton, foam, or fiber-fill of acetate or polyester.

Embroidery and Quilted Fabrics in Use

The beauty and distinction of hand-done embroidery and quilting should not be overlooked.

Innovative design and workmanship of the highest quality are available throughout North America, and, for both conventional and unconventional applications in interiors, they are worth seeking out.

Machine-embroidered and quilted fabrics find many uses as interior textiles. Care must be taken to assure that threads and sewing techniques are durable, as broken threads are both unsightly and allow the layers to shift.

Crewel embroidered fabrics make outstanding upholstery, and plain or patterned fabrics, when quality quilted, add interest, texture, and durability to furnishings.

Laminated Fabrics (Bonded Fabrics)

Laminated, or bonded fabrics are made with a multitude of materials of variable quality. These compound fabrics must be assessed carefully to determine that:

- the layers are securely bonded
- adhesives have not penetrated the surface or backing
- the grain lines (if applicable) of the two fabrics are compatible
- there is no stiffness, off-color, or unusual odor
- adequate care instructions are available

Fabrics are intimately bonded together in two basic ways: (1) the wet-adhesive method and (2) with foam-flame bonding.

Wet-Adhesive Method

In the wet-adhesive method, rollers apply a carefully controlled quantity of adhesive to the underside of the face fabric, which is then pressed to the underside of the backing fabric. Two types of adhesive are used:

WATER-BASED ACRYLICS require a cure temperature of 148°C (300°F). It is the lower cost method, but applicable only to fabrics or films that can stand the temperature.

SOLVENT-BASED URETHANES cure without heat, but the moment of contact between the tacky adhesive surface of one fabric and the fabric being bonded to it is crucial, and the bonding process must be done in smaller batches. A good bond, however, has excellent durability, and fabrics bonded with this adhesive may be washed or dry cleaned.

Foam-Flame Bonding

In foam-flame bonding, one surface of a layer of foam is flame melted as it is brought into contact with the underside of the face fabric; the alternate surface of the foam layer is melted as it is brought into contact with the underside of the backing fabric.

Common Laminations

FABRIC-TO-FOAM AND FILM-TO-FOAM LAMINATES are also known as 'foambacks.' A layer of foam is bonded to the underside of a layer of fabric, or film, by either of the two methods.

FABRIC-TO-FABRIC BONDS are composed of any two fabrics (e.g., wool blend face and nylon tricot backing) bonded by either of the two methods. Fabric may also be bonded in this manner to a layer of fibers to produce fabric for special end uses.

FABRIC-TO-FOAM-TO-FABRIC BONDS: In this combination, the intention is to retain a foam layer. Thicker foam and the foam-flame bonding technique are used.

OTHER COMPONENTS combined by lamination techniques are: metallic polyester film bonded to clear film (Mylar® is the trade name), Polyester Fiberfil® batting bonded to a face fabric, open-net backing bonded to open lace-type fabric, open-faced fabrics bonded to metallic films, sheer lace-type fabrics bonded to clear vinyl.

Laminated Fabrics in Use

Use of laminates is highest in the apparel field, where the insulating, self-lining, and reversible characteristics are very attractive. For interiors, laminates have very wide acceptance: shower curtains, wall coverings, tablecloths, furniture coverings, draperies, and casement cloths.

FINISHING

Finishing is a term that encompasses a vast array of activities and materials. Unfinished textiles are virtually nonexistent. Most fabrics, by the time they are finished, have undergone a minimum of a dozen processes. The exceptions to this broad generalization are some of the nonwoven fabrics and films manufactured for specific uses.

The bulk of woven and knitted fabrics are produced as *greige*, or *gray* goods. They are not literally gray, but may be any degree of off-white or even colored, with impurities and blemishes, and totally devoid of character. Finishing transforms them into fabrics we can identify.

There are hundreds of trademarked fabric finishes, and more appear each year. As these finishes relate to interior textiles, labels are important. Usually, they are informative about the finish, explicit about maintenance, and have a guarantee of effectiveness and/or permanence. Finishes fall into various categories—basic finishes, surface treatment, and functional finishes.

Finishes are determined by their longevity. Permanent finishes (mercerized cotton) maintain their effectiveness over time, durable finishes (such as wrinkle resistance) last the lifetime of the textile but are less effective over time, say 40-50 launderings. Semi-durable finishes such as static control may endure for 5-10 launderings. Semi-temporary finishes can be re-applied by a dry cleaner, and temporary finishes are substantially less effective after one laundering.

If the *greige* goods have not been produced in an integrated operation, goods are sent or sold to a *converter,* a firm that 'converts' or finishes textiles.

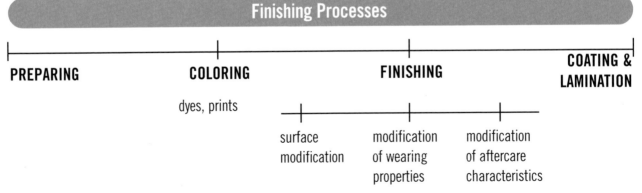

Basic Finishes

There are a number of basic finishes that must be applied to textiles throughout the production process. Natural fibers tend to have impurities that, if not removed, impede the process of fabric production. Stabilization must occur early in the processing of natural fiber textiles in order to meet the minimum requirements for production.

The following are considered basic finishes:

Cotton and Linen: boiling, singeing, sizing, desizing, bleaching, optional mercerizing, preshrinking, stabilizing, tenter drying, brushing, fixing

Wool: perching, carbonizing, fulling, scouring, crabbing, preshrinking, stabilizing

Silk: boiling, bleaching, drying, optional weighting

Rayon and Acetate: singeing, scouring

Manufactured fabrics: scouring, dry heat setting

Blends pose particular problems for finishers. Combining manufactured fibers and natural fibers requires attention to how both classifications react to certain processes.

Finishes

APPLYING FINISHES: The types of finishes used in fabric production depend on desired characteristics and the intended end use. Finishes may be **mechanical, chemical,** or a **combination** of the two. There is no set order to adding pretreatments. The progression of basic finishes varies with both the fiber content and the planned finishes. Most fabric converters combine several finishes in one continuous automated line.

BASIC FINISHES	
Boiling	Cotton, linen, and silk are boiled in water to remove the natural gums, pectins, and waxes.
Bleaching	Bleaching with chlorine, peroxide, and oxygen all work to whiten natural greige goods, preparing them for accepting dyes more evenly.
Sizing	Often added to the warp yarns in the weaving process to keep fine yarns manageable and separate. These products may be starch, wax, gelatin, oil or chemical polymers.
Desizing	In the desizing treatment, special enzymes are applied to convert the sizing to compounds that will easily wash out. Usually done in tandem with singeing.
Brushing	This is a mechanical process to remove short fine fibers from the surface, carried out by passing the fabric over a revolving drum equipped with fine bristles. The procedure is sometimes used in conjunction with singe PCT or shearing.
Singeing	The surface of the fabric is singed with gas jets or white hot metal to burn off the protruding fuzz and surface fibers. Immediately after singeing, the cloth is immersed in water. The water bath often contains enzymes that break down any remaining starches into soluble sugars, which are easily washed out in subsequent steps.
Tenter Drying	This procedure follows various wet treatments that leave the fabric damp and pulled out of shape. The tenter frame holds the fabric by the selvages and exerts tension, if needed, while carrying the cloth over a heat source to set it to its proper width. If the cloth has gone off-grain in the manufacturing process, cloth straighteners on the tenter frame will automatically sense it, and adjustments may be made to pull the cloth square.

BASIC FINISHES, cont'd	
Preshrinking	This procedure varies for different fibers. **Cotton:** Preshrinking gets the fabric back to its original size after many wet treatments have stretched it out of shape. This is done with compression and heat and, sometimes, the addition of ammonia, which penetrates the fibers and changes the molecular structure. The ammonia swells and then relaxes the fibers. Once removed, the stable cotton will not shrink. **Rayon:** The fabric is saturated with caustic soda that swells the fibers permanently and sets them in position. **Wool:** Controlling shrinkage in wool is complicated. No single process will achieve this. Methods include mechanical compacting and cold-water baths. Chemical treatments may be applied, such as the wet-chlorination process, which is designed to change the fiber surface by altering the frictional properties, thus preventing felting. Additives, such as resin, rubber derivatives, and polymers, are also used to impregnate and/or coat the wool fibers.
Stabilizing	This is a process for setting the woven or knit fabric in a particular size configuration. It is sometimes considered synonymous with shrinkage control. Dry heat is used at temperatures up to 204°C (400°F) to lock the construction dimensions in place. Application of synthetic resins is an alternate method of stabilizing.
Mercerizing	Mercerization is a patented process first developed by English chemist John Mercer in 1844. It improves strength, luster, and dyeability of cotton. Under tension, **cotton** is saturated with caustic soda. This transforms the fibers from irregular to round and even. Mercerization helps the fabric take up dye more evenly along the entire surface.
Perching	This is an early examination procedure. Cloth is passed over a frame (called a perch) of frosted glass lighted from above and below. Individuals carry out visual inspection, and flaws, stains, knots, etc., are marked.
Fixing	This takes place after dyeing when steam or hot wash fixes the color to the textile.
Carbonizing	Carbonizing is a **chemical** finish. A solution of sulfuric acid is used to saturate the wool fabric in order to burn out vegetable matter. Fabric is briefly heated and the acid converts the vegetation to carbon, which can then be brushed out.
Fulling	Fulling softens and compacts woven **wool** fabrics. The fabric is agitated or twisted in warm soapy water and rinsed thoroughly in cold water. The yarns shrink together and the fabric softens.
Scouring	This is washing with soap, alkalis, or detergents in water, or, alternately, chemical solvents may be used.
Crabbing	Crabbing is a mechanical finish applied to **wool** to set the weave. The fabric is immersed in hot, then cold, water and fed into pressing rollers with the warp and filling yarns carefully set at a 90° angle to each other. Improper crabbing can set a fabric **off-grain**.
Weighting	Weighting is a sizing technique applied to **silk**. After boiling off the natural gums, silk fabric is very soft and light. Because the fibers are very absorbent, weighting with metallic salts such as stannous chloride is possible, and is done to make the silk fabric heavier. If overdone, the silk fabric tends to crack and split. Additionally, weighted silks are less durable and more sensitive to sunlight, air, aging, and perspiration. The amount of weighting is controlled by law and is usually less than 10-15%. Sericin, or other organic gums, may be used legally to weight silk, but fabrics must then be dry cleaned, as washing will remove the gums. In addition, sericin or gum-weighted silk is subject to spotting with water.

Surface Treatments

Surface treatments are those that affect the appearance and/or hand of the fabric. Many are traditional mechanical treatments, others are durable resin finishes, and some are a combination of chemical and mechanical processes to effect a particular appearance or touch.

Mechanical Finishes		
Heat Setting		This process is used on **synthetics** to introduce or increase dimensional stability in a smooth, flat shape. Heat setting is also used to set creases. The physical characteristics of the polymer are changed when heated, set occurs while cooling, and the fabric is not degraded in any way.
Sueding		This procedure involves 'sanding' the surface with abrasive rollers to produce a soft, very low, pile.
Napping		Also called **brushing, gigging, raising,** or **teaseling**, this procedure results in formation of a nap (or pile) by subjecting the surface to a vigorous brushing action with wire bristles mounted on rollers. Fabrics may be napped on one or both surfaces. Sweatshirt fabric is napped.
Polishing		Polishing is applied to pile fabrics to straighten the fibers and impart luster. A felt blanket is used as a base, and the surface is brought into contact with a heated cylinder set with serrated fluted blades that comb the pile fibers into alignment.
Plissé		This wrinkled effect is obtained by printing cotton with concentrated caustic soda applied with a roller. The parts of the fabric that are printed shrink while the rest of the fabric stays stable. This finish creates a puckered or crinkled effect.
Shearing		Shearing is a mechanical process where surface fibers are sheared (cut off) to even out the nap or pile. The machine is a spiral cylinder fitted with blades (similar to a lawn mower).
Decating		This is a mechanical process used on **wool, silk, rayon,** or **blends** and can be performed wet or dry. The object is to set a luster on wool, to soften the hand and reduce the shine of silk and rayon, and to increase stability of all. The wet process forces hot, then cold, water through the fabric, followed by pressing.
		In dry decating, steam and then cold air are forced through the fabric, followed by pressing. The intensity of the heating-cooling cycles, and the degree of pressure in pressing, are variable. The most intense procedure is called **full decating**. This is followed by **semi-decating**, and, least severe, **continuous decating**. The fabric's end use will determine which method is used.
Corduroy		The long filling floats woven into the fabric are not always cut in manufacturing. This process cuts the floats, and the resulting pile is repeatedly brushed and treated with oils and waxes to set the corduroy luster.
Calendering		Calendering is an important final finishing process and is done on nearly all natural and manufactured cellulosic fabrics. Heavy steel rollers are heated to variable temperatures and exert pressure up to 140 kg per square centimeter (2000 pounds/square inch). The fabric passes between the rollers in order to smooth the surface, compact the surface, improve luster, or emboss a pattern. The machine uses two to seven rollers, and the type of roller determines the fabric's finish. Following are some effects that can be achieved with the calendering process.

Mechanical Finishes, cont'd

| Calendering, cont'd | | EMBOSSING is achieved by using one steel roller with an engraved design and one solid roller.

MOIRE looks like old watermarked cloth. Moiré is used on many ribbed fabrics such as taffeta and failles made of silk, rayon, acetate, polyester, and nylon. The effect is characterized by a soft luster and texture. The process involves two rollers, one engraved and one solid. This process only works on ribbed fabrics as the pressure flattens the ribs in a predetermined pattern and helps to create the effect. Synthetic fabrics are heat set in the process, but cotton and rayon must be treated with resin to increase durability of the effect.

SCHREINER uses a roller on which very fine lines have been engraved. This gives the fabric extremely fine ridges, which reflect light and simulate mercerized cotton. |
|---|---|---|

Flocking

Flock fibers are cut to 6 mm (1/4") lengths and charged so that there is an attraction to the electrically charged base fabric. When the base fabric, printed with adhesive, moves along the conveyor, the tiny flock fibers are immediately attracted to it and stick to the fabric in predetermined patterns.

Flocking

| Electrostatic Flocking | | This is an extremely fast and efficient system, and it is flexible to changes in fabric and flocking. The fibers to be used for flocking are chopped less than 6 mm (1/4") in length and treated to make them electrostatically responsive. The machinery carrying the base fabric is electrically charged and the flocking fibers adhere in an upright position.

The process is used to produce upholstery fabric, draperies, carpets, blankets, pool and game table covers, wall coverings, and outdoor surface coverings for putting greens, swimming pool surrounds, and tennis courts. |
|---|---|---|

Durable Finishes

Durable finishes have been used since the Everglaze process for making durable glazed chintz was introduced by Jos. Bancroft and Sons in 1938. Many of the traditional methods are used, but adding chemical substances to the fabric before or during treatment renders the finish as durable as the life of the cloth. Durable finishes usually last throughout the life of the textile, but diminish in effectiveness over time.

Durable Finishes

Synthetic Resin	This was the first material used to produce durable finishes. Resin is an adhesive synthetic substance and, properly cured, is insoluble. It is applied to cloth in liquid form and contains a chemical catalyst to stimulate the resin to polymerize when exposed to heat. This process of polymerization (joining monomers end to end) locks the resin into chains and cross chains on and between the individual fibers to make the finish durable.

Durable Finishes, cont'd

Durable Press		
		Durable press finish is used on fabrics that have poor resilience and crease easily. Resin is added before calendering and adheres to the fabric in the processing. The fabric maintains a very flat surface during use, but also becomes stiff. **Embossing** adds a permanent textural pattern to fabric. Double embossing calenders are used where the pattern or texture is engraved onto one roller, while the other remains a solid paper roller. When the fabric is passed between the rollers, the engraved roller imprints into the solid paper roller, and the pattern is created on the fabric. This can be done on thermoplastic or cotton fabrics. **Durable glazing** is done with friction calendering of resin-treated fabrics. **Dimensional stability, crispness,** and **resistence to wrinkles** are added to fabrics given durable resin finishes.

Effect of Resin on Fabrics

Resins generally have a beneficial effect on fabrics. However, the effectiveness depends on the quality of the cloth, the quality of the chemicals, and the care taken with the mechanical finish. Resins weaken the fibers slightly, and the stiffening of the fabrics with resin contributes to a decrease in abrasion resistance. Resin may also make a fabric brittle and less absorbent.

CHEMICAL FINISHES

Chemical finishes are used to change the performance of a textile and can be added at any stage of production. The finish name usually reflects the function of chemical treatments. Chemicals may adhere to the surfaces of the fibers, creating a barrier, or the chemicals may absorb into the core and alter its internal chemical structure. Different chemicals make for very different wear life in the finish. Some commonly used chemical finishes are described below.

Chemical Finishes

Acid Finishes		Used on cotton to produce a transparent or parchment-like effect. **Sulphuric** acid can be used to create 'burn out' patterns on selected parts of the fabric, or it may be used in a bath form where the entire fabric piece is submerged and then quickly neutralized. This burns off some of the cellulose, but not all, and makes a stiff translucent fabric. The technique is also used with blended fabrics, in which case the acid completely destroys one fiber but not the other, leaving intricate designs.
Caustics or Phenol		These may be used to produce irregular texture effects on specific fabrics. Use must be carefully controlled to avoid destroying the fabric.
Stiffening Finishes		In addition to the sizing, various thermosetting resins, cellulose, and plastic compounds are used to produce fabrics with durable stiffness.
Softening Finishes		Many products are used as softening agents. Oil, fat, wax, soap, detergent, substituted ammonium, and silicone are used to improve hand and drape of fabrics. These softeners work by coating and lubricating the fibers so they slide past one another easily. The silicone finishes are relatively durable.

Chemical Finishes, cont'd		
Delusterants		This effect can be obtained by treating fabric with titanium dioxide. Other delustrants are barium sulphate, china clay, aluminum oxide, zinc oxide, and methylene urea. These external delusterants are deposited on the fibers to subdue the luster.
Optical Brighteners		Optical brighteners make fabrics appear brighter or whiter. Liquid blueing was often used to remove yellowing from white cotton, adding a blue white to create the illusion of whiter white. Dye molecules attach themselves to the fabric and, when exposed to sunlight, selectively absorb ultraviolet light and reflect it as visible blue light. More visible light is emitted from treated fabric. Cotton remains bright as the finish is renewable in the washing process as most detergents contain optical brighteners. Synthetic fibers can be manufactured with optical brighteners added to the solution before the fiber is spun. This makes it a permanent finish.

Functional Finishes

Functional finishes affect a fabric's performance more than its appearance or hand. These finishes include water repellents, flame retardants, antistatics, bacteriostats, and mothproofing. These finishes also affect care of the fabrics and include soil and stain resistants or minimum-care finishes.

Functional Finishes	
Water-Repellent Finishes	These finishes coat or seal a fabric so that water cannot pass through. Early coatings included wax, rubber, oxidized oil, and varnish. Some of these are still used, but silicone products are most popular and durable for fabrics. Cost and wear-life of these finishes vary. Silicone can be applied to most fabrics and creates a durable finish, but it is expensive. Fluorochemical finishes such as Scotchgard® also provide some oil, stain, and soil repellency. Scotchgard® can be applied inexpensively with a simple application from an aerosol can. Organic chromium water repellents work well for synthetics and wool, and they are fairly durable for regular cleaning. Pyridinium-based finishes rely on long-chain fatty amides and wax resin to repel water. They are not expensive and are durable under normal washing conditions. Wax finishes are the least expensive but are difficult to maintain and care for.
Flame Retardants	Some fabrics are inherently flame retardant: aramid, asbestos, glass, novoloid, and modacrylic. Most textiles burn when exposed to flames, and if the fabric construction is open (with space between the yarns), fabrics will continue to burn. Flammability legislation restricts the use of flammable textiles in public spaces and certain apparel. Beds, draperies, and upholstery fabrics are treated with flame-retardants that help slow the burning, though they are not considered flameproof. Flame-resistant fabrics should be made in a close structure with little air in between the yarns, and these fabrics can also be treated chemically with flame retardant to slow ignition and prevent quick spread of flames. Synthetic fibers can have the finishes added before spinning, while others have a topical finish applied once the fabric is woven. Adding a finish will change the hand and flexibility of fabrics. Fabrics that are commonly treated topically are theater curtains, draperies, airplane upholstery, and public seating.

Functional Finishes, cont'd

Flame Retardants, cont'd	Care of flame-retardant treated fabric should be carefully outlined by the manufacturer and, of course, followed by the user in order to retain the effectiveness of the finish. Fabric softeners, soaps, and chlorine bleach may destroy topical finish.
	WATER-SOLUBLE COMPOUNDS include borax, boric acid, ammonium phosphate, ammonium sulfate, and some mixtures of these.
	INSOLUBLE SALTS include metal oxide such as ferric oxide, stannic oxide, and manganese dioxide.
	OILS, WAXES, OR RESIN with incorporated chlorinated substances, phosphorus compounds, or antimony compounds are used, as well as substances that react with the fibers, to produce molecular changes in cellulosic fabrics.
	Finishes must be carefully matched to fabrics, and the selection of appropriate chemicals is a particular textile science.
	Cellulosic fibers, natural and manufactured, are among the most flammable.
	Blends have been a challenge for manufacturers. In some cases, the two fibers in a blend cannot be treated with the same solution and accept finishes differently. In the 1970s, a topical fire retardant known as Tris was used in children's sleepwear. It was eventually taken off the market because it was potentially a carcinogen, emitting fumes when wet. Other flame retardants also emit fumes.
	Some trade names for flame-retardent finshes are as follows: Banfire®, CM Flame Retardant®, Fi-Retard®, Firegard®, Firemaster®, Firemaster 200®, Firestop®, Fvrol 76®, Proban®, Pyropel®, Pyrovatex CP®, THPC. X-12®.
	It is important for designers to inform clients of the proper care for flame-retardant treated fabrics. Certain processes can damage the finishes and stain the fabric. For this reason, topical finishes are being replaced with fibers where there have been molecular changes that will not be affected by care and use.
Light Stabilizers	Some fabrics are prone to damage by exposure to ultraviolet rays of the sun. Interior fabrics are especially susceptible to damage through glass. In order to diminish the rates of disintegration from UV light, light-stabilizing chemicals are added to filter out the sun.
	Research has been strong in this area recently. With the depletion of the ozone layer and the dangers that come from exposure to the sun's harmful rays, textiles are seen as a good protective barrier to the sun. Making sure the fabrics filter the rays of the sun and are not damaged by them is leading to more innovative fabric construction and finishes.
Antistatic Finishes	Static buildup in fibers and fabrics is a problem for manufacturers and consumers alike. In the factory, humidity, lubricants, and various antistatic finishes are used to control the buildup of electrons during the manufacturing process. It is important to reduce static because the equipment gets very hot and sparks could ignite the fibers, causing a fire hazard.
	Antistatic finishes prevent, dissipate, or reduce electrical charges within the fabric. Adding antistats to spinning solutions of manufactured fibers and incorporating fine metallic yarns to carpeting can reduce static buildup. Nylon carpets, made from fibers with poor conductivity, allow the buildup of electricity and must be treated.
	Some trademark brand antistatic finishes include 3M brand Static Control®, X-Static®.
	Dependable, long-lasting antistatic finishes have yet to be devised for fabrics that must undergo frequent laundering or dry cleaning. For these, commercial fabric softeners are effective in reducing static. Softeners coat the fibers, preventing buildup and improving conduction.

Functional Finishes, cont'd

Antistatic Finishes, cont'd	Other durable finishes are based on polyethylene glycol or polyalkylene glycol ethers. Trade names for these include Aston®, Nopcostat®, Permastat®, Stanax®, and Valstat®.
Mothproof Finishes	Protein fibers are especially vulnerable to moth larvae. Wool is the most susceptible and frequently damaged protein fiber. A mothproof finish can be applied that is toxic to the insect. It may be added to the fiber during fulling or dyeing. Toxicity levels in DDT, an effective mothproofing finish, caused its use to be banned. Other compounds are suspected to harm humans. Mothproof finishes are not durable, and longevity is never sufficient as the finishes wear off easily. Permethryn® is one commercial mothproofing finish. Research is being done into other preventative methods. Scientists believe that making a fiber indigestible to larvae would stop them from eating it. These finishes are not yet widely used in commercial wool production. Other trade names include Crestocide®, Hartocide®, Mitin®, Neocide®, and Repel-O-Tac®, and the effects of these products are considered durable. Proper care of untreated wool or wool blends is essential. Carpets and upholstery must be kept clean; soiled wool is particularly subject to attack. Napthalene, in the form of crystals or mothballs, repels the mature moth and prevents the deposit of eggs. However, the offensive odor of napthalene is a deterrent to its use. Damage to wool products by moth larvae and carpet beetles costs hundreds of millions of dollars each year. As a result, research is ongoing to develop new, effective mothproofing systems. Studies are underway to find ways to make wool's keratin protein unpalatable, and to find substances to add to the sheeps' diet to make their wool inherently mothproof.
Antimicrobial Finishes	Mildew, mold, and rot on textiles are caused by microorganisms. Bacteria, fungi, and microbes all develop and spread on fibers that are exposed to moisture. They lead to the destruction of a wide range of materials, the spread of disease, skin irritation, infections, and unpleasant odors. Polyester, being oleophillic, tends to build up bacteria very easily. It is hydrophobic, so water will not penetrate the fiber to help remove the oils that are absorbed. Over time, bacteria feed off the absorbed oils and cause skin irritation or unpleasant odors. Antimicrobial finishes can reduce the possibility of infection by reducing bacterial counts and buildup of fungus by 75-99%. They are applied to yarn surfaces to prevent mold and mildew growth. Renewable finishes are widely used on apparel and household materials by dry cleaners, and in commercial and home laundry products. Some trade names are Borateem®, Dowicide®, Sanitized® and Sanitone®, Shirlan®. Durable finishes are composed of amines, acids, and metallic salts (zirconium, copper, mercury, and silver). Some trade names are Sylgard®, Intersept®, Ultra-Fresh®, Guardsan®, Hyarnine®, Marcocide®, Nuodex®, Permacide®, and Vancide®. Antimicrobial finishes are especially important for textiles used in interiors of commercial spaces where there is a chance viruses and disease will be deposited onto the fabric (on upholstery, for example.) These finishes are especially important for any textile being used in a healthcare facility. Carpet manufacturers often combine finishes, and when an antimicrobial finish is paired with a soil repellent, as with Lees Commercial Carpeting, it carries the trademark Bioguard®.

Functional Finishes, cont'd

Antimicrobial Finishes, cont'd	There are two types of antimicrobial finishes. **Unbound** finishes are consumed by the microorganism and are not bonded to the fabric. They act as poison to the bacteria. This type of finish is not durable over the long term and is not effective against all forms of bacteria. **Bound** antimicrobials are chemically attached to the fiber. They kill organisms on contact and remain effective over long-term use. There is little worry about toxicity levels with bound antimicrobials, whereas unbound finishes tend to vary with safety and toxicity levels. Fabrics routinely treated with antimicrobial finishes are sheeting, mattress fabrics and paddings, carpet padding, carpeting, blankets, tents, tarpaulins, upholstery fabrics, fabrics for healthcare facilities, institutional or commercial use, and a range of apparel and footwear.

Soil- and Stain-Resistant Finishes ———

There are a number of finishes used to protect a fabric from oily stains and soils. They can shield the fabric from absorbing soils, they can assist in the release of soils, or they can do both at the same time. All soil and stains should be removed as soon as possible as the finishes do not claim to resist soil or stains indefinitely.

Soil- and Stain-Resistant Finishes

Soil-Repellent Finishes	Fabrics finished with soil-repellent are less prone to absorbing oily soils that stain. Oil and water will remain on the surface of the fabric longer, rather than absorb into the core. This allows time to wipe up the soil before it has a chance to enter inside the fiber, where it is harder to remove. These repellents can be applied in the manufacturing of the fabric or after the fabric has been bought. Examples of these include Zepel® (DuPont) or Scotchgard® (3M), which are formulated to protect a variety of different fabrics. A mix of silicone and fluorocarbons is applied as a good barrier to oily soils and water-based soils as well.
Soil-Release Finishes	With the presence of soil-release agents, oily soil can more easily be removed in laundering without pretreatment with detergents. Visa® (Milliken and Company, Inc.), Come Clean®, and X-it® and Scotchgard Stain Release® (used on carpeting) are all effective. Their function is to facilitate the release of stains or soils during laundering. They operate in one of two ways: provision of a hydrophilic surface that attracts water, allowing it to lift out the stain or soil; or coating the fibers so that soil does not penetrate. The finishes are most often included in durable press finishes, but are also available for untreated, and/or synthetic, fabrics. Chemicals used are fluorocarbons, acrylates, and hydrophilic copolymers. These finishes often provide other benefits such as antistatic, anti-pilling, and fuzz prevention. They also reduce soil redeposition, and soften hand. Because soil destroys fabric when left on for too long, fabrics treated for soil release make fabrics more durable. Carpets and Stain Resistance: Wool carpets are sometimes protected by Invecta Wool Shield®. This covers the fibers with a long-lasting coating after they have been dyed. Recently, nylon carpets have been the subject of many studies aiming to find ways to protect them from soiling and staining. The finishes protect the carpet long enough for potential staining sources to be wiped up, thus avoiding the attraction of molecules within the fibers. Resin is often used, and its natural yellow color can lead to yellowing of the carpet fibers over time. Stainmaster® carpet by DuPont is nylon carpet that has been treated with both stain-resist finish and soil-release finish.

Minimum Care Finishes

Often textiles are more appealing to consumers if little care is required. In order to facilitate the use and wearing of fabric manufacturers regularly, apply a large number of easy-care finishes to products. Anti-wrinkle, wash and wear, and permanent press are all finishes designed to reduce the work of the user in maintaining the textile.

Minimum Care Finishes	
Wrinkle Recovery/Crease Resistance	Indicates the ability of a fabric to recover from deformation while the fabric is dry.
Wash and Wear	This was a breakthrough of the 1950s as a result of the new thermoplastic fibers (nylon and polyester) that could be heat set to build in optimum appearance and superior recovery from laundering.
Permanent Press	Permanent press or durable press was introduced in 1964. It refers to a fabric's ability to retain presses and creases or a smooth appearance through repeated laundering.

Polyester is inherently permanent press. The following discussion is limited to finishes applied to fabrics that are prone to wrinkling.

Wrinkle recovery and durable press are closely related. Both properties can be added to cellulosic fabrics with resins. The resin reacts chemically with cellulose molecules to form a system of cross linkages that holds the fabric in a particular configuration. Wrinkling is inevitable in cotton and linen fabrics. In the 1920s, research started in earnest to find ways to alleviate the problem, and the resin finish was developed at that time. Early finishes had a serious drawback in that they drastically reduced strength and abrasion resistance in treated fabrics. By the 1960s, 100% cotton fabrics could be treated for crease resistance with 'acceptable' (about 40%) loss of strength.

Durable press finishes use the same cross-linking techniques, and these finishes are now most often applied to fabrics (or ready-made apparel) of cotton blended with polyester. The polyester adds the strength lost by treating the cotton.

Durable press can be done before garment production (precured) or after garment production is complete (post-cured). |

DYES AND PRINTS

The appeal of color is universal, and fabric has been colored for centuries. Some colors, like purple, were so rare and costly that they were reserved for royalty. Until the mid-nineteenth century, all dye was obtained from natural sources such as plants and insects. Reds, such as madder, came from a Mediterranean plant root; cochineal came from a Mexican insect; blue came from indigo leaves; yellow from the stigmata of the saffron plant. These, and many other, natural sources still yield dyes and are used for small dyeing jobs.

In 1856, in England, Sir William Perkins accidentally produced the first synthetic dyestuff, mauve, from a coal tar derivative. Since then, development of dye types and dyeing technology has been rapid and steady, and now there are thousands of dyes available.

Dye is any natural or manufactured organic substance or compound that can be fixed on another substance to evoke the visual sensation of color. The molecular structure of the dye determines which colors are absorbed and which are reflected. For example, a red-dyed fiber absorbs all colors except red, which is reflected and, therefore, can be seen.

Color can be applied at any stage in the textile production process. Color can be added to synthetic **solutions** of manufactured fibers before they are spun. **Yarn dyes** are popular for checked fabrics or plaids, and the color is added to the yarns. Dyeing the fabric—**piece dye**—is the quickest, most cost-effective and popular method.

Dyes

For dyes to satisfy the customer's needs, the fiber type, yarn structure, fabric structure, and finishes must all work together. Fabric dyes are classified by color, chemical type, and method of application.

Synthetic fibers usually require dyestuffs to be added early in the manufacturing process. For example, nylon 6,6 is first extruded as a colorless or greige fiber.

Acid dyes or cationic dyes work best on this fiber although direct dyes and disperse dyes can be used.

Dyes may be reactive, in that they form a chemical bond with the fiber, or they may be held on the fabric by chemical attraction.

The following types of dyes relate to specific fibers or groups of fibers.

Classifications of Dyes ━━━━━━━

Direct Dyes

Direct, or substantive, dyes form the largest and most commercially important group. They are water soluble and are used primarily on cellulosic fibers and, to a lesser degree, on protein and polyamide fibers.

Direct dyes are dissolved in water, and a salt is added to control the rate of absorption into the fibers. The dyes are relatively colorfast to sunlight, but colorfastness to washing may be poor unless finished with resin. Resin finished, direct dyed fabrics are colorfast to washing. Direct dyes produce bright colors and are generally used for fabrics in the medium to low price range.

Used for: cotton, linen, rayon, wool, silk, polyamides (nylon and aramid)

Azoic or Napthol Dyes

Color is produced in the fiber by applying a colorless diazo compound, followed by napthol. Reaction with the fiber produces the colored effect. These compounds are applied cold, and the fabric is then washed with detergent in hot water.

Brilliant colors are possible with this dye method, which is relatively inexpensive. The colors produced with azoic or napthol dyes have good colorfastness to light, washing, bleaching, and alkalis. These dyes have a tendency to **crock**, or rub off onto other fabrics.

Used for: cotton, linen, rayon, acrylic, nylon, polyester, olefin (polypropylene)

Vat Dyes

Developed in Europe in 1910, vat dyes are among the older dye methods. Vat dyes are colorfast and wear well, and the dyeing procedure must be carefully controlled. Vat dyes are used on cellulosic fibers and some manufactured fibers but never on wool or silk. Because of their dependable colorfastness, they are often called **fast dyes**.

Used for: cotton, rayon, linen, some manufactured fibers

Sulphur Dyes

Sulphur dyes produce fair to good colorfastness for dark shades on cellulosic fibers. If not properly applied, the dye may break down on the fabric causing the fabric structure to weaken or disintegrate. Sulphur dyes are relatively low cost.

Used for: cotton, rayon

Reactive Dyes

Introduced in 1956, these dyes combine with the fiber molecule in a complex system using a reactive molecule. Reactive dyes produce bright colors with excellent colorfastness to washing and sunlight. A drawback is their susceptibility to damage from chlorine. Colorfastness to dry cleaning, fume fading, crocking, and perspiration is good to excellent.

Used for: cotton, linen, rayon, nylon, wool, silk, acrylic, blends

Acid or Anionic Dyes

These dyes are mainly organic acids produced as salts. They are called acid dyes because they are applied to the fibers in the presence of an acid, such as a solution of sulfuric, formic, or acetic acids. Acid dyes are ineffective on cellulosic fibers and on fibers sensitive to acids.

Acid dyes are noted for their superior colorfastness, excellent fixation, and wide range of available shades.

Used for: wool, silk, modified rayon, modified acrylic, nylon, modified polyester, some polypropylene (olefin)

Disperse Dyes

This group of dyestuffs was formerly called acetate dyes, as they were originally developed to dye acetate fibers. The dye particles are present in the spinning solution and attach to the fiber, dissolving into it to produce good colorfastness to light, laundering, and dry cleaning. The dye requires fixing with heat (205°C/400°F) in hot air, in infrared heat zones, or on a hot surface.

Disperse dyes on acetate, nylon, or polyester are subject to change or color loss in the presence of atmospheric fumes, particularly gaseous oxides of nitrogen. For this reason, fabric finishes have been devised to

Affinities of Dyes and Fibers

DYES	FIBERS
DIRECT	cotton, linen, rayon, wool, silk, polyamides
AZOIC (naphthol)	cotton, linen, rayon, acrylic, nylon, polyester, polypropylene
VAT	cotton, rayon, linen, some manufactured fibers
SULPHUR	cotton, rayon
REACTIVE	cotton, linen, rayon, nylon, wool, silk, acrylic, blends
ACID	wool, silk, modified rayon, modified acrylic, nylon, modified polyester, some olefin
DISPERSE	acetate, nylon, polyester, modified polyester, acrylic
METALLIZED ACID	wool, silk
BASIC	acrylic, nylon, polyester

counteract fading. The finishes are produced by various tertiary amines and are comparably durable. They are called fume fade-resistant finishes.

Used for: acetate, nylon, polyester, modified polyester, acrylic

Metallized Acid Dyes

These are acid dyes with added metal particles—mostly chromium, sometimes cobalt, aluminum, nickel, or copper. The effective fiber range is the same and the addition of metal results in an insoluble dye with improved colorfastness to light, laundering, and dry cleaning. The dry cleaning colorfastness is important for metallized dyes used on wool and silk.

Used for: wool, silk

Basic or Cationic Dyes

These dyes are salts of colored organic bases. There is a chemical reaction between the dyes and fibers, which results in excellent colorfastness. Basic dyes are also used in cross dyeing where they produce the lightest and brightest shades in the combination. They are exceptionally effective on acrylic and nylon fibers.

Used for: acrylic, nylon, polyester

Methods of Dyeing

Color may be applied to textiles at almost any stage of manufacture, from fiber to yarn to **finished goods.** Although the specific techniques vary, all of the dyeing methods listed below (except for solution dyeing) have four general steps. These are:

1. fiber preparation
2. dyebath preparation
3. dye application
4. finishing

FIBER PREPARATION differs for natural and manufactured fibers. The natural fibers are cleaned and bleached before processing; manufactured fibers are treated with spinning lubricants.

DYEBATH PREPARATION varies with the application method. In general, the dye or dyes are first mixed in a water solution. Other chemical agents are added to the dyebath to control the dyeing process and to ensure uniform dye absorption.

DYE APPLICATION introduces the dye to the fiber and promotes absorption. The dyebath is kept at specific temperatures, and the fiber is immersed for a specified length of time. When dyeing Nylon 6,6 it is important that the dyebath not be too alkaline—no more than 7.0 pH—or any cationic dyes will be adversely affected.

FINISHING the dye process requires rinsing off excess dye and dyeing agents in water. The dyed fiber is then dried before further processing.

Solution Dyeing (Producer Coloring, Dope Dyeing)

This method uses **pigment** colors added to the polymer solution before extrusion into fibers. While they are not technically dyes—they are insoluble in water and have no affinity for fibers—pigments are used to color fabrics through solution dyeing. Pigments are added to the fiber solution or molten polymer, and the fiber is extruded in a colored state. Solution dyeing provides excellent colorfastness to laundering, dry cleaning, light, perspiration, and crocking.

Solution dyeing is more expensive and less versatile than other dye methods. Final color decisions have to be made before the fiber is spun, which is very early in the process of fabric production. This limits the speed of response to changes in fashion trends. This method is primarily used to color fibers for outdoor carpet that cannot be dyed by any other method. The term *color sealed* identifies solution dyed goods.

Acetate, rayon, nylon, polyester, glass, and other manufactured fibers may be colored in this way.

Fiber Dyeing

This dyeing process takes place at the raw fiber stage, and it provides excellent color penetration and colorfastness. It is also called **stock dyeing** or, in the case of wool fibers in the sliver stage, **top dyeing.** Masses of fibers are submerged into the dye and absorb the color thoroughly. Fiber dyeing is sometimes combined with yarn production to produce unusual color effects; for example, two or more colors of fibers can be distributed through the spun yarn. This effect is called **heather.**

Yarn Dyeing

COLORING YARNS is one of the oldest methods of dyeing. There are several yarn dye methods.

SKEIN DYEING subjects small amounts of loosely wound coils of yarn (skeins) to a dye bath. It can produce either solid color yarns or multicolor yarns when two or more fiber types are used in the yarn bundles.

PACKAGE DYEING involves winding the yarn onto perforated cylinders (called **packages**) and stacking them on posts in the dye vat. The dye is forced up through the inside of the posts and through the cylinders, coloring the yarns from the inside out.

BEAM DYEING takes place after yarns are reeled onto a warp beam and loaded onto the beam-drying machine. Dye liquor is forced through the yarns, inside to outside and vice versa, allowing the color to fully penetrate the fibers.

SPACE DYEING produces random colors and patterns along the length of the yarn. The effect is a variegated coloration. For years, space dyed yarns

(variegated yarns) have been used in hand and machine knitting for clothing. These yarns are now being used for interior textiles such as upholstery and carpets. Carpet manufacturers can achieve this look by tufting the fabric, printing with color, and then de-tufting.

Piece Dyeing or Fabric Dyeing

This method refers to dyeing greige goods (unfinished fabric) and is generally the easiest and least expensive way to produce solid color fabric. Piece dyeing works best on single fiber fabrics, but blends can be dyed in this manner as well. Blended fabrics might have a heathered effect with flecks of light and dark color, depending on the up-take of the dyes for each fiber type. Selecting dye class is important when coloring blends. Different fiber types react differently to dyes, and there may be variations in the color.

BECK DYEING involves putting the greige goods in huge dye vats (becks) and then adding color. Dye becks can typically color 137 linear meters (150 linear yards) per batch. However, the goods may vary slightly in color from dye lot to dye lot.

JIG DYEING winds the fabric from one roll through the dye bath and onto a second roll. The number of passes back and forth determines the intensity of the color.

PADDING is another method of dyeing full-width goods. The fabric is run through a dye box, then through squeeze rollers that force in the color and remove excess liquid. Padding is the system used for all continuous dyeing procedures.

PRESSURE JET DYEING is a system specifically used for synthetic fabrics. Pressure jet dyeing uses a high pressure, high temperature, dye application system and sets the dye at a high temperature.

UNION DYEING involves carefully balancing dyestuffs so that one dyeing of a fabric composed of two or more fibers results in one even color. Usually, dye classes can be combined in one dye bath, and the appropriate dye is then picked up by the fiber for which it is intended. Other dyes in the same bath simultaneously 'meet up with' their target fiber. This is called a **one-bath process.** If separate baths are required to union dye a fabric of multiple fibers, a **two-bath** process is used.

CROSS DYEING takes advantage of blended fibers to produce different colors in one fabric in one dye bath. Many interesting effects may be obtained by this method. It is particularly effective with acrylic and polyester fabrics.

Polychromatic Dyeing

This is a flexible technique for dyeing in random patterns. It is sometimes listed as a method of printing.

In either dye weave or flow form, the dye applicator (jets or roller) can be moved sideways to add diagonal or horizontal pattern to the finished fabric. Speed of application, speed of the cloth, and amount of color are all variables. Tufted carpeting takes these methods very well, as dye penetration is excellent. Interesting furnishing fabrics are also polychromatic dyed.

DYE WEAVE forces dye through jets onto the top edge of a metal plate set at a 45° angle to the fabric. The dye runs down at irregular speeds and hits the moving fabric in a random manner. The pattern formed has sharp and blurred areas.

FLOW FORM uses a pierced roller filled with dye. The dye is rolled onto fabric giving it a marblized effect.

TAK PRINTING adds dye to precolored carpet surfaces. The dye liquor is contained in a sheet that flows downward and is cut by laterally oscillating chains. The dye is sprinkled or deposited at random on the moving fabric. Textile engineers have developed new equipment to meet today's preferences for color and design. The Multi-TAK® unit developed by Kusters is more versatile than the Tak operation and can deposit the dye in simple geometric and wave-like patterns.

JET PRINTING has expanded in use with computerization allowing detailed designs to be added to fabrics. Jet printing is used to color soft floor coverings.

Nozzles, jets, or blowers are used in a precisely controlled manner to create detailed designs or pattern repeats. The engineering is so sophisticated in some systems that the intricate color placement and elaborate patterns of authentic Oriental rugs can be replicated. This method requires high capital investment. A high rate of production, however, combined with less need for water, dye, and energy, make jet printing a comparatively cost effective and environmentally sensitive process. Millikin Carpets developed a system called the MILLITRON®. This is an electronically controlled system that uses hundreds of dye jets to 'print' the carpet surface as it moves through the process.

FOAM DYEING is used for coloring carpets. Foam (dye suspended in air rather than in water) is dispensed in a planned pattern, the bubbles burst, and the dye penetrates into the pile yarns.

Foam dyeing is attractive to carpet manufacturers because it reduces water consumption and energy use and is, therefore, cost effective and environmentally sensitive.

Carpet Dyeing

In carpet manufacturing, dyeing may occur in any one of three stages: fiber stage, yarn stage, or as finished goods.

In the fiber stage, methods include solution dyeing, stock or fiber dyeing, skein dyeing, and package dyeing. These methods produce solid colors.

In an alternate first-stage method, the fibers are densely packed into vats, and dye is forced through them. This is less expensive than solution dyeing but still offers uniform coloration and very good colorfastness.

When color is added after the fibers have been spun into yarns, the most common methods are skein dyeing, package dyeing, and space dyeing. All are less expensive than first-stage methods, yet offer good dye penetration and uniform coloration. In addition, higher dyeing temperatures can be used to promote fastness and ensure quicker drying times.

The third stage at which color can be added is after the yarns have been made into carpeting. The three major methods are beck dyeing, padding (continuous dyeing), and printing. All are easier and cheaper to perform than fiber or yarn spinning methods.

Carpet manufacturers employing third-stage methods need only stock greige yarns, thereby reducing their inventories. Carpets can be custom colored after they have been ordered. This enables manufacturers to offer shorter lead-times for delivery.

Printing

Printed fabrics have a design, pattern, or motif applied to the finished fabric. Methods include liquid dye baths (resist printing), pigment dispersions in paste, and techniques using paper, photographic, and computer transfers. Printing is normally done with **dye paste** pigments, but regular dyes are used for resist prints. Pigments in paste or other media are used for direct printing, which may be done by block or roller and for stencil and screen printing. Discharge printing reverses the procedure by removing color from a colored fabric in a pattern. Fabric designers are almost without restriction in having their designs committed to fabric. All of the automated printing processes are flexible and accurate. The range of colors is large and the intricacy of designs almost unlimited.

Print Methods

Resist Prints

Resist prints are created by allowing color to penetrate in specified areas of the fabric, while being resisted in others.

Tie-Dye

This method, which has had a recent revival as a contemporary craft, uses various means to shield parts of the fabric from the dye.

PLANGI TIE-DYE uses waxed thread to tie circles of fabric in bunches or to secure bunched folds. The fabric is immersed in the dye bath where loose fabric absorbs color, and the areas where dye cannot penetrate remain uncolored.

TRITIK is a technique similar to tie-dye, except hand stitching is used to gather the fabric together in intricate designs.

IKAT (OR KASURI) is a Japanese and Indonesian method of resist dyeing in which warp yarns are tie-dyed on the loom. When the cloth is woven, a pattern appears at fixed intervals.

Batik

Batik uses wax to resist dye absorption. The craft, originated and perfected by the Javanese, makes intricate designs in many colors. It is not amenable to automated production.

Intricate batik dyeing uses a *tjanting*, a copper cup afixed to a wood or reed handle with a small spout in the cup for measured application of the wax. The design is drawn in wax on the fabric, and the fabric is then piece dyed, coloring the exposed material and leaving the areas penetrated by wax. After thorough rinsing, the wax may be removed with hot water or by hot ironing between absorbent surfaces. The process is repeated many times, blocking (by wax penetration) different or additional portions of the fabric to produce a variety of colors and patterns.

A method to speed up fine design printing was devised by Javanese women, using a *tjap*. This is a block with the design worked in copper wires affixed to the surface. The block is dipped in hot wax to coat the wires, which are then pressed to the fabric, transferring the design in wax to the surface of the material.

Intricate batik is a lengthy process—it can take up to two months to complete a 1.8 meter (2 yards) length using tjanting; up to fifteen days using the tjap.

Simple batik is done by painting on larger sections of wax with a brush. Sometimes the cooled waxed portion is deliberately cracked so that fine lines of color appear in the uncolored portions.

There is such a demand for authentic block, batik, or ikat print fabric that manufacturers produce look-like-hand-printed patterns with high-speed printing techniques. This meets the need of large quantities of yardage at an economic cost.

Stencil Prints

This method was developed in Japan and can be considered the forerunner of screen printing. To stencil print, designs are cut into a film of oil-coated paper or thin metal. The stencil is then secured to the

Color Prints Key Terms

BLOTCH is a term signifying a printed solid color background. It sometimes presents problems with dye penetration.

COVER is the percentage of printed area on a given cloth. It may be as little as 10% or overprinted with colors to obtain up to 140% coverage.

DYE AFFINITY is the compatibility between specific fibers and dyestuffs.

GRINS are slices of ground fabric showing through a printed cloth. Grins usually signify off-registration.

HALFTONES are subtle shadings from one color to another.

MOTIF is the single pattern element, such as one flower, simple geometric shape, or a whole bouquet of flowers.

OVER-LAYS (OR FALL-ONS) are areas that are printed more than once. They may darken an existing color or produce a new one. (Blue overlaid on red will produce purple, for instance.)

PATTERN repeat is a complete pattern unit—one row of polka dots or a complete floral design—that it repeated over and over again along the length of the fabric.

PENETRATION is the degree of absorption of the color in the fabric. Poor penetration results in incomplete coverage in some cases, or it may be the cause of later color abrasion as the dye wears off the surface.

PIGMENTS are alternates to dyestuffs. They are cured on the fabric with heat so do not require the washing and rinsing of dyed fabrics.

REGISTRATION is the alignment of successive color printing. Failures in alignment are called off-registration and may show unintentional overlays, grins, or both.

SELVAGE legend is the information printed on the fabric edge. It may include the pattern designer's name, copyright, manufacturer, and blocks of the colors used in printing. Authentic historic patterns are identified on the selvage.

STRIKE OFF is a trial printing of one or more pattern repeats. It is a factory procedure used to establish color lines, check pattern, and to test cloth/dye affinity and finish.

---

cloth surface and color is applied with a brush or spray gun. Additional color is applied using separate stencils. A multicolored design requires careful fitting of each stencil so that the design registers properly.

Screen Prints

Screen printing is a stencil process adapted to a fine screen rather than to a solid plate. The design is cut into a solid film, and this film is laid over the fine mesh. Dye is then forced through the mesh into the fabric and prevented from reaching the fabric where the film had been left intact. Chemical blocking substances are often used to cover areas where color is not wanted.

In automatic screen printing, the mesh screens are prepared by engraving, chemical substance blocking, or photochemical processes. To screen print, the prepared screen is fitted to the fabric and the dye forced through the open mesh areas with a rubber squeegee. Multicolor prints are made with several screens, and there must be careful registration of each screen.

Flat Bed Screen Prints

Flat bed screen printing is usually used to make large designs on fabrics, which are repeated every 6.4

meters (7 yards). The cloth is automatically moved, intermittently, across the print table, and the screens are fixed and colors applied.

Rotary Screen Prints

Rotary screen printing, which developed in the 1960s, is a fast printing method. It is more accurate, more economical, and produces a more uniform coloration. It is capable of printing roughly 25-100 meters (27-110 yards) per minute. Over 60 percent of printed fabrics are printed in this way. The screens are seamless and shaped into cylinders that are similar to the original rotary printers, but not as heavy and cumbersome. Patterns are made on the screen roller where the circumference of each roll determines the size of the pattern repeat.

Thousands of meters (yards) of fabric per day may be continuously printed in this manner. The number of rollers determines the number of colors. One color is contained within each roller. Automated squeegee (rubber blade) devices force a controlled amount of dye through the screen, and it comes in contact with the fabric. The fabric is carried on a backing belt that minimizes distortion, an especially important factor with knitted fabrics.

Rotary screen printing is similar to direct roller printing, and results are identical. Screens used for rotary screen printing are easier and cheaper to make than the engraved rolls used for roller printing. Rotary screens may be very wide, up to 5.1 meters (200 feet), and they can be arranged in pairs to simultaneously print both sides of a fabric.

Direct Prints

This is the most common method of color printing and ranges from handcrafts to full automation.

Block Prints

Block printing dates back to around 2500 B.C.E. It is a method of stamping colored patterns on fabrics by means of carved blocks of wood or other solid material. The blocks are usually small, the largest for handcrafting being around 30 x 45 cm (12 x 18"). Each block stamps one color at a time on the flat fabric; the dye paste may be used as a block dip or be applied to the block surface with a rubber roller.

Flat Bed Prints

Flat bed printing was an outgrowth of block printing. In the thirteenth and fourteenth centuries, block printing was an established craft in some European centers. By the seventeenth century, textile centers in Germany, Holland, Switzerland, Spain, France, and England featured intricate block printed designs on linen and cotton. As demand for the prints grew, the technique was eventually replaced with a flat table and a flat bed press engraved with a design. The system reached a pinnacle with Christophe Phillippe Oberkampf, who originated the **Toiles de Jouy** prints in Jouy, France, in 1760. The prints were notable for their well-drawn, attractive designs, which depended on events of national interest for their fashionable patterns. Oberkampf's death, and the Napoleonic Wars, caused the eventual dissolution of the Juoy factory in 1830.

Roller Prints

Roller printing was used following the invention of a roller print machine by Thomas Bell, in Scotland, in 1783. It combined metal engraving techniques with color printing, and it is the basis of modern roller printing.

Today, the design is etched into metal with acid or photoengraving techniques, and the engraved metal

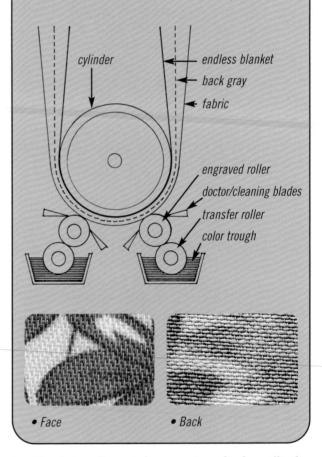

Roller Print Method

Thousands of meters/yards of fabric per day may be continuously printed in this manner. At the center is the main powered cylinder.

Greige fabric that is to be printed is delivered over guide rollers and into contact with the cylinder. A backing cloth cushions the contact. As the cylinder moves the fabric, it is brought into contact with the engraved printing rolls, each of which is coated with dye solution from individual color baths.

'Doctor blades' remove excess dye from each printing roll so that only the recessed, engraved details carry dye for deposit on the moving fabric.

The fabric then proceeds to drying, steaming, pressing, or other final finishing steps. In actual production, there may be sixteen or more print rolls operating on a single machine.

cylinder

endless blanket
back gray
fabric

engraved roller
doctor/cleaning blades
transfer roller
color trough

• Face   • Back

is affixed to rollers. A large main cylinder rolls the fabric into contact with the smaller printing rollers, which are arranged around it. Each printing roller has an individual dye bath, which applies color to the deeper engraved area and scrapes dye from the smooth metal areas. (This is in reverse to block printing, where dye adheres to the high areas.) As the padded cylinder rolls the fabric past each printing roller, the dye is transferred from the engraved sections to the fabric. Roller machines can print up to sixteen colors at one time at a rate of about 182 meters (200 yards) per minute. Automation assures accurate printing. As in rotary screen printing, the size of the pattern repeat is limited to the size of the printing roller.

This process has been largely replaced with rotary screen printing because of the labor and time required for etching the pattern on the copper roller, and the cost of the cylinder is very high. Setting up and changing the cylinders is cumbersome compared to the much lighter rotary screen-print method.

The color usually only penetrates the surface of the fabric, and the back is distinctly different. The pattern might be visible from the back, but the colors will not be as vivid and the outlines of the images will not be as sharp.

Duplex Prints

Duplex prints are a modification of direct roller printing, producing an identical print on both sides. Duplex prints may resemble fabrics usually made from dyed fiber or yarn.

Photographic Prints

Photographic prints are applied by a technique similar to printing photographs on paper. The fabric is treated with a light-reactive dye. When the photographic negative (black and white or full color) is placed on the fabric, and light is transmitted through it, the photograph print appears on the cloth and needs only stabilization and washing to make it permanent.

Transfer Prints (or Heat Transfer Prints)

This is a variation of decal decoration, first used in the 1970s. First the fabric dye is fixed on a special paper. The paper is then laid on the fabric and subjected to heat and pressure, which transfers the color pattern from the paper to the fabric. This method uses only disperse dyes, so fabrics amenable to this process must have this dye affinity. Transfer printing is also called **sublistatic printing**, as the transfer process sublimes the dye from solid to gaseous form and back to solid on the fabric surface.

Flock Prints

Flocking fibers (tiny staple fibers) are attached with adhesive onto the fabric surface in a predetermined pattern. The adhesive is printed in a pattern, and the fibers are blown over the surface, sticking only to the adhesive-treated portions of the fabric. Nylon and rayon fibers are the most popular flocking fibers. The type of adhesive determines the durability of this print method.

Discharge Prints

Rather than apply color, discharge printing removes color from an already dyed fabric. It is done with a rotary screen printing device, which applies a bleach or chemical dye remover to the fabric in a particular design. Small white designs, such as polka dots or tiny florals on dark fabrics, are usually discharge printed. Recent developments allow both color removal and color printing in one simultaneous operation.

• Face   • Back

Warp Prints (Shadow Prints)

Warp prints are characterized by a hazy design or pattern. The print is placed only on the warp yarns, before the fabric is woven. The filling yarns contain no print or design and are sometimes left white. This helps to achieve a subdued, smoky pattern with dull outlines. It is extremely important that the warp yarns remain perfectly aligned or the pattern will be ruined in the weaving process.

Etching or Burn-Out Prints

This variation of discharge printing is applied to blended fabrics with a combination of acid-resistant and acid-degradable fibers. Acid is used to burn out patterned sections of a fabric. This method leaves sheer sections of design on a textured background.

• Burn-Out Print

PART
THREE

IO

SELECTING TEXTILES

Today's built environment sometimes displays anonymity, which is in contrast to earlier eras when buildings were custom designed and had unique construction materials, structure, and joinings. Moldings, cornices, paneling, and multi-paned windows contributed to a feeling of individuality and often had a more human scale. Today's textiles may be effectively used to create that same sense of individuality. Large-scale glass-walled interiors now often depend on textile furnishings to provide warmth and comfort.

The range of textile products available to consumers is vast, and demand for furnishings, clothing, and industrial goods continues to grow. The textile industry is one sector of the economy that has consistently exhibited steady growth. Research and development are constant and demand for innovative products is greater than ever. Designers, who are in a position to specify textiles, have a clear understanding of what is available and how to make the best choices for their clients. While specifying textiles for floor covering, window treatments, or upholstery the designer is specifying textiles for people. Intelligent and thoughtful combining of fabrics and other materials is a challenge.

Considerations for Selecting Textiles

An interior's aesthetic is made up of a number of components: the textile design, the specification of textiles relative to other furnishings and equipment, the volume of the space, and the adjacent environment.

When textiles are being selected, human behavior must be considered. Studies of the near environment (home, office, or workplace) show that our immediate surroundings affect productivity, behavior, and mood. People often change their behavior without conscious thought when their surroundings change. The designer, therefore, must consider the users' unconscious needs when selecting textiles or other components of an interior.

When selecting textile products, designers have to consider:

- Aesthetics
- Functional Performance
- Health and Safety
- Economics Considerations

Criteria for Aesthetic Performance in Textiles

Textiles for interiors often have color and patterns that change and follow particular fashion trends. But selection of interior textiles also affects *psychological and physical needs*.

To some extent, the needs that affect selection are subliminal and relate to a perception of harmony and

Unconscious Needs of Users

ENVIRONMENTAL PERCEPTION: Gathering information on brightness, color, depth, perceptual constancy, and movement.

ADAPTATION: Many personal and physical factors influence the perceptual process. For instance, a familiar pattern or color is not consciously seen after a while, or, over time, a glaring pattern may produce environmental numbness.

SPATIAL COGNITION: Past association has an impact on spatial cognition. For instance, a user may have fond memories of, or bad experiences with, a situation/environment with similar color, texture, or pattern.

COGNITIVE ERROR: How the user applies geometry that is not really there is important; for instance, connecting points and patterns into lines, holes, or obstructions. Three-dimensional dishonest patterns may imply high and low areas on a factually level surface. Knowledge of cognitive errors is of special concern to design professionals in order to prevent their own perceptional mistakes. When working with a small piece of patterned textile, for example, design professionals need to envision the larger pattern, which may be quite different, or realize how the application of different colors, values, etc. changes the effect of the pattern.

SENSORY PERCEPTION: This should also be recognized in such *imaginary* situations as those induced by warm and cool colors, closeness of heavy textures, and so on.

VISUAL PERCEPTION: This is more than pure sensory perception, and it is also more than simply seeing and recognizing something for what it physically is. Each visual experience contains reference points that evoke unconscious memories that, in turn, create emotional and, sometimes, conscious responses.

---

balance as expressed through the **elements and principles of design.** Needs are sense-perceived—the eye sees and the hand reaches out to touch—and answer the user's need for a sense of well being. The verbalization of these needs should be solicited from the client and encouraged at an early stage, as needs will be a determining factor in the client's final approval of the design.

Aesthetics (appearance and touch) are related to the visual qualities the fabric possesses and how well the

Fundamentals of Design

Lack of design is chaos.

Design is order.

Elements of design are to visual expression what sound is to music. When organized and governed by the principles of harmony, balance, and rhythm, design is created.

PRINCIPLES OF DESIGN:

Harmony, agreement, a quality of oneness, as expressed by **line/shape/color/texture**

Balance: equilibrium due to equal opposition or equal attraction
           symmetrical or formal balance
           asymmetrical or informal balance

Rhythm: movement in regular measures
           definite direction
           progression
           repetition

ELEMENTS OF DESIGN:

Harmony, balance, rhythm, as expressed by **line/area/value/color/texture/volume**

Line: delicate or bold
         angular or curved
         flowing

Area: surface surrounded by contour or shape

Value: quantity of visible light reflected by a tone
         the lightness or darkness of a tone
         tone is the value of a color

Color: quality of visible light reflected by a tone
         a tone of color has: Hue: the particular color reflected
                        Value: lightness and darkness
                        Intensity: saturation of hue
         a neutral tone has volume but no hue

Texture: minute structure of a material
         appeals to sense of touch

Volume: three dimensional
         mass occupying space
         implies solid form or void

fabric maintains its original look. The fabric construction (open or closed structure) and the method of yarn spinning (tight, loose, smooth, or fuzzy) help determine durability of aesthetic qualities. Color, texture, pattern, luster, pilling propensity, proneness to static, and hand, all affect the aesthetics of the fabrics.

Color

Color offers enormous design potential, and textiles are a major vehicle for introducing color to an interior. Differences in tone and hue cover the full color spectrum. Colored textiles have become more colorfast and, therefore, more dependable. Coloring textiles is a difficult and technically complex process with some dyes taking up to ten months to produce. Our wonderland of cheap, effective color—everywhere around us—should not be taken for granted.

Colors need not appear flat or dull when used on textiles. Nature's colors are composed of minute color particles, and textiles can have similar depth and interest by 'fracturing' color. This breakup may be achieved in many ways: manufacturing cloth with yarns of different colors, cross dyeing, space dyeing, etc. The light source—artificial, natural, or reflected—in an interior space is very important when determining the choice of color.

Perception of color is a highly complex human faculty. Electromagnetic waves of light, measured in millimicrons, strike the retina of the eye. This stimulates the optic nerve to transmit an electric impulse to the brain where it is interpreted as a particular color. Perception of color is a changeable sensation, dependent on light and the juxtaposition of other hues within a space. Even the intensity with which an individual looks at a color can alter perception of the shade. Colors engender psychological or emotional responses. Often, universal reactions are indelibly stamped on the collective unconscious—feelings of warmth if the color resembles the sun; feelings of coolness if it stirs memories of water. Color is also a cultural construct; perceptions of meaning and color vary widely from culture to culture.

Color Changes

Color should maintain its original intensity regardless of light sources. Understanding what can cause changes in color on certain fabrics helps when selecting a fabric.

FADING may occur if a textile's fibers are affected by sunlight or other atmospheric conditions. Dyes should remain colorfast to sun exposure, strong light, air pollutants, or recommended cleaners. Acetates, colored with disperse dyes, for instance, are subject to gas-fume fading unless treated to resist such fumes.

CROCKING, the rubbing off of excess dyestuff from a fabric's surface, results from too much dye being used. In some cases, using a dye with imperfect affinity to the fiber will cause crocking to occur. Color transferred from one fabric to another by crocking (or rubbing) will ruin both fabrics—one will fade, and the other will take on a different shade.

COLOR LOSS can occur during laundering or dry cleaning if the manufacturer treated the fabric with an inappropriate dye or dyeing method. If colorfastness is not known or guaranteed by the manufacturer, fabric samples must be tested before assembly to assure colorfastness to the recommended cleaning method.

A Rainbow of Symbolism

RED	**HEALTH AND VITALITY**
bright red	passion
dark, grayed red	evil
pure pink	delicacy, festivity
warm, medium pink	innocence, calm
ORANGE	**ENTHUSIASM, ZEAL**
light orange	intensity
dark orange	ambition
YELLOW	**INSPIRATION**
medium yellow	goodness, wisdom
strong, light yellow	stimulation
dark-medium yellow	love of humanity
gold	luxury, glory, distinction
GREEN	**SOCIABILITY**
yellow-green	youth, freshness
medium green	honesty, practicality
BLUE	**IDEALISM**
strong blue-green	restlessness, nostalgia
grayed blue-green	placidity, repose
dark, grayed blue	kindness, sincerity
light-medium blue	peacefulness
PURPLE	**MAGNIFICENCE**
strong purple-blue	sternness
light purple	fragility, softness
medium purple	poise

Texture

All materials have texture. Texture is, in essence, a pattern of lights and shadows caused by elevated portions of the surface. It is most apparent in coarse fabric, but texture may be described as smooth or rough, soft or hard, level or uneven, shiny or dull, in any combination and degree. All of this is determined by the fiber content, the elements of construction, and how the textile is produced. A manufactured fabric may also be finished to provide additional texture by embossing, pressing, or the addition of surface finishes such as flocking. Texture does not need a direct tactile connection to create a textured effect; it also may visually impart an imagined sensation of texture that is both pleasing and appropriate to the end use.

Pattern

Pattern, like color, can reflect many moods. It can become an integral part of the fabric as it is constructed, or it may be applied to a finished surface. Pattern is a specific arrangement of shapes and colors. It may be immediately eye-catching—a bold floral or geometric—or so subtle as to be almost missed—a tone-on-tone chevron. A **motif** is a pattern unit that is repeated over and over again. It forms the **pattern repeat**, which may be as small as a centimeter (inches) or as large as 1.5 meters (1.64 yards).

Stripes, checks, and dots are ancient, common patterns. Yet, they are as effective and popular today as ever, lending themselves to myriad interpretations in scale and mood, from subtle to psychedelic. Geometrics, florals, scenes, paisleys, brocades—the range of patterns is practically limitless, and each may be used for textiles.

Luster

Luster refers to the sheen and is caused by light rays breaking and reflecting from the fabric surface. Silk fibers have high luster; cotton, linen, and wool fibers have low luster. Manufactured fibers have degrees of luster dependant on how the fiber is spun and what finishes are applied. Both fabric construction and finish affect luster; silk can be made to have a matte finish if it is a crepe weave, for example. Wool, conversely, can be combed, tightly spun, and woven in a closed structure to create higher luster.

Feng Shui

Feng Shui is an ancient Chinese art that combines folklore, religion, and science. It is a guide to creating harmony in interior spaces, and has recently become very popular in North America and Europe. Feng Shui identifies peoples' energy types and manipulates the living and working environment to suit them. Lighting, furniture design, furniture placement, and color are all used to create optimum balance and harmony in the design. According to practitioners, energy runs through a space and affects human behavior and well-being.

Five Feng Shui elements—fire, earth, wood, water, fire—provide guidelines to help improve the energy flow and create harmony. Color is closely linked to the elements and has meaning in the art of feng shui.

RED
Youth
Element: fire
Activating, dynamic, soaring

ORANGE
Motion/Productive
Elements: fire/earth
Lively, sociable, rooted

YELLOW
Long life
Element: earth
Positive, stability,
 productive, calming

GREEN
Growth
Element: wood
Creativity, clarity, positive

BLUE
Truth
Element: water
Flowing, descending, supple

PURPLE
Loyalty/Truth
Element: fire
Powerful

WHITE
Aging
Element: water
Purity, rigid, concentration,
 clear thinking

Pilling and Fuzzing

Fuzzing is the result of fibers breaking and working out of the fabric and protruding above the surface. *Pilling* occurs when fuzz is tangled and rolled into tight balls that stick to the surface, held on by a few tenacious fibers. Both are unsightly. When hydrophilic (absorbent) fibers—such as wool—fuzz and pill, it is generally temporary and the pills are easily removed; when hydrophobic (non- absorbent) fibers—such as polyester—pill, they are persistent and difficult to remove. Fabrics made from short fibers pill more easily than fabrics of longer fibers, and filament fibers are inherently fuzz- and pill-resistant.

Static Electricity and Textiles

Static contributes to safety hazards and also tends to attract dust, thread, hair, fur, and lint to a fabric's surface. If a static-prone fabric is used where these elements are present, the fabric will be more difficult to maintain. Particles cling to the fabric tenaciously; sometimes they are difficult to vacuum and must be removed manually. Physical comfort is also affected by electrical attraction. A static-prone fabric used as upholstery will cause a user's clothing to cling to the furniture surface; when the user leaves the seat, the clothing, especially if made of hydrophobic materials, will carry static and cling together or to other clothing layers.

Hand

Hand denotes the way a fabric feels when it is touched or handled. Hand is determined by a number of characteristics including flexibility, resilience, elasticity, fiber density, and the surface contour of the fabric. Terms such as *soft, crisp, silky, waxy, rough* describe the hand of a fabric. Fiber shape, yarn construction, fabric construction, and some finishes or dyes affect the hand of a fabric. Fabrics with the best drape include those that are soft, limp, and pliable. Stiff fabrics do not hang well and have a rigid drape.

Criteria for Functional Performance

The function of a textile is to behave in a planned, predetermined way. The fiber choice, yarn, and fabric structures and finishes all contribute to the overall performance satisfaction of the fabric. The product must be amenable to maintenance and cleaning for a reasonable time period. Overall needs of the space must also be considered. Whether the requirements call for sound deadening, insulating, brightening, low cost, luxury, bacteria control, or minimal maintenance, careful research of the specific needs gives the design team clear parameters with which to focus on the solution.

All textile performance is relative to use. Exposure, climate, levels of abuse, and maintenance must be considered. In some cases, the safest possible solution will not prevent deterioration; in other applications, gentle use and care can assure long life to a fragile fabric. As a general rule, institutional settings require fabrics that are durable and easy to maintain; residential, ceremonial, and occasional public-use areas may allow for more flexible fabric choices in order to arrive at an innovative or especially decorative solution. Good communication between the design professional and client is the essential ingredient for best selection.

Durability and Maintenance

Durability is the capacity of a textile to last or endure for a reasonable length of time without deterioration or destruction, and with minimal *loss of appearance*. *Maintenance* refers to the ongoing treatment necessary to keep a textile clean. Cleaning refers to periodic efforts to renew abused or soiled textiles. The two processes are collectively known as *maintenance*. Maintenance is measured in ease or difficulty, required frequency of attention, and by what continual and/or periodic care methods are undertaken.

Durability and maintenance are linked, and are considered together as a performance aspect of any textile. They must be assessed based on the performance data available. Performance data from the testing of fibers, yarns, fabrics, dyes, and finishes are available to designers either through the manufacturer or through independent testing in a textile-testing facility. The test results and other information help form the reference points for textile selection.

Interpreting the performance data, balancing the pros and cons, weighing the alternatives, and choosing the best textiles are satisfying tasks. Assessment starts with the fiber and progresses through all the subsequent processes to build the necessary composite picture of the finished textile's attributes. The following summaries of fibers, yarns, fabric structures, finishes and coloring may help in the selection process.

Each of the following affects durability and may be assessed for performance:

FIBER CONTENT determines durability to a large extent. Fibers may be chosen for their ability to resist abrasion or to maintain a soft hand and soft drape. Often, strength and flexibility are the most important qualities for interior fabrics, especially for carpets and upholstery.

YARN STRUCTURES contribute to durability. Simple ply yarns or multifilaments are generally most durable; complex or novelty yarns are less resistant to abrasion and are generally weaker.

- *Spun yarns* are composed of staple fibers, and they may be either singles or ply. Single yarns are inherently weaker than ply yarns and are more easily abraded. Staple yarns are spun with relatively short fibers and have a fuzzy surface. **Carded** cotton yarns are spun with the shortest cotton staple fibers removed by a simple combing process. **Combed** yarns are spun exclusively of longer staple cotton fibers (the shorter yarns are combed out by a second combing process), and they are the finest and smoothest spun yarns. **Woolen** and **worsted** yarns are made of wool and undergo similar processing to carded and combed cotton. **Tow** and **line** refer to linen and other bast fibers. Tow fibers are the short, broken bast fibers, and line fibers are the longer, higher quality bast fibers.

- *Yarn twist* may be S or Z—clockwise or counter-clockwise—and the yarns may be balanced or unbalanced. The balanced yarn does not exceed the optimum twist level for holding fibers together. An unbalanced or over-twisted yarn, when slackened, will then twist back on itself. It will be significantly weaker than balanced yarn because the individual fibers begin to break from the stress of the twist. *Yarn count* is a method of stating the weight of a measured amount of yarn. The *yarn number* reflects this weight.

FABRIC CONSTRUCTION is an important factor. Generally, plain, firm, and smooth surface fabrics are the most durable. Decorative fabrics may snag or run, and may or may not be durable depending on the application. With suitable placement (in low traffic areas, for instance) and proper care and handling, however, such fabrics are appropriate.

Woven fabrics are generally composed of one of three basic weaves or combinations of them. Woven fabrics are formed by interlacing yarns at 90° angles to each other, with yarns in the *warp* direction and yarns in the *filling/weft/pick* direction.

- *Plain weaves* have yarns interwoven on a one-to-one basis or in balanced or unbalanced variations, such as 2 x 2, 2 x 3, 4 x 4, etc.

- *Twill weaves* form a diagonal line on the cloth by moving the weaving pattern one yarn crosswise with each row.

- *Satin weaves* have yarns in one direction that float over a number of other yarns going in the other direction. This weave creates a smooth, lustrous surface.

- *Special effect* weaves use one or more of the above basic weaves to form a cut or loop pile, a pebbly surface, a multicolored design, or special texture.

Knits are formed with needles rather than with yarns intersecting each other at 90° angle.

- *Weft knitting* is based on hand-knitting techniques, and the fabric is formed by crosswise looping of a single yarn. Weft knit fabrics are flat or tubular single knits, double knits, or pile fabrics.

- *Warp knitting* is done on a very fast machine that produces plain or decorative tricot knit fabrics in a variety of weights. Raschel knits are made on a flexible machine and produce light lace-like decorative fabrics or heavy industrial fabrics.

Nonwoven fabrics are neither woven nor knit. They are produced directly from fibers or from polymer solutions. Felt was traditionally made of wool. The wool fibers, subjected to heat, moisture, and agitation, open, and the outer scales hook onto one another. This forms a closed, usually dense, fabric. Felt can also be made from manufactured fibers such as polyester. These felts are often mechanically produced by the needle-punching process, which tangles, compresses, then heats the fibers to form a flat fabric.

- *Bonded fabrics* are made from fibers held together with adhesives, heat, or a combination of both.

- *Foams* are produced from polymer solutions that incorporate sponge-like air bubbles before the solution is cooled or cured.

- *Films* are produced from polymer solutions, extruded into flat sheets that may be very thin or relatively thick. Expanded films have a slight cellular structure that is introduced at the solution stage. Supported films have a fine fabric backing. Films may be textured, colored, or printed.

Compound fabrics are composed of more than one component, joined by various means.

- *Embroidery* is any fabric with yarns securely stitched in a decorative pattern on the fabric's surface.

- *Quilting* is an old technique where three textile layers are sewn together in a decorative stitch pattern. The bottom layer is fabric, the middle is a loose tangle of fibers, and the top layer is usually the decorative layer.

FINISHES fall into several categories, and they make appreciable differences to the properties of fabric. Finishes can be semi-durable, durable, or permanent. They may be applied to fibers, yarns, or fabrics. Finishes can affect durability, sometimes weakening a fiber in order to obtain a different property (softness, for example).

Basic finishes may be characterized as preliminary finishes. They are basic steps to clean the cloth and stabilize the size and shape to allow for further processing.

Surface treatments affect the appearance and/or hand of fabrics.

- *Mechanical finishes* are used to produce a nap, smooth or polish the surface, or produce texture.

- *Flocking* is a technique for adhesive bonding bunches of fibers to a fabric surface. Flocking may be applied in a pattern, or it may cover the entire surface.

- *Durable finishes* are chemical or mechanical finishes that add permanent press, crease resistance, crease retention, durable glazing, or embossed designs to fabrics.

- *Chemical finishes* are used on fabrics to stiffen, soften, deluster, or optically brighten.

Functional enhancement finishes affect the performance criteria of fabrics.

- *Water repellent* treatments seal a fabric so that water cannot pass through. Water-based stains are held on the surface for a considerable period of time.

- *Flame-retardant finishes* are applied to flammable fabrics (such as cotton, linen, acetate, and triacetate) that normally ignite and burn freely. Designers need to be acutely aware of the details of the flame-resistant finishes they specify in textiles. Expected life span, maintenance, and the efficacy of the finish must be fully understood in order to protect the users from harm due to fire and smoke.

- *Antistatic finishes* are only semi-durable for fabrics that will be frequently laundered or dry cleaned. It is more effective to have static inhibitors built into the manufactured fibers that are the most prone to static buildup.

- *Mothproofing* is an effective finish for protein fabrics to make them unpalatable as moth larvae food.

- *Bacteriostats* protect fabrics made of fibers that are adversely affected by microorganisms. The various finishes are effective and durable, and they prevent the growth and/or spread of fungi and bacteria.

- *Soil- and stain-resistant fibers* are normally the same as water-repellent finishes.

- *Soil-release finishes* are used to facilitate the removal of soil or stains. These finishes may coat the fiber so that soil does not penetrate, or the finishes may provide a water-attracting quality (surfactant) to the fiber that allows detergents in water to lift out the soil.

- *Minimum-care finishes* are identical to durable finishes. These finishes are used to make wrinkle-prone fabrics, such as cotton and rayon, more wrinkle resistant.

DYEING or **PRINTING** matches fibers to particular dye types and dyeing processes in order to produce colorfast colors. Dyeing may be done in the polymer solution, fiber, yarn, fabric, or product stage. Printing is normally done at the fabric stage, but can also be applied on the warp threads before weaving actually takes place.

- *Fiber dyeing* or solution dyeing is done by adding pigments to the polymer solution before extrusion of the fibers. The extruded fibers can also be dyed.

- *Yarn dyeing* can be done by immersing yarns in the dye solution. They may be space dyed to produce variations of color and to dye fibers of varying lengths.

- *Piece dyeing* is where the untreated fabric (greige goods) is dyed. Piece dyeing involves several methods for immersing the fabric in dye baths or otherwise exposing it to the coloring solution. Union dyeing carefully balances dyes to produce one color in a fabric of two or more fiber types. Cross dyeing takes advantage of the fiber differences to produce different colors in one fabric and one dyebath. Polychromatic dyeing applies color in random patterns on finished fabric.

- *Printing* applies to fabrics where pigment is used instead of water-based dyes. The thick colored paste is applied to fabric to form a design motif or pattern on the surface. There are many printing techniques. Printed fabric may not be as colorfast as some other dye methods. Print paste does not absorb as deeply into the fiber, but usually sits on the surface of the fabric. Coloring and printing do not radically alter the performance of a fabric, although a fabric may be slightly weaker, stiffer, or more susceptible to light and chemical damage.

Abrasion Resistance

Abrasion resistance is the ability of the textile to resist wear from flat rubbing, flexing, or edge abrasion. Abrasion resistance contributes to textile durability and resistance to splitting and tearing. Damage from abrasion may be the result of certain inherent fiber properties or problems with yarn or fabric construction. Fabrics made from fibers that possess both high breaking strength and abrasion resistance can be used for a long period of time without showing signs of wear. Also, fabrics with flat, compact yarn structures and optimum interlacing are less subject to damage than those with very open structures and irregular surfaces.

Absorbency

Absorbency is the ability of the fabric to take in moisture. Most textile fibers have a certain amount of moisture as part of their structure. The absorbency of a fabric is determined by the fiber components and is influenced by modifications or finishes and by the fabric structure. Fibers that absorb moisture easily are called **hydrophilic** fibers. Fibers that do not readily absorb moisture are called **hydrophobic** fibers.

The relation of fiber strength to moisture absorption is an important consideration in evaluating fabric behavior. Some fibers are stronger wet than dry, others are weaker when wet, some show no change; these factors influence care and maintenance. Fabrics with no moisture regain, such as fiberglass casements, wash and dry easily and quickly. Absorbency is also related to static buildup, stain removal and spotting, and dimensional stability when wet.

Absorbency in fibers is measured with two factors: (a) moisture regain, or amount of moisture contained in a fiber at standard conditions of 21.1°C (70°F) at 65% relative humidity, and (b) moisture absorption, or the water holding capacity at 100% humidity. Both are expressed as percentages of the weight of the bone-dry specimen.

Elasticity, Elongation, and Recovery

ELASTICITY is the ability of a fabric to increase in length when under tension and then return to the original length when tension is released. Good elasticity tends to increase the breaking strength of a fabric.

ELONGATION is the amount of stretch or extension that a fabric will endure before it breaks. Excessive elongation may cause sagging if recovery from elongation is poor. It is important that elasticity and elongation be considered together in fiber evaluation.

RECOVERY indicates the degree of return to a fabric's original shape after elongation, and it is closely related to elasticity. Good recovery will prevent bagginess from occurring in upholstery fabric—even after many hours of use.

Resiliency

Resiliency is the ability of a fiber to return to shape following compression, bending, or other deformation. It is evaluated on a comparative basis from excellent to poor. Usually good elastic recovery indicates good resiliency and wrinkle recovery. Resiliency is very important in carpet fabrics and is measured by how quickly a flattened carpet pile will regain its shape and restore its appearance.

Dimensional Stability

Dimensional stability is the capacity of a fabric to retain shape. It is an important element for all textiles, particularly those fabrics that are hung or used as coverings. Absorbency, elasticity, elongation, recovery, and the construction of the fabric all affect dimensional stability. Free-hanging fabric may sag, shrink, or hike (alternately sag and shrink) when exposed to changes in humidity. Elongation (sagging) should not be greater than 2 percent. A loosely constructed fabric, particularly one of heavy yarns, will sag more than a tightly woven one. Casements or draperies made from hydrophilic fibers that absorb moist warm air may suddenly shrink, sag, and hike when subjected to dry, cool air-conditioning. Fabrics used for upholstery, wall coverings, or carpeting need dimensional stability to prevent them from stretching, which results in loose or buckled surfaces. Shrinking may result in puckered seams and excessive tension. In variable climates, fabrics should be chosen carefully and tested for dimensional stability.

Cover Efficiency

Cover is the ability of a fabric to occupy space or to conceal with a minimum of fibers and weight. It is dependent on the density of the fiber and the structure of the cloth or carpet. An efficient fabric covers well with the least amount of bulk and weight. Cover can be determined by (1) holding a fabric up to the light and observing how much of that light shows through or (2) bending a sample of carpet to see if the backing shows.

FIBERS with high density (weight per unit volume), such as fiberglass, are compact and heavy compared to fibers of low density, such as wool or crimped synthetics. Low-density fibers are lighter, have more loft or bulk, and cover more efficiently with fewer fibers and less weight.

FABRIC STRUCTURES with closely packed yarns and high-thread counts offer more cover than open construction with lower thread counts.

Textile Geometry

Most fabrics are made of fibers or yarns that are geometrically arranged into a finished fabric shape. The geometry of a textile contributes to its eventual performance as a finished drapery, upholstery fabric, or carpeting. Geometric factors influence the transmission of air and moisture through fabric. They affect the dimensional stability, abrasion resistance, hand and drape, and the tendency to retain soil. Finishes can also alter these characteristics.

Airflow

The ability for air to pass through the fabric is desirable where the textile will be in contact with the body, such as in upholstered seating. Fabrics that **breathe** are more comfortable against the body than those that do not breathe. Fabric that is impermeable can trap body heat and cause discomfort. In a warm climate or overheated room, or if the person using the seating is overheated (in sports club lounges, for instance), fabrics with no airflow can be uncomfortable to sit on. Materials that have good airflow are often loosely spun yarns that are thick or fluffy and have irregular or rough surfaces.

Sometimes airflow is not desired. Window casements that are meant to insulate a room should not have significant airflow. A window radiates hot or cold air so a smooth, densely woven fabric leaves minimal spaces in the fabric interstices for air to pass through.

Moisture Permeability

The same geometric characteristics that permit or prevent airflow also affect the passage for water vapor or moisture (known as wicking) through a fabric. The sorptive qualities of the fiber(s) play a significant part in a fabric's wicking ability. Cotton absorbs moisture and holds it within the fiber. Some microfiber fabrics pull moisture through the fabric (rather than into the fiber's core), making the surface moisture-free and more comfortable. This excellent wicking ability has made microfiber fabrics popular in products from furniture to lingerie and workout apparel.

Water repellency is influenced by a tight geometric configuration with only miniscule interstices where moisture cannot accumulate and saturate the fabric. A closely constructed cloth of hydrophobic fiber, such as nylon, will prevent water from penetrating.

Reactions to Sunlight

The harmful ultraviolet rays of the sun may discolor, fade, or rot fabrics. The amount of degradation of the fabric depends on the fiber content, the types of dyes and finishes, and the type of exposure to which the fabric is subjected. Sun rot is a serious matter; susceptible casements or draperies may totally disintegrate in laundering or dry cleaning after a period of exposure to the sun.

Criteria for Health and Safety Performance

The factors mentioned under this general category are also important as aesthetic and functional considerations. However, where health or safety is a requirement, the criteria are of prime importance.

Fire Resistance

Fire resistance depends on fiber content and, to some extent, on fabric structure. Fibers have various reactions to heat and flame, and these reactions must be carefully noted. Depending on fiber content, an open, loose fabric structure burns more easily and quickly than a closed fabric structure. In a closed structure, the amount of oxygen is reduced so the flame does not propagate as quickly.

Fire-retardant finishes are often applied to interior fabrics, but their wear life and efficacy are variable. Written guarantees from the manufacturer are the best protection for both the client/user and the designer.

Microorganism and Insect Resistance

Some fibers are inherently resistant to mildew, fungus, and bacteria. Other fibers, in the presence of moisture and warmth, are more vulnerable to such attack. Accumulated soil on fibers may foster the growth of microorganisms on fibers that are generally resistant. Anti-microbial finishes are often applied to protect fabric. Mildew, fungi, and bacteria growth are most severe in climates of sustained warmth and high humidity.

Buildup of microorganisms is of particular concern for fabrics used in healthcare facilities, where bacterial growth could contribute to the spread of disease.

Insects such as moths, carpet beetles, silverfish, and weevils are attracted to certain textile products. Cellulosic and protein fibers are natural food sources for these insects, and fabric made with these fibers should have a resistant finish applied to protect them. Wool should be treated with a mothproof finish.

Static Resistance

Resistance to static refers to the capacity of a fabric to act as an effective conductor of electricity. Static accumulates on nonconductors and only in the absence of adequate humidity. The amount of conductivity depends on the fiber type. Nylon is a very poor conductor and builds up electricity easily. Cotton, with a higher moisture content, conducts electricity and does not build up static. Static-resistant finishes are applied to static-prone fibers. Sometimes these fibers are blended with conducting fibers to reduce the ability of the static to build up in the fabric.

Static accumulation is a safety factor wherever flammable materials or sensitive machinery are used.

Environmental Considerations

The concept of environmental sustainability means many things to different people. Environmentally sustainable textiles might, for example, be made with all natural fibers grown with no pesticides or herbicides. Perhaps they are manufactured fibers where the process of production has been modified to reduce consumption of energy or water. The fibers might be recycled or recyclable. Improving interior air quality (IAQ) might be the main concern in choosing textiles. Using fewer toxic adhesives or fabrics with few added chemical finishes might be considered environmentally sustainable.

Design professionals need to be well informed and educated with respect to all materials selection, including textiles. Information can come from sales representatives and manufacturers. Sometimes, though, more objective information is also needed. Independent labs and textile-testing facilities exist where specific performance criteria are analyzed. Carpets and rugs are frequently tested at the Carpet and Rug Institute, for example. Universities and colleges often have teaching facilities that act as textile-testing laboratories for industry or individuals. Often, though, designers rely on past experience with materials to make future specifications on design projects. The designer needs to be a knowledgeable intermediary capable of judicious assessment and good advising.

Economic Considerations in Textile Selection

Cost is very important in textile selection. Relatively high capital and financing costs of renovating or building mean clients insist on value. They must carefully assess the investment/life-span ratio of the materials. Textile manufacturers make sure their products are price competitive with other interior finishes. Textiles can deliver the right texture, color, pattern, performance, safety, durability, comfort, and ease of maintenance to meet increasing demand for a wide range of applications.

Matching the textile to the budget can be a real challenge; the price of the goods per meter or yard is not the only factor to consider in estimating cost. Square meter or yard cost, makeup, and/or installation, ancillary materials, maintenance, and life span must all be taken into account. In addition, an exclusive or custom-made fabric may be desired, which adds to the cost.

Fabric price is not always determined by quality. The price of mass-produced fabrics (such as sheeting) is determined by fiber content, fineness of yarn, closeness of weave, colorfastness, and pattern. Price often, but not always, reflects quality. Other fabrics, however, whether of limited production, or specialty, handcrafted, or imported, reflect higher costs of lower volume manufacturing and marketing. The higher price does not necessarily infer high quality. It must not be assumed that an expensive textile product will pay for itself with long wear. It may, but often luxury fabrics are beautiful, not durable. The designer need not refrain from specifying such textiles—for drama, special effect, uniqueness, or sheer luxury—as long as clients recognizes they may be compromising life span and that the associated costs of maintenance will likely be higher.

Costing

ACCURATE COST: The cost per meter or yard of fabric cannot be used to estimate true cost until the fabric has been converted to cost per square unit. The conversion to square measure is necessary because of the varying widths of goods. As an example, 1 meter/ yard of 90 cm (36") fabric at $20.00 is twice the price of 1 meter/yard of 180 cm (72") material at $20.00. The latter gives twice as much width for the same price.

Fabrics with large pattern repeats must be carefully costed. Patterns need to be matched at the seams to achieve a balanced look. Pattern match sometimes requires a 25 percent increase in length of the fabric.

FABRICATION AND/OR INSTALLATION COSTS: These refer to costs of having casements or draperies made up, furnishings upholstered, or carpets installed. Where there is custom work, costs usually escalate sharply. Even with stock items there will be make-up and installation costs.

ANCILLARY MATERIALS: These include such items as backing material, underpadding, linings and inter-linings, tapes, tracks, and other installation mechanisms.

MAINTENANCE COSTS: Cleaning may be infrequent and the treatment may be less costly, or the fabric may require complete removal and cleaning in a secondary site (such as a dry cleaner), which will escalate the cost of maintenance considerably.

LIFE SPAN: A fabric's durability and life span have a direct bearing on cost. Averaging the initial cost over the number of years of expected satisfactory appearance and use breaks the cost down on an annual cost basis.

Cost Effectiveness

Specification decisions should not be finalized before considering the cost effectiveness of textile components based on requirements and performance criteria.

LIFE-CYCLE COSTING is a method used to estimate the cost over the service life (see below) of materials. The method assesses the projected costs of installation, labor, ancillary materials, and maintenance costs (regular preventative care and corrective treatments over the life span of the product). These amounts are added to the actual cost of the goods. This total is the estimated cost over the expected life span of the item—the **life-cycle cost.** An annual cost is obtained by dividing this total by the service life estimated by the product's manufacturer.

Clients or facility managers use the product life-cycle costs supplied by the design professionals as part of their own financial considerations. The totals may be part of insurance valuations, capital cost budgets, and financing costs, and the total spending will be amortized over the expected life span by the clients' accountants. Although not part of the design team's responsibility, it is important the design team knows that the costs provided to the client or facility manager may be an integral part of mortgage applications, estimated tax savings on interest, or allowable depreciation on capital expenditures.

Service life describes the effective life span of a product. It is sometimes based on test results from the manufacturer and often based on actual experience with long-term use. Accurate life-cycle costing depends on reliable information regarding service life. Written warranties of the life span and detailed care instructions should come from the manufacturer. Care costs are difficult to estimate accurately, and it is wise to add a percentage for inflation in the life-cycle cost estimate.

PEOPLE COSTING is based on how the environment affects human performance. If a designer can indicate and authenticate, with past studies, that a particular solution to an environment will improve efficiency or productivity, the client may be in a position to see an actual return on the investment. Many studies have been done on the office environment and show that a positive change in overall design may improve productivity and reduce absenteeism. The 'tone' of the workspace, including healthier interaction, pride in workmanship, respect for the organization, and less employee dissatisfaction can all be documented following thoughtful, skilled redesign of a space. While these outcomes are attributable to all aspects of a design solution, the textile component (carpet, upholstery, window treatments) is huge and very effective.

Life-Cycle Costing	
Initial Cost	Costs of all materials and components Discounts for quantity Discounts for prompt payment Storage of items if shipment arrives before scheduled installation Transportation from storage to site Installation and/or assembly costs Training personnel to use equipment and furniture Administration expenses of inventory management

Use Life	Reliability, prediction, and verification of service life of components
	    Warranties
	    Service contracts or in-house services
	Recurring maintenance costs required for preventative and corrective maintenance
	    Labor costs
	    Supplies
	    Equipment

Final Cost Factors	Removal costs Recycling costs (if applicable) Residual value from salvageable components Downtime costs (closure due to replacement) Replacement costs

DRAPERY AND UPHOLSTERY

Cloth, in the context of fabrics for interiors, can no longer be narrowly defined—as one contemporary dictionary does—as "a fabric formed by weaving, felting, etc., from wool, hair, silk, flax, cotton or other fiber." In our terms, cloth may be knitted, knotted, or woven and made of virtually any fiber, yarn, or element. The distinction we have chosen to make is between 'cloth' and 'carpeting.' Cloth is any material used for casements and draperies, for applying to walls or ceilings, as hangings, or as coverings for furnishings of any description.

Window Treatments

Many creative methods can be used to treat windows. There are no hard and fast rules; and shutters, blinds, screens, or no covering at all are as viable for particular applications as coverings of cloth. Casements, curtains and draperies, and textile shades and blinds are universally functional, attractive, economical, and flexible, and they deserve first consideration.

CASEMENT is a general term for curtain and drapery fabrics that have medium weight and some degree of transparency. Operation is horizontal.

CURTAIN is a general term for textile window covering fabric hung without linings. Operation is horizontal.

DRAPERIES are lined textile fabric panels hung to drape gracefully at windows or over walls and are operated horizontally.

SHADES are constructed of textile fabrics of varying compactness of construction such as Austrian shades, balloon shades, accordion pleated shades, Roman shades, roller shades, and honeycomb cellular shades. These are operated vertically.

History

Curtains were first used to cover cold walls and open doorways. Their main function was to keep the heat in. Windows, as we know them, were nonexistent; openings in the walls were covered with wooden shutters or oiled linen. When glass for windows was introduced, it was thick, bubbly, and used in small openings in the fortress-like castles of the Middle Ages, where windows were hardly more than slits in the thick walls. With improved heating systems, homes of the wealthy began to open up, and soon multi-paned windows of great height and graciousness appeared. They were largely left uncovered, but gradually simple curtains were devised—cloths hung by metal rings on ornate iron rods. The curtains extended beyond the window opening so that the fabric could be drawn from the window by day and ornament the wall on either side. The fabrics were as ornate as the style was simple, with heavy damasks, brocades, velvets, intricate embroidery on heavy linens, satins and silks, and all trimmed with braids and tassels.

Attitudes toward design in Victorian England also influenced attitudes to design in Europe and North America. For example, heavy drapes covered the windows of many homes. Greater density of population in cities meant that something was needed to cover the windows by day, for privacy, as well as at night, and lace curtains were introduced.

The opulence—or pseudo-opulence—ended in the 1920s. A sparse, modern look came into vogue, with plain fabrics and pinch pleats for every application.

Today, consumers can choose from a wide range of fabrics and options in style—including those from the past. Research into methods of decorating with fabrics is available and may lead to new uses of old styles appropriate to the contemporary context. Window treatments can, and should, reflect *location, lifestyle, individual preferences* and *needs*.

User Requirements

Windows are a sharp visual transition from solid wall to light-filled void. The user or occupant of the space has particular needs. These are, primarily, to control the light, to control the view (from outside as well as from inside), to provide privacy, to ventilate, to insulate, and to protect furnishings from sun damage.

Light Control

During the day, light changes intensity and direction. Glare can be a particular distraction for people with sight problems. Light should be controlled sufficiently for the user to feel comfortable while facing the window, yet should still permit soft daylight to flood the room. For example, casements of mesh, closely woven sheers, or any open construction fabric may be required. Usually these are in white or off-white blends. If the expanse of glass is large and the glare intense, dark sheer casements can be used as an alternative to blocking the light entirely.

Treatments may also be designed to provide varied levels of control throughout the day, ranging from bright exposure to total darkness. There are six factors that influence brightness control as provided by soft window treatments:

1. color characteristics of the coverings
2. number of layers used
3. fullness of the panels
4. addition of fiber delusterant
5. fabric coatings
6. fabric openness

For maximum flexibility, various combinations of shades, curtains, and draperies may be considered. For total blackout, shades or fabrics with opaque coatings may be installed.

View Control

Windows with interesting views need little or no covering during most of the day. Many windows in our environment, however, have no idyllic view, and the requirement is to make the outline of the view, or simply the daylight, as interesting as possible.

Unless the night view is of a lighted garden or a panorama of city lights, the visual transition is from solid walls to black void. If privacy is a requirement, or if the user wants to give the room a changed appearance for nighttime, then opaque draperies could be available to draw across the windows' glass area. The fabric for these can be drawn from a wide range, depending on other requirements, tastes, and budget. Blocking the window at night, if not required for privacy, may be necessary to shut out unwelcome street light or a collage of neon.

The view of the window from outside is usually less important to the occupant of the space, but a window exposed to neighbors or passers-by, particularly in the presence of street lighting, should present a finished look on both sides. Office buildings, hospitals, and hotels focus on a unified appearance from the exterior.

Privacy

Privacy is a precious commodity. In some cases, a hard choice must be made between an unobstructed daytime view and a need for privacy. Fortunately, it is much easier to see out through a sheer fabric than it is to see in.

Night privacy may require an opaque drapery. Some fabrics may reveal the occupants as moving shadows. If this is too 'exposed,' then heavier fabric or lining is required.

Ventilation

Windows that open for ventilation require special attention. Casements must be hung based on the window's method of opening so that the fabric does not block the flow of air and the fenestration hardware is easily accessible.

Thermal Insulation

Even with triple glazing, windows in northern climates lose interior heat in winter. Conversely, direct sunlight penetrates layers of glass and heats every surface it reaches in the interior. Knowing these facts and armed with technical and basic information, window treatments can be specified that conserve heat in winter and/or air conditioning in summer.

Energy conservation has become a specific science. The design team must be sure to analyze the climate carefully and choose the best window style. The following factors should be assessed:

- Exposure: orientation to the sun and wind

- Exterior sun blocks: awnings, shutters, overhead screens, architectural projections, trees, and adjacent buildings that shade the room

- Window components: size, energy efficiency (i.e., single, double, or triple paned), type of operation, slant (if any), glazing, weather stripping, applied film

Window treatments that open and close provide the flexibility needed to control seasonal solar heat gain. On sunny winter days, they can be opened to increase the level of heat transmission; on sunny summer days, they can be closed to increase the level of heat rejection.

Any layer of fabric is effective in slowing heat transfer. Drapery fabric may have **Fabric Fenestration Data**, information relating to the transmission of solar energy through glass to a building interior. Casement fabrics may come with a **shading coefficient**, a numerical rating that measures transmission related

To calculate the shading coefficient, the total amount of heat transmitted by a window and covering is divided by the total amount of heat transmitted by a single pane of clear glass. For example, a clear piece of glass might have a shading coefficient of .93 while a white vertical blind has a value in the range of .30.

to temperature flow. The lower the number, the more effective the fabric is in blocking heat transfer.

Even a sheer fabric can block a significant amount of heat. A practical test is simply to observe whether the fabric prevents the sun's rays from penetrating. If it does, then the radiant effect is blocked.

Heavier, closely constructed fabrics provide greater insulation. The most effective thermal insulation is obtained by using fabrics with linings or interlinings of closely constructed material with a thermal finish. Fiber batting and foam-backed linings are also effective.

Acoustical Insulation

Four types of sounds are heard within interiors:

1. Airborne sounds radiate directly into the air from people talking or working (e.g., food service) or from office machinery such as printers, copiers, faxes.

2. Surface sounds include people walking or pushing something along the floor.

3. Impact sounds (or structurally borne noise) result from vibration due to impacts such as jumping or hammering on walls, floors, or a floor above.

4. Exterior sounds, such as surface or air traffic, may penetrate the interior.

All of these sounds, if they are not wanted, become "noise." Carefully selected fabric and planned air spaces can help reduce these sounds.

Ceiling materials and soft floor coverings absorb sound that travels vertically; window and wall coverings can be installed to absorb sound that travels horizontally. The sound absorbency of drapery fabric decreases as fabric openness increases. For example, in multi-bed hospital rooms, cubicle curtains are hung primarily to provide privacy and to divide the space. However, these interior partitions also lessen horizontally reflected sound when constructed of closed, compact fabrics.

Protecting from Sun Damage

Protecting interior furnishings and carpeting against the ultraviolet rays of the sun may be necessary. The harmful rays of the sun can cause fibers to weaken, and colors to fade. The best solution is to block the sun from entering.

Aesthetics

The primary aesthetic consideration for the occupant is a feeling of comfortableness (not to be confused with comfort). The window treatment should have a comfortable, unobtrusive feeling. Color; texture, and pattern; harmony, balance, and scale; and camouflage all need to be considered when designing to satisfy the aesthetic needs of the user.

Color

Color is a powerful, but often unconscious, source of feeling. Used with discretion, it can lift the spirits and contribute to an overall feeling of contentment or security. Color is used in certain interior spaces to evoke a mood or behavior. Hospitals or other healthcare facilities often use soothing colors to try and placate patients. Because color will change with light behind the fabric, intensity of color and structure of the fabric need to be carefully thought out. Both the site and the exposure dictate whether casements should be nearly neutral, very dark, very light, or colored.

Texture and Pattern

Texture and pattern are most effective in breaking up the large flat expanses in commercial and institutional settings. The range of textured sheers, patterned openwork, extruded film, and novelty yarn fabrics is exceedingly broad and can be used to great effect. Pattern and texture are nearly limitless in fabrics that can be used for any window covering.

Harmony, Balance, and Scale

These design concepts apply as fully to window treatment as to any other area of design. The choice of casements and draperies must complement the surroundings. The development of fabrics with the appearance of weight and strong texture is of interest for applications where excessively strong architectural details (striated concrete, for instance) dictate an equally strong window treatment. Similarly, the production of fabrics in unusual widths assists in the treatment of whole walls of glass or multi-storey windows.

Camouflage

Very often an interior is considerably less than perfect. Irregularly placed or poorly proportioned windows, beams, radiators, air conditioners, all interfere with the overall unity of the space. Often the least arduous and least expensive solution to such problems is the use of draperies and/or casements to conceal the problem.

Performance Criteria

Performance data are essential parts of the information about any fabric. Casement and drapery requirements are specific and different, in some respects from the performance requirements of textiles for other uses.

Dimensional Stability

The ability to retain shape is of paramount importance in fabrics that hang freely. Sagging, shrinking, and hiking (alternate sagging and shrinking) are serious faults that will not be tolerated by any client.

SAGGING is elongation of the fabric and is more common in heavy, loosely constructed cloth. Weight causes sagging, particularly if the fabric is heavier in the weft (filling) direction. Fabrics that hang should have greater strength and weight in the warp direction—lengthwise.

SHRINKING is shortening of the fabric and often does not occur until the cloth is washed or dry cleaned. Most fabrics are either inherently resistant to shrinkage or are preshrunk before being made into a finished product. Shrinking more commonly occurs with laundering, so expensive and/or weighty casements and draperies should be professionally dry cleaned. Shrinking may also occur if the interior atmosphere is mechanically (or, less frequently, naturally) changed too quickly. An air conditioner set at *cool* in a room full of moist warm air can cause shrinkage in some fabrics.

HIKING occurs with **hydrophilic** fibers—those that absorb moisture readily. The hiking, or 'yoyo' effect, results from the fabric shrinking in moist air as the fibers swell with water, and then sagging as the humidity lowers and the fibers release water, and relax. Fabrics with strong warp yarns are less susceptible to hiking. **Hydrophobic** fibers—those that do not absorb moisture—are not affected by shrinking and sagging.

Sun Damage

Direct sunlight fades, weakens, degrades, or disintegrates fabrics, so a fabric's resistance to sun is a prime consideration in choosing fabrics and draperies.

Draperies can be protected with a sun-proof lining. If the drapery fabric is susceptible to sun then the turned-back edge that faces outside will rot. To forestall losing the entire drapery, extra fabric should be obtained at time of initial purchase so that a replacement of the edge can be done when necessary.

Casements or curtains in full sun for an extended time are extremely vulnerable to damage. Sun-resistant fabrics should be chosen, or, alternately, a sun-proof finish should be applied to the fabric.

It cannot be assumed that these protective measures will be completely effective. Sun and the buildup of heat between glass and fabric are both very destructive. Furthermore, the damage is not usually evident until the fabric is laundered or dry cleaned and it falls apart.

Slippage

Slippage occurs mainly n loosely constructed or open fabrics. With smooth fibers, in particular, slippage can cause distortion and, sometimes, snagging. In heavy-use areas such as public places, yarns may be handled more, causing them to separate inside the fabric. This leaves unsightly gaps in the fabric.

Microorganisms

Fabrics in moist warm conditions are prone to damage by microorganism. Some fibers (like cotton and wool) are more prone to attack than others. Air circulation and light discourage attack. As well, bacteriostats—finishes and/or treatments to prevent such damage—are widely used and effective. Untreated wool is likely to be attacked by moths; if this fabric is going to be used, ensure that it has a mothproof finish.

Installation

There are dozens of ways to hang casements, curtains, or draperies, and very specialized fittings are available.

Overall design of a space and the practical problems of interior and exterior elevations, tracking, and hardware are not discussed in this book, but are, of course, intimately related to the successful use of cloth casements and draperies.

Health and Safety

Fire Safety

Flame retardance for casements and draperies, especially those in public spaces, is a safety specification required by law. Interior designers, architects, facility managers, or any specifiers must ascertain if an authority with jurisdiction over materials used in a particular facility has established any mandates governing performance characteristics of window coverings. Today, various municipal, state, provincial, and federal agencies have established fire safety requirements for several types of commercial interiors.

For safety's sake, in applications where there is no legal requirement, precautions should be taken to assure that the window covering is resistant to a lighted candle or sparks. Flammability depends on fiber content and fabric construction. Shaggy or loosely constructed fabrics fuel the spread of fire; smooth, closely constructed fabrics resist flame spread. Flame retardant finishes are often applied to fabrics so they are less prone to igniting, and the spread of fire is slower.

Key terms in this area are as follows:

> **FLAMMABILITY** (or flammable) means ease with which a fabric catches fire (combusts).
>
> **FLAME RESISTANT** fabrics are hard to ignite, burn slowly, and sometimes self-extinguish.
>
> **FLAME PROOF** or **NONFLAMMABLE** fabric will not catch fire (e.g., metal or glass).
>
> **FIRE RETARDANT** is usually a finish applied to fabrics to retard the spread of flame once a fabric has caught fire.
>
> Fire retardant is usually a finish applied to fabrics to retard the spread of flame once a fabric has caught fire.

Specification Checklist—Drapery Fabrication

AREA
- ☐ Location
- ☐ Approximate dimension (bidder/contractor responsible for absolute dimensions on site)
- ☐ Elevator description—extension beyond window area
- ☐ Distance above casing or within casing or valance details

FABRIC
- ☐ Name and manufacturer
- ☐ Pattern number and description
- ☐ Color number and description
- ☐ Pattern repeat
- ☐ Fiber content

CHARACTERISTICS
- ☐ Colorfastness
- ☐ Yarn dyed
- ☐ Resistance to sun damage
- ☐ Fade resistance
- ☐ Flammability resistance ratings

FABRICATION
- ☐ Percentage of fullness
- ☐ Type of pleat
- ☐ Header size and description (e.g., type of stiffening)
- ☐ Hem details (e.g., double hems, weights, wired)
- ☐ Seam details

HARDWARE
- ☐ Type of track or rod, and hooks or rings, etc
- ☐ Separation method: One way
                          Two way
                          Multiple draw
                          Cord operated
                          Motorized

Note: All materials and methods to ensure a first-class installation

INSTALLATION
- ☐ Explicit instructions:
        Wall and ceiling installation
        Above casing or within casing
        Architectural recess or valance or drapery valance

SPECIAL INSTRUCTIONS   (e.g., finished appearance on both sides)

Design Checklist—Soft Window Treatments

USER REQUIREMENTS
- [ ] Viewing
- [ ] Privacy
- [ ] Insulation/energy conservation
- [ ] Ventilation
- [ ] Noise reduction
- [ ] Glare reduction/blockout
- [ ] Protection for other furnishings

AESTHETICS
- [ ] Line direction and character
- [ ] Area
- [ ] Value—light or dark
- [ ] Color
- [ ] Texture
- [ ] Drapery and/or casements or blinds or shades
- [ ] Drapery/casement headers
- [ ] Type of pleats:
  - Box
  - Pinch
  - Pleat-tape-pleat
  - French
  - Cartridge
  - Shirred
  - Loops
  - Scallops
  - Clips
  - Tabs
- [ ] Appearance against daylight
- [ ] Appearance under specific light sources
- [ ] Appearance from exterior

TREATMENTS
- [ ] Vertical or horizontal
- [ ] Drapery:
  - One-way draw
  - Two-way draw
  - Stocking space
  - Center split or side split
  - Hidden track or exposed rod
- [ ] Blinds and shade:
  - Austrian
  - Accordion
  - Honeycomb pleated shades
  - Roman shades
  - Balloon shades
  - Vertical blinds
  - Roller blinds

- *Barrel or cartridge pleats*
- *Shirred*
- *Accordian pleated shade*
- *Austrian shade*
- *Scalloped*
- *Sewn pinch pleats*
- *Looped*
- *French pleat*
- *Clipped*
- *Box pleat*
- *Balloon shade*

DRAPERY AND UPHOLSTERY

Cost Effectiveness

Prior to final selection of the proposed window treatment, many cost factors must be considered, including

- Initial cost of fabrics for casements and/or draperies and/or linings and special fabric finishes (if required)
- Initial cost of ancillary items such as hardware (e.g.,tracks, rods, draw system)
- Fabrication costs (unless treatment is a ready-made solution) of drapery, curtains, overhead treatments, cutting and fitting of blinds, etc.
- Installation costs of track, rods, and so on
- Maintenance costs over the expected life span. The life of textiles is affected by fibers, yarns and fabric of construction, the treatment, exposure, and care.
- Replacement costs of new materials and associated fabrication and installation

Maintenance Costs

When deciding on the type of window treatment, the cost of maintenance should be considered. Most drapery and curtain treatments eventually need to be cleaned in order to remove excess dust or staining from exposure to the elements. To determine the cleaning method the following should be considered carefully:

- Fiber type
- Finishes
- Coloration
- Fabric structure
- Yarn stability

It is essential to obtain care instructions for the fabrics used and to make sure the clients receive them. Labels need to be read carefully and manufacturers' directions followed.

Replacement Costs

The cost of replacing draperies and the effective useful life of a window treatment should be carefully considered. Drapery costs can be high due to the amount of fabric needed and the labor involved in manufacturing them. Appropriate linings are important, as are colorfast fabrics—usually those where more expensive dyeing techniques have been used. An equally important factor to consider is the effect of the window treatment on the furnishings in the space. Having effective barriers to light may save other furnishings from sun damage. The labor and material costs of removal and reinstallation of window treatments, while certainly not inexpensive, are less than those for replacing or reupholstering furniture. The cost over the life cycle of a window treatment should be carefully calculated in these terms.

Environmental Concerns

Energy Conservation

Concern for the environment and awareness of the increasing use and cost of energy have made governments, consumers, and manufacturers look for ways to reduce energy consumption. Window treatments and other interior textile products can play an important role in conservation.

Insulation

The thermal performance criteria for window treatments change as the seasons change. In winter, insulation is necessary to reduce heat loss; in summer, reflection of the sun's radiant energy is necessary to reduce heat gain. Three methods, **convection**, **conduction**, and **radiation**, transfer heat.

CONVECTION is heat transfer through air movement, including wide and forced circulation. For example, in an interior, warm air may be drawn between the window coverings and the window glass, where it is cooled, becomes heavier, and flows under the lower edges of free-hanging coverings and back into the room.

CONDUCTION is the movement of thermal energy through solids, liquids, and gases. Insulation resists thermal transfer and stems conduction. In residential and commercial structures, heat is conducted through walls, doors, floors, and roof areas as well as the windows. However, from 25 to 50 percent of the heat generated in homes is lost through windows alone. To avoid this, heavy fabric draperies, cloth shades, or blinds increase insulation and reduce loss of heat. Venetian blinds and vertical blinds do little to insulate a window. Aluminum is highly conductive, so it is ineffective in reducing heat loss in the winter.

RADIATION transfers heat through rays and waves. Rays emanate directly from the sun or hard surfaces on the exterior of the building, pavement, or other buildings. Some of these waves are rejected at the window; others make their way through the glass to the shades on the interior. Heat energy is transferred as the waves permeate to the interior. In winter, this can increase the room temperature and reduce dependence on heaters in the house. If the rays are not blocked in the heat of summer, however, radiation can cause an air conditioner to work overtime and use unnecessary energy. Closing drapes in the summer to reject the radiant waves cools the interior and reduces dependence on air conditioning.

Upholstery

The bed was probably one of the first pieces of furniture. The bed was made from four substantial posts, fastened together and lashed with cord to support the sleeper. Cushioning and covers were soon added for comfort. Seating, originally made of squared blocks of wood or stone, became more comfortable with the addition of a soft pillows. Backs and arms were gradually added, with padding and distinctive coverings for some. The sofa started as a bed; it was covered to make it appropriate for daytime seating. It, too, evolved into grand forms—some were padded and covered for comfort, others for show. Comfort and appearance were not often combined.

Today, the range of upholstered furnishings is immense, and the quality, cost, comfort, and appearance depend entirely on situation, preference, and budget. While most upholstered furniture pieces are the products of assembly line fabrication, it is still possible to obtain handcrafted pieces from skilled furniture makers/upholsterers to whatever specifications the designer and clients designate.

User Requirements

In the case of upholstery, actual needs and aesthetic requirements are closely related. For purposes of this review, *needs* (function and touch) deal only with actual requirements regarding value and product life expectancy. The many other factors are counted as aesthetics and performance criteria.

Function

The clients/users and the design team together should have a clear perception of the exact functions of the space, who will use it, what degree of use it will receive, where it is to be located, and what particular—and hidden—needs it is intended to serve.

Seating in a hotel lobby, a pediatrician's waiting room, a veterinary clinic, and a restaurant have very different intended use patterns.

Touch

Upholstery fabrics are touched and sat upon; therefore, how they feel to the hand and the body is as important as aesthetic considerations.

HAND CONTACT: Upholstery fabrics can be relatively neutral to the touch, or they can have a definite character. Most are in the neutral range, neither pleasant nor unpleasant. More definitive textures will evoke subliminal responses. If the response is conscious, such as physically drawing away from a prickly plush fabric—the fingernail on the chalkboard effect—then the fabric is wrong for that application. Hand contact should be 'pleasant' whether it is a nubby tweed, glazed cotton, microfiber, velvet, or satin.

FUZZING AND PILLING can add unpleasant texture where it did not originally exist. Fuzz results when abrasion works fibers out of the fabric, creating patches of loose, dirt-collecting surface. Pilling occurs when this fuzz gets rolled into tight balls, or pills, that stick to the surface. Some woolens may pill, but it is temporary, and the pills is easily removed. Some synthetic fibers, however, form pills that are hard to remove because they are anchored to the fabric with strong fibers. Pills on such fabrics may add an uncomfortable feel and look. Fabrics with a tendency to pill should, therefore, be avoided for applications where there will be abrasion through heavy use and wear.

SNAGGING occurs when yarns are pulled out of the fabric. It is a common occurrence with loosely constructed fabrics or those with long floats (satins), particularly if the constituent fibers are smooth and slippery. Pets allowed on furniture can snag yarns with their toenails, and idle or nervous people (children and adults) may unconsciously pick at fabric. The use, and users, of a piece of furniture should be assessed before choosing a snag-prone fabric.

On a more positive note, occasional snags are not serious as long as they receive prompt attention and are mended back, pulled through, or cut off. Fabrics that may snag should not be totally disregarded for upholstery uses.

BODY CONTACT: The degree of comfort or discomfort felt while sitting on an upholstered surface depends on two things: the texture of the cloth and its porosity. When considering these factors, keep in mind that in certain applications either very thin clothing or (depending on current styles) bare skin will come in contact with upholstery.

Texture, if it is so rough or prickly that it affects body comfort, is excessive. Texture that can be felt through thin clothing or is so slippery that leaning back causes the body weight to slide forward is not good. High temperatures accentuate these adverse reactions. In hot weather or in an overheated room, the prickly effect is particularly irritating. Similarly, a slick surface will feel uncomfortably cold in a cool or air-conditioned room.

Porosity is a measure of a fabric's capacity to transmit air and moisture. A fabric's ability to breathe is experienced in direct proportion to the length of time the occupant is in contact with the upholstery. The porosity of a piece of upholstered furniture depends on:

* the fabric's fiber content
* its method of construction
* finishes applied to the fabric
* the density of the cushioning

Fibers that are highly absorbent (**hydrophilic**) breathe well; nonabsorbent fibers (**hydrophobic**) do not breathe well. Open construction allows air and moisture to pass through; tightly constructed fabrics or films do not. Finishes may seal the surface of otherwise porous fibers and may even block the tiny air passages in an open construction cloth. Finally, the cushioning material may not breathe at all, negating to a great extent the effect of a porous covering.

A further disadvantage of lack of porosity is the possibility of generated static. Fibers or fabrics that do not absorb moisture are subject to a buildup of electrons. With friction, this may cause sparking. Static also causes clothing to cling to the upholstered surface or to pass the static from the upholstery to the occupant's clothing.

Where periods of extended seating are expected, as in airplanes, restaurants, conference rooms, theaters, or residential living rooms, fabric texture and porosity should be considered. Where short-term use is anticipated, porosity is less important.

Life Expectancy

Life expectancy means the period of time a fabric looks and feels good, and the time it takes to 'wear out.' The intended use of the fabric will dictate, to some extent, its life expectancy. The client, understandably, wants fabric with a reasonable life span. Depending on the user, this may be a totally unrealistic number of years, or an appreciation of the fact that a change in upholstery fabric will give a new look and extend the life of the seating.

The life expectancy of any fabric must take into account all of its physical characteristics. Many fabrics can endure endlessly, but at some point become faded or uncleanable. Life expectancy should, therefore, be measured in terms of good appearance and responsiveness to cleaning.

Maintenance

Maintenance dictates intended use as well. The clients/users must take into consideration:

* who will be responsible of keeping the upholstery clean
* how often the upholstery is cleaned
* if there will be anyone to spot clean the upholstery, if necessary

Aesthetics

The aesthetics of upholstery fabric choice are distinct and numerous; nearly all of our senses are involved. Users see and feel upholstery, and they may also hear it and smell it.

Appearance

The type of fabric used to cover a piece of furniture helps to determine its character, its impact, its 'staying power,' and its price. For example, change of fabric can make otherwise identical chairs acceptable in both a bedroom and a boardroom.

Color, Texture, Pattern

These factors evoke immediate responses. The elements must be—and must be seen to be—in keeping with the piece of furniture, in tune with the space, and appropriate to the intended use. This is not to say the choice of fabric must be 'safe'; it may be surprising, or different, or unexpected.

Some of the particulars are as follows:

HARD LOOK VS. SOFT LOOK, which can also be stated as tailored vs. casual, severe vs. comfortable, or even, chaste vs. sensuous. The user should be able to discern which side of the scale a particular upholstered piece fits. To a large extent, the construction, padding, and cushioning of a piece dictate whether the covering is taut and square or loose and flexible.

VISUAL FLATNESS is a way of describing fabrics with balanced, structured, compact, or disciplined patterns. These patterns are preferable on pieces of furniture to patterns that seem to have movement or to those with a random, unbalanced, free-floating design.

SCALE refers to the cloth itself, the texture, as well as the pattern. Each must complement the piece of furniture it covers and the environment.

PATTERN is always more difficult than plain fabric to place when used for upholstery. Problems with matching motifs and repeats can make using patterned fabric more expensive due to the extra quantity of fabric and labor involved. Stripes must maintain their thickness when matching cushions side by side. Floral patterns, especially big bold motifs, must be matched to achieve the whole effect of the pattern on the furniture. A pattern's visual line, horizontal or vertical, has to be determined prior to writing specifications and receiving estimates and before upholstering starts, and is vital to placing the various elements on the furniture in the finished piece. Often, a main motif is centered on the back and carried over the seat of the chair, sofa, or lounge. The rest of the elements should be balanced on the arms and sides of the furniture for maximum aesthetic appeal. Use of patterned fabric always entails more fabric than plain fabric. The larger the pattern repeat, the more fabric needed for a balanced appearance.

Performance Criteria

Upholstery fabric needs to have **strength**, **slippage**, **stability**, and **abrasion resistance**. These are the factors that most affect day-to-day use and life span.

Strength

Fabrics may vary in strength depending on their fiber content, yarns, and method of construction. It is unlikely that an inherently weak fabric would be selected for upholstery. It is possible, however, that finishes can adversely affect a fabric's strength, making it prone to damage. Sunlight is capable of completely destroying some fabrics; if placement in the sun is inevitable, then sun-resistant fabrics or those so treated are the only choice.

Slippage

Although seam slippage is not common in upholstery fabric, some slippery yarns within a fabric may have a tendency to give. This will occur at seams, with the seam stitches holding firm and the adjacent fabric yarns pulling apart. Yarns may also ravel from cut edges. These are serious problems. Slippage tendencies should be recognized before the fabric is made up so that workroom procedures can overcome the problem. Such procedures include:

- machine stitching the pattern edge before assembling
- allowing ample seam widths
- reinforcing the seams with fine cotton
- sewing with a double row of stitching

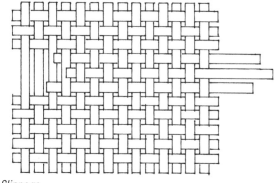

• *Slippage*

Because seam slippage or raveling is virtually impossible to repair, fabrics liable to slip or give under stress should generally be avoided for upholstery purposes.

Dimensional Stability

An upholstered fabric's dimensional stability is its ability to maintain a neat fit without wrinkling, sagging, or tearing. It must have the resilience to expand when weight is put upon it and to contract when the weight is removed.

An important factor here is the **under-cushioning.** If the under-cushion allows for more give than the fabric covering has, the upholstery will be strained in direct proportion to the weight put upon it. The second aspect of under-cushion importance is its shape and size. Large slab cushions, for instance, must depend on the fabric's own resilience to keep them in place. Often, the pattern of use causes the fabric to work itself over an edge, totally destroying a squared look. Similarly, sculptured furniture requires a snug fitted resilient covering. Fabric can be stabilized on the cushioning by buttoning, tufting, or channeling.

> **BUTTONING** is securing, with a minimum of tension, the layers of fabric and cushioning with a thread and a button on the surface.
>
> **TUFTING** is similar to buttoning except that the button is pulled tight, causing characteristic folds in the fabric.
>
> **CHANNELING** involves folding and securing the fabric to the cushioning in parallel rows.

Abrasion Resistance

A fabric's ability to withstand abrasion (rubbing, grinding, and friction) is based on fiber, yarns, fabric construction, backing, and under-cushioning. Positive factors in abrasion resistance are:

- strong, smooth filaments
- tightly twisted yarns
- plied yarns
- close-set weave
- heaviness or thickness of the fabric

Factors peculiar to upholstery applications are points of vulnerability, under-cushioning, and color abrasion.

POINTS OF VULNERABILITY are those areas on a piece of furniture that show wear first: the front and inside edges of upholstered arms, the top front edge of the seat, and any welts used in construction, particularly in the areas just mentioned. These factors, in turn, are influenced by the degree of tautness in the fabric. A tightly pulled cloth is naturally susceptible to abrasive wear.

UNDER-CUSHIONING plays a related role; soft undercushioning permits the fabric to give and thereby resist some of the grinding action. Fabric pulled over a sharp or hard edge is very quickly abraded.

COLOR ABRASION is due to insufficient penetration of the dye into the fabric, and the effect is to show the ground or natural color at points of abrasive wear. This is most noticeable in dark colors and on nubby, textured surfaces. **Crocking**—the rubbing off of dyestuff from the surface of the fabric—is a related problem. It is temporary and does not affect the cloth, but chemical dye inadvertently deposited on clothing or hands is certainly not welcome. To test dry crocking performance, rub a clean piece of white cotton back and forth a number of times on the fabric face. Test for wet crocking using the same method, but with a piece of wet cotton fabric.

The degree of abrasion resistance needed for a particular upholstery application will depend on the anticipated use. A bedroom chair in a home may be covered in a fragile fabric because the degree and type of use will not likely ruin it. In a hotel room, a considerably more abrasion-resistant fabric will be needed. In a restaurant or an airport lounge, use will be constant and relatively careless, and fabric choice will be limited to those with exceptional strength and abrasion resistance.

Construction Features of Upholstered Furniture

Fabrics used on upholstered furniture are referred to as *deck fabric* and *bottom fabric*. The **deck** is the platform, springs, and filling of the seat. **Self-deck** treatment is when the fabric covering the inner structure is the same fabric as the outer upholstery. For upholstery fabrics that are not suited to self-deck treatments (perhaps they are too bulky or textured), a lightweight, strong, smooth, and, often, less expensive fabric may be used.

Cushion and Pillow Treatments

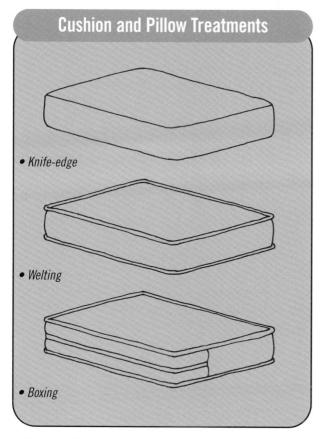

• *Knife-edge*

• *Welting*

• *Boxing*

Fabric is also needed on the bottom of furniture. These fabrics are referred to as **bottom fabrics.** Normally these are nonwoven, spunbonded fabrics that are lightweight, strong, and resistant to bacteria. Polypropylene (olefin) fabrics of different weights are common for bottom fabrics.

CUSHION AND PILLOW TREATMENTS (as illustrated) can be done in three different ways.

• Knife-edge treatment uses a plain seam with no extra detailing.

• Welting involves inserting a cord into the seam for a same-fabric welt, or including a separate fabricated welt of a contrasting color or fabric.

• Boxing is when a strip of fabric is combined with a zipper. This allows the filling to be easily added or removed.

When pillows and cushions can be attached to the frame of the furniture, it is known as **tight-pillow construction.** These cushions cannot be shifted or removed. Alternately, cushions that can be removed are called **loose-pillow style.** It is usually a good idea to make loose cushions the same fabric on both sides so they can receive equal patterns of wear and soiling. Other seating is manufactured with the fabric bonded to the hard material of construction, with little or no cushioning. This provides the look and feel of fabric without the expense of upholstery.

Cost Effectiveness

A client's requirement for upholstery is based on a predetermined need for seating. Given that decisions have been made to incorporate a certain number of chairs, sofas, or specialized seating units, the question that follows is 'what covering?" Usually the investment in fabric and labor fits a predetermined budget and the client/user and designer must assess possible solutions with an eye to value. Whatever the eventual decision, the clients must be satisfied that they have paid for upholstery that will give them a reasonable term of wear, and that they have purchased goods that will return comfort and eye appeal; in other words, they must feel they have received value for their money.

Walls and Ceilings

Cloth may be used on walls and ceilings for a number of reasons. It is not a new idea, but it has never been widely used. Historically, when it was used, fabric was limited to luxurious surroundings; panels of tightly gathered fabric or full wall tapestries provided richly elegant treatment for walls. Tapestries were movable and were transferred from one home (castle or fortress) to another as their wealthy owners moved about. The tent canopy—fabric-draped ceiling—was considered high style in Napoleonic France. Fabric was used for both practical (insulation) purposes as well as aesthetics, as is the case today. Fabric provides excellent insulation against sound and climate, and it is also useful for covering furnishings to update the look of a room or office.

Aesthetics

Against dry-wall construction, factory-made paneling, plain moldings, and square corners, the texture and suppleness of fabric offer a unique combination of a 'strong-yet-soft' appearance. It is impossible for a cloth-covered wall or ceiling to be bland or monotonous. Applied flat, plumply padded, shirred on tracks, or framed in a variety of ways, fabric absorbs and reflects light different from a hard surface so the effect of light is always changing. The visual effect of cloth-covered surfaces is one of warmth and intimacy.

Acoustic Control

Fabric can be used with great effectiveness to absorb sound and to prevent sound transmission from room to room. Fabrics chosen for this purpose should be thick, with a relatively open construction to provide air spaces that will trap and hold sound waves rather than bounce them back into the room. Wall fabrics for this purpose are available, or any deeply textured fabric may be used. Alternately, fabrics that are less bulky may be hung or mounted in such a way as to provide an air trap between the fabric and the wall or ceiling. The deadening effect can be heightened by using foam, batting, or acoustical boards behind the fabric. Besides the actual sound deadening characteristics there is a psychological effect: fabric surroundings have a feeling of intimacy—people tend to talk more quietly and to be conscious of making incidental noise.

Functional Finishes

For increased safety, textile wall and panel coverings may be treated with a flame-retardant compound. To reduce the rate of soil accumulation and to protect the wall coverings from staining, fluorocarbon compounds like Teflon® may be applied. For maximum protection against soiling and general abuse and to make the surface washable, the textile wall covering may be laminated with a clear or translucent vinyl film.

Art

Fiber art (or textile art) can be an exciting and vibrant contribution to an interior space. Fiber art (e.g., tapestries and needlepoint) dates back many centuries. Modern fiber art is a result of the Bauhaus School from the 1930s, but it was not until the 1960s when it became a commonly accepted art form. In the twenty-first century, new fiber technology means there are more possibilities for creativity than ever before.

Fiber art can be free form and use many types and combinations of techniques to make a visual statement. Textile artists use a variety of materials including fibers, yarns, fabrics, ropes, string, ribbons, and many others. The scale of the project depends on the artist, but it may be intimate in size or have gigantic proportions, and may be designed for wall hanging, free hanging, or be self-supporting. The variety of fiber art techniques means that it can be used in many different contexts and have great visual impact. Fiber art often possesses a duality of function and art. Today's artist is less bound by tradition and experiments with chemicals, dyes, finishes, or natural unprocessed fibers.

Representational fiber art is another decorative commodity. Called **soft sculpture**, people and animals are constructed of any combination of mainly soft materials, and are as viable as interior accessories as sculptures of ceramic, stone, or metals.

Fabrics of all types have long been enjoyed as art. Artistic expression has often been combined with utilitarian function. Quilts are an example of this. Delightful combinations of color and pattern mean that this once functional handcraft has excellent aesthetic appeal. Quilts are exhibited in juried shows, and they demonstrate the challenge of combining the tactile and the visual in two- and three-dimensional forms. Often quilts are used as wall hangings rather than for their original purpose as bed covering.

Embroidery and other forms of needlework are also being seen and recognized as art as well as a handcraft. Crewel, floss, pearl, and candlewick yarns are used for embroidery work. Their use results in distinct appearances; embroidery is often known by the type of yarn used, as well as by the difference in stitches. The work of artisans in South America, who appliqué highly stylized animal motifs by combining several layers and colors of fabric, has helped to popularize these textiles.

Tapestries have been an effective form of woven fabric art since the Middle Ages, when well-known artists were commissioned to design them. Completed masterpieces, created by many weavers and depicting important stories, were generally hung in the interiors of churches and castles. These tapestries served two purposes; they transformed the cold stone walls into dramatic backdrops, and they reduced cold air drafts and heat transfer. Surviving medieval works are found in the Victoria and Albert Museum in London, England, and the Metropolitan Museum of Art in New York. Today's tapestries tend to have more stylized motifs or geometric designs than depictions of particular events, and they are often not of the traditional tapestry technique but of highly technical jacquard weaves.

People from the earliest civilizations around the Mediterranean, Persia (now Iran), and China produced art on fabric. Over 3000 years ago in South America, Peruvian natives were weaving intricate fabrics and composing distinctive designs that told of their history and religion.

We enjoy a very long and culturally diverse history of fiber arts: tapestries and rugs, folk artifacts, and contemporary native weavings. For decoration of contemporary interiors, textile art can be used in the same way painted art or sculptured stone. Artists often use traditional methods such as manual dyeing and spinning despite new software being available. Often artists will combine tradition with technology to produce and share their art.

Constantly evolving software technology allows artists to see their work and create sculpture in both two- and three-dimensions. Artists can create and manipulate without committing the resources and time to building the actual piece. This allows for greater experimentation. Complexities of structure can easily be addressed, and changes can be made quickly.

With ease of communication and the ability to transfer images over networks in seconds, communities of textile artists virtually come together from around the world. These networks allow the sharing of ideas and techniques, and give easy access to art that might not have been seen less than 15 years ago.

Maintenance and Cleaning: Drapery and Upholstery

For classification, maintenance is regular ongoing care. This prevents spots and stains and delays the buildup of soil on the fabric's surface. Cleaning is the necessary, periodic removal of accumulated grime. Ideally, cleaning renews the fabric close to its original appearance.

MAINTENANCE: Good maintenance of casements, draperies, walls, artwork, and upholstery fabrics means cleaning is needed less frequently. There should be regular removal of airborne dust by vacuuming and prompt treatment of any substance that may spot or stain. At time of installation, the cloth's composition and finishes should be noted and provided to the client, along with manufacturer's recommended procedures for care. Ignorance in this area may not only compound maintenance problems, but lead to inadvertent disasters if the wrong treatment is applied. Use of the wrong cleaning fluid or water-based cleaner can sometimes result in bleeding dye, dissolved sizing, chemical wicking from interlinings or backings, shrinking, fading, or other calamities.

A fabric's life span is part of cost, and good maintenance is an important factor in life span; for a client to maintain a fabric is economically sound and protective of the initial investment. The designer's responsibility is to make sure that full and complete information, in writing, is given to the client.

CLEANING: Cleaning is done by laundering, dry cleaning, or in the case of upholstered furnishings, artwork, and fabric-covered walls, by specialized treatment by professionals.

Casements and Draperies

Casements and draperies attract dust and absorb air- and moisture-borne particles from cigarette smoke, air pollution, and oily fumes. Depending on the location, casements and draperies may need only one yearly cleaning, or they may require attention much more frequently.

There are two distinct cleaning methods: **laundering** and **dry cleaning**. Laundering involves water plus a cleaning agent; dry cleaning uses organic solvents such as perchloroethylene (perc) or petroleum-based solvents. Each fabric has a best method of cleaning, and labeling on the fabric bolt or information provided by the manufacturer should be followed.

Elaborate styling and multiple components increase maintenance costs of fabric. Separate charges may be assessed for removing and transporting the coverings to the cleaning plant, for ironing and reforming the folds, and for returning and rehanging the treatment. The anticipated frequency of cleaning must be considered when estimating long-term maintenance costs.

THE LAUNDRY PROCESS may use hot, warm, or cool water, and may specify soap or detergent. Soaps are excellent cleansers, but only in soft water. Detergents are more commonly used and often contain water softeners, soil redeposition preventatives, optical brighteners, and antibacterial agents. Bleaches are oxidizing agents (chemical reacting) and may be chlorine or nonchlorine. Chlorine bleaches are fast and effective as whiteners and stain removers if they are recommended for that fabric, but can damage fabrics beyond repair if they are used incorrectly. Nonchlorine bleaches work slower and are costlier, but they are generally safe to use on all washable fabrics. All bleaches weaken fibers, so excessive use is unwise.

THE DRY CLEANING PROCESS immerses fabric in cool or temperate organic solvent (instead of water and cleanser) and mechanically tumbles as in laundering. The principal solvent used is of the chlorinated hydrocarbon type (perchloroethylene) which is nonflammable. A few fabrics specify that petroleum-based solvent (called Stoddard solvent) be used. This is a flammable product and requires careful handling and special equipment.

Solvents remove oil and grease but cannot remove water-soluble soil. To remove both soil types, dry-cleaning solvents are charged, which means that a small quantity of water and detergent are added to remove water-based soil from the fabric. These quantities and the products used are the concerns of professional cleaners.

In addition to the dry cleaning process, **spotting** is used to remove particular stains. The interactions between fiber, stain, and chemical spot removers are exacting.

Vinyl or vinyl-coated fabrics will turn brittle if dry cleaned. Laminated or bonded fabrics carry labels stating whether if the adhesives are solvent soluble.

Upholstery

The most important aspect of upholstery cleaning is knowing the fabric. Materials are so numerous, the range of finishes so large, and the stain removal and maintenance products so diverse that only complete information will guarantee good care. Clients should also know what linings, backings, or under-cushioning have been used. This information, provided by the designer, will be used to direct the intelligent maintenance and the professional cleaning of upholstered furniture. In any event, test cleaning of an inconspicuous area is essential.

Manufacturers of upholstery frequently label their products with a **cleaning code** to facilitate cleaning. The code is based on the level of color migration and bleeding caused by water and solvent. The code used is:

- W: use water-based upholstery cleaner only
- S: use solvent-based upholstery cleaner only
- WS: use water-based or solvent-based cleaner
- X: does not clean with either water of solvent-based cleaner; use vacuuming or light brushing only

These codes are meant for the outer covering fabric only. Avoid over-wetting, which affects the filling materials. Zippered covers should not be removed for cleaning as excessive shrinkage may occur; zippers are used to facilitate filling the cushions, not to facilitate cleaning.

Spot Cleaning	Spots and stains need prompt attention. If immediate action is not taken, some stains may prove impossible to remove. Most stains fall into one of three categories: **water-borne, oil-borne,** or **combination.** The following are some types of stains that fall into each category: **Water-borne stains •** blood, candy, catsup, coffee, egg, fruit, fruit juice, grass, ink, iodine, liquor, milk drinks, mud, soft drinks, tea, urine, vegetables **Oil-borne stains •** butter, candle wax, moisturizer, deodorant, fat, grease, hair oil, ball-point pen ink, lipstick, make-up, margarine, mayonnaise, oil, salad dressing, shoe polish **Combination stains •** chocolate, gravy, ice cream, mustard, soup

RUGS AND CARPETS

In the Near East and Middle East, rugs were used for many purposes, both practical and symbolic. Rugs were used to lie upon, as coverings, and as shelter against the cold and wind. By day, they were easy to roll up and transport to the next grazing site. Rugs were made of wool that was readily available from sheep. Rugs are still used in this way in some countries where nomadic families roam the land.

In time, more colors were added and design became more complex and reflected the cultural tastes of the people who made the rugs. Soon sultans and sheiks directed the making of rugs with distinctive and intricate markings. Rug making spread eastward to China on established trade routes, where it became an important craft. The rise of Islam gave birth to the personal prayer rug and, with the expansion of the Islamic faith, the availability of the rugs spread into Spain and Eastern Europe. Marco Polo's travels brought back to Europe the idea of rugs, and the Crusades of the eleventh to fourteenth centuries furthered eastern rug making in Europe. The British started carpet making in the sixteenth century, with skills taught by Muslim prisoners brought to England by seafaring adventurers.

In Europe, early rug making was exclusively a handcraft. Many workers, tuned to the chanted instructions of the *khaidi,* or chief weaver, would simultaneously loop and knot individual tufts of colored wool into a woven wool backing. The craft developed to a fine art form; patterns were exciting, colors vibrant, and a fine silk rug could have as many as 110 knots per square centimeter (700 per square inch).

The commercial carpet industry began in England, and the names of manufacturing towns like Axminster and Wilton became synonymous with rugs. Power looms were devised to weave carpeting, but 27 inches was the only width available. By 1848, the power loom was used in the United States to produce Wilton carpets. Woven wool carpets with

Oriental designs were popular but were a luxury until after World War II, when mechanical tufting processes were devised. The machinery was fast and efficient, and the product was of excellent quality. In 1950, tufted carpets accounted for less than 10 percent of production; in 2003, their market share was 90 percent.

A carpeted floor creates an atmosphere of warmth, comfort, and quality. A carpet's colors and textures may be used to establish or enhance a particular mood. Carpets are also used for six practical reasons:

1. to reduce fatigue
2. to enhance safety
3. to improve facility of movement for people with disabilities

4. to control sound (carpets are ten times more effective at noise abatement than almost any other flooring)

5. to conserve energy

6. to camouflage worn, uneven, or damaged floors in older structures

Hand Techniques

Rugs

Although they are produced by hand techniques, handcrafted rugs are often the product of sophisticated commercial operations, with strict quality control and well-developed marketing strategies. Oriental rugs and Native American rugs are typical of this blend of manual skill and modern organization.

Weaving is the most common technique for hand-producing rugs, but hooking, braiding, and felting operations are also popular. Because of their appealing designs, handcrafted rugs are used as wall hangings nearly as often as they are used for floor coverings.

ORIENTALS

Oriental rugs were so designated because of the Latin term for 'from the east.' For centuries, this term was satisfactory to central Europeans and later to North Americans. Today, it is known that carpets from this huge geographical area are distinct in their traditions and are a source of cultural pride. For convenience in the trade, 'Oriental' is still used as a descriptor of all the carpets from the area, and the rugs are an important factor in contemporary interiors.

A fine Oriental is often used as a focal point in a formal residential living area or as an outstanding addition to a corporate boardroom or luxury hotel lobby. A good Oriental rug has the qualities one looks for in a work of art and evokes the same kinds of responses in the viewer. From an aesthetic point of view, the designs are fascinating, the colors are fantastic, and the craftsmanship is stupendous. These rugs have been brought from their lands of origin in the east—Turkey and the eastern shores of the Mediterranean through the Middle East to India and China—to the West because they add life and 'a sense of the exotic' to a space. They are practically indestructible, look good even when well used or extremely old, and are considered to be a good investment. Their popularity continues to grow.

The rugs have distinctive designs, formed by knotting wool or silk yarns onto a woven backing. Two types of knots—the Senna or Sehna (Persian) and the Ghiordes (Turkish)—are used, but there are no visual distinctions on the face of the rugs. Both types of knots are tied to the base warp yarns.

Carpet and Rug Key Terms

RUGS are carpets that can be moved.

ROOM SIZE RUGS are loose rugs that are close to the actual size of the room. A border of 5-30.5 cm (2-12") should be left around the rug, exposing the floor underneath. These rugs are easily moved to accommodate traffic wear and can be moved from room to room more easily than a fixed carpet.

AREA RUGS are available in a variety of sizes, shapes, colors, and textures. Area rugs are either placed on bare floor or used as a decorative rug on top of wall-to-wall carpeting.

RUNNERS are long narrow rugs used in hallways and on stairs. Runners must be secured to the floor when they are used on stairs.

MATS are small rugs.

SCATTER RUGS are small rugs used mainly in residential design. These rugs protect areas where there is heavy traffic (e.g., front entrances) or as decorative accents in a room. These rugs can be a safety hazard or a barrier to wheelchair access. People often trip on these rugs, and wheels can get caught.

CARPET is soft floor covering made in a continuous roll or tile form and intended for permanent installation. Both means of manufacture indicate 'carpeting,' and the terms are used interchangeably by manufacturers, merchants, and the design community.

In all authentic Oriental rugs, each pile tuft is hand knotted. The Sehna knot can be tied either to the left or right, but the direction must be consistent throughout the rug. When other construction features are equal, the Sehna-knotted rug is finer than a Ghiordes-knotted rug, and it has a more sharply defined pattern.

Pile yarns are knotted in horizontal rows, and one or two filling or weft yarns are used in plain-weave interlacing between each crosswise row of pile knots. Increasing the number of filling yarns increases pile density.

The quality of Oriental rugs is determined by the number of yarns per square centimeter (inch). Antique rugs often had yarn densities as high as 78 knots per square centimeter (500 per square inch), while modern rugs range from 16-35 knots per square centimeter (100-225 per square inch), with 50 knots per square centimeter (324 per square inch) found in exceptional cases. Other quality-related factors are **pile height, fiber content**, and **luster level.** While natural dyestuffs used in antique rugs had a subdued, mellow luster, the synthetic dyes developed in the 1850s simplified dyeing and resulted in brighter colors. Chemical treatments will simulate the luster of older rugs but often at the price of degrading the fibers and carpet life.

Oriental rugs display intricate motifs and many colors. Traditionally, the straight-line designs indicated tribal or village source, while curves, floral patterns, medallions, and animals designated town weavers. Historically, weavers produced only their ancestral designs. Today's weavers working for mass-market sales adapt patterns from around the world, so it is not always possible to identify a rug's origin by its design. Modern rugs from Afghanistan and Pakistan incorporate images of tanks, bombs, landscapes, and buildings that tell stories of war (known as **war rugs**). With those rugs, particular motifs and designs act as a signature that can be used to trace the maker to a particular village or refugee camp. Often there is writing along the edges of these rugs that further identify the maker.

Antique rugs were named after the city or area of origin. Many names, such as Kerman, Sarouk, Kazak, Dazvin, Heriz, Serapi, Gorevan, Mehrevan, Tabriz, Meshed, Teheran, Saraband, and Yezd designate particular traditional designs, choice of colors, and material. The basic Oriental patterns are medallion on an open field, medallion on a designed field, and an overall design. Borders take many forms. It is difficult to differentiate between the origins of these carpets and their quality. It is essential, therefore, to seek the advice of well-respected experts before recommending use of an Oriental rug. There are also many authoritative books on the subject. Today, machine-made Oriental-style carpets are available in a wide variety of styles and at reasonable prices from home-improvement stores.

OTHER HAND TECHNIQUE RUGS

Handcrafted rugs of various styles originate in many parts of the world.

SAVONNERIE AND AUBUSSON rugs were first produced in France. They feature classic designs and soft colors and often use hand carving to give texture and emphasize the design. Aubusson rugs use a fine, loop pile.

RYA rugs originate in Scandinavia. These are hand-knotted, long pile, wool rugs made with the Ghiordes knot found in some Oriental rugs. The pile height ranges from 2.5 cm- 7.62 cm (1" to 3"), and is controlled by the length of the rya stick, used in the construction process. Producing a Rya rug by hand is very labor intensive and requires large amounts of wool yarn.

FLOKATI rugs are long pile, hand-pulled, woven, wool structures from Greece. The pile length is controlled by the weaver, and the finished rug is immersed in a deep vat where the wool fibers become felted.

KHILIM (KELIM, KILIM) rugs are nonpile rugs from eastern European countries. They have graceful, stylized designs featuring flowers, animals, and other natural motifs. The construction is similar to tapestry weaving except the ends of all filling yarns are woven in, so the pattern is reversible.

NAVAJO, HOPI, AND CHEYENNE rugs are produced by native North Americans. Since the ends are woven in at each color change, the rugs are reversible. Unlike Khilims, however, the filling yarns are woven to avoid slits. Bold graphic symbols or detailed patterns on these rugs represent tribal life.

DHURRIE (DURRIE, DURRY) rugs are made in India. These nonpile, hand-woven rugs have a plain, twill, or tapestry interlacing. They may display crosswise striations or stylized design.

FLOOR MATS can be composed of various grasses, sisal, coir, linen, hemp, or jute. Often twill interlacing creates diamond, herringbone, and other geometric shapes. Rag rugs are woven in plain-weave interlacing, using rolled and twisted fabric.

MACHINE-MANUFACTURED RUGS

FABRICATED RUGS are produced when pieces of pile carpet are cut, assembled, and carved and/or beveled in a pattern. This method is sometimes used to recycle old carpets that have worn out unevenly.

Once the carpet is removed from the original space there are often meters/yards of usable material left. Sections are cut from the leftover carpet and then pieced together into new designs. This process can be used for custom-designed rugs (with logos, for example).

Machine-woven rugs, such as those made on the Van de Wiele loom, are popular. They provide limitless possibilities of patterns and designs that suit most interiors. They are usually reasonably priced for the quality, and are part of several designer collections.

Carpet Materials and Construction

The use of the word *carpet* to describe a carpet manufactured by modern techniques is somewhat of a misnomer. *Carpet System* is a more accurate term, since there are several components involved. These include the carpet itself (the pile yarns, backings, and adhesives) and the cushion and topical treatments.

Carpet Materials

The material used in carpets is one of the most costly components of the finished product. Since prices of materials tend to fluctuate more sharply than either labor or production, carpeting is considered to be a **material cost-sensitive product.**

THE PILE FIBER is the most important component material; it forms the walking surface, and, thus, it determines the aesthetic and performance value of the carpet. It also has the major impact on cost.

THE PRIMARY BACKING SYSTEM or, in the case of woven carpets, backing yarns, anchor the pile fibers.

A SECONDARY BACKING SYSTEM is often used to lock the pile fibers into the carpet and also to attach the secondary backing system to the main body of the carpet.

AN ADHESIVE SYSTEM is used to lock the pile fibers into the carpet and to attach the secondary backing system to the main body of the carpet.

TOPICAL TREATMENTS are used for specific purposes, such as soil or stain resistance, static control, or anti-microbial protection.

Each of the material components is important, but the type of components used varies with the manufacturing system. For example, Axminster carpet does not require a primary or secondary backing system. Instead, it uses a system of backing yarns.

Construction

Fibers are shipped to manufacturers in one of two forms: staple or continuous filament. **Staple fibers** are shipped in bales; **bulked continuous filament** (BCF) is wound on tubes.

The thickness of the yarn depends on the thickness of the individual fibers and the thickness of the number of fibers in each bundle. The thickness of the bundle can be controlled by winding two or more yarns together to make plied yarns.

The size of BCF yarns is measured in **denier**, which is the weight in grams of 9000 meters of yarn. The amount of twist a yarn has is also important. In general, the more twist, the stronger the yarn, although every yarn has a limit beyond which it will start to twist back on itself (like crimped yarn) and become weaker due to stress and tension.

The three major styles of carpets are:

1. loop pile (uncut pile)
2. cut pile
3. combination of cut and uncut pile

Loop pile carpets are produced with BCF yarn, cut pile uses staple yarns, and cut-uncut may use both forms or just BCF.

The most common manufacturing methods are tufting, fusion bonding, and weaving.

Fusion bonding is only used to make cut pile carpet; tufting and weaving are used to manufacture all types of carpet.

Tufted carpets are used extensively in 95 percent of commercial projects. Loop pile is the most popular tufted carpet style, encompassing 54 percent of the tufted market, followed by cut pile (38 percent), and cut-uncut (8 percent).

Carpet Types

Contemporary carpeting may be divided into seven main types:

1. woven
2. tufted
3. needle punched
4. flocked
5. fusion bonded
6. knitted
7. modular

Needle-punched, flocked, and fusion-bonded carpeting have limited markets.

Woven Carpets

Woven carpets were originally made exclusively of wool. They are now constructed in nylon, acrylics, rayon, polyester, and blends. More and more manufacturers are producing carpets made from recycled fibers—either post consumer or post industrial. Old carpets are deconstructed and reprocessed into polymer chips then spun back into usable fibers for new carpets. Even soda pop bottles are recycled into polyester fibers and used in some carpets. These synthetic fiber carpets feature extremely dense pile on closely woven backing. They are frequently specified for commercial installations and can be produced in custom-designed patterns.

Axminster

A complicated loom is required to weave Axminster carpeting. The backing is heavy jute, cotton, or a manufactured fiber, and forms lengthwise ribs. Spools of yarns deliver the various colors to the weaving area in predetermined patterns. The carpet has a smooth cut-pile surface.

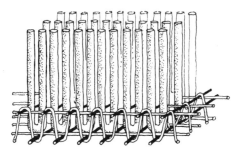

• *Axminster*

Wilton

Wilton carpeting is produced on a jacquard loom and features a variety of surface textures, from level cut pile to multilevel loop pile. Computers are used to control the pattern and feeding of yarns to the pile surface. Yarns are woven one at a time and bury the previous woven yarns, enhancing the carpet's body.

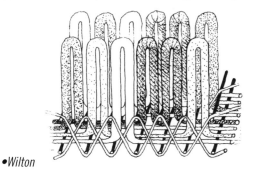

•*Wilton*

Velvet

These carpets are not patterned, but they may feature various colors in an overall tweed look. Textures may be tight and pebbly, cut pile, or multi-loop.

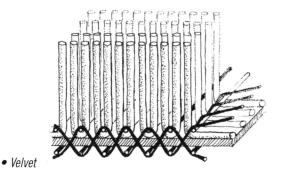

• *Velvet*

Chenille

Chenille carpets were devised in 1839 by James Templeton, from Scotland. The carpets are thick and soft, and can be woven in widths up to 9 meters (30 feet).

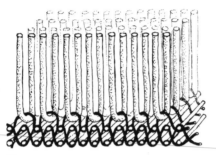

• *Chenille*

Tufted Carpets

Tufting is by far the most common construction method. The tremendous growth in broadloom began in the 1950s and now accounts for approximately 90 percent of all carpet sales.

Manufacture

The tufting process is described under Fabric Construction (see chapter 7). The same method is used to produce tufted carpeting. Wide, multi-needled machines can manufacture 3.65 meter (12 foot) widths in a variety of patterns, gauges, and colors.

LOOP PILE construction results in a surface of continuous loops.

CUT PILE construction has each loop cut as part of the production process, and the surface reveals the cut ends of the yarns.

CUT AND LOOP PILE combines both cut pile and loop pile construction techniques in the same carpeting.

PILE DEPTH is controllable by automatic machine adjustment of two factors:

1. the tension on the feeding yarn

2. the distance between the backing and the loop-catching hooks

PILE DENSITY is a factor in durability and cost, and is a measure of the number of tufts per unit square. This variable is controlled by machine adjustment of the tufting gauge and the stitch rate.

VERSATILITY is an important feature in tufting equipment and allows for a selection of style effects. For an embossed surface, photoelectric cells activate a translucent acetate pattern drum to regulate the yarn supply, resulting in simultaneous construction of a low and high pile. Twist can be introduced at set intervals to give various texture effects. The machinery is also adaptable to a wide range of carpet yarns in any fiber and blend.

BACKING MATERIALS may be jute, cotton, or synthetics. Polypropylene, woven or nonwoven, is the most widely used backing. Backing materials are also made from recycled carpet backing or used car tires. These are broken down and re-processed into new backing material. Jute is still commonly used as a carpet backing.

Needle-Punched Carpets

This system of manufacture is based on the fiber web method of needle felt fabric construction (see Nonwoven Fabrics, chapter 7). Webs of synthesized fibers are crosslaid for adequate strength. The heated barbed needles mounted in the needle board then repeatedly punch the web to produce a firm mass of entangled fibers. The heat melts the fibers, which when cooled, stick together and form a web. Latex is usually applied as a backing.

Needle-punched carpet is the familiar indoor-outdoor type.

Flocked Carpets

The electrostatic flocking process (described in chapter 8) is used to produce this carpeting. Flocking is fast, efficient, and flexible, and contemporary machines are capable of producing more than 15 meters (50 feet) of fabric per minute. The depth of the carpet is determined by the length of the flocks—the chopped pieces of fiber—that are adhered to the backing. Predyed, manufactured fibers are most commonly used for flocked carpets. Natural fibers are also used to a lesser extent, and these fibers may be dyed or printed after production.

Fusion-Bonded Carpets

Pile yarn is inserted directly into liquid vinyl, which locks the yarn in place when it hardens. Fusion-bonded carpets exhibit outstanding tuft lock and a continuous impermeable back. This method can

Carpet Surface Contours

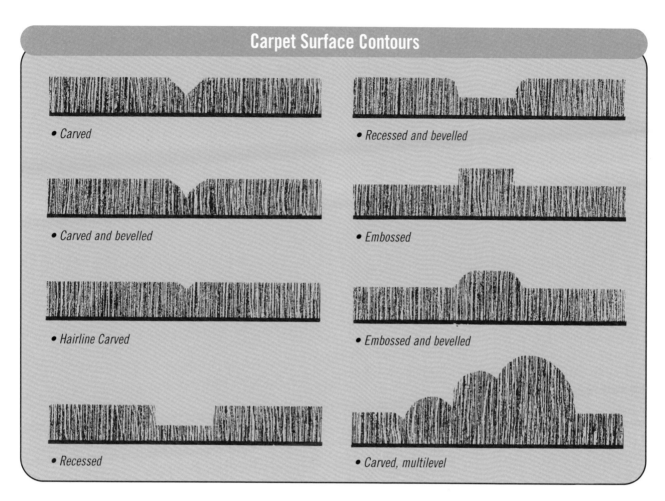

- *Carved*

- *Carved and bevelled*

- *Hairline Carved*

- *Recessed*

- *Recessed and bevelled*

- *Embossed*

- *Embossed and bevelled*

- *Carved, multilevel*

produce solid colors, heather cut piles, and print-base carpeting.

Knitted Carpets

Knitted carpeting is made on a raschel machine. This flexible warp knitter's capacity to stitch and lay-in yarns with multiple control bars produces plush carpets of various densities; textured, patterned, or plain in a wide range of yarns. Knitted carpets are fast and simple to produce and economical in their use of yarn.

Modular Carpet Systems

Computer technology has helped make modular carpets possible. Customers can create their own carpets. Once a product is chosen from a manufacturer offering this process, a base construction and color are chosen. One design and up to five overprint colors are specified (company logo, for instance), and colors are assigned to each element of the design. The specifier receives carpet samples and a photographic image of

the carpet design as it would appear in the actual interior before shipment, to confirm the details. Custom-carpet designs can now be produced much more easily than in the past.

Carpet Tiles

Carpet tiles, or squares, are often an excellent alternative to continuous carpeting. Carpet tiles have been improved greatly since their introduction in the 1960s, and now offer greater dimensional stability, ravel resistance, and appearance retention qualities. Carpet tiles are available in cut pile, level loop, and cut-uncut constructions.

Pressure-sensitive adhesives have helped increase the popularity of carpet tiles; the tiles can be anchored firmly and still allow easy replacement. These properties make carpet tiles a recommended choice for some installations—for instance, when floor access is necessary or in extreme traffic pattern situations.

Tufted Carpet Pile Variations

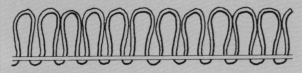

Level loop pile is formed with loops of yarn of uniform height. It usually has a tight, dense surface and may be solid color, multicolored or printed. Usually made of continuous filament yarn, it is durable and easy to maintain.

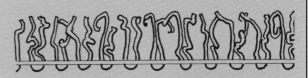

Hardtwist, or frieze pile is formed of tightly twisted, heat-set yarns, either of staple or continuous filament fibers. It has a somewhat shaggy appearance, but with greater durability and resilience. It has good soil hiding characteristics and is easily maintained.

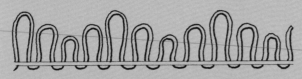

Multi-level loop pile is formed of at least two levels of loops to produce random patterns, ripples or ribs. It has better soil hiding characteristics than level loop, but is slightly less durable as the longer loops take a disproportionate share of wear. It is usually constructed of continuous filament yarn.

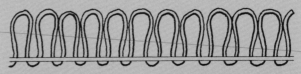

Level tip shear pile has both loops and cut pile at a uniform height. It combines the long-wearing practicality of level loops with some of the luxuriant qualities of plush. It may be made of staple or continuous filament yarn.

Plush pile has all loops cut to a uniform height, giving a more luxurious appearance than loop piles. Shading the apparent change of color depending on the direction of the pile—may occur in plush carpeting. Usually made of staple fiber yarns, it requires more regular and thorough maintenance but it is long wearing. Plush pile is also called saxony or velvet. The plush surface may also be cut to form various surface contours.

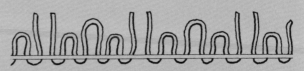

Random shear pile is a variation of the multi-level loop, but may be constructed of staple or continuous filament yarns, with the highest loops sheared to form cut pile. The texture is similar to multi-level loop, and it may be similarly patterned.

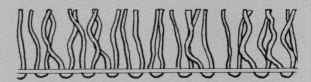

Cut and loop pile may be similar in texture to random shear, or it may present a carved or sculptured appearance. It is made of either staple or continuous filament yarns.

Shag pile has long cut tufts and is less dense than plush. It is subject to shading and crushing. Although it hides soil and footprints, it is time-consuming to maintain. Even in low usage residential areas, its popularity is limited. It may be constructed of spun or continuous filament yarns.

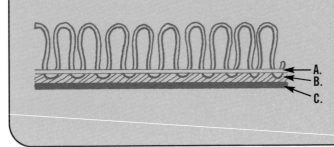

A.
B.
C.

Backing on tufted carpet generally consists of two of three separate layers. The primary backing **(a)** is the pre-formed fabric into which the tufts are stitched; **(b)** represents a latex of thermoplastic layer which is heat set onto the primary backing to lock the tufts in place. These two layers may complete the backing, or a third layer **(c)** may be added. It is called the secondary backing abd can be pre-formed fabric, either natural of manufactured, or a foam material.

User Requirements

The use of carpeting in spaces formerly reserved for hard-surface flooring has been made possible by the increased range of fibers, engineering of fibers, and manufacturing techniques. The scope of possible application leads to an even wider range of aesthetic and performance requirements.

Basic Considerations

Some basic considerations for carpet use are:

- location
- usage
- visual pleasure
- comfort
- noise level
- maintenance
- initial costs and life-cycle costs

Location

Applications for carpeting have extended so greatly that soft surface flooring can be installed almost anywhere—indoors and out. Interior use is not restricted to selected areas in residences, offices, stores, schools, restaurants, and institutions; it has moved into kitchens, bathrooms, stockrooms, school hallways, and restaurant service areas, and onto walls. With easy-care carpet (treated for microorganism control and stain resistance) available, carpeting is now used in hospitals, care facilities, and food-service areas.

Usage

Usage dictates the type of carpeting installed. There is, for instance, a significant difference in use between a residential bedroom and the public areas of a large bank.

Visual Pleasure

This factor is a matter of aesthetics. The **elements of design**—color, texture, line, area, and scale—must be successfully applied with regard for the **principles of design**—harmony, balance, order, rhythm, and emphasis. All of these factors must be considered to obtain the desired 'character' and fit between the aesthetics of the carpet and the aesthetics of the space—its volume, furniture, and fitments.

Visual pleasure is a matter of individual preference. Generally speaking, however, a carpet that can maintain a neat appearance is preferable to one that shows overall grime, shedding, pile shading, or browning (becoming flattened and off-color) in traffic paths. The quality and color of the carpet must be appropriate to the location and end use in order to be maintained in a clean, like-new condition.

Comfort

Compared to hard-surface flooring, any carpet is more comfortable to walk on and stand upon. Carpeting adds comfort and helps to reduce fatigue. The desired degree of comfort depends on personal preference and realistic appraisal of the area to be carpeted. The degree of comfort depends on the type of subflooring, the choice of underpadding, and the type and quality of the carpeting.

SUBFLOORING dictates the degree of comfort in some applications. If nonpiled carpeting is glued to concrete or other hard surface, it will certainly be more comfortable to the user than a hard surface, but the major benefit will be in acoustic control rather that comfort.

UNDERPADDING has a great effect; even the highest-quality pile carpet is made much more resilient with suitable padding.

CARPET TYPES vary from very thin and nearly solid, through tightly woven low-looped pile, to thick, dense, and luxurious cut pile. Comfort varies accordingly.

Noise Level

An enormous acoustic benefit results when **impact noise** and **surface noise** (footsteps, furniture movement) are reduced with carpeting. In addition, carpeting muffles **airborne sound** within an area: equipment noise (music systems, printers, copiers), activity noise (food preparation, eating), and conversation. Applications such as classrooms, open offices, healthcare facilities, restaurants, and so on are sources of their own 'noise,' and the acoustic insulating properties of the proposed carpeting system should be assessed accordingly.

Any carpet is effective for acoustic control, absorbing a minimum of 10 percent of airborne noise. The degree of sound-deadening depends on the carpet type, carpet backing, and underlay.

CARPETS with dense pile and those with deep pile absorb sound very well. A deep, dense piled carpet is, therefore, the best for sound deadening.

BACKINGS of woven wool, jute, cotton, or kraft cord add to acoustic effectiveness. Latex backings have a lower noise-reduction coefficient.

Foam may be applied as a secondary backing. Urethane or other foamed material is laminated to the carpet back and forms an effective cushion for applications where no separate underlay is possible, such as in direct glue-down operations.

UNDERLAYS make a difference in sound muffling, with thick foam rubber, urethane, foam, and hair felt being most effective.

Maintenance

This is a factor in appearance and cost effectiveness as well as a concern in its own right. Particulars of maintenance and cleaning are dealt with later in this section; however, the issue must be considered at the time of specification. Obvious maintenance concerns are color selection, fiber choice, carpet construction, and placement of the carpet. The requirements of use and location determine the range of choices available for suitable maintenance.

Maintenance of many of the new manufactured fiber carpets, particularly those with the absence of pile, is almost as routine as hard-surface flooring. High-power vacuums and Wet-Vac® systems are effective in removing even tracked-in street dirt.

Costs

Cost effectiveness is a performance factor relating to value: the investment in carpeting is a large one, and initial cost, installation, maintenance, and expected life span must be taken into careful consideration based on needs of the user and the

requirements of the space. The life-cycle costs of installing and maintaining carpeting are competitive with many hard-surface floorings. In extremely hard-use areas, carpeting does not have the staying power of slate, ceramic, or heavy-duty vinyl with a comparable degree of care, but is considerably less expensive than these surfaces and can be replaced as needed. If acoustic control, accident prevention, or glare reduction is important, a good argument can be made for frequent replacement of industrial-style carpeting as opposed to a lifetime investment in one of the extremely durable hard-surface floorings.

An important part of the life-cycle cost of carpeting is its removal and recycling. Many manufacturers—like DuPont's Carpet Reclamation® program—routinely remove and recycle old carpet, and the industry has embraced this practice. CARE[sm] (Carpet America Recovery Effort) is a joint industry and government effort in the United States to recycle and reuse carpet in order to reduce waste going to the landfill. (See chapter 2 for more information on this topic.)

In normal-use areas, consumers generally opt for the quietness, comfort, insulation, and visual warmth of carpeting, and here investment in quality and in underpadding is undoubtedly a good one.

Performance Criteria

The performance of any carpeting depends on the fiber(s) selected, the method of construction, and the funcltional qualities of the finished product. Undercushioning and installation affect performance as well, and these factors are addressed later in this chapter.

Fiber Selection

A review of the programming for any project will reveal the major functional requirements, traffic levels, environmental conditions, thermal and acoustical needs, maintenance, and costs. Determining the fiber best suited to these needs should be the first selection decision, before yarn and carpet construction factors are considered.

Fibers used in carpets for contract interiors include:

- wool: has a small but stable part of the market
- nylon: in staple or bulked continuous fiber is the most popular choice

Performance Checklist: Carpeting and Rugs

TYPE OF TRAFFIC

- ☐ Light
- ☐ Medium
- ☐ Heavy
- ☐ Foot Traffic
- ☐ Wheel Traffic

USE

- ☐ Concentrated Traffic Patterns
- ☐ Stairs
- ☐ Ramps
- ☐ Age of Users
- ☐ Special Activities
- ☐ Food and Drink Service
- ☐ Healthcare Facility
- ☐ Fixed Furniture
- ☐ Movable Furniture

ENVIRONMENTAL CONDITIONS

- ☐ Exposure to Natural Light
- ☐ Exposure to Artificial Light
- ☐ Exposure to Fluorescent Light
- ☐ Exposure to Incandescent

Exposure to Humidity:

- ☐ Consistent
- ☐ Changeable

HEALTH AND SAFETY

Flammability:

- ☐ Sprinklers
- ☐ Other Fire Prevention Systems
- ☐ Smoking Permitted
- ☐ Off-Gas Factors

ACOUSTICS

- ☐ Control of Airborne Noise
- ☐ Control of Impact Noise

Acoustic Issues re: Theatrical Performances

- ☐ Speeches
- ☐ Presentations
- ☐ Concentration of Seating

INSULATION

- ☐ Subfloor
- ☐ Necessary Access to Subfloor
- ☐ Importance of Pattern as a Design Feature
- ☐ Carpet Seaming re: Traffic Pattern
- ☐ Off-Gas Issues

STATIC

Static-Control Issues:

- ☐ Human Comfort
- ☐ Equipment (computers or other equipment)

MAINTENANCE

- ☐ Installation at Street Level
- ☐ Control of Walk-Off Traffic

Maintenance Program:

- ☐ Daily
- ☐ Weekly
- ☐ Emergency Spot Removal Program

LIFE-CYCLE ISSUES

- ☐ Maintenance Schedules
- ☐ Replacement Schedule

ENVIRONMENTAL SUSTAINABILITY ISSUES

- ☐ Recycling Programs Available
- ☐ Reuse Programs Available

- acrylic: is used to a small degree and in fiber blends with nylon

- polyester: fibers are primarily used in the residential sector

The material used in a carpet is one of the most costly components of its production. The types of materials (fibers) have a major impact on the overall cost and also reflect on the performance.

Wool was once the most popular carpet fiber. Increased demand for carpeting has meant synthetic fibers have largely replaced wool as the most commonly used fiber for floor covering. Wool has many good qualities. It is highly resistant to greasy stains, both because the stains show less and are comparatively easy to remove from wool. Abrasion resistance is good. Fuzzing may be a problem with new carpet, but the shed fibers are easily removed, and wool carpets may wear nearly threadbare and still retain their appearance. Wool is inherently, initially, fire resistant.

Nylon is an exceptional carpet fiber. Manufactured in a variety of cross sections, it has good opacity, nice sheen and hand, excellent colorfastness, bulk without weight, and excellent recovery from crushing. Continuous filament nylon is inherently resistant to pilling and shedding. Staple cut nylon fibers, manufactured in round cross section with microscopic voids within the fiber, are used in a blend of deniers in cut pile carpets.

Nylon 6 and nylon 6,6 are the most popular types of nylon for carpeting. Nylon 6,6 is stronger than any natural fiber and very lightweight. Nylon can be manufactured in a variety of strengths depending on the end use. It also has good resiliency, compressibility, and heat resistance. Nylon 6,6 derives its name from its molecular structure. It is a combination of adipic acid and hexamethylene diamide (HMD), each of which have six carbon atoms.

Nylon 6,6 originally had poor antistatic properties, but addition of a carbon-core fiber to each yarn

Fiber Selection for Carpets

Multicolored carpet yarn construction showing the plied look where three or more colored yarns are twisted together. Each color remains quite clearly defined. The heather look is achieved by entangling colored filaments. Multiple colors may be used and the result is an integrated color union, or 'heather effect.'

• *Plied*   • *Heathered*

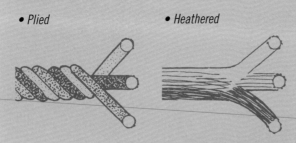

Fibers for carpet yarns are similar to those for cloth yarns but are generally of greater weight and, in the case of synthetic fibers, have a larger cross section, which gives them greater crush resistance. Carpet fibers look very much alike, but their properties vary greatly.

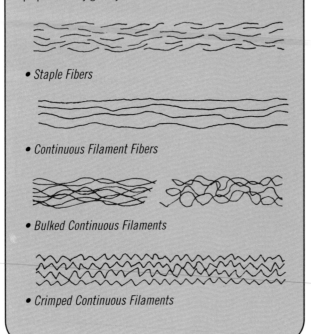

• *Staple Fibers*

• *Continuous Filament Fibers*

• *Bulked Continuous Filaments*

• *Crimped Continuous Filaments*

Modacrylic carpeting uses mechanically crimped staple cut fiber. It has excellent weather and fire resistance.

Polypropylene (Olefin) fibers are widely used for indoor/outdoor carpets and as an alternate to jute for carpet backing.

Polyester is a relatively new fiber for carpet use. It has good durability, good crush resistance, and high resistance to waterborne soils. Polyester is often successfully blended with nylon for carpeting.

Carpet yarns are usually either plied (multiple ends twisted together) or heathered (more than one fiber entangled).

Producers have modified yarns, especially nylon, to improve appearance retention and maintain performance. The chemical structure has not been altered, however, so durability, resilience, and flammability have not changed. Blending fibers can improve overall performance, but individual constituents must comprise at least 20 percent to have any significant effect.

A major advantage of manufactured fibers is the ability to control the fiber's physical properties. Because of its unique combination of properties, nylon has captured over 80 percent of the market share.

Construction

The factors for consideration are:

- yarn count
- yarn structure (ply, sinlge, cord)
- carpet construction

YARN COUNT is the fineness or coarseness of the finished yarn and is measured by two systems:

- Woolen count refers to the number of running yards in 1 ounce of finished yarn.
- Denier count refers to the yarn weight, measured in grams based, on a standard 9000 meter length of yarn.

YARN PLY refers to the number of single yarns that are twisted together to form one plied yarn. Manufactured fiber yarns may be twisted in a continuous filament. Yarns given added fullness by various means are called *bulked yarns*.

bundle has provided permanent static dissipation ability. Other improvements have been in dyeing properties and colorfastness.

Acrylic carpet fibers are staple cut, mechanically crimped, or of bicomponent self-crimping. Acrylic fibers have very good durability and good crush recovery, and are usually modified in the solution stage for fire retardance.

CARPET CONSTRUCTION is based on density factors. These are accumulated by the following measurements:

- Stitches or tufts per square measure refers to the count of stitches or tufts per square inch or centimeter. The more stitches per square inch or centimeter, the denser the carpet.

- Gauge is the distance between rows of tufts across the width of a tufted carpet.

- Pitch is the distance between rows of tufts in a woven carpet, but is counted on a 68.6 cm width (27-inch).

Strength

The strength of a carpet structure has a great deal to do with overall durability. Strength comes from a combination of factors.

PILE HEIGHT refers to the distance from the backing to the top of the yarn. Generally, a lower pile height requires more stitches per centimeter (inch) to obtain adequate coverage.

PILE WEIGHT, or face weight, is the weight of pile yarns and is measured, in the industry, in ounces per square yard. The **finished pile weight** includes the pile and all backing fabrics.

PILE DENSITY may be obtained by the following formula:

36" **x** finished pile weight in ounces per yard **divided** by the average pile height in inches

Alternatively, the stitches per centimeter (inch) and the gauge or pitch may be assessed. Visually, the density can be estimated by bending the carpet sample. Whether the backing can be seen and by how much are good indications of density.

CONSTRUCTION STRENGTH is based on:

- **tuft bind:** how firmly the tufts are secured to the carpet back

- **delamination strength:** a measure of how well the secondary (laminated) backing is adhered to the primary backing

- **dry breaking strength:** how well a sample withstands mechanical pulling force.

Carpet manufacturers mechanically test the strength, and test results are available to design professionals for assessment purposes.

Abrasion Resistance

This is perhaps the most important factor in durability. Resistance to abrasion depends on:

- the carpet fiber

- the thickness and twist of the yarns

- the density of the pile

CARPET FIBERS rated in order of resistance to abrasion are nylon polyester and olefins, acrylic, modacrylic, and wool.

YARN THICKNESS AND TWIST: The thicker the yarn, the better the abrasion resistance. Twisted yarns expose less continuous fiber surface to abrasion.

DENSITY of the pile is naturally a factor—the more yarns, the less total abrasion.

Compression Resiliency

This is the capacity of carpet fibers and yarns to return to their original shape after compression. Heavy traffic and furniture legs exert a crushing force on carpets. In overall recovery, nylon recovers best, wool second, then acrylic and polyester. Recent research and development with polyester as a carpet fiber have improved its performance in general, and polyester is expected to become more widely used.

Appearance Retention

The major factors in appearance are:

- soiling

- stain resistance

- shedding and fading

- crush resistance (mentioned above)

SOILING is strongly fiber dependent and has two elements: real and apparent.

Real soil is the deposit of dust, dirt, and grime on fibers. Soil is naturally more visible on pale colors than on neutral or dark colors. Soil retention is also affected by the electrostatic properties of fibers. A buildup of static causes dirt to be attracted and cling to the fibers.

Apparent soil is a term used for the magnification of real soil that occurs when deposited on individual manufactured fibers that are nearly transparent, as is some nylon. Round fibers are the only ones subject to apparent soil, as the dirt shows through easily and is

Soil-Hiding Synthetic Fibers

The first synthetic fibers were produced in round, smooth filaments. As these filaments were often nearly transparent, soil that collected on one surface was magnified and appeared on all surfaces. The phenomenon is called 'apparent soil.'

Several methods have been introduced to overcome apparent soil. Additionally, reshaping the filament's cross-sectional contour was discovered to have an effect on the fiber's ability to shed soil.

• *Clear Round Filament*

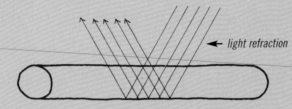

← *light refraction*

Color added to the round filament helped in overcoming the magnification of soil. However, a somewhat chalky appearance was the result of the opaque pigment. As well, eventual soil buildup made the carpet look very dirty.

• *Colored Round Filament*

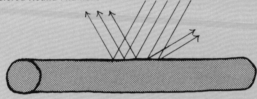

This modification mimicked the soil-hiding efficiency of wool. The filament was produced with lengthwise voids in the round fiber surface. While it was successful in hiding soil initially, the carpet darkened greatly when dampened, and re-soiling after cleaning was faster than before cleaning.

• *Treated Fiber With Voids*

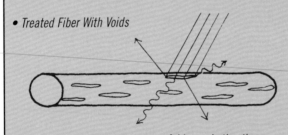

This development was very successful in combating the magnification phenomenon. With sustained use, however, the indentations trap and hold soil.

• *Multilobal Filament*

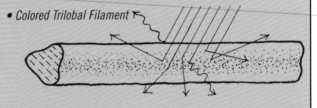

This variation of a multilobal filament eliminates the indentations found in other trilobal fibers, exposing less soil-trapping surface.

• *Colored Trilobal Filament*

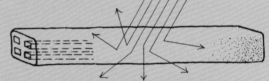

A popular cross-sectional shape is the round-cornered square. The smooth surface does not trap soil. The longitudinal tunnels refract light from the inner surfaces and avoid the apparent soil effect.

• *Square With Longitudinal Tunnels*

Four-hole hollow filament fiber (such as DuPont Antron®) minimizes the surface area. The smooth, uniform surface with round corners means there are no crevices where dirt can attach. The hollow interior (four hollow channels) diffuses and refracts light to hide soil.

magnified by the fiber's contour. Carpet fibers made more opaque by a change in cross-sectional dyeing methods show less apparent soil. Using delusterants sometimes assists by making the fiber seem more opaque, but these may also give the carpet fibers a more chalky appearance. The problem of apparent soil is well known and manufactured carpet fibers now have a trilobal or other cross-sectional shape. In addition, nylon carpet fibers are now generally manufactured with voids within the fiber that scatter light and make see-through magnification impossible (e.g., Antron® by DuPont).

STAIN RESISTANCE is most effective when it is fiber dependent. If staining is a possibility, the types of anticipated stain must be matched to the type or types of fiber that are both best able to withstand them and recover from stain-removal techniques. Applied stain-resistant finishes can be effective but need thorough investigation and testing by the mill/supplier to ensure the quality of the finish and application.

SHEDDING is a problem with carpet yarns made from staple fibers. Some shedding is to be expected. Depending on the fiber type, this may be temporary and easily removed or too persistent and difficult to remove. Continuous filament fibers are inherently resistant to shedding.

COLORFASTNESS is the term used to indicate resistance to fading. Fading can be of two types: **on-tone fading** and **off-tone fading**. In on-tone fading, the color fades to a lighter shade; in off-tone fading, the fiber actually changes color, such as from dark blue to light green.

Fading can occur if a carpet is exposed to sunlight, air pollution, or frequent and extensive wet cleaning. Use of improper cleaning agents is one of the major causes. Crocking, the mechanical removal of dye from fibers by pedestrian or wheeled traffic, also causes fading. Manufacturers' tests are sources of information for these particular situations.

Colorfastness to light is measured by a Fade-0-Meter. Carpet samples are exposed to high-intensity xenon arc lamps for predetermined periods. Afterwards the samples are compared to a standard gray scale to determine how much fading has occurred.

Colorfastness can be enhanced at the design stage by selecting dyes and fibers that are resistant to fading. In general, acid dyes are more resistant to fading than cationic dyes. Fibers with a dense molecular structure resist fading better than less dense fibers. Nylon 6,6 is one fiber with high molecular density, which explains its wide usage in carpeting.

HEALTH AND SAFETY ISSUES

Clients will have certain specific requirements of the carpet system for the benefit of the day-to-day users. The design team should be prepared to use the following points to identify the best solution for the particular application.

Fire Safety

In any carpet specification, **flame retardance** is an essential consideration whether regulated by law or not.

The increased use of carpet in commercial buildings has raised the issue of flame resistance. Carpets need to be self-extinguishing and have the ability to shrink away from a flame. There are two tests for determining resistance to flame spread:

- Methenamine Tablet Test
- Radiant Floor Panel Test

Methenamine Tablet Test

In this test, eight carpet samples of identical size and shape are placed in test chambers. A methenamine tablet is placed on each sample and ignited. The samples are allowed to burn until they self-extinguish, and the burnt area of each sample is measured. If two or more samples have burned for three inches in any direction, the carpet fails the test.

Radiant Floor Panel Test

In this testing technique, samples of a carpeting system are placed in a test chamber, and a radiant heat panel is placed above one end of the sample. The distance that the sample burns is measured, and the **Critical Radiant Flux** (CRF) is calculated. Each system is tested three times and an average CRF is calculated. The higher the CRF, the greater the flame resistance.

The Methenamine Tablet Test is used to evaluate carpets to be used in rooms and other locations besides corridors. The Radiant Floor Panel technique is for corridors. Nylon 6,6 offers high-flame resistance and the highest melting point of all manufactured fibers.

Fatigue Reduction

A carpet's compressibility determines the degree to which the impact of walking is absorbed and cushioned. For users of the space who will spend most of the day walking or standing, this factor is important. The cushioning effect will reduce fatigue, lessen orthopedic and back strain, and thus increase the user's productivity and satisfaction.

Safety

Safety needs to be one of the main considerations when specifying carpets. A soft floor covering may reduce injury and frequency of falling.

Compressibility of the carpet along with low, dense pile increase the margin of safety from injuries such as falling or tripping; if a fall does occur, the severity is lessened. Users with mobility or sight problems also benefit from this type of carpet as it provides a glare-free, slip-resistant surface for persons using canes, walkers, or wheelchairs. All seams and edges must be securely anchored.

Static Control

Static electricity in carpeting may be an occasional annoyance or continuing concern. In some situations—computer and data processing areas, care facilities where oxygen or heart monitors are used—its control is of vital importance.

In electrical terms, **conductors** are substances that offer little resistance to the flow of electricity. They do not generate or hold static. **Insulators** are nonconductors—substances that offer very high resistance to current flow. Insulators are, therefore, the prime targets for static buildup.

STATIC ELECTRICITY is so named because it remains stationary (or static) on some surfaces rather than flowing through as an electrical current. When materials that are carrying dissimilar charges (negative or positive) are brought into contact or close proximity, the excess of electrons jumps to the grounded or less charged object, causing the characteristic jolt or spark.

STATIC GENERATION in carpets is based on fiber and pile type, backing, atmospheric conditions, and the types of materials in contact with the carpet.

> **Fibers:** Fibers with no moisture content or ability to absorb moisture are poor conductors. They offer more resistance to electrical current flow and are more susceptible to static buildup. Hydrophilic fibers (those that absorb moisture) are better conductors and less prone to static accumulation in the presence of sufficient humidity. Cut pile generates more static than loop pile.

> **Carpet Backings:** Carpet backings may be made into better conductors by the addition of carbon or metal fibers.

> **Atmospheric Conditions:** When relative humidity is 50 percent or higher, static is seldom a problem.

CONTACT MATERIALS: Leather shoe soles and rubber heels usually generate more static than other types, but this depends on the carpet fiber as well. Steel and plastic furniture tend to generate static, especially in low-humidity.

EXTRA SENSITIVITY: Computers are particularly sensitive to static. Static discharges may occur on the equipment frames or the machine's high speed, or frictional action may attract sparks from across a room. Incorrect data entries, memory data changes, and malfunctioning terminal displays on computers have all been linked to static. **Flammable** or **explosive materials** need protection from static discharge. Ground conductors protect areas where these materials are stored or used. The designer must be aware of the problem in case it is overlooked at a later date (for instance, the renovation of a hospital area with the addition of carpeting).

CONTROL METHODS include increasing humidity and introducing conductive materials to the carpet. One of the first techniques used to control static was the addition of a conductive compound (such as polyethylene glycol) to the polymer solution prior to extrusion. Fine metal filaments can be incorporated into the fiber, or nylon filaments can be coated with a conductive material such as silver. Some manufacturers use the conductive properties of carbon black to produce nonuniform filament structures. One such application is a filament comprised of a carbon black core with a sheath of nylon. In another application, a round carbon black filament is plied with trilobal nylon in proportions of 95% nylon and 5% carbon to form a yarn bundle. Conductive materials are also added to latex and backings to provide a conductive underlayer that prevents pooling of static charges.

The effectiveness of coating fibers diminishes over time as traffic wears the conductive layer off. Metal filaments can break with repeated bending or compressions, which can also limit effectiveness. Adding conductive material to backings and latex is expensive, and there are concerns about negative effects on tuft bind and secondary backing adhesion. The most reliable control technique available now is the sheathed carbon core, since the nylon protects the conductive material and prevents it from being washed or worn away. It is also the least visually obtrusive option.

Sanitation

Carpet in healthcare facilities is a comparatively recent phenomenon. Careful research comparing bacteria growth in carpets to hard-surface flooring indicates that vacuuming carpets reduces the number of bacteria present in hospital settings, while wet mopping resilient flooring actually fosters bacteria growth in dirt-clogged seams. Years of testing have led to safe use of carpeting in hospital and nursing home corridors and patients' rooms.

Benefits of carpeting in these institutions are:

- increased safety for patients
- noise level reduction
- lower maintenance costs
- better appearance
- thermal advantages
- better bacteria control

Comparing specifications is a necessary part of the carpet selection process.

Cost Effectivness

Cost effectiveness is a performance factor relating to value. The investment in carpeting is a large one and includes:

- initial cost
- installation costs
- maintenance costs

INITIAL COST: The number of meters or yards required is multiplied by the dollar cost per square meter or yard. Extra material is required for matching pattern repeats, direction of nap, etc. In advertisements, carpeting is often quoted in per square meter/foot prices, in order to compare it with hard-surface and resilient flooring.

INSTALLATION COSTS: These include labor to install the carpet and cushion, cost of installation materials, and cost for floor preparation in advance of installation. Costs may be estimated as a total price or as a price per square meter or yard.

MAINTENANCE COSTS: These include the cost of care over a specified time period to keep the carpet clean and attractive. The largest portion of this cost is labor. Equipment and supplies need to be factored in as well.

Cushions

The structure placed between the carpet and the floor is known by many names—cushion, pad, padding, lining, foundation, underlayment—but the terms **cushion** and **carpet cushion** are most descriptive. Cushions vary widely in properties and the benefits they contribute to the carpeting system. Some cushions can only be used separately, while others can either be separate or permanently attached to the carpet backing.

The type of cushioning depends on:

- the type of carpet selected
- the "feel" preferred underfoot
- environmental and traffic conditions
- cost

Cushions fall into three broad categories:

1. fibrous cushions
2. cellular rubber
3. urethane foam

In areas where low traffic is anticipated, a low-density cushion could be selected for greater comfort. In high-traffic areas, a thin, high-density structure should be used. It should be remembered that a high-quality cushion will not compensate for a low-quality carpet, and vice-versa.

Cushioning Requirements

Traffic Classification

The amount of wear a carpet and cushion installation receives is perhaps the most important consideration. **Heavy traffic** is expected in entrance foyers and halls in commercial buildings, hotels, schools, etc. If the traffic is constant, day and night, and if carts, for example, are wheeled through, as in hospital entries and transportation terminals, the classification would be **extra-heavy traffic**. **Medium traffic** and **light traffic** areas are other classifications.

Note must also be taken of considerations such as the type of traffic, where the raffic is coming from (e.g., from the street), and factors such as spillage or staining from icy, salt-treated sidewalks.

Acoustic Control

Noise levels and, if applicable, any other noise-reducing components in the space must be evaluating. These factors should be considered in conjunction with the user's anticipated sound-deadening expectations.

Thermal Consideration

Carpeting/cushioning combinations contribute to insulating value on a varying scale. The relative importance of this factor must be considered. Cushioning also adds insulation from noise, especially between floors.

Life Span

Carpet life is extended with cushioning by up to 50 percent. A cushion prevents loss of carpet thickness due to abrasion, pile crushing, and the cutting and fraying of fibers that occur as dirt is ground in. Carpet maintenance is also assisted by a cushion, which allows more effective vacuuming. Cushioning also adds insulation to a room—from both noise (between floors) and extreme temperatures. Rooms are more comfortable when carpets have adequate cushioning.

Installation Assistance

Cushions may be effectively used as a camouflage for less-than-perfect flooring—cracks, nail holes, trowel marks. Over time, such surface imperfections have a tendency to show through uncushioned carpet. Cushions permit carpet installation without repair of these faults.

Cushion Types

Three types of carpet padding, and many subtypes, guarantee a wide selection of cushioning materials for different needs and situations.

Fibrous Felt

Carpet felts are formed either by heat and agitation of natural fibers or, more commonly today, by needle-punching. Felts provide a very firm, dense cushion for heavy, moderate, and light traffic classifications. Antimicrobial agents are recommended, and because the fibers are subject to moisture damage, latex sheets are recommended as protective barriers if below-grade installations are planned. The surfaces of the fibrous batts and latex sheets are usually embossed for skid resistance and to compensate for low compressibility and resiliency. Felts are available in various weights, from about 1200-3200 grams per square meter (32-86 ounces per square yard) and in widths up to 3.7 meters (12 feet).

HAIR FELT is composed of 100% animal hair, usually washed cattle hair.

COMBINATION FELT is made of animal hair and other compatible fibers.

FIBER FELT is composed of manufactured fibers.

RUBBERIZED FELT may be any one of the above with the addition of a rubber coating on one or both sides.

Sponge and Foam Rubber

Cellular rubber cushions can be either foam or sponge rubber, and may be manufactured of natural or synthetic rubber with various fillers and a 'blowing agent' that forms the characteristic cells. Recently, car tires have been reclaimed and recycled to use as carpet cushioning as part of sustainability efforts in building design. The cellular structure is responsible for the buoyancy and softness of the cushion, and this aspect is enhanced if a three-dimensional structure—often called waffle, ripple, or bubble sponge—is used. Sponge cushions produce the plushness often sought for residential applications, but they do not stand up to heavy commercial traffic. In addition, the clay or ash fillers might grind against other components and cause crumbling.

Foam rubber contains smaller cells and is, therefore, firmer. The smaller cells can contribute to odor retention, a factor to consider where spills are likely. A spunbonded fabric is applied to the top of foam and sponge rubber cushions to facilitate installation.

Sponge and foam rubber are available in 3.7 m (12 feet) widths. Sponge rubber weights range from 1535-4500 g/sq.m (41-120 oz/sq.yd.), in thicknesses from 1.6-8 mm (1/16" - 5/16").

FLAT SPONGE is formed in a continuous sheet and has a smooth surface.

WAFFLED SPONGE is formed and then expanded on a chain belt to form the desired rippled or waffled surface.

FOAM RUBBER is a medium-weight padding that provides a good degree of firmness. It is manufactured in flat sheets from a latex rubber base that is natural, synthetic, or a blend. Weights are from 1086-2168 g/m (28-65 oz/sq./yd.). Thickness varies from 3.2-15.9 mm (1/8-5/8").

Urethane Foam

Urethane foam is manufactured by various methods and provides padding to suit light to heavy traffic.

PRIME URETHANE FOAM is manufactured by mixing polymeric materials and curing in blocks. The blocks are cut into sheets of various thicknesses (6.4-19.1 mm or 1/4-3/4") and densities, and a facing is applied to one or each side. Prime urethane foam has comparatively large, ellipse-shaped cells, and the foam struts are vertically aligned. Density determines the compressibility. Under load, these structures may 'bottom out,' a term referring to the flattening of the cushion. These foams may contain powdered fillers and polymer additives for stability.

DENSIFIED PRIME URETHANE FOAM has a modified structure, with various densities controlled by cellular configuration. The cellular structure is finer, more elongated, and has somewhat horizontal struts. No fillers are used. These cushions offer improved resiliency and resistance to bottoming out. The foam is formed and then cut into rolls of the desired thickness, and a facing material is added

to one side. Thickness varies from 6.4-19.1 mm (1/4-3/4").

BONDED URETHANE FOAM is made from trimmed waste material of prime urethane foam. The term **rebond** is sometimes used to describe these cushions. The foam is granulated and bonded together in blocks, sheets, or rolls. Some debris may be used as additives—vinyl, fabric-backed foam, wood chips, paper—and coloring may be added. Designers should not permit a debris content of over 1 percent, and they should be cautious that added color is not of a type that may bleed into the carpet.

Cushion Specifications

While specification listings for cushions are less extensive than those typically prepared for carpets and rugs, they still must detail the composition, construction, and performance features. In some cases, the designer must specify test methods and levels of performance to ensure that the cushion conforms to legal requirements. In other cases, the data is required to facilitate decisions based on anticipated traffic conditions and other factors. Sample specifications are provided below.

Specification for Attached Latex Foam Cushions

Weight ....38 oz/sq.yd.

Thickness ....1/8"

Density ....17lb/cu.ft.

Compression Loss ....Max. of 15% loss

Compression Deflection ....Not less than 5 psi
    (pounds per square inch)

Delamination Strength ....2 lb/in.

Accelerated Aging
(a) Heat aging: 24 hours at 135°C (275°F); after flexing, should remain flexible and serviceable.

(b) Fade-O-Meter aging: 20 hours exposure; sample should show only slight crazing.

Ash Content..............................Maximum of 50%

—Courtesy of the Carpet and Rug Institute

Specifications for Densified Prime Urethane Foam

Coating ....Spunbonded polypropylene olefin

Density ....5.0 lb/cu.ft.

Thickness ....0.265 inch

Compressive Load

  Deflection..........25% deflection: 1.5 psi minimum

          65% deflection: 6.5 psi minimum

          75% deflection: 11.0 psi minimum

Compression Set ....Maximum of 15% at
                     50% deflection

Tensile Strength ....25 psi minimum

Elongation ....50% minimum

Flammability
(a) FF 1-70/tablet test: passes

(b) Flooring radiant panel test: greater than 0.25 watt/cm^2

Performance Evaluation

Some performance features apply to only one cushion type. Aging applies exclusively to cellular rubber, and delamination strength is important only for permanently attached cushions. Other features, such as compression loss and elongation, apply to all cushion types.

ACCELERATED AGING is a concern with cellular rubber cushions. In one procedure, latex cushions are placed in a circulating air oven at 135°C (275°F) for 24 hours. In another, a sample is placed in a Fade-0-Meter for 20 hours. Foam latex samples should withstand these tests with no more than slight discoloration or surface degradation.

COMPRESSIBILITY evaluations measure to what degree a cushion resists being crushed under a static (nonmoving) load. The force required to compress the specimen a given percentage of its original thickness is measured. The force is reported in **psi** (pounds per square inch). Firmer cushions should be used for high- traffic areas.

COMPRESSION SET, OR COMPRESSION LOSS, indicates by how much a sample fails to recover its original thickness after static compression. Usually, specimens are layered to a thickness of 2.54cm (1 inch), and compressed 50 percent. The sample is then put in an oven at 70°C (158°F) for 22 hours. The load is removed, and the specimen is allowed to recover for 30 minutes. The thickness is measured and compared to acceptable levels. A recovery of 85 percent is acceptable.

TENSILE STRENGTH is measured according to prescribed test methods such as FTMS 191 A, Method 5100. The indicator is the force per unit area required to cause rupture of the specimen. Values typically range from 8 to 20 psi.

ELONGATION is related to tensile strength. It describes how long a specimen stretches before breaking.

Because cushioning is a hidden element, extra care must be given to its specification and installation to forestall problems in the carpeting that may become evident later. Padding should be installed in the largest possible lengths, with a minimum of seaming. It should be placed flush with tackless strips and have the applied facing (if any) on top. If installed over concrete, it should be cemented down; over wood, it may be stapled in place. Seams should be taped together and should not occur directly under carpet seams.

Installation

The specifier needs to be familiar with the terminology and basic methods of installation in order to specify the appropriate method of installation. Carpet manufacturers, however, recommend installation methods for specific carpet types, and this should be taken into consideration. The three methods of installation are:

1. trackless strip
2. glue down
3. free-lay

To ensure the long-term serviceability of any carpeting system, specifiers should consider installation factors as thoroughly as they do

---

Cushion Underpad Specification Checklist

CUSHION UNDERPAD

Composition
- ☐ Cushion composition

Structure
- ☐ Coating, if applicable
- ☐ Density
- ☐ Thickness

Performance Levels

- ☐ Compression load deflection
- ☐ psi @ specific deflection percentage
    25%   50%   75%

- ☐ Compression set: expressed maximum percentage of set @ percentage of deflection
- ☐ Tensile set: acceptable minimum expressed in psi
- ☐ Elongation: acceptable minimum expressed in percentage
- ☐ Flammability: @ CFR
    @ flooring radiant panel test

performance and appearance factors. Without proper installation, ripples, bubbles, prominent seams, and mismatched patterns may occur. Insecure installations present an obvious accident hazard and can result in undue stress in the carpet system itself.

Familiarity with the basic procedures used in wall-to-wall installations prepares the specifier for an accurate analysis of the factors to consider in choosing a method of installation. This knowledge is the basis for properly planning the carpet layout, determining the quantity required, and estimating the cost of the project.

The site must be properly prepared before any installation; it must be dry, clean, and free of grit. Removal of previously installed carpet is an essential part of site preparation. If left in place, old carpet prevents proper installation and results in severe flexing of the new assembly, reducing its life.

In glue-down installations, sheet vinyl and linoleum must be removed for the new system to adhere well. While subfloor dryness is always important, it is critical for glue-down operations. New concrete, on-grade (ground level) and below-grade applications are of particular importance. New concrete may take up to four months to dry.

Traffic conditions, planned space use, concern for noise reduction, and energy conservation are also factors in choosing the installation method.

Tackless Strip

This method involves stretching the carpet and securing the edges with tackless strips. They are 3.81 cm (1.5") wide, with rust-resistant metal pins pointing upward at an angle of 60 degrees. The strips are up to .952 cm (.375") thick, coordinated with the cushion thickness. Three rows of pins are recommended for heavy-traffic areas, while two are enough for other areas. The strips are located around the perimeter of the carpet, pins angled to the wall, and allowing a small gap between the strip and the wall. On wood floors, the strips are nailed down with closely spaced nails long enough to hold the strips securely. On cement floors, strips may be applied with adhesives, by drilling holes through the strip and into the floor and plugging them together, or by direct nailing into the floor.

When joining seams or when pattern matching is required, the edges of the floor covering must be aligned carefully and trimmed to fit tightly. Factory edges should not be butted since they may be irregular. After the carpet is cut, a thin bead of adhesive should be applied to the edge to prevent raveling. Seams may be stitched or secured by hot-melt tape. Sometimes a pressure-sensitive tape combined with a latex bead is also used.

After seaming, the carpet is stretched and anchored over the wooden strips. The degree of stretching is usually 1 to 1.5 percent of length and width. A power stretcher is often used to provide uniform stretching, and a knee-kicker is used to grip and anchor the edges over the pins. Tackless strips are used across doorways, and if there is a transition to a hard surface, the carpet edge must be covered and secured with carpet molding strips.

Glue-Down

Glue-down installations use an adhesive to secure the carpet system to the floor. **Direct glue-down** refers to installations with no cushion, while **glue-down** refers to installations using a cushion. The method for both types of installation is the same except that when direct glue-down is used the carpet is rolled onto the adhesive, while in glue-down the carpeting system is pressed into the adhesive. Layout and seam placement must be carefully planned. If the carpet is too small, separation of seams may occur; if it is too large, buckles and ripples may develop.

This method of installation is useful in extra-heavy traffic areas, and in any other installation involving tight, low-surface carpets with high-density foam cushions, those with jute or nonwoven backings, and those with backings coated with latex, polyvinyl chloride, or polyurethane compounds. No separate cushion is used in this method.

Carpet is held securely to the floor with specific adhesives and does not shift under heavy traffic. Occasionally, carpet is adhered to a raised wooden floor may be lifted in sections to provide access that to underfloor services (computer wiring, for instance).

Glue-down is only successful if careful consideration is given to the location's environmental conditions, the condition and preparation of the subfloor, adhesives, the type and quality of carpet construction and its constituent fibers, and the seaming.

ENVIRONMENTAL CONDITIONS must include temperatures and relative humidity. Drastic temperature changes may cause buckling, and excessive humidity may stretch or shrink the fibers.

SUBFLOOR PREPARATIONS are important for glue-down installations because of surface irregularities and adhesive bonding criteria. Concrete is commonly the flooring surface for glue-down installations. It is classed as suspended if it is above-grade, on-grade if it is in contact with the ground, and below-grade if it is under the soil line. Moisture transmission from the ground up through below-grade or on-grade concrete must be blocked by prepreparation compounds. Wood, terazzo, ceramic, or quarry tile will necessitate floor preparation techniques to fill cracks or grout lines. Radiant heated floors must be maintained at specified temperatures while adhesives dry after installation.

ADHESIVES used for carpet glue-down are of four types: natural latex, synthetic latex, solvent-based rubber, and alcohol-solvent resins. Each has particular characteristics, compatabilities, and application techniques.

CARPET TYPES used in carpet construction should be tight, with a good face weight. Generally, low-level loop surfaces are amenable to this installation technique and the areas where it will most likely be applied. The carpet's backing must be one that will remain stable and provide a secure bond with the adhesive. Jute and nonwoven synthetics are among the most successful. Fibers should be selected for abrasion resistance.

SEAMING must be secure. The carpet should be tightly constructed to prevent edges from fraying. Seams should be sealed with latex-type glue before installation.

Free-Lay

When designers want to maximize the flexibility of the carpet system, free-lay installations may be considered. This option may only be considered, however, when heavy rolling traffic such as hospital gurneys are not expected. (Chairs with carpet casters are not a problem.)

Superior dimensional stability is a prerequisite for free-lay use. The application of a heavy secondary backing will often achieve this feature. Some free-lay

Performance of Major Carpet Fibers

	WOOL	NYLON	NYLON 6,6	ACRYLIC	MODACRYLIC	OLEFIN	POLYESTER
Abrasion Resistance	good	excellent	excellent	good	good	excellent	good
Resliency	very good	very good	very good	very good	very good	good	fair
Color Retention	fair	very good	very good	good	good	excellent	good
Pattern Retention	good	very good	very good	good	good	good	fair
Texture Retention	good	very good	very good	good	good	good	fair
Stain and Soil Resistance	good	good	excellent	good	good	excellent	good
Heat/Flame Resistance	excellent	very good	very good	good (if treated)	very good	good	good
Moisture Absorbency	high	low	low	low	low	very low	low
Mold/Mildew Insect Resistance	high (if treated)	high	high	high	high	high	high
Static Resistance	low	low	high	medium	medium	excellent	low

tiles alternate layers of heavy-gauge vinyl with layers of glass fiber scrims.

Prior to installation, a control grid is prepared to maximize the size of perimeter nodules. Within this grid, selected lengthwise and crosswise rows of nodules are secured to the floor to minimize shifting. This selective glue-down leaves up to 90 percent of the modules in free-lay mode. Free-lay modules permit easy access to floor and under-floor utility systems and maximum convenience in changing modules.

Other Carpet Particulars Affecting Installation

Nap

Carpet nap is the direction that the pile tends to lie. The nap direction affects the appearance of the carpet—a slightly different color is seen when the carpet is viewed with the nap and against the nap.

Ideally, nap should run in the same direction for an entire installation. Cuts and sides, where seaming has been necessary, must not show a nap change. On stairs, the carpet should be installed with the nap running downward. This provides for longer wear and a most pleasing appearance.

Seam Placement

Planning the seam placement in a carpet installation is one of the most important considerations. Designers should request that the contractor or installer submit a seaming diagram prior to work being undertaken. Seams should be avoided across areas of heavy traffic such as halls. Seams should not run into doorways, although across a doorway is often necessary. Seams should not be placed in positions where people change directions or pivot.

Carpet seams must be strong enough to withstand stretching during installation or during use.

HAND SEWING with coarse linen thread and curved needles is an exacting task, and it is only feasible on carpet with backing that can be penetrated. The completed seams are heated with a special ironing device and coated with latex adhesive.

HOT-MELT TAPE produces a flat, invisible seam that is very strong. An adhesive-surfaced tape bonds the seams together when heat is applied. It is used only on specified fibers and must not be used on fiber with low melting points, rubber or latex backings, or in conjunction with foam or sponge underlays that permit the seam to become apparent on the carpet surface. Seams should be accurately fitted before the tape is applied.

LATEX TAPE is a method where no heat is necessary, and the latex becomes the bonding agent.

Patterned Carpet

Patterned carpets present special problems in seaming. The patterns must be accurately measured and the match planned accordingly. Patterned carpets are designed in three ways:

1. **SET MATCH** indicates that the pattern elements are in a straight side-by-side match across the width of the carpet.

2. **DROP MATCH** indicates that the pattern elements are situated in a diagonal across the carpet.

3. **QUARTER DROP MATCH** is usually found in 68.5 cm (27") woven carpets, with four pattern blocks (4 quarters) in every length repeat, with one block (1 quarter) dropped in each repeat.

Loose-Laid Rug Installations

Cut edges of rugs and runners should be bound, either by sewing twill-woven tape over the edges or by serging the edges. Cushions should be thin and 2.54-5.08 cm (1-2") shorter than all carpet dimensions.

Maintenance and Cleaning

Carpet maintenance has changed over the years from a semi-annual cleaning to programmed regular cleaning to prevent dirt and abrasive soil from settling in the fibers.

Effective carpet maintenance retains the original appearance and texture of the carpet for as long as possible by keeping the soil content and stains to a minimum. Traffic by itself does not wear out most carpets; it is the soil and dirt in and on the carpet, often having sharp edges, which, with traffic, presses against the fibers. This continual abrasion eventually severs some fibers from the pile.

The type of soil in the area must be considered with the maintenance program. The carpet's color and texture must aid in soil hiding, while its properties must be compatible with the maintenance program considered.

To prolong carpet life, regular and systematic cleaning is essential. The type of cleaning equipment used will depend upon the area to be cleaned, the number of obstructions, the type of carpet, traffic load, availability of utilities, and cleaning frequency required.

No saving results from neglecting or downgrading carpet maintenance. A neglected carpet is more expensive to restore and wears out sooner. In addition, if excessive soil is allowed to accumulate in high-traffic areas, it will be tracked to other areas.

Preventative Maintenance

A program of maintenance, based on knowledge of the expected soil sources and areas of the carpet that will receive extra wear, may be planned.

Types of Soil

These have been defined as **water-soluble soils** and **solvent-soluble soils.** The sources of the soiling are airborne, shoe surface, and spillage. If any of these are extensive and not removable by vacuuming, cleansing (and thorough removal of the cleansing agent and the soil) should be done as soon as possible.

Soil Areas

Areas that require daily maintenance and more frequent special attention are:

TRACK-OFF AREAS: This is where people walk in from the outdoors or from adjacent hard-surface flooring. These areas should be vacuumed daily, and walk-off mats, both inside and outside, are necessary to prevent the tracked soil from spreading into the carpeted space.

FUNNEL AREAS: These are areas where foot traffic takes a specific, concentrated course, such as the center of a hallway, elevators, water fountains, and vending machines. These areas require daily vacuuming, spot cleaning as necessary, and frequent cleaning of the whole area.

Traffic in these areas should be identified on a floor plan, along with flow patterns.

Maintenance Systems

An advantage carpeting has over other types of flooring is that it localizes soil. Eighty-five percent of soil is tracked in on shoes, so the traffic study will allow systematic cleaning to be done. By concentrating on the 30 percent or less of floor area that is in heavy use, overall costs can be reduced without detracting from the overall appearance or longevity of the carpet.

In designing a maintenance system, special care should be paid to pattern changes and seasonal variations, and the plan adjusted accordingly.

Maintenance Activities

VACUUMING is the single most important activity related to carpet care. In commercial buildings and institutional settings, it is usually done with a heavy-duty vacuum equipped with brush agitators. The action of the brush lifts the pile fibers and exposes the dirt to the suction of the cleaner. The cleaner should be a heavy-duty one, but not so cumbersome as to be a burden to the operator.

SPOT REMOVAL should ideally be undertaken as soon as spots or spills occur. Many carpet manufacturers make available spot-cleaning kits equipped with the proper chemicals for their product, along with instructions for its use.

CORRECTIVE CLEANING is undertaken with the accumulation of oily airborne soil. Carpeting should first be thoroughly vacuumed, and the floor area cleaned by one of the following methods:

Dry extraction removes dirt by brushing moist granulated or powdered materials into the carpet and allowing them to dry, usually for about 30 minutes. Vacuuming removes both the powder and the soil. It is a good method for high-traffic areas, or areas where traffic can not be stopped.

Wer cleaning, with water-based solvents, takes several days to dry thoroughly, so scheduling is important. It is not advisable to require wet cleaning in areas where traffic cannot be stopped. This carpet care activity is a major undertaking, requiring removal of as much furniture as possible before cleaning, and placing metal foil under the legs of furniture that cannot be moved. The carpet manufacturer usually recommends a detergent solution. If a detergent is used that has not been recommended, it should be tested on an inconspicuous area first. The detergent should have a pH of between 6.5 and 10.0. Wet cleaning should be followed by immediate wet vacuuming.

Dry foam cleaning is a simultaneous procedure. A dry foam agent is deposited on the carpet just before it is wet vacuumed with an agitating reel-type brush. Overwetting is prevented, and use may resume after an hour. Since this method uses less moisture than wet shampooing, it reduces the drying time. It is recommended for lighter soil, since a second treatment is required for heavy soil.

Hot-water extraction uses a hot-detergent solution under pressure to quickly wet the carpet. The solution is immediately extracted by vacuum, along with the soil. This method is particularly good for high pile, plush carpets because it minimizes pile distortion. It also minimizes detergent buildup. Well-trained operators are required, however, or overwetting occurs, involving long delays in the use of the carpet.

Catastrophic cleaning is, unfortunately, occasionally needed in instances where water pipes rupture, or natural disasters such as floods occur. Some cleaning firms specialize in this area; others add this dimension to their services and work on the restoration of premises so afflicted.

The investment in carpeting is a large one, and the installed carpet requires knowledgeable care and attention. Maintenance factors must always be considered both for the user's satisfaction with the carpet's appearance and as a factor in life-cycle costing.

Project Criteria ▬▬▬▬▬

Knowledge is the key to selecting the right carpet for the project. This knowledge is acquired from observation of many different projects and research and investigation of products, or the assistance of an expert carpet specifier can be used when necessary. The user requirements should be prioritized in order of importance to the specific project and the products measured against the requirements. The needs of the physically challenged (mobility, sight, hearing, etc.) are to be considered in all interiors.

The following project categories indicate some of the general concerns in establishing criteria for a given project.

Carpet Specifications

The final factor in assuring that the best carpet has been selected for a project is proper specifications of the product. The specifier can develop the specifications in one of two ways:

1. by performance requirements
2. by construction requirements

The **performance specification** explains *how the carpet is to perform* in a specific application. It does not tell the manufacturer which fiber(s) to use or how to manufacture the carpet.

The **construction specification** explains *how the carpet is to be produced.* The pile fiber, adhesives, backings, dyeing method, and construction method are all determined by the specifier.

With both performance and construction specifications, the specifier must determine the carpet installation method, the undercushion, any special installation procedures, certification or compliance with regulatory requirements, delivery and installation schedule, and recommended maintenance procedures.

Writing a Carpet Specification

The process of specifying carpet is complex because of the multiplicity of fiber choices. Before developing a specification, it is necessary to determine the performance criteria for the specific end use.

There are ten areas to be considered when developing a carpet system.

1. **Budget:** The performance requirements for a specific area must be thoroughly assessed prior to setting the budget for carpet. Budget may limit the choice of carpeting, but it is important for the product to meet the performance requirements.

2. **Codes:** Building codes contain restrictions about the type of carpet that can be used in given situations, and the codes specify the testing procedures considered to be 'authority.' Flammability standards for carpets and large rugs are controlled by the three levels of government: federal, provincial or state, and municipal.

3. **Traffic concentration and traffic flow:** In any building there are different types, levels, and patterns of traffic. One carpet might not be suitable for the entire installation.

4. **Rolling stock:** The presence of rolling stock or wheeled traffic precludes the use of many carpet textures because they will not retain their appearance under heavy use.

5. **In-project soiling:** This situation can occur as a result of anticipated spillage from various sources such as coffee, chemicals, or other fluids, as well as the solvents and waxes that will be used on tile flooring next to a carpeted area. Buildings in which there are work areas may have grit or sand tracked onto the carpet, and this must also be considered.

6. **Types of installation:** See section on installation in this chapter.

7. **Access to wiring:** Subfloor ducting and wiring will influence the type of carpet specified.

8. **Color:** The choice of colors plays a key role in keeping carpet looking new over time.

   Some colors can create the illusion of cleanliness by camouflaging soil. Consider that:

   - color is affected by lighting
   - the extremes of the color spectrum tend to show more soiling
   - solid colors reveal more dirt and foot traffic than multicolor or random pattern carpets
   - the 'color mix' obtained through combinations of fibers with different dye affinities helps conceal soil

9. **Texture:** Texture is an important factor in the character, performance, camouflage, and specification of carpet. Choose a surface that can stand up to prevailing conditions, retain a high level of appearance, and be aesthetically pleasing.

10. **Maintenance:** Before a carpet is specified for any project, it is imperative to know that it has been developed with an appropriate maintenance program in mind.

Once project criteria have been established, the construction details of the carpet can be developed. These can be separated into segments such as:

- fibers and yarns
- carpet construction
- performance minimums that involve many parameters that should not be treated independently

Fibers and Yarns

Once the generic fiber type(s) has been selected, the yarn construction details must be consistent with fiber form. When specifying a BCF yarn, it is important to identify the size, or decitex, of the yarn. If the yarn is plied or air entangled, the component types used to obtain the final yarn should be stated. With a staple or spun yarn, the twist level must be specified as well as the number of ends plied. These parameters affect both the performance and the aesthetics of the carpet.

Carpet Construction

Construction parameters and how they relate to one another should be understood to ensure the best selection of carpet for the job. The number of tufts per 100 cm² (the product of the number of needles and the stitches per needle in a square area) is an indicator of the carpet's potential performance. An increase in either variable will increase the number of tufts per 100 cm². The density rating is also a performance indicator. It depends on the decitex of the yarn, the machine gauge (the number of needles per 10 cm) and the stitch count. The density is expressed in a kilotex per square centimeter rating. It cannot be assumed that carpets with the same density rating but different fiber types will have similar appearance retention.

Pile weight and pile height affect the carpet performance. **Pile weight** is defined as the weight, as tufted, of face fiber, expressed in grams per square meter (g/m2). **Pile height** is measured in millimeters from the primary backing to the surface of the carpet. The standard primary backing is polypropylene. The secondary backing is normally a jute or woven polypropylene material. Patented methods of unitary backings are available in which the synthetic backing is heat treated onto the primary backing and can offer increased tuft bind and delamination strength.

Performance Minimums

After specifying the fiber, yarn, and construction method, the performance minimums should be stated. These include:

- static control level
- tuft bind
- delamination strength or peel adhesion
- colorfastness
- flame resistance

Project Criteria

Corporate	**OFFICES, EXECUTIVE SUITES, BOARDROOMS, RECEPTION AREAS** *Performance considerations:* attractive appearance, durability, resistance to stains and soiling, acoustics, permanent static control, amount and type of traffic. Solutions: Office carpeting should have low, dense pile. Tufted carpet is the most common type and loop pile or twisted pile is often the most effective for heavy traffic. Patterns, tweeds, and heather effects also assist in camouflaging traffic areas.
Hospitality	**HOTELS, MOTELS, RESORTS, AND RESTAURANTS** *Performance considerations:* attractive appearance, durability, resistance to stains and soiling (from heavy traffic directly from the street). *Solutions:* Carpeting for the hospitality industry should be chosen based on fiber, texture, color, and pattern that combine to hide traffic patterns and stains, resist wear, and create pleasant aesthetic appeal. A heavy denier fiber will resist stains and soiling and provide easy maintenance.
Retail	**SMALL BOUTIQUE TO MULTI-LEVEL DEPARTMENT STORE** *Performance considerations:* traffic heavy or extra-heavy traffic, hide wear, durability, resistance to stains and soiling. *Solutions:* Carpeting should provide a backdrop for the merchandise.
Healthcare	**HOSPITALS, PERSONAL CARE HOMES, ASSISTED-LIVING FACILITIES** *Performance considerations:* nonallergenic; inhibit the growth of most common fungi, bacteria, and mildew; resistant to spills and stains; control odor; flame resistance; good traction; high-abrasion resistance. *Solutions:* Carpets should not impede foot or wheelchair traffic. Installation should be carefully planned to avoid ridges between hard surfaces and carpet.
Education	**PRESCHOOL, ELEMENTARY, SECONDARY, POST-SECONDARY, TECHNICAL** *Performance considerations:* Student ages and purpose of institution must be considered. Educational facilities have heavy pedestrian traffic in corridors and circulation areas. They also have distinct areas with specific needs—cafeterias and sports facilities, for example. Carpets must have exceptional abrasion and stain resistance, flame resistance, and acoustics. *Solutions:* Pattern, texture, and color are useful elements to withstand the abuses of traffic while retaining an attractive appearance.
Industrial	**AIRPORT, BUS AND TRAIN STATION CONCOURSES AND TICKET COUNTERS AND SALES SERVICE AREAS** *Performance considerations:* heavy pedestrian and wheel traffic, resistant to stains and soiling, flame resistance, static control, fade resistance, good colorfastness. *Solutions:* Very dense level loop constructions and durable pile fibers are often recommended.

The level to which static electricity buildup should be controlled must be specified (e.g., 3.5 kv at 20% RH and 20°C).

Tuft bind determines how well the individual tufts are locked in the carpet system. Only a minimum acceptance number should be specified. The C.G.S.B. standards are 13 Newtons (force) for cut pile and 25 Newtons for uncut pile carpets.

Delamination strength or peel adhesion measures the strength of the bond between the secondary backing and the rest of the carpet. A minimum acceptable figure should be specified, not an average value.

The International Gray Scale (L 1 to 8) is the standard scale for colorfastness. Carpets are tested and rated against this scale to measure color retention. Minimum values of L 5 are common for commercial carpets.

Environmental Considerations

Carpet manufacturers are among the most environmentally conscious in the textile industry. The industry has embraced the green movement. Manufacturers have dedicated resources to devising programs and processes to reclaim, reuse, or recycle carpets and carpet backing in the hopes that the landfill sites (the traditional place of disposal) will not see any carpets dumped in the future. Carpets that are removed from buildings can be deconstructed and the fibers melted down to be respun into new fibers, the carpet can be redye, or a pattern can be applied to change the look. Carpets can also be cut down and used in carpet tiles. There are many ways of reusing carpeting. Throughout the construction business there are numerous programs (CARE℠ and LEED®, for example) that are helping to improve the environmental sustainability of building and renovating structures.

LEED® Certification Standards: Carpets

Leadership in Energy and Environmental Design (LEED®) criteria for carpet specifications involve a number of ways that buildings can earn valuable credits toward certification. LEED® is a self-assessing system of the United States Green Buildings Council (USGBC) that is designed to rate new building construction and major renovations of commercial buildings. Points are given for:

- choosing sustainable sites
- water efficiency
- energy and atmosphere
- materials and resources
- indoor environmental quality

Carpet can help a building earn credits toward LEED® certification. Carpets must meet standards of indoor air quality and materials and resources. Carpets have a certain amount of off-gassing after they have been installed. This is mainly due to adhesives and new materials. The carpet must be installed with enough time for it to emit the gasses before occupancy, so the users are not working in a polluted indoor environment.

The life cycle of the carpet must have the least possible impact on the environment. Producing the carpet must not use excessive energy or water. Maintenance must not mean excessive use of water and chemical cleaners. The carpet must contain recycled carpet material in all components, including backing and cushioning. Facing can be made from recycled pop bottles (polyester) or nylon from other carpets. Backing can be made from recycled car tires. A number of systems have developed recently to help designers have easy access to these materials. Manufacturers are working with the design industry to help make carpeting more sustainable. The carpet must also be removable and recyclable once it is no longer wanted for the original purpose. Essentially, the life cycle of the carpet must have as little possible environmental impact from the time that it is manufactured to its disposal (landfill or recycling). If the carpet meets LEED® criteria it can help contribute one point to certification of a building.

Energy Conservation

As with drapery, cushioned carpeting helps provide insulation and increases thermal resistance. With warm colors and plush carpeting people sometimes feel warmer, even though the ambient temperature is the same. This means that people will leave the thermostat at a lower temperature, still feel comfortable, and help preserve precious energy.

Specification Checklist for Rugs and Carpets

AREA

- [ ] Location
- [ ] Approximate Dimension

CARPET

- [ ] Name of Manufacturer
- [ ] Pattern Number
- [ ] Color Number
- [ ] Color Description
- [ ] Surface Texture
- [ ] Face Fiber Content
- [ ] Yarn Size
- [ ] Pile Height
- [ ] Pile Yarn Weight (g/m²)
- [ ] Total Weight
- [ ] Average Density (ktex/cm²)
- [ ] Weight Density
- [ ] Carpet Structure
  - [ ] Gauge
  - [ ] Stitches per Inch
  - [ ] Primary Backing
    - [ ] Type
    - [ ] Weight
  - [ ] Backing Characteristics
- [ ] Structural Stability
  - [ ] Tuft Interlacement
- [ ] Delamination Strength

CHARACTERISTICS

- [ ] Colorfastness (Gray Scale)
  - [ ] Crocking
    - [ ] Fume Fading
  - [ ] Ozone Fading
  - [ ] Wet Cleaning
  - [ ] Light Fastness
- [ ] Flammability

- [ ] Methenamine Tablet Test
  - [ ] Tunnel Test
  - [ ] Radiant Floor Panel Test
- [ ] Static Generation (kv @ 20% RH & 20°C)
- [ ] Wear Resistance
  - [ ] Texture Change
  - [ ] Pilling Propensity
  - [ ] Stain Resistance
  - [ ] Crush Resistance
- [ ] Acoustic Qualities
- [ ] Light Reflection
- [ ] Azoic Control

UNDERPADDING

- [ ] Type
- [ ] Weight
- [ ] Characteristics
  - [ ] Acoustic Qualities
  - [ ] Service Life
  - [ ] Thermal Qualities

INSTALLATION

- [ ] Description
- [ ] Type
  - [ ] Tackless
  - [ ] Glued
  - [ ] Fringed
- [ ] Flooring Materials
  - [ ] Pattern/pile Direction Instructions
  - [ ] Seam Type
- [ ] Seam Locations
- [ ] Doorways
  - [ ] Edges
  - [ ] Preparatory Work
  - [ ] Re-stitching Following Installation
  - [ ] Fittings to be Accommodated
  - [ ] Clean-up
  - [ ] Request for Maintenance Instructions

PROFESSIONAL PRACTICE

Every individual lives, works, and interacts within the built environment. Home is that important place where we find rest and renewal, appreciation and stimulation. For most of us there is a separate place for work where we are productive, efficient, and fulfilled. All of us find places where we are entertained, educated, and inspired.

Interior Design Professionals

Design professionals are qualified by education, experience, certification, and continuing education to design interiors to improve the quality of life, increase productivity, and protect the health, safety, and welfare of the public.

- analyze clients' and users' needs, goals, and life and safety requirements

- formulate preliminary design concepts that are appropriate, functional, and aesthetic, and present recommendations to clients

- prepare working drawings and specifications for nonload bearing interior construction materials, finishes, space planning, furnishings, fixtures, and equipment

- work within a set budget

- integrate barrier-free design and elements to enhance the health and safety of the occupants of the space

- provide solutions to material specifications that are environmentally friendly

- collaborate with professional services of other licensed practitioners in the technical areas of construction

- prepare and administer bids and contract documents as the client's agent

- review and evaluate design solutions during implementation and upon completion of a project

The design community specializes in the creation of places to meet all of these needs. Through education and practice, design professionals cultivate their natural talents to become experts in the development of harmonious places to meet the emotional, aesthetic, and practical requirements of the occupants. Design professionals have a social responsibility to affect the built environment in a positive way.

The design community caters to a diverse, international client base and works on projects in every corner of world. Firms are often based in one city, but have satellite offices, with design associates working in several other countries and cities. Designers are being called on to understand cultural and aesthetic preferences of a diverse clientele with different tastes and expectations. This makes the design professional's job interesting and challenging.

Good design comes from a cooperative effort between the design professionals and the client. The design team analyzes and interprets the client's needs, communicates and guides the choices to be made, and emerges with a functional and aesthetically pleasing space. The work is a great challenge and a satisfying accomplishment when done well.

Professional Ethics

Design professionals are accorded a significant level of trust—personal, financial, and otherwise—by clients, the general public, and members of other professions. It is imperative that this trust be backed by competence, honesty, integrity, and objectivity.

To provide models of conduct for design professionals who deal with complex personal/business relationships, various codes of ethics have been formulated. These codes combine business practices with moral principles, enabling designers to uphold this trust in the practice of their profession.

Codes of ethical behavior exist within professional organizations. The concept of professional ethics is apparent in various rules, regulations, and prohibitions, but the codes particularly specify a minimum standard of acceptable behavior. It is in the best interest of design professions to strive for total commitment to good conduct and to continually improve their competence and the quality of service they provide.

Among other things, ethical conduct deals with what is disclosed or not disclosed to clients and the public. A list of **disclosure** items may include:

- refraining from making misleading, deceptive, or false statement or claims

- conforming to all existing laws, regulations, and business procedures as established by municipal, state/provincial, or federal governments

Responsibilities to Clients, Colleagues, and the Professions

Design professionals should be fair and candid with their clients. Design professionals should serve them to the best of their abilities with professional concerns that are in the clients' best interests and consistent with their responsibilities to the public.

They should conduct themselves in a manner that promotes cooperation and good relations within the design professions. The interchange of technical information and experience between the allied professions and respect for others' interests and contributions are important to good relations and, ultimately, good solutions. Some general guidelines for professional practice are as follows:

- Designers should not undertake any work that they cannot reasonably expect to complete with professional competence.

- In the performance of professional services, design professionals should not allow their own financial or other interests affect the exercise of independent professional judgment on behalf of their clients.

- Should designers become involved in projects that seem unsafe, economically unfeasible, environmentally unsound, or about which they have serious legal reservations, the clients should be given a written notification of the designers' concerns.

Specification of Textile Products

The textile component is an integral part of virtually all design of interior spaces; it may comprise the major solution to requirements for floors, walls, and

Types of Projects for Professional Interior Designers and Facility Managers

DESIGN PROFESSIONALS ARE INVOLVED IN DESIGN FOR:

- offices and other work settings

- the hospitality industry: restaurants, hotels, resorts

- health-related facilities: hospitals, clinics, personal care homes

- retail: chain stores, specialty shops

- places of worship

- educational facilities and libraries

- entertainment facilities

- museums

- government facilities: post offices to submarines

- transportation: terminals, trains, ships, airplanes, spacecraft

- residential

- other specialization: set design for stage/screen/television productions, lighting design, product development, marketing research, teaching, journalism, illustration, programming, space planning, facility planning, historic preservation, and color consultation furnishings. New materials have added a demanding dimension to specifications in this area, and designer liability is an increasingly important issue. Designers, architects, and facility managers are held responsible for the performance of the products they specify in the areas of function and safety. Understanding the benefits and risks of certain design solutions is the responsibility of the designer.

Reading labels and fact sheets and asking questions are invaluable aids to keeping knowledge current, and the designer must never assume that what was known yesterday applies today.

Quality Safeguards

The best safeguard against errors with textile specification is a good understanding of the elementary facts and relationships. The specification process is based on product life span and evaluation of the materials being considered.

User Interface

The specified textiles should meet the aesthetic needs of the users and provide the expected degree of safety, comfort, and/or privacy while meeting their visual needs. Other components of the interior like color and geometric coordination are also important aesthetics. The textiles must also meet the practical combination of good looks and long life in the circumstances into which they are placed.

To design considering the health, safety, and welfare of the public requires particular knowledge in the following areas:

- anthropometrics and ergonomics
- proxemics and behavioral theory

- requirements for special populations, such as the disabled and the elderly
- construction detailing
- lighting
- heating, ventilation, and air conditioning
- physical attributes of materials, installation methods
- building codes
- fire codes and life-safety requirements
- industry product standards
- business practices
- specifications writing for interior construction and furnishing

---

ANTHROPOMETRICS: the branch of anthropology that deals with measurement of the human body

ERGONOMICS: the scientific study of the relationship between humans and their working environment

PROXEMICS: human's perception of social and personal space

A general framework for understanding threats to safety is necessary. In general, hazards can be defined in terms of actions involved in the injury. Design-based hazards regarding textile use can be classified as:

MECHANICAL: Falls onto floor, downstairs, etc.

ELECTRICAL: Shocks experienced from electric static discharge.

THERMAL: Burns from flammable materials.

CHEMICAL: Inhalation of toxic gases and other materials produced by fire, smoke, or other reaction.

PHYSIOLOGICAL: Sensory loss from loud noise, or other causes.

Economic Feasibility

To specify textiles within a client's budget requires consideration of the following.

Stability and Durability

The proposed cloth or carpeting must be assessed as appropriate for the function. While this may seem elementary, it sometimes occurs that a client has unrealistic expectations of a textile product's capacity to endure hard use. The designer must feel confident that the material can fulfil the expected function for a reasonable period of time, and should be able to give the client an accurate appraisal as to a textile's stability and a good approximation of its durability.

Maintenance

Specified fabrics have care and maintenance instructions that must be passed on to the client. Textile components should not require costly maintenance or frequent replacement, but should be relatively easy to maintain over the expected life span. Flexibility should be carefully considered if relocation of the textile components is likely.

Evaluating Textile Performance

Testing of textiles may be required to meet code, or it may be part of normal production where the testing results are used to supply further information to clients.

Some tests are easy to perform and can be done without the expense of using a testing lab. Simple burning tests can help identify different fibers through smell, residue, and general burning behavior. Feeling, crushing, rubbing, and deconstructing fabrics and untwisting yarns can reveal information about the fabric. Colorfastness can be checked by rubbing a clean, white piece of cotton on the fabric and checking it for color transfer. These methods establish some basics and provide quick evaluation of some everyday performance requirements. Designers, however, need to supplement this type of hands-on experience with more specific and exacting tests. Access to testing labs in universities and independent agencies is relatively easy, though there is a fee for the service.

The **hang test** is one such lab test. Material is left to hang and the draping quality, transparency/opacity, shrinkage, and elongation are assessed. Cleaning tests, fading tests, wear tests, bacteria and insect resistance tests, and fire retardance tests are all also useful tests for fabrics.

Performance Test Methods

Performance testing methods are usually grouped into three categories:

PHYSICAL TESTS are used where compliance with specified requirements can best be established with tests that simulate the intended *use condition.*

CALCULATION METHOD is used where compliance with requirements can be established by means of graphic and/or numerical calculations, using accepted engineering practice and applicable codes.

OBSERVATION is used where compliance with performance requirements can only be established by observing the textiles under specified conditions. Visual evaluation should be based on unanimous agreement of a panel of at least three independent observers.

Performance testing is undertaken by many different agencies. A number of scientific agencies help to establish standards for textile products of all kinds. These tests are to protect the users from harm or death due to fire or other safety concerns. The tests are also meant to provide critical information about care and use to make sure the textile product has a long use-

Terminology of Flaws and Faults

A FLAW is an individual inconsistency in a fabric. Quality-control inspectors might find these flaws in the factory inspection process, and the flaws are sometimes repaired. Flawed fabrics are often tagged '**Imperfect**' and offered at discounted price.

A FAULT is inconsistency in an entire piece or lot of fabric. These fabrics are sometimes changed so substantially that they no longer suit the standard for the intended end use.

Flaws	A BAR, BARRE, or BAR MARK is the most common and visible flaw. It is a horizontal band varying in size from a single weft yarn (either too heavy or too light). If a whole bobbin of flawed yarn has been used, the bar may be 5-15 cm (2-6") in depth, or occasionally greater.
	BROKEN WARP ENDS frequently occur due to tension on the threads in the weaving process. These are usually mended before the fabric is shipped. If the broken warp ruins a design or causes mispicks or warp floats, the fabric is tagged.

Terminology of Flaws and Faults, cont'd

Flaws, cont'd	BURR is a common term for any vegetable matter, cottonseed, stick, or residue left in a natural fabric.
	DIRT or GREASE is usually removed in scouring, but occasionally some is left in the fibers and found when the fabric is made.
	FLOAT flaws may be horizontal or vertical. A horizontal float (in the weft/pick direction) is a mispick; a vertical float (in the warp direction) is a warp float. Very short floats usually do not ruin a fabric and are acceptable. Longer floats may be mended.
	FLY is yarn contamination by other fiber or lint. If it is slight, it is usually picked out with a needle.
	A HOLE is a major flaw, and it is the result of either a smash—the beater falling on a shuttle trapped in the warp during the weaving process—or a broken end in warp-knit goods. Depending on the size, a hole may be successfully mended.
	KNOTS, if they are small, may be pushed to the back of the fabric. If they are large, they must be untied and darned into the fabric.
	A REED MARK is a vertical streak caused by a distorted wire in the reed or comb.
	A SKIP PICK is a horizontal flaw caused by a missed pass of filling yarn. In a plain weave, it results in two filling yarns running as one.
	A SLUB is an overly heavy area in a yarn; it may be vertical or horizontal.
	A SLUG is a loose filling yarn. The slack may be pulled to the selvage, or it may be darned into place.
Faults	COLOR VARIATION is any off-standard color in the cloth. It may or may not be acceptable, but usually cannot be matched.
	OFF-GRAIN is a finishing fault in which the horizontal yarns run at an angle. This fault shows up most often in a striped fabric. Off-grain fabric is very hard to work with, and sewing is extremely difficult.
	MISPRINT is a finishing flaw of printed goods where the print is either off-grain, overlapping, or in the wrong direction. It is generally not acceptable.
	PILE LOSS may occur during dyeing, printing, or finishing. It may be slight or extreme. End use will determine whether pile loss is an acceptable fault.
	SELVAGE PROBLEMS, if they are extensive, are usually not acceptable as they affect the hang and shaping quality of the fabric. Selvages may be too tight (short) or too loose (long). If the problem is slight or intermittent, it is considered a flaw.
	SLIPPAGE of warp yarns during finishing may distort the fabric.
	TENDER GOODS is a term used to designate fabric that has lost strength because of improper use of heat or chemicals. It is an uncommon, yet serious, problem.

life. Testing is done by each of the following organizations, and often the tests have the same method but different reference numbers, usually starting with the organization's acronym followed by a number.

- American Association of Textile Chemists and Colorists (AATCC)

The AATCC is an internationally recognized society concerned with testing dyed and chemically treated fibers and fabrics. The AATCC works with issues of colorfastness of all types and develops test methods to measure performance in this area. A monthly journal called *Textile Chemist and Colorist* presents recent innovation and information on matters related to dye, printing, and finishes.

- American Society for Testing and Materials (ASTM)

  The ASTM tests all materials including textiles. Standard test methods are outlined and numbered then published in the *Annual Book of ASTM Standards*. These books are divided into volumes depending on the material, so textiles has its own book as does concrete, for example.

- National Fire Protection Association (NFPA)

  The NFPA is concerned with any matter related to fire safety, including textiles. Committees are formed to establish standards to reduce loss of life, injury, or loss of property due to fire.

- International Organization of Standardization (ISO)

  The ISO was established in 1947 and is a worldwide federation that includes national standardization bodies from over 140 countries. International agreements on standards are published as international standards. The mission of the ISO is to promote standardization around the world to help facilitate international trade of both goods and services. The ISO covers all spheres of intellectual, technological, scientific, and economic activity, including textile product development and testing.

Verifying Test Results

Performance testing presents many problems. Predicting a fabric's performance under various conditions is sometimes impossible to determine in a laboratory setting. Often, several test methods are used to fully understand how a material will function in a particular situation. When requesting technical data from a manufacturer, the design professional outlines the intended use of the material, specifying exactly how and where a textile product will interface with other components. It is important to obtain test information in written form.

To verify the claims made by manufacturers, millions of dollars are spent yearly evaluating performance test methods. To assure that tests provide valid results, the following criteria have been established:

- Test methods should simulate, as closely as possible, conditions typical of actual use.

- The test should provide reliable and quantitative results.

- It should be possible to repeat and reproduce test results. Tests conducted on a given material in the same laboratory, under the same conditions, should reveal continuity of results.

- The test method should be cost effective. The size and cost of testing equipment, the time required for the test, and the sample size or quantity required for testing must be considered.

- Test results should be reported in terms that are understandable by the people who will read them.

- Interior designers, architects, and code officials must be able to apply test findings in their practices.

Virtually every functional aspect of a textile may be tested by one or more of the methods outlined. Documented test results are often made available by the manufacturers. Except in unusual circumstances, where the slightest deviation may be a hazard to health or safety, guarantees of performance should be acceptable to both the designer and client. Written warranties cover such aspects as breaking strength of carpet, static resistance, flame retardance, guaranteed durable finishes, etc.

For textiles such as carpeting, testing determines sound transfer, resistance to force, pill resistance, adhesive strength, static load resistance, surface flame spread, smoke density, colorfastness, shrinkage, and effective cleaning methods. Tests to ascertain shading coefficients, shrink/sag tendencies, insulating values, and heat transfer may be available from casement and drapery fabric manufacturers or independent testing laboratories. Abrasion and exposure tests for upholstery fabrics may also be undertaken to determine specific performance criteria.

Colorfastness and Maintenance

Colorfastness and maintenance methods are two areas that are often questioned and may need independent testing. (Fire regulations are dealt with in the following section.)

Colorfastness	Textiles may change color for a number for reasons. **Environmental factors** such as sunlight and wear or use may result in color alteration. Laundering or dry cleaning may also cause fading or color change. *Colorfastness* is how well the fabric maintains its color when exposed to conditions such as light, wear, or maintenance. All are more of a problem with intense or dark colors. Lighter shades do not show fading as dramatically. In a patterned or multicolored fabric, one color may be less colorfast than the others, which will cause problems.

Chemical fumes, oily substances, and other specific agents may cause staining, and resistance to these particulars needs consideration. Cigarette smoke is one of the worst offenders in changing a textile's color. If smoking is permitted in an area being designed, special attention is essential to devise a satisfactory solution.

When assessing color change of any kind, the light sources used for testing purposes should match the full range of light sources in the area of the textile's use—direct sunlight, incandescent light, halogen light, or fluorescent light.

Crocking is the transfer of color from one fabric to another by rubbing. Dark colors and printed textiles are more likely to have poor crocking performance. The paste used on printed textiles does not normally absorb deeply into the core of the fiber, but simply attaches to the surface making it easy to rub off.

A simple test, on a device known as a **crock-meter**, subjects the fabric sample to a measured amount of abrasion of weight with a small white testing cloth attached. This test is conducted wet and dry, and the two methods often show very different outcomes. The transfer of color onto the white testing cloth is matched for intensity with a gray scale, which helps determines the class or degree of colorfastness to crocking. Class 1 indicates a high degree of crocking; Class 5 indicates negligible or no crocking.

Frosting is similar to crocking, but shows color loss only in areas subject to relatively severe localized flat abrasion, such as the welt on the top front edge of an upholstered cushion. Union-dyed fabrics or printed materials are most susceptible. A test for frosting may be conducted on a surface abrader that subjects the sample to a multidimensional rubbing action and then compares the color of the abraded sample to the original.

COLORFASTNESS TO LIGHT is tested on a Fade-O-Meter, which accelerates the ultraviolet light exposure effect to approximate weeks or months of exposure to sunlight. Fabrics may be exposed for 10-200 hours, depending on the expected real-life exposure. Drapery fabric is usually tested for 80 hours and a fade rating given.

COLORFASTNESS TO WASHING is tested in a variety of ways because there are so many different methods of laundering fabrics. The following variables must be taken into consideration:

- Presoak or no presoak
- Washing temperature: cold to hot
- Cleansing additives: soap, detergents, bleaches—all of various strengths and types
- Proportions of cleansing agent to water
- Mechanical action
- Washing time

From these laundering tests, a recommended method and methods or products that should be avoided are determined. |

	Colorfastness and Maintenance, cont'd	
Colorfastness, cont'd	*COLORFASTNESS TO DRY CLEANING* is tested with perchloroethylene for three reasons: 1. it is the most common commercial dry cleaning solution 2. it is more severe in solvent action than Stoddard solvent (petroleum base) 3. color that is unaffected by perchloroethylene will also be unaffected by Stoddard, while the reverse is not the case. *COLORFASTNESS TO FUME FADING* is a concern with fabrics that will be exposed to the oxides of nitrogen contained in heating or illuminating gases. The most susceptible to fading is acetate dyed with disperse dye. Finishes to prevent fume fading may be applied but these are usually temporary. Samples of new or cleaned fabric may be tested in a gas-fading chamber and the results assessed visually.	
Maintenance	The same laundering, dry cleaning, and spot tests used to test colorfastness are used for checking other factors such as dimensional stability (shrinkage and stretching) and changes in hand or texture. Repeated treatments are necessary to accumulate a true picture of the long-term effects of maintenance.	

Laws and Regulations

Textile laws and regulations, and the industry's quality programs, are stringent and, therefore, a dependable source of information for the design community. Identification and marketing are controlled by government trade or commerce departments; industry guarantee programs are self-imposed and regulated for the benefit of both manufacturer and consumer.

Identification

The most important law for textile specifiers and buyers is the **Textile Fiber Products Identification Act** (TFPIA), which was first adopted in the United States in 1960. It is the standard for all American textile producers. The Canadian Act is called the **Textile Labelling and Advertising Regulations.** Similar regulations are in force in most countries that require identification of fibers in foreign textiles. The main purpose of these regulations is to protect consumers and manufacturers from misbranding and false advertising of the fiber content of textiles. Textile labels must contain the following information:

- generic name(s) of the fiber(s) present in the fabric (trademark names may or may not be included)

- percentage of fiber content by weight

- country of origin

- manufacturers name or registered identification number (in Canada this is the ca number)

Product Warranties

The terms *warranty* and *guarantee* are commonly, but incorrectly, used interchangeably. A **guarantee** is a collateral agreement for the performance of another's undertaking. This most often takes the form of a financial guarantee. The correct term relating to the performance of a textile product is **warranty**. This is a written statement by the seller that certain facts are as they have been presented. The seller may promise that the product is of a certain quality or will perform in a certain manner. The warranty is part of the contract of sale.

> **GUARANTEE:** a written pledge that something is as represented and will be replaced if it does not meet specifications
>
> **WARRANTY:** a written statement by the seller that certain facts are as they have been presented
>
> All warranties are, or should be, *limited* with respect to certain conditions such as time, condition of use, or liability. Reasonable quality for use is implied in most warranties; that is, a product is sold for a broad category of normal end uses.

Legally binding agreements for long-term satisfaction are frequently demanded by design professionals. Consumers have become used to the protection and expect fabrics to be replaced if they are not satisfied with performance. Manufacturers (particularly of carpets) have started to use their warranties as marketing tools to win customers. This is an excellent market-driven consumer protection.

Consumer protection laws may be more stringent than any warranty provided by the seller. In most jurisdictions, products have implied warranties of being free of manufacturing defects for a reasonable period of time unless this is specifically excluded in the contract of sale.

Manufacturer guarantee programs often offer restitution to the purchaser if the textile fails to meet stated performance criteria. Labeling, hang tags, or selvage legends refer to the textiles' warranties and also may refer to guaranteed finishes. A manufacturer might have a five-year free replacement anti-shock guarantee program for antistatic carpets, for example. The designer should ensure that the client is aware of any such programs.

If topical sprays are applied to textiles after installation, the manufacturer warranty may be voided since such treatments are outside their control and can be improperly applied.

Care Instructions

Governments require that instructions for care be attached—permanently on apparel or as hang tags and handouts for roll goods. The textile industry is responsible for accuracy of care instructions and the manufacturers are liable if these instructions, are incorrect. The manufacturer, by attaching a care label, is indicating that these instructions are correct and, when followed, will not substantially affect the use of the textile. Designers have the responsibility of ensuring that the goals of the regulation will be met. They must instruct clients/users to follow the care instructions given to them with the textile product and to let any legitimate dissatisfaction be known to the source where the textile was purchased and/or the manufacturer. The manufacturer can be traced through the identification number that is part of the label. In Canada, consumers can use the **ca** number to find the customer-service representative.

Fire Regulations

Regulations for fire safety are set in order to help reduce the threat to life and property. Fabrics can be flammable and/or produce quantities of smoke and/or toxic fumes, and they often burn or melt easily (in relative degrees) unless treated or engineered to reduce their combustibility. Flammability standards exist for carpets, rugs, and mattresses. Certain expectations of standards also exist for upholstered furnishings, but these are not regulated as stringently as other textile products. Mattresses and furniture are tested for ignition from cigarettes and other sources, and programs exist to oversee the results and disseminate the information. The Upholstered Furniture Action Council (UFAC) is an organization that monitors and tests interior furnishings.

The stages in the development of fire need to be understood in order to understand the basis of fire regulations in the textile industry.

STAGE 1 refers to the time of ignition and the initial fire growth. If the fire remains in the area of ignition (say, a wastepaper basket), it is considered a stage 1 fire. At this stage, material characteristics that may contribute to the further development of fire are very important; the ease of ignition, flame-spread qualities, and the amount of heat and smoke released by a material will play a large part in determining either the eradication or spread of the fire.

STAGE 2 is considered the growth stage when an entire compartment or room becomes involved in the fire. During this stage, **flashover** occurs—most combustible material reaches high enough temperatures that they burst into flame in an explosive manner. Flames spread, oxygen is depleted, and smoke and toxic and volatile gases are created. Interior sprinkler systems will help reduce the damage and chances of injury or loss of life.

STAGE 3 is a fully developed fire. Flashover has occurred. The fire becomes an ignition source for adjacent materials, and new fires develop. The fire continues to spread rapidly throughout the building. Lateral spread may occur through doors, ceilings, and horizontal ducts. Vertical spread occurs through stairs, elevators, open windows, and building ducts and shafts.

Hazardous Materials

The degree of combustibility, flame-spread rate, smoke release, and fume toxicity are all facets of hazardous materials. Potential fire hazards are numerous. Natural and manufactured cellulosic fabrics and underpaddings, if not treated with flame retardants, ignite on contact with a flame and burn easily. Perhaps the greatest interior fire hazards are the abundance of plastic in interior finishes and furnishings and synthetic fibers that are chemically related to plastic.

Plastics

Plastics are everywhere in the built environment, and it is useful to consider their potential danger. They present three major areas of fire hazard.

COMBUSTION SPEED: Plastics burn much more rapidly than natural products, causing faster flame spread.

HEAT: Burning plastics produce intense heat, causing greater fire severity and spread of ignition. One pound of polystyrene releases 10 000 more BTUs (British Thermal Units) than one pound of pine.

SMOKE: Plastics produce great quantities of dense black smoke. Toxic and/or flammable gases are released throughout the combustion period.

Fire Codes

Codes are laws that specify particular standards of performance that are required for buildings to be approved. Codes are set to protect occupants of the buildings from harm and are enacted by federal, state or provincial, and municipal levels. Meeting codes is mandatory, and if a code is not met, it is the designer, architect, or engineer who is liable if any damage or injury occurs because of faulty construction or material selection. Consumers are demanding safety in residential and commercial buildings, and the safety standard is constantly changing. Voluntary quality control helps the textile industry and consumers keep in step with each other to ensure safety and satisfaction with the products.

Fire departments, fire protection associations, members of scientific associations, and consumer safety agencies are united in the goals of educating and regulating, and of preventing injury and fatalities from fire and smoke inhalation. Regulations are numerous, and standards now exist in most countries for carpets and mattresses, as well as apparel.

Application of Code Standards

Everyone involved in the design community must become familiar with codes. Design professionals should be aware that index ratings are confusing and vary according to test method. In some tests, a high index rating indicates greater hazard; in others, it represents a lower hazard. Fire-code officials are faced with extremely difficult decisions, and it is important that design professionals realize that their decision-making process is not easy.

Test methods evaluate flame-spread factors, ease of ignition, amount of smoke, heat production rate, and heat potential. All of these separate factors must be assessed and combined with knowledge of how materials interface within the space.

The safety decisions of design professionals are complex and are complicated by concerns for function, aesthetics, and costs. Evaluating textile selection choices related to a particular project may result in combining factors—X textile, Y finish, Z underpadding or lining, etc.—to achieve an adequate level of fire safety.

Flammability Testing

Flammability tests are invaluable in determining the potential hazard of materials. Some of these tests look at fire safety but also measure sensitivity to heat without flame. The long lists of flammability performance tests shown on many interior products may be confusing. However, each test serves a particular purpose. The following is an outline of some current testing methods.

NFPA 701

The **National Fire Protection Association** 701-1999 Standard Methods of Fire Tests for Flame Resistant Textiles and Films may be used to evaluate the effectiveness of polymer additives and finishing compounds in reducing the flammability of textile window coverings. There are two test methods for use with textiles and films treated with flame-retardant agents or composed of flame-resistant manufactured fibers. Fabrics are expected to retain their flame-resistant qualities through dry cleaning, laundering, weathering, or other exposure and are subjected to accelerated exposure prior to testing. This regulation is revised on a regular basis; specifiers should always check for latest revision date.

NFPA 701 Small-Scale Test Method

This method is used to test fabrics that do not exhibit excessive shrinkage or melting when exposed to a flame.

TEST PROCEDURE: Ten specimens of the covering are cut 2.5 inches x 10 inches. Five have their long dimension in the direction of the filling and five in the direction of the warp. The specimens are then conditioned in an oven at a temperature of 140°F for 1-1.5 hours, or, if they would melt or distort in the oven, they are conditioned at 60-80°F and 25-50% humidity for a minimum of 24 hours. Next, each specimen is placed in an open-ended specimen holder and suspended in a vertical flammability tester. Finally, the flame from a burner is applied to the lower edge for 12 seconds.

In order to pass the test the specimen must meet the following requirements:

1. No specimen shall continue flaming for more than two seconds after the test flame is removed from contact with the specimen.

2. The vertical spread of flame and afterglow on the material as indicated by the length of the char "shall not exceed a length of 3.5-5.5 inches, depending on the weight of the material being tested."

3. At no time during or after the application of the test flame shall portions or residues of textiles or films that break or drip from a test specimen continue to flame after they reach the floor of the tester.

NFPA 701 Large-Scale Test Method

This method is for use with materials that show excessive shrinkage or melting. It is also useful for evaluating the fire behavior of coverings hung in folds.

TEST PROCEDURE: Specimens of the covering material may be tested in single, flat sheets or hung in folds. For flat testing, ten specimens, 5 inches x 7 feet, are cut. For testing with folds, four lengths of the fabric, each cut 25 inches x 7 feet, are folded longitudinally to form four folds, each

approximately 5 inches wide. Half the specimens are cut with the length in the warp direction and half in the filling direction. The specimens are conditioned as described for the small-scale test.

The specimens, flat or folded, are suspended in the tester, which is a sheet-iron rack 12 inches x 12 inches x 7 feet. The lower edge of the specimen is 4 inches above the burner tip and an 11 inch flame is held under the specimen for two minutes.

The material must meet the following requirements to pass the test:

1. No specimen shall continue flaming for more than two seconds after the test flame is removed from contact with the specimen.

2. The vertical spread of burning on the material in single sheets shall not exceed 10 inches from the tip of the test flame to a horizontal line above which all material is sound and in original condition, except for possible smoke deposits.

3. The vertical spread of burning on the folded specimens shall not exceed 35 inches above the tip of the test flame, but the afterglow may spread in the folds.

4. At no time during or after the application of the test flame shall portions or residues of textiles or films that break or drip from a test specimen continue to flame after they reach the floor of the tester.

Methenamine Pill Test

This test was developed by the National Bureau of Standards and adopted by the United States Department of Commerce in 1970. The test method has numerous test codes that cross a number of different methods employed by different agencies. They are ASTM D2859, BS6307, ISO6925, and IWS141. The test is applied to all types of textile floor coverings and is best thought of as a screening test rather than as the final word. Most products need numerous tests to cover the various conditions of fire.

A small ignition source, which in this case is the methenamine pill, is placed in the center on the surface of the conditioned test specimen. The test measures the distance from the location of the fire source to the edge of the affected (burned) area. The ease of ignition is measured.

All carpeting produced in the United States must pass this test. Some regulatory agencies require tests on the back as well as on the top surface and, occasionally, on carpet underpadding.

TEST PROCEDURE: A carpet sample, 22.9 cm², is placed on the bottom of a 30.5 cm draft-protected square box, open at the top. The sample is held in place by a 22.9 cm² metal plate, with a 20.3 cm diameter hole in the center. A highly flammable, timed methenamine pill is placed in the center of the carpet and ignited. Surface flame should not show considerable spread. If the sample burns to within 2.5 cm of the metal plate, it fails the test. The test is repeated 8 times and 7 out of 8 samples must pass to qualify for approval. Rating is straightforward: pass or fail.

In Canada, the Methenamine Pill Test method is found in the National Standard of Canada CAN-2-4.2.

This test is modified in Canada and Canadian design professionals should check the National Building Code and equivalent provincial and municipal codes. As far as carpets and other interior finish materials are concerned, these are only regulated in the code in terms of their burning properties (FSR—Flame Spread Rating) and smoke emission characteristics (SDC—Smoke Developed Classification.) These properties are determined in accordance with (a) CAN4-S12.2-M80 (Standard Method of Test for Surface Burning Characteristics of Flooring, Floor Covering and Miscellaneous Materials) if the carpet is to be installed on the floor of a room, (b) CAN4-S102-M80 (Standard Method of Test for Surface Burning Characteristics of Building Materials) if the carpet is to be installed on a wall or ceiling. S102.2 is a modification of the Steiner Tunnel Test used by some authorities in the United States and described below. It is not identical to the Steiner Test and Steiner results are not acceptable as proof that the product meets Canadian codes.

Steiner Tunnel Test

This test was developed by A. J. Steiner for the Underwriters Laboratories Inc. in the United States and is known under the following testing designations: ASTM E-84, UL 723, UBC 8-1. The test was originally devised to test the comparative surface-burning characteristics of building materials and interior finishes. It is designed to simulate a fully developed fire, and it provides data on flame-spread, fuel contribution, and smoke density. It is currently required by many regulatory agencies. This test does not purport to give complete flammability information and should be used in combination with other tests.

The carpet industry opposes the Steiner Tunnel Test method for carpet for the following reasons:

- Primarily designed for wall and ceiling finish materials, the tunnel test requires carpet to be tested upside down, which causes many fibers to melt and drip at an early stage in the test procedure.

- Research has proven that temperatures during a fire are much higher at ceiling level than at floor level.

- Testing carpets with this method is inconclusive, as it has been difficult to establish repeatable test results.

TEST PROCEDURE: A sample of the material to be tested, 20" x 24', is secured to the ceiling of a 25' tunnel. A double jet gas burner at one end is lit and burns for ten minutes at 300,000 BTU/hr. Air is induced into the tunnel to pull the flame upstream for about 4 feet. The distance of the burn along the test sample is measured visually to determine the flame-spread rating. Materials are rated according to flame-spread range: 0 indicates no burn; 100 is a moderate burn rate. Smoke density is measured by the optical cell mounted at the tunnel's exhaust.

The Chamber Test

This method was developed as an alternative to the Steiner Tunnel Test. The Chamber Test determines the flame spread and flame propagation of carpet. It is used by some regulatory agencies.

TEST PROCEDURE: A carpet sample, 0.6 m x 2.4 m (2" x 8") is installed on the floor of a chamber. A gas flame is then applied to the carpet for 12 minutes, along with a controlled air draft. Calculations for rating are based on the length of the flame spread and time of flame travel. The rating index has not been accepted as relevant as it divides material into two groups and continuous classification is difficult.

Radiant Floor Panel Test

This test is *highly recommended* for testing floor-covering systems; it measures radiant exposures that are very important in corridors and exits. The flooring system is tested on a horizontal plane in the same way as a carpet is used. The test procedure is simple, and the apparatus is simple and compact and uses only a small test sample. Reproducibility and repeatability of test results are excellent.

The test simulates and measures the flame spread in a corridor or in an exit that is under the influence of a fully developed fire in an adjacent room. In building fires, the fully developed fire can transmit heat and radiant energy to the ceilings and walls of an adjacent corridor, igniting the carpet and blocking what might be the only means of escape. Most major regulatory agencies have adopted this test: EN ISO 9239, ASTM E 648, NFPA 253.

TEST PROCEDURE: A sample, 20 cm x 99 cm, is mounted horizontally and receives radiant energy from an air gas-fueled radiant panel mounted above the sample at a 30° angle. After the sample is preheated, a gas-fired pilot burner ignites the flooring sample. The distance burned is measured and converted into a flux number that becomes the *flame-spread index*, expressed in watts per square centimeter (watts/cm^2). The higher the number, the more resistant the material is to flame propagation. A *critical radiant flux* rating is the minimum energy necessary to sustain flame in the flooring system. Class II average minimum is 0.22 watts/cm^2 for corridors and exits of day cares, existing correctional facilities, hotels, dorms, and apartment buildings. Class II minimum is 0.45 watts/cm^2 for corridors and exits of healthcare facilities (hospitals and nursing homes) and newly constructed correctional facilities.

A smoke-measuring system is mounted on a separate frame at the exhaust stack.

Smoke Density Chamber

This test was devised to measure the smoke potential of solid materials.

TEST PROCEDURE: The chamber is an enclosed cabinet 61 cm x 91.4 cm x 91.4 cm. A 7.6 cm^2 square sample of material is secured vertically in a holder while exposed to heat under conditions with flame present and conditions with heat, but no flame present. A photometric meter measures light density in the resulting smoke. The rating is from 0-800, with most regulatory agencies who use this test method requiring a smoke density of 450 or less (flaming).

In the United States, the federal government, the industry, and design professionals are trying to develop upholstery flammability testing methods. Proposed flammability standards have been put forth by the Department of Commerce (DOC) to standardize upholstered furniture under the alpha numeric code PFF 6-81 (16 CFR 1633).

Other new standards related to interiors are FF 1-70, proposed by the DOC in the United States for large carpets and rugs, FF 2-70 for small carpets and rugs, and FF 4-74 for mattress pads and mattresses. These are all worth becoming familiar with, as they impact material selections.

Professional Responsibilities

Designers have a responsibility to see that various regulations aimed at consumer safety are followed. Risk management is concerned mostly with fire regulations and the decisions that designers, as well as code officials, have to make regarding product specification. The following are basic fire risk-management guidelines that should be reviewed frequently:

Guidelines for the Specifications of Upholstered Furniture: Fire

Designers specifying upholstered furniture for commercial and institutional use should be aware of particular installations that may present special fire hazards. These include:

- areas where smoking is permitted
- areas that accommodate seating for periods of time, such as planes, buses, rapid transit systems, transportation terminals, cocktail lounges, bars, restaurants and lounge areas in public buildings
- areas where the lighting level is low
- live-in accommodations (Areas that include bedding as well as seating are particularly vulnerable to fire hazard.)

For any of the above commercial or institutional situations, and particularly where there is a combination of all four factors, special upholstery flammability considerations are in order.

Burning Behavior of Fibers

FIBER	WHILE APPROACHING THE FLAME	WHILE IN THE FLAME	AFTER REMOVAL FROM FLAME	RESIDUE	ODOR
NATURAL					
Protein					
Wool	Curls away from flame	Burns slowly	Self-extinguishes	Small, black, brittle bead	Similar to burning hair
Silk	Curls away from flame	Burns slowly	Self-extinguishes	Crushable, black bead	Similar to burning hair
Cellulosic					
Cotton	Ignites upon contact with flame	Burns quickly	Continues to burn; has an afterglow	Light, feathery, gray ash	Similar to burning paper
Linen	Ignites upon contact with flame	Burns quickly	Continues to burn; has an afterglow	Light, feathery charcoal-colored ash	Similar to burning paper
MANUFACTURED					
Cellulosic					
Acetate	Melts away from flame	Burns quickly and melts	Continues to burn and melt	Brittle, black bead	Acid-vinegar
Rayon	Ignites close to contact; does not shrink away	Burns quickly; does not melt	Continues to burn; afterglow	Light, fluffy ash	Similar to burning paper
Mineral					
Glass	Shrinks away from flame	Melts, glows red	Glowing stops	Hard, white bead	No odor
Metallic-pure	No reaction, or may shrink away from flame	Glows red	Glowing stops; hardens	Hardened fiber	No odor
Noncellulosic					
Acrylic	Shrinks away from flame	Burns and melts	Continues to burn and melt, then self-extinguishes	Brittle, black bead	Acrid
Modacrylic	Shrinks away from flame	Burns slowly and melts	Self-extinguishes	Hard, black bead	Chemical, acid
Nylon	Shrinks away from flame	Burns slowly and melts	Self-extinguishes	Hard, round gray bead	Celery
Aramid	Shrinks away from flame	Ignites at very high temperatures only	Self-extinguishes	Thick char	Chemical
Olefin	Shrinks and curls away from flame	Burns and melts	Continues to burn and has sooty smoke	Hard, tan bead	Chemical
Polyester	Shrinks away from flame	Burns slowly and melts	Self-extinguishes	Hard, black bead	Chemical
Saran	Shrinks away from flame	Burns slowly in yellow flame, melts	Self-extinguishes	Hard, black bead	Chemical
Spandex	Fuses, but does not shrink away from flame	Burns and melts	Continues to burn and melt	Soft, crushable fluffy ash	Chemical
Vinyon	Shrinks away from flame	Burns slowly and melts	Self-extinguishes	Hard, black bead	Acrid

- Fabric with a high thermoplastic fiber content or a form of flame-retardant or heat barrier should be specified.

- Areas where a cigarette may lodge and burn should be minimized. These include tufting or other decorative surface treatment used on horizontal seats and arms; welt cording, which should be composed of a treated material or PVC and used only where necessary; and the crevice where back and seat areas join.

- Seams used across the seat area should be avoided; they tend to pull loose under heavy use, which exposes the inner filling material to possible ignition from a cigarette.

Designers should not use inappropriate terminology in dealing with fire-related terms. Descriptive expressions such as *nonburning* and *noncombustible* are not part of the accepted terminology and tend to be confused with phrases that have definite and precise meanings.

In the United States, the Federal Trade Commission (FTC) has warned that certain cellular plastic products present serious hazards in case of fire. They produce significantly higher flame-spread in actual fire conditions. Designers should be cautious about specifying these materials as furniture components: polyurethane foam, polystyrene foam, polyvinyl chloride foam, ABS foam, cellulose acetate foam, epoxy foam, phenolic foam, polyethylene foam, urea foam, polypropylene foam, silicone foam, and foamed latex.

The Upholstered Furniture Action Council has devised a program to help reduce the cigarette ignition of upholstered furniture. A hang-tag identifies items that comply with Council's standards. Products with this tag are safer, but are not completely fireproof.

Specifying Flame-Resistant Materials

When specifying a flame-resistant textile, the following information should be requested from the manufacturer:

1. What is the fiber content?

2. What type of flame-retardant chemical has been used if the fabric is labeled *flame resistant?*

The designer will then have to establish whether or not the flame-retardant chemical meets the required standard of the local authorities. The same checklist of information will be necessary for all textiles being specified, whether linings or face fabrics.

When specifying flame-resistant upholstered furniture, the following is a checklist of information that must be obtained from the manufacturer:

√ The fiber content of the upholstery covering

√ If the fabric is labeled *flame resistant,* the type of flame retardant used

√ If welt cording is used, its fiber content

√ If fabric is to be specified *customer's own material* if the fabric will accept a chemical retardant treatment, if the treatment will adversely affect the soil resistance of the fabric, and if any shrinkage will occur

√ The filling materials used in the horizontal areas, vertical areas, deck areas, and for loose cushions

√ If any of the above filling materials are to be treated with flame retardant

√ If a heat barrier is to be used, the type and how it will be applied—as a liner, backcoating, or encased around the filling

√ If the flame-retardant chemical used or proposed meets the required standards of the authority within the jurisdiction

√ If flame retardants are added to upholstery fabric, filling material, or welt cording, what the cost for each component is

Risk-Management Guidlines

General:

√ Obtain up-to-date, pertinent fire-code standards for type of project and location of project.

√ Know who to contact for specific and detailed information.

√ Attend fire-safety seminars provided for architects, designers, and facility managers.

√ Keep informed on new test methods as they are developed.

Project Specific:

√ Early in any design process, determine the potential fire hazard of the project.

√ Obtain up-to-date, pertinent, fire codes for job site.

√ Determine the performance test method that will provide the level of fire protection information required for the project.

√ Use concise fire terminology in specifications.

Documentation

Acquire information about material performance in writing. Warranties are available through the manufacturer or the supplier—be sure to receive them. Each warranty stipulates certain installation, operational, and maintenance requirements that, if neglected, invalidate the warranty agreement. The design professional should pass this information on to the client, in writing, and keep a copy on file.

If specific warranty agreements are not available, the design team should note and record all pertinent information that is written on carpet backs, hang tags, or other sources, and keep a complete file on the project and, in particular, correspondence to manufacturers and the client.

The design team's own checklists and matrix forms (if used) can also illustrate a conscientious effort to investigate a product's reliability. Success in establishing compliance with standards governing professional liability will be, in most cases, in direct proportion to the quantity and quality of the documentation of professional concern.

The development of a checklist is very useful in summarizing all the information accumulated through the performance evaluation process. Items such as carpet, drapery, wall covering, seating, and space dividers can be listed with the necessary fire-safety requirements and test methods. Requirements determined by prescribed federal or local codes should be matched to the test methods acceptable for meeting codes, regulations, and/or local standards—along with the designer's own tests. All results should be recorded and filed with other project details. The location of certain components is important because many code requirements vary with the proposed use or location of the material. This should also be noted and recorded.

Other checklists may be devised to measure individual components against all the performance requirements: health and safety, maintenance, durability, and functional effectiveness.

These forms provide an accurate record of performance requirements for each design project. As the project proceeds, the checklist could help prevent oversights in compliance with various code requirements. Most important, the written record documents accountability and professionalism.

Performance Requirements of Interior Textiles

	Fire Resistance	Strength	Abrasion Resistance	Dimensional Stability	Resilience	Color Stability	Crockfastness	Lightfastness	Glare Resistance	Privacy	Cleanability	Static Control	Acoustical Control	Thermal Control	Hand
Carpet	*	*	*	*	*	*	*	*			*	*	*	*	*
Casements	*	*		*			*	*	*	*				*	
Drapery	*	*		*		*	*	*	*	*			*	*	
Upholstery	*	*	*	*	*	*	*	*			*	*			*
Wall Coverings	*			*		*					*	*	*	*	

PART
FOUR

FUTURE OF TEXTILES

Technology builds on knowledge from the past to create advancements for the future. The textile industry is constantly making changes to existing products, inventing new products, and improving the processing technology. The entire textile complex—from fibers, to yarns, fabrics, dyes, finishes, and marketing—is affected by technological advances. Fiber engineering is fusing with traditional manufacturing techniques to create aesthetically pleasing and high-performance textile products in all segments of the industry, including interior textiles. Research is no longer dedicated only to making production less expensive; it is also focusing on making fabrics more interesting and useful in our lives. Environmental concerns also dictate the direction of much of the research. Textiles are being produced in safer conditions with fewer polluting emissions and less run off. Such products are referred to as 'environmentally sustainable,' 'eco-sensitive,' or 'green.' And in the end the textiles still must perform well, feel good, and look beautiful.

Much of the textile research occurs in Europe, North America, and Japan. Some of the more interesting and innovative fabrics are adopted first in Japan, and then eventually in the rest of the world. In Japan, **ultramicrofiber**, for example, is replacing microfiber—new processing techniques make fibers even smaller in diameter than microfibers. **Smart fabrics** are also gaining acceptance. Spinning processes for yarns are being adapted, as are weaving techniques, but much of these two areas are limited to manipulations of the machinery.

Nonwoven fabric production has been using innovative fibers for years, but new fibers are transforming the end uses of nonwoven fabrics. Recent innovations are concentrated in the areas of finishing, coloring, and fiber engineering. Products are aiming to be more consistently uniform with better performance characteristics while expanding the range of products or adding novelty to the fabrics. The original goals of synthetic fiber scientists were to imitate natural fibers in performance, hand (feel), and aesthetics. Rayon, for instance, was intended as a replacement for silk, but, as a cellulosic fiber, it also had many of the same performance characteristics as cotton or linen. Nylon and polyester were both meant to imitate the continuous filament of silk, but with better wear and easier care. Today, researchers no longer try to imitate natural fibers, but try to improve the performance and processing technology of older manufactured fibers. Fibers are now being used as conductors of electricity. State of the art equipment is being developed to help textile researchers and manufacturers progress in the areas of high-performance textiles and environmental sustainability of the whole industry.

Fibers and Information Technology

The future of high-performance fiber technology is in the area of bicomponent fibers. Production technology will allow for multiple fibers to be spun simultaneously and in layers and give the fiber multiple performance characteristics. The sheath and core construction produce electroconductivity in fibers, for example. A polyester filament can be coated with conductive polyurethane, which contains carbon black. The fibers remain more flexible than the chrome or nickel wires, previously used as conductors of electricity in textiles. Alternately, aramid can be spun with ultrafine steel fibers dispersed throughout. Electronic capabilities in textiles enable fabrics to become extensions of our senses and how we interact with them in our built environment.

Already, smart fabrics can sense heart rate or even hormone levels. The fibers are beginning to be used in the medical profession, helping doctors monitor patients from a distance. Information technology (IT) textile products, such as wearable computers and cellular telephones, are not far in the future. They might sound like gadgets in a spy movie, but it may not be long before they are incorporated into our daily lives.

Smart clothing is being tested and slowly adopted, and *smart rooms* are in the experimentation stage. Already, lighting technology allows lights to react to human presence in a room, turning on when someone enters and turning off when the last person leaves. Computers can also monitor and eliminate indoor pollution and toxic substances in the air, and help reduce exposure to harmful ultraviolet rays of the sun. In England, researchers are creating walls made entirely of computer screen that can be changed to whatever design the user desires, at any time. With specific instructions, a computer will change the wall 'treatment' to different designs, colors, or patterns. With research well underway, software constantly changing, and prototypes continually being produced and tested, it is only a matter of time until smart products are available to a wide consumer base.

Fiber Blending

Thirty years ago, blending fibers meant blending entire polyester fibers with entire cotton fibers. This is still done, and polyester—which does not absorb water, but is extremely strong— and cotton—which is weaker, but hydrophilic—take on each other's positive characteristics and minimize their less desirable ones. Today many different variations of synthetic fibers are spun at the same time to create ultrafine denier fibers or bicomponent fibers. These fibers can be treated with finishes or spun to create craters that improve on their deficiencies and result in fine, highly technical fibers. Microfiber technology will have a great impact on the future of textiles. As production techniques change and allow fibers to be spun in smaller denier (fiber size), they move further away from natural fibers in their inherent properties and performance. Microfibers have a denier of less than one, and are more often closer to .01, or even less. These fibers can be used in very dense fabric structures, where the yarns are packed closely together. The fibers are lightweight, crease resistant, soft, strong, and have excellent drape. They can be used in fabrics for apparel or interiors and bring new characteristics to the fabric and final products.

Fiber Technology and Renewable Resources

The chemical composition of most manufactured, or synthetic, fibers has remained unchanged since they were first introduced. These fibers are coal- or oil-based, and they are not particularly environmentally sustainable. One of the newest innovative fiber types is made from chitin, the safe, natural substance that gives stiffness to a crab's shell. Chitin (N-acetylglucosamine), is a polysaccharide, but has a strong positive charge, which allows it to bind to other negative charges. Chitin, a renewable resource, is likely to become a mainstay of future textiles. Billions of tons of crustaceans are available to fill any future demand. Chitin is often blended with rayon (Crabyon® by Omikenshi of Japan) or with cotton. The fiber is resistant to chemicals; has antibacterial, antifungal, and antiviral properties; and is nonallergenic. These properties make chitin an excellent fiber for use in the healthcare (medical) field for wound dressing, sutures, and grafts. Chitin is biodegradable and, depending on finishes and dye methods, safe for the environment. This fiber has great potential in the textile field, and it is more environmentally sustainable than early synthetic fibers.

Fabric Production Technology

Knit and woven fabrics rely heavily on traditional production methods. While production is much faster and more efficient than ever before, equipment is used much as it has been for the past century. Fabric makers must adapt equipment to suit the needs of new fiber technologies that affect yarn types and fabric construction needs. Fabric producers adapt to new fiber technology or to new finishes that will be applied after they have finished with the product. Looms and knitting machines are adapted for smaller denier fiber, and spinning equipment is adapted to spin the yarn without breaking the fine filaments. Ultramicrofibers create fabrics that are highly packed and have excellent drape. Advancements in this area are likely to continue to focus on reducing costs and increasing production speeds. Other goals are to improve uniformity in fabrics and to create lower-cost, higher-quality fabrics. Uniformity is important when considering durability and how long the textile product will be used.

Nonwoven fabrics are usually in the forefront where new fiber technology is applied. The nonwoven segment remains a growing area with new end uses (often for temporary one-time-use textiles), for cleaning and maintenance, and healthcare. These new fabrics are more durable, sometimes washable, and chemical resistant. They do not fray and can handle complex cutting patterns and treatments. They are inexpensive to produce and can be finished to imitate regular woven fibers. Future research in this area will be in the disposable products market, which is accepting these products readily. Producing convenient, high-performance nonwovens that also satisfy growing demand for environmental sustainability could be a promising direction in this area.

Finishing and Coloring Textiles

Types and application techniques for finishes seem endless. The future of textiles is highly concentrated in this area. Textiles will be made to end-use specifications more than ever before. Fabric treatments are poised to change the world of textiles in terms of comfort, beauty, and performance. Newer finishes make fabrics more beautiful; affect health and wellness, color intensity and luster; and even make clothing smell more pleasant.

COLOR ENHANCING finishes are applied in the form of silica particles and alkaline. They work when the silica reacts with the alkaline and creates microcratering on the fiber surface. These are depressions or spacings in the fiber and are similar to wavelengths of light. The craters redirect major fractures of light toward the inside of the fiber, rather than away from it, making the color appear more intense. This process requires no extra dye or processing.

Colorless compounds are being used in experiments where microencapsulation is combined with bicomponent fibers. The microencapsulation contains clear compounds that react with ambient temperatures. A textile might be clear or translucent inside (at room temperature), but turn a very dark color, such as navy or dark gray, when exposed to cooler, outdoor conditions.

PRINT TECHNOLOGY is also advancing. While traditional screen-printing creates detailed prints, flaws in the process make the prints less uniform once the entire length of fabric is printed. The basis for future textile printing is related to the same computer printing technology that we use every day at work and school. Prints can be designed and tested on computers (with computer-aided design (CAD) programs), then printed on ink-jet printers. Exact replicas of the computer pattern are printed, with textile print pigments, and are more consistent than traditional methods. Print technology is equipped to handle wide widths of fabrics and infinite lengths of pattern repeats.

BACTERIA DYES are being developed to create the look of indigo blue used in denim fabric. Traditional indigo (made from leaves of indigo plants) has a trace of red; for centuries, producers have been trying to eliminate it. Bacteria-produced indigo dye is infused with bacteria that removes any trace of redness from the blue. The blue dye is more like plant-derived indigo than other synthetic processes have been. This type of indigo production is also more environmentally sustainable than other indigo production methods, which use vast amounts of water or harmful and unsustainable raw materials such as coal or oil byproducts.

SCENTED FIBERS have been used for decades, but have never been durable or widely accepted. Scent can be a positive mood enhancer and can add to the pleasure of using certain textiles. Compounds related to health and wellness are also being used. Sleep enhancers, for example, can be added to bedding and pajama fabrics to help with insomnia. Scented bedding and home furnishings can help maintain freshness in an interior, and scent on clothing can have a positive effect on the wearer.

Advances in bicomponent fibers are key to producing scented and medically charged fibers. The core-sheath fiber helps prevent the loss of scent by placing the perfumed particles on the inside core of the fiber, hidden so as not to be affected by high heat processing and spinning. Dispersal of the scent occurs with use and friction when fibers release the substance to the surface.

Microencapsulation is being used on different types of fabrics, both in the apparel sector and in the interior

sector. Polyurethane or urea-formaldehyde resin capsules strong enough to withstand production are being used to contain scent (or medicins). Silicone binders hold the perfume inside the fiber during laundering and maintenance of the fabric. The capsules are weak enough, however, to rupture when there is friction applied to the fabric during regular use. Extra fragrance-loaded strips are sometimes placed in areas where offensive odors might occur. Interior upholstered furniture is a good end use for this type of finish. Flower scents, such as rose or lavender, are often used, but future applications of microencapsulation could include health promoting substances to improve our lives. Vitamins, minerals, and even mosquito repellent might soon be part of everyday fabrics.

Antibacterial finishes that fend off bacteria and fungi growth are presently used and well researched. The finishes fight offensive odor buildup in fibers that come in contact with skin or other sources of bacteria. The healthcare industry, apparel industry, and interior industry all benefit from these finishes. Antimicrobial finishes can be added to the fibers or to finished fabrics. New in this area are the bicomponent fiber structures. Finishes can be added to the core of the fiber or can be microencapsulated in the same way as scent. With use, the finish is released and attacks bacteria that are growing on the fiber, reducing chances of infection and buildup of bad odors.

The annual Frankfurt TechTextil Fair in Germany showcases the most up-to-date technological advances in the textile industry with some very exciting and sometimes bizarre ideas presented. Some ideas eventually become widely accepted, and some do not. But the fair provides an opportunity to see the direction technical textile fabrics is headed. Constant innovation in university labs and at textile firms means that the technology is constantly being updated. Environmental issues, geotextiles (textiles used in the outdoor environment), and industrial textiles are often the focus of initial research.

BIBLIOGRAPHY

Adrosko, R. J., Cooper, G. R., *Spinning and Weaving,* Smithsonian Institute Press, Washington, D.C., 1977.

Aff Encyclopedia of Textiles, 3rd ed. by editors of American Fabrics and Fashion Magazine. Prentice Hall, Inc., Englewood Cliffs, N.J., 1980.

All About Textiles, American Textile Manufacturers' Institute, Charlotte, North Carolina, 1978.

American Association for Textile Technology, Textile Fibers and Their Properties, Burlington Industries Inc., Greensboro, North Carolina, 1977.

Bennett, W., *Designs Textiles for Brickel Associates, 3rd ed.* Brickel Associates Inc., New York, 1981.

Berkovich, J. E., *Trends in Japanese Textile Technology,* U.S. Department of Commerce, 1996.

Braddock, S.E., O'Mahony, M., *Techno Textiles: Revolutionary fabrics for fashion and design,* Thames and Hudson Ltd., London, 1999.

Burnham, D. K., *The Comfortable Arts, Traditional Spinning and Weaving in Canada,* National Gallery of Canada/National Museums of Canada, Ottawa, 1981.

Bumham, H. B. and Bumham, D., *Keep Me Warm One Night,* University of Toronto Press, Toronto, Canada, 1972.

Coen, L., Duncan, L., *The Oriental Rug,* Harper and Row, Publishers, New York, 1978.

Contract Carpet Manual, The Canadian Carpet Institute, Ottawa, 1988.

Crane, C. C., ed., *Residential Interiors Today,* Whitney Library of Design, New York, 1977.

Caplan, R., *The Design of Herman Miller,* Whitney Library of Design, New York, 1976.

Collier, B.J., Torotora, P.G., *Understanding Textiles, 6th ed.,* Prentice Hall, New Jersey, 2001.

Craft House, Williamsburg Reproductions, The Colonial Williamsburg Foundation, Williamsburg, Virginia, 1976.

Eberle, H., Hermeling, H., Hornberger, M., Menzer, D., Ring, W., *Clothing Technology,* Verlag Europa-Lehrmittel, Haan Guiten, 1995.

Eisler, B., *The Lowell Offering,* J.B. Lippincott Company, Philadelphia and New York, 1977.

Eldringhoff, S. K., *A Survey of Factors for Drapery Specification,* Thesis, Faculty of Graduate School, University of Missouri, August 1968.

Facts About Fabrics, DuPont DeNemours & Co. Inc., Textile Fibers Department, Wilmington, Delaware.

Faulkner, R. and Faulkner, S., *Inside Today's Home, 4th Ed.,* Holt, Rinehart and Winston, New York, 1975.

Fiber Expressions: The Contemporary Quilt, Quilt National, Schiffer Publishing Ltd., West Chester, Pennsylvania, 1987.

Friedman, A., Pile, J. F., Wilson, F., *Interior Design— An Introduction to Architectural Interiors, 2nd ed.* American Elsevier Publishing Company, New York, 1976.

Gohl, E.P.G., Vilensky, L.D., *Textile Science; an explanation of fibre properties, 2nd ed.,* Longman Cheshire Pty Ltd., Melbourne, Australia, 1983.

Guide to Man-Made Fibers, Man-made Fiber Producer's Association Inc., Washington, 1977.

Gutcheon, B., *The Perfect Patchwork Primer,* Penguin Books Ltd., New York, 1977.

Hatch, K.L., *Textile Science,* West Publishing Company, St. Paul, MN., 1993.

Heckenlaible, D. F., *Development and Documentation of a Catalogue of Historic American Textiles in the Related Art Division Permanent Collection,* Thesis, Faculty of Graduate School, University of Minnesota, August, 1969.

Hollen, N., Saddler, J., *Textiles, 4th ed.,* Macmillan Publishing Co. Inc., New York, 1973.

Hudson, P.B., Clapp, A.C., Kness, D., Joseph's *Introductory Textile Science, 6th ed.,* Harcourt Brace Jovanovich College Publishers, New York, 1993.

Interplay—The Story of Man-Made Fibers, Man-made Fiber Producers Association Inc., Washington, 1975.

Joseph, M. L., *Essentials of Textile Science, 3rd ed.,* Holt, Rinehart and Winston, New York, 1984.

Kadolph, S., Langford, A., Hollen, N., Saddler, J., *Textiles, 7th ed.,* MacMillan Publishing Co., New York, 1993.

Klapper, M., *Textile Glossary,* Fairchild Publications, Inc., New York, 1973.

Klein, B., *Eye For Colour,* Bernat Klein, Scotland, with Collins Landau, England, 1965.

Lanier, M. B., *English Oriental Carpets at Williamsburg,* The Colonial Williamsburg Foundation, Williamsburg, Virginia, 1975.

Larsen, J. L. and Weeks, J., *Fabrics for Interiors,* Van Nostrand Reinhold Company, New York, 1975.

Lewis, A. A., *The Mountain Artisans Quilting Book,* Macmillan Publishing Co., Inc., New York, 1974.

Liebetrau, P., *Oriental Rugs in Colour,* Macmillan Publishing Co., Inc. New York, 1963.

Lubell, C., *Textile Collections of the World, Volume 1—United States and Canada,* Volume II—United Kingdom and Ireland, Volume III —France. Van Nostrand Reinhold Company, New York, 1976.

Man-Made Fibers Fact Book, Man-Made Fiber Producers Association, Inc. Washington, 1978.

McKendry, R., *Quilts and Other Bed Coverings in the Canadian Tradition,* Van Nostrand Reinhold, New York, 1979.

Miller, E., *Textiles, Properties and Behaviour.* B.T.Batsford Ltd., 1968.

Pizzuto, J. J., *Fabric Science, 5th Ed.;* revised by Arthur Price and Alien C. Cohen. Fairchild Publications, New York, 1978.

Propst, R. and Wodka, M., *The Action Office Acoustic Handbook, 2nd Ed.,* Herman Miller Research Corporation. 1975.

Reed, S., *Oriental Rugs and Carpets,* Octopus Books Limited, London, England, 1972.

Reznikoff, S. C., *Specifications for Commercial Interiors, Professional Liabilities, Regulations and Performance Criteria,* Whitney Library of Design, New York, 1979.

Scobey, J., *Rugs and Wall Hangings,* The Dial Press, 1974.

Shoshkes, L., *Contact Carpeting,* Whitney Library of Design, New York, 1974.

Snook, B., *The Creative Art of Embroidery,* The Hamlyn Publishing Group Limited, London, 1972.

Swan, S. B., *Plain and Fancy, American Women and Their Needlework 1700-1850,* Holt Rinehart and Winston, New York, 1977.

Textiles From Start to Finish, American Textile Manufacturers' Institute, Charlotte, North Carolina.

Textiles Our First Great Industry, American Textile Manufacturers' Institute, Charlotte, North Carolina.

The Textile Industry and Burlington's Position in It, Burlington Industries Ltd., Greensboro, North Carolina, 1975.

Thorpe, A. S., Larsen. J. L., *Elements of Weaving,* Doubleday and Company, Inc., New York, 1978.

Tortora, P., Merkel, R., *Fairchild's Dictionary of Textiles, 7th ed.,* Fairchild Publications, New York, 1996.

Yeager, J., Teter-Justice, K., *Textiles for Residential and Commercial Interiors,* Fairchild Publications, New York, 2000.

GLOSSARY / INDEX

A

abaca fiber obtained from the leaf stalk of the banana plant. Also called Manila hemp. (35, 54)

abrasion resistance ability of fabric to withstand damage from rubbing and wear. (44, 59, 80, 81, 86, 88, 107, 122, 142, 143, 157, 158, 175, 184, 189)

absorbency the ability to take in moisture. (36, 38, 44, 47, 49, 50, 52, 53, 56, 58, 61, 63, 67, 69, 70, 72, 74, 75, 77, 78, 81, 142, 149, 184)

acetate generic term for a manufactured fiber composed of acetylated cellulose. (35, 43, 60, 62, 63, 108, 111, 113, 116, 124, 125, 126, 137, 141, 168, 199, 205, 206)

acid dyes class of dyes used primarily for protein and nylon fibers. (123, 124, 125, 177)

acoustical insulation employed to reduce the sound or noise. (149)

Acrilan® trade name of an acrylic fiber produced by Monsanto. (70)

acrylic generic term for fiber composed of acrylonitrile units which are derived from petrochemical by-products. (23, 35, 39, 44, 70, 71, 72, 73, 85, 111, 118, 124, 125, 127, 167, 173, 174, 175, 184, 205)

additive finishes general term for finishes that are chemical rather than mechanical, typically used to modify a fabric's appearance, hand, or function. (5, 9, 12, 31, 36, 37, 58, 65, 66, 68, 69, 76, 89, 112, 113, 115, 116, 117–22, 123, 124, 125, 138, 139, 141, 142, 143, 144, 151, 154, 156, 157, 160, 161, 162, 177, 192, 197, 199, 200, 201, 203, 211, 212, 213, 214)

adhesives chemicals used to bond pile yarns to primary backings and secondary backings. Also referred to as latex backing. (10, 12, 87, 106, 107, 110, 111, 140, 144, 162, 166, 169, 183, 184, 187, 190)

alpaca long, fine, natural protein hair fiber obtained from the domesticated South American alpaca, a member of the camel family; a wool variant. (35, 57, 59)

angora goat native to Turkey from which the natural protein fiber, mohair, is obtained; a wool variant. (35, 59)

animal fiber general term for natural protein fiber of animal origin, such as wool (sheep) or silk (silkworm). (15, 33, 36, 57, 59, 180)

antibacterial finishes chemical treatments (bacteriostats) applied to finished cloth to repel mildew and other microorganisms. (120, 214)

antique satin cloth of sateen construction with an exaggerated slub filling and a fine warp. (100)

antistatic finishes chemical treatments for reducing static electricity in synthetic fibers. (119–20, 141)

Antron® DuPont's trademarked term for nylon carpet fiber, a strong, soil-hiding fiber with four hollow tubes within the fiber. (23, 33, 64, 176, 177)

apparent soil term used for the magnification of real soil deposited on individual, nearly transparent fibers. (175, 176)

aramid generic term for a modified nylon fiber. (24, 35, 67, 118, 124, 205, 212)

Arnel® trade name for a triacetate fiber produced by Celanese. (43)

asbestos natural mineral fiber used for its inherently flame resistant property. (36, 118)

ASTM the American Society for Testing and Materials. ASTM Standards minimum standards set by the ASTM. (32, 197, 202, 203, 204)

Axminster cut pile woven woolen fabric used for carpeting. (21, 163, 166, 167)

azoic dyes (naphthol) class of dyes used on cellulosic and selected manufactured fibers. (124, 125, 191)

B

backfilling supplementary filling yarn used to pad or support a cloth.

backing a semi-liquid latex or plastic sprayed or rolled on fabric back to increase stability and prevent seam slippage. (2, 105, 111,149, 158, 166, 168, 172, 174, 178, 181, 183, 185, 188)

backing fabric fabric that is bonded or laminated to the reverse side of a face fabric. (104, 105, 111, 145, 166)

bacteriostats general term for microorganism repellents. (118, 141, 151)

Banlon® trade name of a process for adding texture to filament yarns, licensed by Joseph Bancroft. (89)

bar, barré, or **color bar** a flaw in cloth—line of off-shade color running crosswise in a fabric caused by a change in loom tension or irregular dyeing. (195)

barathea twill variation with a broken rib weave on one face and a pebbly texture on the other. (100)

bark cloth a) roughly woven drapery fabric with a bark-like texture b) non-woven material made from soaked and beaten inner bark of tropical trees such as tapa. (109)

basic dyes class of synthetic dyes effective on acrylics, modified nylon and modified polyester. Also called cationic dyes. (125)

basket weave balanced plain weave in which two or more warp yarns interlace with two or more filling yarns. (97, 100)

bast fibers woody fibers from the stems of plants such as flax, jute and hemp. (140)

batik resist print in which wax is drawn or blocked onto a fabric before dyeing. (10, 18, 19, 128)

batiste fine, sheer, plain-woven cloth of combed and carded long-staple cotton. (100)

batten see 'beater'.

batting layers or sheets of fiber used for lining quilts. (83, 110–11)

BCF (bulked continuous filament) continuous strands of synthetic fiber, which are spun into yarn and textured to add bulk and cover. (166, 188)

beaker dyeing dyeing of small fabric samples during color development.

beam cylinder attached to a loom, on which the warp is wound. (95)

beater movable frame on a loom that holds the reed and packs the filling yarns into place. (196)

Bedford cord a weave with padded ridges parallel to the lengthwise grain of the fabric. Originally made of wool, now made in a variety of fibers. (98, 99)

Bemberg® trade name of a process for producing cuprammonium rayon fibers. (60, 100)

Berber yarn hand- or machine-spun wool yarn with a mottled, natural color and irregular diameter.

Beta® trade name of an extremely fine bulked-glass fiber with improved abrasion resistance and flexing properties, manufactured by Owens-Corning. (80)

bias invisible line at a 45° angle to the grain of a fabric; the diagonal. (96)

bicomponent fiber single fiber formed by extruding two different modifications of a polymer solution as one filament. (41, 212, 214)

biconstituent fiber single fiber formed by extruding two generically different polymer solutions as one filament. (42)

bird's eye a dobby loom weave. Pattern is a diamond with a small center dot. (100)

blanket a textile sample showing a series of patterns or colors all on the same warp.

bleaching basic finishing process to whiten gray (greige) goods. (47, 113, 124)

bleeding a fault in which dye runs from one pattern area into another. (161, 162)

blend a) yarn of two or more staple fibers spun together b) fabric containing blended yarns in the warp and filling. (43–44)

block printing general term for a hand-printing process using wood or other solid material blocks into which patterns have been cut. (26, 130)

blotch printing open-screen roller-printing process by which the plain background of a printed fabric can be colored. (129)

bobbin lace single-element construction, originally handmade on a pillow with numerous threads. (105)

bolt an entire length of fabric, usually rolled full-width on a tube; sometimes folded before rolling. (4, 161, 163)

bonded fabric fabric formed by combining an outer face fabric with a backing fabric using an adhesive or thin foam lamination. (106–7, 162, 180)

bonded web bat of loose fibers that is compressed with heat and an adhesive. (107)

bonding process of laminating two fabrics, or a fabric and a backing. (111)

bouclé a) a looped and crimped novelty yarn b) fabric with a knotty, looped surface, woven with a bouclé yarn. (89, 90)

braid flat or round, woven or plaited fabric used for trimming. (94, 105, 147, 164)

breaking load maximum force applied to a fabric in a tensile test. (5, 33, 38, 48, 50, 52, 53, 58, 85, 142, 175, 182, 197)

broadcloth tightly woven, lustrous cotton fabric in a plain weave with a fine crosswise rib, or wool fabric with a close twill weave, brushed and sheared to give a uniform, slightly felted, smooth appearance. (21, 100)

brocade jacquard-woven fabric with a supplementary warp and/or filling which creates an all-over design: background is satin or twill weave. (100, 138, 147)

brocatelle satin-faced jacquard-patterned cloth in which a supplementary backing weft is used to raise the surface. (100)

broken end a cut or untied warp yarn in a fabric. (196)

brushing finishing process in which fibers are raised to obscure the construction of the fabric. (113, 115)

buckram plain-woven, sleazy cotton fabric stiffened with sizing.

bulking chemically or mechanically plumping up filament yarns to increase their loft. (40–41, 70, 88, 89, 166, 174)

burlap plain-woven cloth of retted, single-ply jute. (50)

burn-out printing process to produce an opaque or translucent pattern by applying acid which dissolves fibers supplemental to the ground cloth. (131)

bursting strength a measurement used only on fabrics having nonaligned yarns such as knit or lace curtain or drapery fabrics. A hard steel ball is forced through a fabric held under an O-shaped plate. The maximum force required to burst through the specimen is recorded.

buttoning method of securing upholstery fabric on a padded surface or cushion. (158)

C

calendering standard finishing process in which cloth is pressed heavily and/or repeatedly under steel rollers to produce a polished surface also used to emboss fabrics. (115–16)

calico ancient, basic woven cotton cloth. (17, 18, 22, 26, 100)

camel hair natural protein fiber obtained from the undercoat of the Asiatic camel. (35, 59)

carbonizing finishing process to destroy vegetable matter in wool cloth. (113, 114)

carded yarn yarn spun from a carded sliver of fibers. (87)

carding process used for all natural fibers, in which they are separated and brought into general alignment prior to spinning. (48, 87)

carpet general term for fabric constructed to be used as floor covering. (2, 11–14, 163–91)

casement cloth general term for sheer drapery fabric. (143, 145, 147, 148, 149, 150, 151, 153, 154, 161–62, 197)

cashmere fine, natural protein fiber obtained from the undercoat of the Himalayan Kashmir goat. (57, 59)

cationic dyes see basic dyes. (124, 125, 177)

cavalry twill smooth-surfaced, 63° diagonal twill fabric with pronounced ribs, usually of worsted wool. (100)

cellulose organic fibrous substance found in all vegetation that is the basic constituent of both natural and manufactured fabrics. (12, 32, 34, 36, 46, 47, 48, 49, 50, 51, 52, 53, 54, 60, 61, 62, 64, 117, 122, 206)

cellulosic fibers such as cotton, linen, jute and rayon. (119, 124, 214)

chain stitch ornamental stitch resembling the links of a chain. (109)

cheesecloth cotton in loose, plain weave with a very low thread count, originally used to wrap cheese. (111)

chemical finishes additives used to modify the appearance or hand of fabrics. (117–18)

chenille a) fuzzy, caterpillar-like yarn of cotton or manufactured fibers, produced by locking short, cut fibers at right angles to the core thread; b) fabric woven with chenille yarn in the weft, producing a cut-pile surface c) as carpeting. (90, 100, 168)

chevron twill weave with a zigzag repeat. (138)

chiffon sheer fabric, especially of silk. (100)

chintz close, plain-woven cotton, either printed or dyed, with a glazed surface. (100, 116)

chitin substance from shells of crustaceans used to produce antibacterial, antifungal fiber. (212–13)

ciré high luster glaze on silk, cotton or synthetics, produced with wax or resin and hot rollers.

cleaning a) dry: immersion of fabric in petroleum or synthetic solvents to remove oil or grease b) wet: removal of waterborne soil or stains by a soap or detergent and water process, done usually on a flat surface with a brush, not to be confused with laundering by immersion. (12, 48, 58, 69, 109, 118, 119, 124, 125, 126, 137, 139, 143, 145, 154, 156, 161–62, 172, 177, 185, 186, 187, 195, 197, 198, 199, 201, 213)

cloth general term used for any pliable material whether woven, knitted, felted, knotted, or extruded. (3, 15–26)

cloth count see thread count. (96)

coated fabric fabric coated, or treated, with a substance such as rubber, vinyl, plastics or oil that is applied on both sides of a fabric. (110, 128, 130, 162, 178, 183, 185, 212)

cohesiveness ability of fibers to adhere to one another in yarn manufacturing process. (32, 39, 46)

coil term used to describe a type of configuration given to a yarn in order to make it stretchable. (89)

coir coarse and extremely durable fiber obtained from the outer husks of coconuts. (35, 36, 54, 166)

color a hue, as contrasted with white, black or gray. (39–40)

color abrasion loss of color, particularly in pigment prints or from poor dye penetration. (158–59)

colorfast term applied to fabrics colored in such a way to prevent color fading from light or cleaning. (5, 22, 124, 125, 126, 127, 137, 141, 142, 145, 152, 154, 173, 174, 177, 188, 189, 190, 191, 195, 196, 197, 198, 199)

color card a series of swatches attached to a sample of fabric to show the complete color line. (5)

color line the range of colors available in a particular fabric.

colorway one individual coloration from the full color line. (5)

color value the lightness or darkness of a color. (36)

C.O.M. customer's own material. (206)

combed yarn yarn spun exclusively of long fibers in parallel conformation which produces the strongest, smoothest staple fiber yarn. (87, 140)

combination dyeing general term for a dyeing process involving cloth made of two or more different fibers. (125)

combination filament yarn yarn composed of two or more different filaments.

combing the process of making carded fibers parallel and removing impurities and short fibers before spinning. (3, 48, 57, 87, 140)

complex yarns any yarns constructed in such a way as to produce a bulky or uneven or otherwise special appearance. (89)

compound cloths cloth layered in two or more thicknesses.

construction the particular manner in which yarns or fibers are interlaced to form fabric. (31, 32, 36, 37, 44, 88, 89, 90, 91, 94–111)

conversion broad range of processes such as finishing, dyeing, printing, embroidering or embossing which change the basic appearance of a fabric. (3, 32, 80, 85, 88, 145)

converter individual or company that buys greige goods, applies finishes, and sells the finished fabric to a wholesaler or retailer. (3, 4, 112, 113)

copolymer polymer composed of two or more repeating units, e.g. spandex, acrylic. (121)

cord fabric general term referring to a fabric with a pronounced horizontal or vertical rib. (86)

corduroy cloth made of either natural or manufactured fibers, with cut-pile ribs (or wales) running the length or width of the fabric. The ribs are produced by weft yarns that are carried over the fabric face and then cut. (98, 100, 115)

cord yarn yarn made of two or more ply yarns twisted together. (86)

core a base yarn which is wrapped with a second and sometimes a third yarn. (78, 91)

core spinning yarn spinning process in which a filament, under predetermined tension, is enrobed in a sheath of staple fibers. When tension is removed, the sheath fibers are pulled into a compact formation, and the yarn is thereafter stretchable to the extent of the pre-determined tension of the core filament. (3, 83)

cotton natural vegetable fiber composed of cellulose. (3, 12, 16, 17, 18, 19, 21, 22, 25, 26, 31, 32, 33, 35, 36, 37, 39, 41, 43, 46, 47)

count see thread count.

course the horizontal element in a knitted fabric. (101, 102, 119, 151)

covert medium or heavy-weight wool fabric, usually of two colors, closely woven with a steep twill, and finished with a smooth face. (100)

crease a line in a fabric caused by a fold. (38, 68, 103, 117, 122, 141, 212)

crease resistant finish a resin finish heat-set on cellulosic fabrics to inhibit wrinkling. (122)

crêpe a) yarn that is overtwisted to create a crinkled profile and stretchy resilience b) fabric woven of crêpe yarn, which has a matte surface texture and slight stretch. (103, 212)

Creslan® trade name for an acrylic fiber. (70)

cretonne plain-woven printed cloth similar to unglazed chintz. (100)

crewel a hand embroidery technique from Kashmir in which fine, loosely twisted two-ply yarn is stitched on cotton. (109, 111, 160)

crimp the waviness in a fiber, either natural (as in wool) or imposed on manufactured (nylon, etc.). (40, 41, 42, 57, 68, 70, 72, 88, 89)

crimping process in which natural or synthetic fibers are set in wavy coils for resilience, wrinkle resistance, and natural cohesion in finishing. (40–41)

crocking the rubbing off of color due to improper or insufficient dye penetration or fixation. (108, 109, 124, 126, 137, 158, 177, 191, 198)

Crocking may occur under wet or dry conditions. (109, 124, 126, 137, 158, 177, 191, 198)

cross dyeing piece-dyeing fabric composed of two generically different fibers with two different dyes to produce a pattern characteristic of yarn-dyed fabric. (125, 127, 137, 141)

cross section shape of the fiber determined by the shape of the spinneret holes through which it is spun; common shapes are round, trilobal, mulitlobal, dogbone, serrated. (33, 39, 40, 64, 70, 88, 176)

crushed fabrics pile fabrics treated with heat, moisture and pressure to distort the pile formation. (58, 182)

cuprammonium rayon a type of rayon made from cellulose dissolved in an ammonium copper solution. (60, 61, 63)

custom services work performed to special order. (41, 127, 135, 145, 166, 167, 169)

cut the cutting module or unfinished panel length of a window or wall fabric. (4, 98, 168)

cut and loop a tufted carpet pile variation. (168, 170)

cut order fabric ordered to a specific measurement. (4I)

cut-pile fabric cloth with a three-dimensional surface produced by double weaving or by looping an additional warp or filling thread into the basic weave, and then cutting the loops. (167)

cutting a small sample of fabric. (85, 154)

cut wire rod a blade that is inserted under the extra warp or filling yarn during the weaving of a cut-pile fabric. As it is withdrawn, it cuts the loop, producing a cut-pile surface.

crystallinity parallel, orderly arrangement of monomers within a polymer chain. Laying parallel means a fiber has a high degree of orientation.

D

Dacron® trade name of a polyester. (64, 68).

damask woven pattern based upon contrasting warp-face and filling-face cloths. (100, 147)

decating (decatizing) basic finishing process that includes light scouring and single calendering. (115)

degumming removal of natural gums from silk yarn or fabric by boiling in a mild alkaline solution. (53, 55)

delamination undesirable separation of the components of bonded or laminated fabrics; delamination strength term used in testing how securely the secondary backing is adhered to the primary backing of carpeting. (175, 181, 182, 188, 190, 191)

delustering chemical process in which the luster of manufactured yarn or fabric is reduced by changing the character of its light-reflecting capacity, either before spinning, by inserting colorless pigments into the solution, or during spinning, by altering the contour, cross-section, or density of the filament. (34, 40, 61)

denier a unit of weight indicating the size of a filament. The higher the denier the heavier the yarn. (32, 38, 42, 43, 46, 92, 166, 173, 174, 189, 212, 212)

denim yarn dyed cotton cloth woven in a warp-faced twill, usually with a dyed warp and a natural filling. (100, 214)

density the measure of the set of a cloth—the total number of ends and picks. (32, 38, 40, 46, 49, 50, 52, 53, 56, 58, 61, 63, 65, 67, 69, 70, 72, 74, 75, 77, 78, 81, 88, 105, 139, 143, 148, 156, 165; Pile Density, 168; 175, 181, 188, 191, 197)

diaper all-over repeating pattern produced by combining herringbone weave and a reversed twill. (100)

dimensional stability ability of a textile to maintain its original shape and size. (38)

direct dyes class of dyes used for cellulosic fibers: needs no fixatives. (123, 124)

direct glue down a type of carpet installation when no cushion is used under a carpet and it is glued directly to the floor. (172, 183)

direct printing general term for a process in which color is applied directly onto the fabric. (128)

discharge printing process in which pattern is obtained by bleaching portions of already dyed cloth. It may be left white or dyed another color. (131)

disperse dyeing process for coloring acetate, acrylic, nylon and polyester in which a slightly water soluble dye is dispersed in the fiber solution. Sometimes subject to fume-fading and sublimation. (39, 123, 124–25, 131, 137, 199, 212)

dobby a mechanical loom attachment that can regulate as many as forty harnesses to produce small, geometric patterns. (99, 100)

dope dyeing see solution dyeing. (125–26)

dotted swiss sheer cloth with a spaced dot pattern, produced by dense areas of supplementary filling in a swivel weave. The dots may also be clipped. (100)

double cloth compound cloth based on two sets each of warp or filling yarns held together at regular intervals by a warp or filling thread passing from one fabric to the other. (98)

double knit knitted fabric made with a double set of needles to produce a double thickness of fabric which is consequently denser and has greater stability than a single knit. (102)

double weave fabric woven with two sets of warp and filling yarns, with an extra yarn to loosely hold the two cloths together. The connecting yarn is cut, and two cut-pile fabrics are produced.

doubling joining together an S twist yarn with a Z twist yarn to create a plied yarn free from torque. (44, 92)

douppioni silk yarn reeled from two cocoons that have grown together, resulting in a slubbed, interrupted texture.

downtown house fabric house in New York that sells to retailers and uptown and regional houses. (4)

draft chart indicating the relationship of warp and weft yarns of a cloth. (44, 85)

Dralon® trade name of acrylic. (70)

drapery general term for fabric used as opaque window or other surface covering. (147)

draw a) to shape or stretch out a fiber or yarn b) in weaving, to move warp threads through the heddles in the proper order to produce a pattern. (35, 39)

drill strong cloth, originally cotton, of twill construction.

dry cleaning removal of dirt from fabrics by treatment with solvents. (162)

dry spinning a) spinning fiber, when dry to produce a lofty, soft yarn; b) extruding manufactured filaments from a spinneret into warm air. (34, 62, 67, 70, 78)

duck cloth compact, durable plain-woven cotton fabric. (100)

durable press finish applied to fabric by means of resins in solution or gaseous form, and cured under conditions of controlled heat to set the shape and make it wrinkle-resistant in machine laundering. Also called permanent press. (117, 121, 122)

dye affinity the susceptibility of a fiber to various dye-stuffs. (85, 129, 131)

dye house facility where greige goods are dyed or printed.

dyeing the process of applying color to fiber, yarn or fabric with natural or synthetic coloring agents. (123– 131) See also: cross, jig, package, piece, skein, solution, space, stock, top, union and yarn dyeing.

Dynel® trade name for a modacrylic fiber. (72)

E

ecology relations and interactions between organisms and their environment. (11)

ecological textiles textiles that are less harmful to the natural environment. (11–12)

Egyptian cotton fine grade of cotton known for its long staple. (16)

elasticity ability of a stretched material to recover its original size and shape. (142)

elastic recovery a factor in the dimensional stability of fabrics. See also: recovery. (38)

elastomer elastic synthetic fiber with the physical properties and strength of natural rubber. (35, 36, 78, 79, 81, 91)

electronic textiles textiles that incorporate fiber optics in yarns and fabrics. (9, 212)

element a single yarn or set of yarns in a constructed fabric. (86, 90, 91, 174)

elongation the stretch capacity of a fiber, yarn or fabric. (38, 46, 48, 50, 52, 53, 56, 58, 61, 63, 67, 68, 71, 72, 73, 75, 77, 78, 81, 85, 88, 101, 103, 107, 142, 150, 181, 182, 195)

embossing decorative fabric finish produced by patterned rollers. (108, 109, 116, 117, 138)

embroidery basic cloth embellished with ornamental needlework. (16, 99, 109, 111, 140, 147, 160)

end a) a single strand of warp yarn b) a short length of fabric. (94, 177)

Enkrome® trade name of an acid-dyeable rayon. (60)

environmental sustainability refers to making choices that will not adversely affect the natural environment or ecosystem; sustains the health and well-being of organisms in the natural environment. (2, 11–14)

extruded fabric nonfibrous fabric, related to film that is made directly from a polymer solution. (108)

extrusion a process for manufacturing synthetic fibers and filaments. In this process, the solid pellets or flakes of polymer are dissolved and forced through spinnerets for shaping and then cooled. (34)

F

fabric general term for any woven, knitted, nonwoven, knotted, felted or otherwise constructed material made from fibers or yarns. Cloth, carpet, caning and matting are all defined as fabric. (1–8)

fabric construction (31, 32, 37, 44, 89, 91, 94-111, 118, 119, 138, 139, 140–41, 151, 158, 168, 213)

fabric width crosswise measurement of cloth. (5, 96, 101, 110, 113, 126, 145)

face the side on which a fabric is finished. (97, 206)

Fade-O-meter a testing machine that determines the colorfastness of a fabric to ultra violet light. (177, 181, 198)

fading color loss due to light, pollutants, cleaning, etc. (124, 125, 137, 161, 175, 177, 191, 195, 198, 199)

faille lightweight fabric, originally silk, with a pronounced transverse rib. (100)

fastness resistance to fading or change in color, also referred to as color fastness. For carpeting, the important types of fastness include light fastness, crocking, chemical fastness and ozone fastness. (207)

fault an inconsistency in an entire piece or lot of fabric. (127, 191)

felt a) non-woven fabric made of fibers joined through the application of heat, agitation and moisture, or by mechanical treatment b) woven fabric that has been treated with heat, moisture and pressure to achieve greater strength and fullness. (15, 106, 107)

fiber the basic element of cloth. Any tough, hair-like substance, natural or manufactured, that can be spun or thrown to form yarn, or felted or otherwise joined into a fabric. (1–5)

Fiberglas® trade name of a glass fiber. (80)

fiberglass manufactured mineral fiber extruded in continuous filaments. (142, 143)

fiber web fabrics cloth constructed from a mat of fibers secured with adhesives and/or heat. (106)

fibril a minute fibrous element that makes up a fiber. (41, 42, 55)

fibroin the main organic constituent of silk. Is a protein of several amino acids. (55)

filament fiber of indefinite length, either natural (silk) or manufactured. Silk filament is the thread of a silkworm's cocoon; manufactured filaments are produced by forcing a solution through a spinneret. (32, 34, 55, 75, 85, 176)

filling (or weft or woof) in weaving, the crosswise yarn or yarns that interlace at right angles with the lengthwise warp. (27, 95, 96, 97, 98, 99, 100, 196)

filling-faced a term used to describe fabrics in which the filling picks predominate over the warp ends. The filling may conceal the warp completely. (98)

film non-fibrous textile, primarily used as a substrate or laminate. (75, 86, 107, 108, 111, 128, 129, 149, 150, 160)

finish any treatment given to a fiber, yarn or fabric to alter its original or greige goods state. (1, 3, 13, 108, 112–22). See also: additive finish, beetling, bleaching, calendering, carbonizing, decatizing, delustering, mercerization, mothproofing, napping, pre-shrinking, shearing, silicone finish, tentering, weighting, wet finish. (118, 120, 141)

fireproof fabric cloth which is impervious to burning. (206)

flame lamination see foam flame bonding flame-resistant fabric a fabric whose fiber content or topical finish makes it difficult to ignite and slow to burn. (111)

flame-retardant fabric manufactured fabric whose fiber content is officially acceptable for most situations. (42, 60, 118, 119, 141, 151, 160, 201, 206)

flammable, or **inflammable** easily set on fire. (118, 119, 141, 144, 151, 162, 178, 194, 200, 201, 203)

flammability code specifications indicating the highest amount of burning, charring, smoke density, or flame spread a fabric may exhibit to meet an approved standard. (24, 47, 49, 51, 52, 54, 56, 58, 60, 62, 63, 65, 67, 69, 71, 73, 74, 76, 77, 79, 81, 118, 151, 152, 173, 174, 181, 182, 187, 191, 200, 201, 203, 204)

flammability test any one of several tests to determine a fabric's resistance to burning, conducted under specific atmospheric conditions. (177-78, 201-7) See also: Methenamine Test, Steiner Tunnel Test.

flannel medium weight, slightly napped plain or twill-woven cloth, most often of wool or cotton. (100)

flaw defect in a fabric. (195–96)

flax plant from which linen is produced. (19, 22, 26, 35, 36, 48, 50, 51, 53, 83, 84, 88, 147)

fleece a) the woolly coat of a sheep, usually clipped in one large piece; b) fabric with a deep soft pile. (21, 57, 214)

flexibility capacity to be bent repeatedly without breaking; pliability. (16, 33, 38, 50, 52, 53, 58, 61, 63, 80, 93, 103, 105, 107, 118, 139, 139, 148, 149, 184, 195)

float portion of warp or filling yarns covering two or more adjacent yarns to form a design or satin surface. (98, 102, 140, 198)

flocked fabric fabric in which the entire surface is covered with flocking to produce a velvet-like or suede-like texture. (90, 108, 116, 131, 167, 168)

flocking process by which a velvety pile surface is formed by securing short fiber ends to a fabric with adhesive. (90, 116, 131, 168)

foam manufactured, no-element fabric primarily used as a substrate or backing for another fabric. (108, 111, 127, 170, 172, 179, 180–206)

foam flame bonding one of the two basic processes used in fabric-to-fabric lamination. (The other is wet adhesive bonding). The foam takes the place of an adhesive and is made tacky by heating with a gas flame. In the process, the thickness of the foam is reduced but not eliminated entirely. This method may also by used to build up face fabrics. (111, 206)

Fortisan® trade name for a filament rayon. (60)

Fortrel® trade name of a polyester fiber. (68)

Free-lay installation a type of carpet installation which allows 80 to 90 percent of the carpet to be moved. A control grid of adhesive or double faced tape is used. (182, 184–85)

frieze (or frise) durable uncut warp-pile fabric often woven with a wool face and cotton back. (100, 170)

fulling a finishing operation dependent on the felting properties of wool, that shrinks the fabric to make it heavier and thicker. (87, 113, 114, 120)

fume fading term used to describe color loss or change caused by gases or other pollutants. Also called atmospheric, or gas fading. (124, 137, 191, 199)

functional finishes improvement of the factors which affect durability, strength, life span, etc. (118–22)

fusing process in which thermoplastic fibers or yarns are melted together, as in ribbons, or heat-sealed, as in joinings, to form a fused edge. (106, 211)

fuzzing gradual raising of fiber ends in a fabric due to wear on the surface, forming patches of matted fibers. These retain soil, are unsightly in appearance, and may lead to pilling. (138)

G

gabardine fabric of fine worsted yarns closely woven in a diagonal twill and finished with a high sheen. (87, 100)

gas fading see fume fading.

gauze openly constructed, transparent cloth of any fiber.

generic fibers universally accepted classifications of chemically distinct families of fibers. (64)

gimp a silk or metallic yarn spiral-wrapped closely around an inner core to cover it completely. (90)

gingham yarn-dyed, combed or carded cotton fabric woven into a series of simple patterns in two or more colors, such as checks, stripes and plaids. (100)

gin removes seeds and impurities from raw cotton. (21, 46)

glass raw material from which fiberglass fibers are made. (22, 35, 36, 64, 80-81, 114)

glazing general term for a polished finish on cloth, often using waxes or resins and hot rollers. (117, 141, 149)

glue down a type of carpet installation when a cushion is attached to a carpet that is installed with adhesive. (172, 182, 183–85)

geotextiles textiles used to stabilize roads, dams, other structures. Often helps with water drainage. (214)

green textiles textiles that are environmentally sustainable and do not adversely affect the natural environment. Textiles may be reused or recycled in a closed loop system to avoid products ending up in the landfill sites. (2, 11-14, 47, 190)

grain the alignment of vertical (lengthwise) and horizontal (crosswise) elements in a fabric to form a right angle relationship. (96, 103, 104, 109, 111, 113, 114, 196)

grass fibers general class of fibers that includes abaca, sea grass, grain straw, bamboo, rattan and cane. (15, 23, 162, 166)

grey goods (or greige goods) woven fabric as it comes from the loom: unbleached, not dyed or printed, unfinished. (3, 100, 112–113, 123, 126, 127, 130, 141)

grin a) ground cloth of a pile fabric visible when it is folded or creased, b) small area of ground color that shows through if the print is off-register.

grosgrain a) heavy, corded ribbon or cloth. b) large-scale frieze cloth with a heavy, regular warp pile. (100)

H

hackling combing process as it applies to flax. (48)

hair fibers animal fibers that lack the crimp and resilience of wool, cashmere, or camel's hair, such as rabbit hair and fur fibers. (59)

hand the tactile quality of fabric. (41, 42, 43, 70, 93)

hand-spun yarn yarn spun by hand on a spinning wheel. (2, 83, 84–85, 140, 188)

handwoven fabric cloth woven on a hand or foot-powered loom, or woven by hand without a loom. (100, 165)

hardtwist a tufted carpet pile variation. (170)

harness rectangular frame on a loom that holds the heddles through which the warp yarns pass.

The harnesses raise and lower the heddles in predetermined patterns so that the filling yarns can be inserted through the shed to produce a desired weave. (95)

Harris tweeds highly durable woolens hand woven in Scotland, rough textured and made in narrow fabric widths.

heather mixture yarn composed of a mixture of fibers dyed in different colors. (126, 169, 174, 189)

heat setting a process wherein yarns are heated to promote twist retention and to stabilize their configuration. (68, 69, 88, 89, 98, 113, 115)

heddles needle-like wires on a loom through which the warp yarns are drawn. They are mounted in the harness, which is raised and lowered during weaving. (95, 99)

Helanca® trade name of a stretch-nylon process. (88, 89)

hemp coarse natural cellulose fiber. (12, 22, 35, 36, 51, 52, 166)

Herculon® trade name of a polypropylene fiber produced by Hercules. (23, 75)

herringbone twill weave which has a zigzag pattern formed by alternating the direction of the twill. The chevron pattern runs selvage to selvage. (98, 100, 166)

high wet modulus rayon a modified rayon with greater dimensional stability in washing. (60, 61)

hiking the alternate sagging and shrinking of casement panels due to humidity changes. (150–51)

homespun originally, a plain-woven, fabric from hand-spun yarns; currently, a machine-woven fabric with irregular yarns to simulate the original textures. (100, 109)

honeycomb hexagonal woven pattern, resembling the cells of a honeycomb. (100, 147, 153)

hopsacking coarse basket-weave fabric of jute, hemp or cotton. (100)

horizontal operation a textile business involved with a single aspect of fabric production, which it sells to a varied market. (3)

horsehair narrow upholstery fabric woven with a filling of long, single tail hairs. (34, 35)

houndstooth variation of a twill weave, with a broken check pattern. (100)

hue color, shade or tint of a color hydrophilic moisture absorbent. (136, 137)

hydrophilic moisture absorbant (38)

hydrophobic moisture repellent. (38)

I

Ikat fabric woven with tie-dyed yarns. (128)

indigo natural vegetable dye used to color fabric blue. (20, 214)

ink jet printing printing process applied to fabrics where ink is forced into the fabric through electronic ink jet printers. (214)

insulating general term for any material used to lessen the transfer of noise, heat or cold. See also acoustic and thermal insulation. (106, 108, 111, 139, 172, 180, 197)

intensity the brightness or darkness of a color. (115, 126, 136, 137, 148, 150, 177, 198, 213)

interlining a layer of fabric between the outer, decorative fabric and the lining. (107, 149, 161)

International Grey Scale standard used to measure color fading on a Fade-O-meter.

intimate blend blend of two or more compatible fibers that are carded together so that no one characteristic dominates. (43, 44)

J

jacquard loom attachment that uses a punched card system to raise and lower single heddles. It permits the weaving of fabrics with complex patterns such as tapestry and brocade. (21, 99, 100, 161, 167)

jean sturdy cotton twill fabric. See denim

jobber person or organization that buys large lots of finished fabrics for resale in smaller quantities. (3, 4)

jute coarse natural cellulose fiber, used primarily in burlap and carpet backing. (35, 50, 51, 84, 166, 167, 168, 172, 174, 183, 184, 188)

K

kapok natural cellulose fiber, extremely light, which is used 'as is', not spun. (35, 54)

knit fabric textile produced by continuous interlooping of one or more yarns. (68, 88, 102, 103, 114, 140)

knot weaving flaw; broken yarns which are tied, and usually pulled through to the back of the fabric. (114, 196)

L

Laminates textiles made of two or more heat bonded materials. (106, 107, 109, 111, 160, 162, 172, 175)

lambswool first fleece sheared from a young sheep. The previously undipped fiber ends are tapered, producing a very soft texture. (57)

laminated fabric fabric created by bonding two or more layers of material together. (107, 111)

lappet three-element woven fabric similar to discontinuous brocade. (99, 100)

lawn lightweight, sheer, fine cotton or linen fabric. (100)

leno weave open weave used for casements, which achieves extra stability by twisting the warp yarns around each other and inserting the filling yarn. (90, 99, 100)

level loop a tufted carpet pile variation. (167, 169, 170, 189)

level tip shear a tufted carpet pile variation. (170)

lightfastness performance with exposure to sun or light. (207)

lifecycle the length of time a textile is used before it wears out; often associated with costing and maintenance. (146, 156, 172, 173)

line long linen fibers that have great luster and strength. (48, 86, 88)

linen a) natural cellulose yarn made from flax fibers, noted for strength, cool hand and luster; low resilience; b) fabric woven from linen yarns. (12, 15, 16, 19, 20, 21, 22, 26, 27, 31, 32, 35, 36, 39, 43, 48–50, 51, 52, 88, 113, 122, 124, 125, 130, 138, 140, 141, 147, 166, 185, 205, 211)

lining material attached under the principal material of a cloth or article. (1, 18, 111, 148, 151, 179, 201)

llama South American animal of the camel family whose fleece is produced in a variety of colors, similar to but coarser than alpaca. (35, 59)

loft bulk or resilience of a fabric, yarn or fiber. (38, 143)

loom machine that produces woven textiles by interlacing warp and filling yarns at right angles to each other (21, 61, 94-97, 99, 100, 106, 128, 163, 166, 167)

Lurex® trade name of a slit-film metallic yarn. (81)

luster the gloss or sheen on the surface of a fiber, yarn or fabric. (12, 38, 39, 44, 46, 48, 50, 53, 54, 55, 57, 68, 73, 77, 78, 80, 93, 114, 115, 116, 118, 137, 138, 165, 214)

Lycra® trade name of a spandex fiber. (33, 37, 78)

M

macromolecule (polymer) large molecule formed by joining together many monomers. (37, 64)

Malimo nonwoven multiple element fabric construction in which hundreds of stitching yarns knit the weft onto the warp. (104)

manufactured fiber inclusive term for manufactured fibers of natural or synthetic in origin. (12, 24, 32, 33–34, 37, 39, 40, 43, 44, 59, 60, 62, 64–77, 83, 85, 86, 87, 88, 106, 113, 119, 123, 124, 125, 126, 138, 140, 141, 144, 167, 168, 172, 174, 175, 180, 211)

marquisette leno weave, sheer cotton or synthetic yarn used for casement cloths. (99, 100)

match the relative constancy of shade from one dye lot to another; also pattern match. (196, 198)

matelassé jacquard-woven cloth with a quilted-like surface, usually cotton or rayon. (100)

melt spinning extruding manufactured filaments through a spinneret in a melted form, which immediately harden when cooled. (34, 75)

memo sample sample of fabric, generally 30 cm. (1 ft.) square. (5)

mercerization caustic soda treatment for cotton and linen, which makes the yarn or cloth stronger, and increases luster and dye affinity. (46, 112, 113, 114, 116)

Merino breed of sheep yielding a high grade wool used for fine woolen and worsted cloth. (17, 20, 21, 25, 26, 57)

metallic descriptive term for any fiber, yarn or fabric using a metal (gold, aluminum, steel, etc.) as part of its structure. (36, 81, 91, 111, 114, 119, 120, 205)

Methenamine Pill Test a flammability test. (202–204)

microfiber extremely fine fibers of 1 denier or less. Fibers are often spun in bicomponent form and excess material is dissolved, leaving fine, strong fibers. (23, 34, 42, 43, 68, 108, 143, 155, 211, 212, 213)

mildew-resistant fabric fabric of inherently resistant fibers, or one treated to resist deterioration by mildew and mold. (13, 109, 120)

mineral fiber natural or manufactured fiber derived from a mineral, such as asbestos or fiberglass. (81–82)

Mitin® trade name of a permanent mothproofing process for wool and wool blends. (120)

modacrylic generic term for a modified acrylic fiber composed of copolymers of acrylonitrile and other materials such as vinyl chloride, which enable the fiber to be softened at low temperatures. (35, 72–73, 118, 174, 175, 184, 205)

Mohair processed fiber of the long, silky hair of the Angora goat b) velvet or plush fabric with a mohair pile and cotton back. (35, 57, 59)

moiré a wavy, watermark pattern added by calendering to ribbed thermoplastic fabric. (116)

moisture regain term used to designate the moisture content of a fiber under prescribed conditions. It is expressed as a percentage of the bone-dry weight. (38, 47, 49, 52, 53, 56, 58, 61, 63, 65, 67, 69, 70, 72, 74, 75, 77, 78, 142)

monk's cloth basket-woven cotton fabric. (100)

monofilament single synthesized filament; fishing line is one example. (2, 32, 34, 83, 86, 93)

monomer single unit, or molecule of low molecular weight that can combine with other molecules of low molecular weight. When joined end to end they form polymer chains or polymers, the basis of fibers. (31)

mordant a metallic salt used to fix dyes. (31, 32, 64, 70, 116)

mothproofing general term for any additive finish which makes natural fibers unappealing to insects.

motif a pattern unit, usually repeated. (128, 129)

multi-level a tufted carpet pile variation. (169)

multifilament yarn composed of several, or hundreds of, extruded filament fibers.

muslin plain-woven, uncombed cotton fabric, ranging from sheer to coarse.

N

nap the cut pile or fuzzy surface finish of a cloth or carpet. (108, 115, 141, 179, 185)

natural fiber any textile fiber obtained from an animal, vegetable or mineral source, such as wool, cotton or asbestos. (3, 12, 37, 43, 46, 47–65)

Naugahyde® an expanded vinyl leather-look fabric. (108)

needle-punching form of nonwoven fabric structure in which webs of fibers are laid down in various ways and stitched together by hundreds of barbed needles, which push the fibers into a closely entangled arrangement. The thickness of a web determines its end use—from light, open-work effects to a dense mesh used for carpeting. (140)

net a) general term for a lacy diamond-shaped mesh b) coarse, open-mesh fabric made by diagonal square knotting. (94, 111)

ninon smooth, sheer, plain-woven fabric for casements. (100)

Nomex® trade name for a flame-retardant and heat-resistant aramid fiber. (67)

nonwoven fabrics fabrics made from techniques other than weaving or knitting. Usually made directly from fibers rather than yarns. Can be spun bonded, needle punched or felted among other methods. (1, 2, 3, 5, 37, 42, 94, 106–11)

novelty yarns see complex yarns.) (89–91, 100, 140, 150)

novolid generic term for a new type of manufactured fiber with inherently high flame resistance.

nub random clot of short, dense fibers incorporated during spinning. (90, 155, 158)

nylon generic term for synthetic polyamide fiber; nylon 6,6 has 6 carbon atoms. (22, 23, 34. 34, 35, 37, 38, 39, 42, 43, 44, 64–66, 86, 88, 92, 110, 111, 116, 119, 122, 123, 124, 126, 131, 143, 144, 167, 172, 173–78, 184, 190, 205, 211)

O

off-grain finishing fault in which the horizontal structure is not at right angles to the vertical. (96, 113, 114, 196)

olefin generic term for synthetic fibers produced from either polyethylene or polypropylene. (23, 35, 73, 75–76, 124, 125, 159, 174, 175, 181, 184, 205)

oleophilic tendency to absorb and retain oily substances. (23, 69)

organdy sheer, plain-woven cotton cloth with a crisp hand. (100)

organza similar to organdy, but made of silk, rayon or nylon.

Oriental rugs term generally used alone to denote a type of rug first handwoven in the Middle East. (127, 163, 164–65)

Orion® trade name of an acrylic fiber. (70I)

ottoman heavy, horizontal-ribbed fabric, usually with a densely set warp of silk, acetate or rayon, and a cotton or wool weft. (100)

outline quilting form of quilting in which the stitching follows the motif of a printed fabric. (110)

P

package dyeing form of yarn dyeing in which the dye fluid and the rinse bath are forced through a large number of 0.45 kg. (1 lb.) packages of yarn. (126, 127)

panné mechanical finish for velvets and velours in which heat and pressure lay the pile on a steep diagonal, thus increasing pile cover and luster. (100)

pattern a) the arrangement of form, design or decoration in a fabric b) guide for cutting fabric. (3, 5, 10, 12, 19, 25, 99, 100, 102, 103, 105, 107, 109, 110, 111, 115, 116, 117, 126–214)

pattern repeat a total design unit. (5, 100, 127, 129, 131, 145, 152, 157, 179, 214)

peel bond strength see delamination strength.

percale fine, plain-woven cloth of closely set, combed and carded long-staple cotton. (100)

pick in weaving, a single passage of filling yarn through the warp shed. (94, 96, 97, 140, 196)

piece one entire length of woven cloth, usually 30, 45 or 55 meters long (33, 50 or 60 yards). (3, 4, 117)

piece dying dyeing of cloth after construction. (126, 141)

pigment insoluble powdered coloring agent carried in a liquid binder and printed or padded onto the surface of a cloth. (39, 65, 67, 68, 70, 73, 91, 125, 128, 129, 141, 142, 176, 214)

pile raised surface produced by an extra set of filling yarns that form loops, which may be cut and sheared or left uncut. (90, 98, 99, 100, 102, 104, 105, 106, 115, 127, 140, 165–96)

pile fabric cloth with a three-dimensional raised surface of cut or uncut loops of yarn. (98, 102,104, 105, 115)

pile weave construction in which cut or uncut loops protrude from the ground cloth; loops may be warp or filling yarns, and be produced by a double weave or with wires. The wire method uses round-tipped, removable wires to raise loops for uncut pile, and sharp-edged cut wires for cut pile. (98, 100)

pilling as a fiber breaks up, the two free ends tend to roll back in the opposite directions, forming a fuzzy ball on the fabric surface. Depending on the fiber, pills may or may not be easy to remove. (39, 44, 85, 108, 121, 137, 138, 155, 173, 191)

pina crisp, grassy fiber from the leaves of the pineapple plant. (35, 54)

piqué durable fabric, either ribbed or in a honeycomb or waffle weave. (99, 102)

plaid pattern of unevenly spaced repeated stripes crossing at right angles (100, 123)

plain weave simplest method of interlacing warp and weft yarns to make cloth. Each filling (weft) passes alternately under and over the warp yarns to produce a balanced construction. It is strong, inexpensive to produce, and the best ground cloth for printing; the thread count determines the fabric's strength. (97, 99, 100, 140, 165, 166, 196)

plastic as fabric, extruded vinyl plastic sheeting comes in various weights from very thin to fairly heavy. It may be fused to a knit backing for greater pliability and stability. (86, 91,108, 117, 178, 201, 206)

plied yarn yarn formed by twisting together two or more single strands. (158, 166, 174)

plissé puckered design effect formed by shrinking fabric in selected areas with a caustic soda solution (cotton) or with heat (synthetics). (115)

plush a) cut-pile construction with higher, less dense pile than velvet and velour b) a tufted carpet pile variation. (59, 100, 103, 155, 169, 170, 187, 190)

ply a) a single strand of yarn; b) to twist in one or more strands of yarn together. (86–90, 91, 92, 96, 139, 140, 174)

polished cotton combed and carded fabric, usually of twill or satin construction, which is calendered to produce a high luster. (141)

polyester generic term for a manufactured fiber in which the fiber-forming substance is a long-chain synthetic polymer composed on a complex ester. (4, 12, 23, 23, 34, 35, 39, 42, 42, 44, 68-69, 81, 85, 87, 88, 91, 108, 110, 110, 116, 120, 122, 124, 125, 126, 127, 138, 140, 167, 173, 174, 175, 184, 190, 205, 211, 212)

polymer chemical compound consisting of repeating monomers joined end to end to form a polymer chain. (31, 32, 34, 35, 42, 43, 64, 67, 68, 70, 86, 87, 107, 108, 115, 125, 140, 141, 167, 178, 181, 201)

polymerization process of joining monomers into large molecules or polymers. (31, 32, 34, 39, 64, 70, 75, 77, 116)

polypropylene olefin fiber made of propylene. (75, 76, 86, 124, 125, 159, 168, 174, 181, 188, 206)

pongee plain weave raw silk fabric with an ecru heather effect caused by natural color variation within the fibers.

poplin plain-woven, warp-faced fabric with a fine crosswise rib. (100)

porosity the ease with which air and water can pass through a cloth. (108, 156)

preshrinking deliberate shrinking of a fabric during manufacture to reduce later shrinking in laundering. (113, 114)

primary colors red, yellow and blue. All other colors are derived from combinations of these.

printing application of color designs to the surface of cloth. (3, 26, 112, 115, 126, 127, 128–31, 141–42, 196, 197, 213, 214)

protein fiber natural fiber originating from an animal such as a sheep (wool) or silkworm (silk). (120)

PVC (polyvinyl chloride) or vinyon generic term for a synthetic fiber composed primarily of vinyl chloride, (72, 77, 206)

Q

quilting compound fabric construction of two layers of cloth with a layer of padding (batting) between, stitched through all three. (109, 110–11, 141)

R

ramie fine, oriental bast fiber. (35, 53–54)

random shear a tufted carpet pile variation. (55, 106, 107, 170, 188)

raschel knit fabric woven on a raschel warp-knitting machine. (102, 103, 104, 105, 140, 169)

ratiné a) novelty yarn constructed by twisting a heavy yarn around a fine yarn. b) textured fabric woven in a plain weave with ratiné yarns. (90)

raveling fraying of yarn at the cut edge of a fabric. (100, 158, 183)

raw fiber textile fiber in its most natural state. e.g., cotton before ginning, wool before scouring. (83, 126)

raw silk silk that is not fully degummed. It is stiff, tacky and caramel in color. (22)

rayon generic term for a manufactured fiber derived from regenerated cellulose. (12, 22, 23, 34, 35, 39, 41, 43, 44, 53, 60–61, 88, 91, 100, 113, 114, 115, 116, 124, 125, 131, 141, 167, 205, 211, 213)

reactive dyes class of dyes that react chemically with fiber molecules and produce fast, bright colors. (124)

recovery ability of a stretch yarn or cloth to return to its original shape or size. (38, 46, 48, 50, 52, 53, 56, 58, 61, 63, 65, 68, 70, 72, 73, 78, 81, 88–89, 91, 104, 107, 122, 142, 172, 173, 174, 175, 182)

reed comb-like device on a loom through which the warp ends pass. See beater. (94, 95, 96, 99, 128, 196)

reed mark vertical streak in woven fabric caused by a bent wire in the reed. (196)

reeled silk continuous filament silk as it is reeled off the softened cocoon of the cultivated silkworm. (55)

regenerated cellulose cellulosic material derived from cotton linters or wood pulp and dissolved, purified, and extruded to form rayon, lyocell, acetate and triacetate. (12, 60–62)

registration the alignment of print screens or rollers to make a precise pattern. (129)

remnant leftover yardage from a bolt of cloth; usually less than three meters or yards.

rep plain-woven fabric characterized by distinct ribs. (100)

running crosswise, produced by weaving large filling yarns through the warp yarns. (99, 174, 196)

repeat the amount of surface a single pattern covers on a fabric. (5, 129, 131, 138, 152, 157)

reprocessed wool wool produced by re-carding and re-spinning shredded scraps of unused fabric and yarn. (106, 167)

resilience a fiber's or fabric's ability to return to its original shape after stretching or crushing. (32, 36, 48, 68, 73, 117, 139, 158, 170, 174)

resin synthetic finishing substance applied to fabric to add water repellence, resistance to crushing, luster or other durable finish. (22, 107, 114, 115, 116, 117, 118, 121, 122, 124, 214)

resist printing general term for printing processes in which the motif or the ground is treated with a dye-resistant substance before dyeing the fabric. (128)

retting soaking of bast fiber plants to permit bacterial or chemical breakdown of the outer bark, which loosens the fibers. (48, 50, 51)

reused wool wool spun from shredded used fabrics, commonly blended with other fibers. (106)

rib raised ridge running lengthwise, crosswise or diagonally on a fabric, usually formed by the insertion of a heavy thread, also formed by embossing with rollers. (97, 101, 102, 103)

rib weave a) modification of plain weave in which fine warp ends are closely set and two picks (or one heavier pick) interlace as one b) any woven fabric construction with a horizontal rib or cord. (97, 101, 102, 103)

roller printing mechanical printing of fabric with engraved rollers. (130, 131)

rotary-screen printing a fast and accurate printing process in which the cloth moves under a series of large, patterned cylinders. (129–31)

roving bundle of fibers that are carded and combed and arranged in parallel alignment before spinning. (84, 85, 87)

rubber generic term for fibers composed of natural or synthetic rubber. (32, 33, 35, 36, 78, 79, 91, 114, 118, 129, 130, 172, 178, 179, 180, 182, 184, 185)

S

sagging elongation, common to many fabrics and dependent on fiber content and cloth structure. (69, 142, 150–51, 158)

sailcloth lightweight, plain-woven cotton duck cloth. (100)

Sanforizing® trade name of preshrinking process for cotton and linen fabrics.

saponified rayon rayon filament created by reconverting cellulose acetate to cellulose. (60, 61)

saran generic term for a manufactured fiber composed of at least 80% polymerized vinylidene chloride. (23, 36, 73–74, 205)

sateen filling-faced satin-woven fabric with horizontal rather than vertical floats. (98, 100)

satin warp-faced fabric in a satin weave. (97, 98, 100, 140, 155)

satin weave basic weave in which the fabric face is composed almost entirely of warp or filling floats, producing a smooth, lustrous surface. (97–98, 100)

schiffli embroidery machine-made embroidery in which the decorative yarns are held in place by a binder thread on the reverse side of the cloth. (109)

Scotchgard® trade name of a fluorochemical stain- and water-repellent finish. (118, 121)

scouring washing of fiber, yarn or fabric to remove grease, dirt, sizing or color. (113, 114, 196)

screen printing hand or machine printing process in which a pattern-making stencil or screen held in a frame is positioned on the cloth and coloring agent applied. (128–131, 213–14)

scrim theatrical gauze of sheer, plain-woven linen or hemp. (185)

seam placement a factor in the proper installation of carpeting and underpadding. (185)

seam slippage the pulling apart of sewn fabrics at the seams because of loose fabric construction or slippery yarns. (157–58)

secondary colors orange, green and violet, obtained by blending two primary colors.

seconds imperfect fabrics having weave, finish or dyeing flaws.

seersucker plain-woven cloth, often striped, with puckered or blistered vertical rows produced by a shrinking differential in two groups of warp yarns. (100)

selvage reinforced edge on either side of a woven or flat knitted cloth, finished to prevent raveling. (96, 97, 129, 196, 200)

selvage legend printed copy (firm, designer, pattern, color key) sometimes found running lengthwise on the fabric edge. (129)

serge smooth-finished fabric in a balanced twill weave, identical on face and back. (100)

sericin gummy substance that holds silk fiber together as they are spun (in pairs) from the silk worm. Is removed from silk before spinning. (55, 114)

sericulture raising of silkworms and production of silk. (15, 18, 19, 22, 55)

set density of a fabric's warp and filling. (41, 98, 102, 103)

shade dark variation of a color. See hue. (137, 137, 149, 177)

shading apparent gradations of color in cut-pile fabrics caused by variations in light reflection. It is not a defect but a desirable characteristic of these fabrics. (149, 170, 171, 197)

shading coefficient the amount of heat and light deflection achieved by a casement cloth, a factor in calculating a room's sun resistance and/or air-conditioning requirements. (149)

shag a tufted carpet pile variation. (170)

shantung dense, plain-woven silk cloth with a slightly irregular surface due to uneven, slubbed filling yarns.

sheath fibers fibers which form a sheath around the elastomeric fiber used in core spinning. (41, 42, 43, 87)

shed the space formed as the harnesses of a loom raise some warp yarns and lower others, through which the shuttle passes to lay in the filling. (95, 96, 97, 99, 173, 176)

sheer very thin, transparent, or semi-opaque fabric. (80, 103, 111, 131, 148, 149)

sheeting plain-woven cotton of various qualities, the traditional ground for chintz and a basic cloth for printing. (14, 100, 121, 145)

shot see pick.

shrinkage contraction of fiber, yarn or fabric due to heat and/or moisture. (12, 41, 42, 58, 61, 70, 76, 114, 150, 162, 195, 197, 199, 202, 206)

shuttle device on a loom to carry the filling yarn through the shed to interlace it with the warp. (27, 95, 96, 97, 99, 105, 196)

shuttleless loom loom on which the filling is carried across the warp by means other than a shuttle, allowing faster production. (96, 97)

silicone finish applied finish to resist dry and water-borne soil. (117)

silk natural protein fiber unwound from the cocoon of the silkworm. (12, 15–23, 25-52, 54-56, 60, 70, 83, 85, 86, 91, 92, 113, 114, 115, 124, 125,138, 164, 205)

singeing basic finishing process, particularly for wool fabrics, in which unwanted surface fibers are burned off by passing the cloth under gas jets. (113)

single a single-ply yarn. (55, 86, 90, 91, 92)

sisal strong natural cellulose fiber used in making cord and matting. (35, 36, 54, 166)

sizing a) starch applied to warp threads to strengthen them for the weaving process, usually removed by scouring during finishing: b) starch applied to cotton or linen cloth that is removed when the fabric is washed. (96, 113, 114, 117)

skein a loosely coiled length of yarn. (126, 127)

slippage the sliding of filling threads over ends, or the shifting of warp threads which results in open spaces in the fabric. (151)

slit film ribbon-like yarn in which metallic and other films are commonly available; see tape yarns.

sliver continuous ropelike strand of loosely assembled fibers before twisting into yarns. (41, 84, 85)

slub lump or knot in a yarn; may be a defect or purposely spun to produce a textured surface in cloth. (90, 196)

slug fabric flaw caused by filling yarn doubling back on itself. (196)

snagging yarns or fibers catching or pulling out of the cloth surface. (151)

soil release finish chemical finish applied to fabrics to facilitate the release of soil during laundering. (121, 122, 141, 184)

soil resistant see stain and spot resistant. (121, 184)

solution dyeing dyeing process in which color is added to manufactured fibers before extrusion into filaments, resulting in a tendency to superior colorfastness. (125–26)

space dyeing dyeing technique in which parts of a long skein are dipped into different color baths. (126–127)

spandex generic term for synthetic elastic fibers composed of segmented polyurethane. (205)

special finishes finishes that determine the character of a fabric. (69)

specific gravity ratio of the weight of a material to the weight of an equal volume of water.

specification a) detailed description of a fabric's composition, including style, width, pick and end count, weight per meter or yard, color and finish; b) directive to choose. (5, 9, 14, 44, 91, 135, 144, 145, 151, 152, 155, 157, 172, 177, 179, 181, 181, 182, 187–92, 192, 204, 207, 213)

spinneret metal disc with numerous fine holes through which a chemical solution is extruded to produce synthetic fibers. (34, 41, 42, 60, 90)

spinning a) drawing out and twisting fiber into yarn or thread. b) extruding manufactured filaments through a spinneret; See dry spinning, melt spinning, wet spinning. (3, 15–18, 83–85)

spunbonding filament or staple fibers are randomly spun into a sheet form and then heat set to form a nonwoven fabric. (107)

spun yarn yarn spun from staple-length fiber, either natural or cut synthetic filaments. (2, 78, 83, 85, 86, 87–88, 91, 93)

squeegee a heavy rubber blade used to push color dye onto the fabric in screen printing. (129)

stability retention of size and shape in a fabric. (31, 38, 44, 48, 50, 52, 53, 56, 58, 62, 63, 65, 67, 69, 70, 72, 73, 75)

stabilize to treat fabric to retain size and shape. (88–89, 141, 158)

stain and **spot resistance** ability of a fabric to resist water and oil-borne stains, either through natural fiber characteristics or treatment with a resistant finish. (13, 69, 76, 118, 121, 141, 142, 161, 162, 166, 171, 175, 177, 184, 189, 191)

standard accepted quality and color of a fabric. (87, 92, 190)

standard conditions in laboratory testing, 65% relative humidity at 21.1°C (70°F). (38, 142)

staple natural or manufactured fiber that has a relatively short length. (32, 35, 41, 43, 44, 46, 64)

static the build-up of electrons on any surface; the release of electrons which have built up on any surface. (40, 44, 65, 81, 112, 119, 137, 139, 141. 142. 144, 156, 166, 173, 174, 175, 178, 182, 184, 188, 189, 190, 191, 194, 197)

Steiner Tunnel Test a flammability test (203).

stock dyeing dyeing a staple fiber prior to spinning. (126)

strength see tensile strength. (32)

stretch fabrics fabrics constructed of stretch yarns to have much greater than normal stretch and recovery characteristics. 'Comfort stretch' is a designation for fabrics with up to 30% stretch and recovery; 'power or action stretch' describes fabrics with 30-50% stretch and recovery. (44, 58, 60, 61, 64, 65, 69, 70, 88, 89, 91, 101, 102, 108, 114, 142)

stretch yarn yarn with a durable, springy elongation and exceptional recovery. (91)

Strike off a trial for color or pattern. (129)

stripe narrow section of a fabric differing in color or texture from the adjoining area. (103, 138, 157, 196)

S twist clockwise direction in which yarn is twisted. (87, 92)

sublistatic printing see transfer printing. (131)

substrate fabric underlayer, generally of synthetic foam. (107)

suedecloth woven fabric with a flat, napped surface finished to resemble suede. (108, 109)

sulphur dye dye that produces heavy shades of black or brown in cellulosic fabrics.

sun rot deterioration caused by sun or light. (124)

surface treatment any mechanical or chemical finishing process that affects the appearance or hand of a fabric. (112, 115–16, 141, 206)

swatch card see color card.

synthetic fiber textile fiber made from a petrochemical rather than a natural base. All synthetic fibers are manufactured, but not all manufactured fibers are synthetic. (3, 12, 23, 33, 34, 37, 38, 118, 123, 155, 167, 176, 201, 211, 212)

T

Taber Test textile abrasion test; the specimen is placed on a rotating platform and is mechanically rubbed by two abrasive wheels.

tackless strip method of installing carpet which is secure but easily removed. (182, 183)

taffeta crisp, plain-woven fabric in which the filling is heavier than the warp, producing a fine, lustrous rib. (100, 116)

tapestry jacquard-woven fabric with supplementary multi-colored yarns which form a design. (100, 161, 165)

tape yarns yarns produced by finely slitting an extruded sheet of polymerized chemicals. (86)

tear strength the force required to begin or continue a tear in a fabric. (107)

Teflon® trade name for a highly heat-resistant fiber. (160)

tender goods fabric that is especially susceptible to tearing, usually because of improper finishing. (196)

tensile strength ability of a fabric to withstand tension without tearing or breaking. (107, 181, 182)

tentering controlling fabric width by stretching the selvages on tenterhooks during finishing. (113, 114)

terrycloth uncut warp-pile fabric, plain or jacquard-woven of cotton, linen or rayon. (99, 100)

Terylene® trade name of a British polyester fiber. (68)

tertiary colors colors obtained by mixing three primary colors, or by mixing one or two secondary colors with black.

testing standard procedures used to determine the specific performance characteristics of a fabric. (195–99)

textile orginally, a general term for any woven cloth; now, a general term for any fabric made from fibers or yarns, natural or manufactured. (1)

textured yarn manufactured yarn that has been mechanically or chemically bulked or crimped. (88–89)

texturing, or **texturizing** process by which a fiber is given a permanent curl to make it lofty, resilient, and more natural in appearance. (40–41)

thermal insulation insulation used to reduce heat. (149)

thermoplastic fiber a fiber that breaks down and becomes fluid at a certain temperature. Thermoplastic fabrics can be heat set in permanent pleats or shapes and can not be altered unless a higher heat is used to break and reform the bonds within the fiber. Examples include polyester and nylon. (69, 88, 122, 206)

thermosetting see heat setting. (117)

thick-and-thin yarn complex yarn that is given an uneven profile in spinning. (90)

thread a strand of plied and twisted yarn with a smooth finish that is used in sewing and stitching. (88)

thread count the number of warp and filling yarns per square measure. (96, 98)

throwing slight twisting of filament yarns. (25, 85)

ticking heavy, strong, linen or cotton twill with a colored warp stripe, used in upholstering and as a covering for mattresses or pillows.

tint a pale variation of a color.

toile plain, coarse twill-woven fabric, often linen. Most noteworthy were the toiles de Jouy. Eighteenth century French fabrics printed in scenes with one color on pale cotton, linen or silk. (130)

top dyeing form of stock dyeing in which a loose rope of parallel wool fibers is dyed prior to spinning. Also, dyeing over another color. (126)

tow a) short or broken fibers of flax, hemp or synthetic materials used for yarn, twine, or stuffing; b) thick bundle of continuous filaments assembled without twisting into a loose ropy strand for cutting into staple. (32, 41, 48, 85, 88, 140)

trade name name given by manufacturer to distinguish a product produced and sold by that manufacturer. (4, 33, 37, 89, 91, 107, 108, 111)

trademark word, letter or symbol used in connection with a specific product originating and owned by a particular manufacturer. (4, 119, 199)

transfer printing printing process in which a pattern is printed on waxed paper and transferred to the cloth under heat and pressure. (131)

trapunto decorative quilted design in high relief that is worked through two or more layers of cloth by outlining the design in a running stitch and padding it from the underside. (110)

treadle lever or pedal on a loom that activates the lowering or raising of a harness. (84)

Trevira® trade name of a multilobal-polyester fiber. (68)

triacetate generic term for a manufactured fiber that is a modification of acetate with a higher ratio of acetate to cellulose. (35, 60, 62, 63, 141)

triaxial weave woven fabric composed of three sets of yarns meeting at 60° angles. (100)

tricot plain, warp-knit fabric with a close, inelastic vertical knit. (102, 103, 104, 105, 111, 140)

tuft soft, fluffy threads in a fabric which are cut off short and used as a decorative feature. (104, 165, 168, 175, 178, 188, 190, 191)

tufted fabrics fabrics, especially including carpeting, constructed by a tufting process. (104–105)

tufting system of securing yarns at right angles to a woven or knit backing, extensively used for the production of carpeting. (104, 105, 126, 158, 163, 167, 168, 206)

Tunnel Test a series of three tests to measure the flame retardance of carpeting and wall coverings. (191, 203)

tussah brownish silk fabric from uncultivated silkworms. (55, 56)

tweed medium-weight, rough woolen fabric, usually twill-woven. Named tweeds such as Donegal, Connemara, Harris and Galashiels are produced in Ireland and Scotland. (87, 100, 155, 167)

twill basic weave that produces a surface of diagonal lines by passing filling threads over two or more ends in a regular progression. (97, 98, 100, 140, 165, 166, 185)

twist the tightness and direction of the twist spun into a yarn. S twist is a clockwise twist and is the most common Z twist is a counter-clockwise twist. (83, 84, 85, 86, 87, 88, 89, 90, 91–92, 96, 98, 140, 166, 168, 175, 188)

twisting winding two or more strands of fiber or yarn together to make a multiple-ply yarn. (33, 43, 83, 84, 85, 86, 87, 90)

twistless yarn yarns formed by combining fibers by means other than twisting. (85, 87)

U

ultramicrofiber extremely fine fiber used in extremely soft, dense fabrics; finer than microfiber. (211)

uniformity similarity in length, width, flexibility and spinning quality. (32, 33, 38, 43, 85, 86, 93, 213)

union dyeing general term for a dyeing process in which a solid color is obtained in a cloth made of two or more different fibers with different dye affinities. (126)

upholstery general term for fabric intended for use as a covering for furniture. (147, 155–59)

uptown house a fabric house in New York that sells cut orders to the trade. (4)

urethane chemical family of cross-linked polymers subject to reactions which cause foaming. The foams are used for bonding and laminating fabrics. Also called polyurethane. (107, 172, 179, 181)

V

vat dyeing process in which alkaline-soluble dyes are oxidized to produce excellent colorfastness in cellulosic fibers. (124, 125, 126, 165)

v-construction in a pile weave, catching the pile loops under one shot of weft.

vegetable fibers natural textile fibers of plant origin, such as cotton, flax or hemp. (36, 114, 196)

velour cut warp-pile fabric, usually of cotton or wool, with higher, less dense pile than velvet. (100)

velvet a) close-cropped, warp-pile fabric with a smooth, rich surface, produced by double weaving or with wires. Originally woven in silk, now made with cotton or synthetics as well b) a type of carpeting. (98, 100, 155, 167, 170)

velveteen single-woven weft pile fabric with a dense cut surface, usually cotton. (100)

Verel® trade name of a modacrylic fiber. (72)

vermicelli machine quilting technique that produces an overall pattern of noodle-like squiggles. (110)

vertical operation a business involved with the entire production of fabric. (3)

vicuna small, wild Andean animal of the camel family, from the undercoat of which is derived a fine, lustrous fiber. (35, 59)

vinal generic term for a manufactured fiber composed largely of vinyl alcohol. (35, 42)

vinyl non-woven fabric made from a petrochemical solution; thick or thin, it is usually soft and pliable. (22, 70, 72, 108, 111, 160, 162, 168, 172, 181, 183, 185)

vinyon see PVC. (22, 35, 42, 77, 205)

virgin wool new wool; not reused, reprocessed or respun. (57)

viscose rayon the most common rayon, formed by converting cellulose into a soluble form and regenerating it into fiber. (107)

voile soft, sheer cloth, plain-woven of fine crepe yarns. (100)

W

waffle weave three-dimensional rectangular pattern woven on a dobby loom. (97, 100)

wale a) a horizontal, vertical, or diagonal rib in a fabric; b) the vertical rib on the face of a knitted fabric. (97, 101)

warp lengthwise yarns in a woven fabric, running vertically through the loom parallel to the selvages. (95–97)

warp-faced fabric woven cloth in which the warp yarns predominate over the filling yarns. (98)

warp knit fabric produced on a knitting machine in which the yarns run in a lengthwise but zigzag direction, producing excellent lengthwise stability. (101, 102–104)

water-repellent fabric cloth that repels water. (57)

water-repellent finish additive finish to make cloth impervious to water. (118, 141)

w-construction in a pile weave, catching the pile yarns under one weft and over another and tying them down on the third to keep them from pulling out of the face of the cloth.

weave structural pattern in which yarns are interlaced to produce fabric. (97–101)

weaving process of making a fabric on a loom by interlacing horizontal yarns (weft) at right angles with vertical yarns (warp). (97–101)

weft horizontal or crosswise element in a woven cloth. (44, 94, 101–104)

weighted silk silk treated with metallic salts to increase the weight and apparent value, strictly controlled and now virtually obsolete. (23, 114)

welt fabric-covered cord sewn into an upholstery seam for aesthetic reasons or to improve the durability of the construction. (159)

wet adhesive bonding process used in fabric-to-fabric bonding; a liquid adhesive is applied to the fabric and the bond is cured with heat. (111)

wet spinning a) spinning fiber, particularly linen and hemp, while damp to produce a smooth, wiry yarn; b) extruding manufactured filaments through a spinneret into water or a chemical solution. (34, 60, 70, 77)

wet strength the relative resistance of a wet fiber, yarn, or fabric. (47, 48, 55, 57, 58, 61, 63, 65, 68, 70)

wickability fiber property that allows moisture to move rapidly from one side of the fabric to the other. (42, 143)

Wilton multiple-element cut-pile carpeting. (21, 163, 167)

woolen fuzzy, loosely twisted yarn spun from carded short wool fibers. Woolen cloths are generally simple weaves and show coarser finishes than worsteds. (14–18, 57-58, 87)

woolen system spinning process in which short wool fibers are carded and spun into soft, fuzzy, loosely twisted yarn. (57)

Wool Mark stamp of approval issued by the International Wool Secretariat to denote selected 100% pure virgin wool. (58)

worsted smooth, compact yarns spun from carded and combed long wool fibers. Worsted cloths are more closely constructed and have smoother finishes than woolens. (57, 84, 87, 92, 140)

worsted system spinning process in which long wool fibers are carded, combed, and spun into smooth, compact yarns with average to high twist. (87)

woven-double fabric velvet or plush fabric in which two ground cloths are woven one over the other, with the pile yarns woven up and down between them, and later cut to form two fabrics. (98–99)

Y

yarn any form of spun, twisted or extruded fibers, natural or manufactured, that can be used in weaving, knitting or knotting; may be monofilament, multifilament, or spun—single or plied. (2, 3, 5, 16, 25, 31–38)

yarn dyeing dyeing at the yarn stage of production, as opposed to solution, stock or piece dyeing. (126–27)

Z

Zefran® trade name of an acrylic fiber. (70)

Z twist counterclockwise direction in which a yarn is twisted. (87, 92)